NAHUM

Zondervan Exegetical Commentary on the Old Testament

NAHUM
The Divine Warrior as Avenger and Deliverer

ZONDERVAN
Exegetical Commentary
ON THE
Old Testament
A DISCOURSE ANALYSIS OF THE HEBREW BIBLE

DANIEL C. TIMMER

DANIEL I. BLOCK
General Editor

ZONDERVAN
ACADEMIC

The Hebrew text is from Deuteronomy 31:11–13, which highlights the importance of "hearing" the voice of Scripture:

> When all Israel comes to appear before יהוה your God at the place he will choose, you shall read this Torah before them in their hearing. Assemble the people—men, women and children, and the foreigners residing in your towns—so they can *listen* and learn to fear יהוה your God and follow carefully all the words of this Torah. Their children, who do not know this Torah, must *hear* it and learn to fear יהוה your God as long as you live in the land you are crossing the Jordan to possess. (NIV, modified)

ZONDERVAN ACADEMIC

Nahum
Copyright © 2020 by Daniel C. Timmer

Published in Grand Rapids, Michigan, by Zondervan. Zondervan is a registered trademark of The Zondervan Corporation, L.L.C., a wholly owned subsidiary of HarperCollins Christian Publishing, Inc.

Requests for information should be addressed to customercare@harpercollins.com.

ISBN 978-0-310-94242-9 (hardcover)

Cover design: Tammy Johnson
Interior design: Beth Shagene

Printed in the United States of America

26 27 28 29 30 31 32 33 34 35 36 37 38 /TRM/ 20 19 18 17 16 15 14 13 12 11 10 9 8 7 6 5 4

To Andreea, Nathan, and Felix,
my blessings from YHWH (Ps 128:4)

Contents

Series Introduction 9

Author's Preface and Acknowledgments 13

Abbreviations 15

Select Bibliography 19

Translation of Nahum 29

Introduction to Nahum 33

Commentary on Nahum 65

1. Nahum 1:1 65
2. Nahum 1:2–8 69
3. Nahum 1:9–2:1[1:15] 96
4. Nahum 2:2–14[1–13] 118
5. Nahum 3:1–19 146

Scripture Index 181

Subject Index 191

Author Index 197

Series Introduction

Prospectus

Modern audiences are often taken in by the oratorical skill and creativity of preachers and teachers. However, they tend to forget that the authority of proclamation is directly related to the correspondence of the key points of the sermon to the message the biblical authors were trying to communicate. Since we confess that "all Scripture [including the entirety of the OT] is God-breathed and is useful for teaching, rebuking, correcting and training in righteousness, so that [all God's people] may be thoroughly equipped for every good work" (2 Tim 3:16–17 NIV), it seems essential that those who proclaim its message should pay close attention to the rhetorical agendas of biblical authors. Too often modern readers, including preachers, are either baffled by OT texts, or they simply get out of them that for which they are looking. Many commentaries available to pastors and teachers try to resolve the dilemma either through word-by-word and verse-by-verse analysis or synthetic theological reflections on the text without careful attention to the flow and argument of that text.

The commentators in this series recognize that too little attention has been paid to biblical authors as rhetoricians, to their larger rhetorical and theological agendas, and especially to the means by which they tried to achieve their goals. Like effective communicators in every age, biblical authors were driven by a passion to communicate a message. So we must inquire not only what that message was, but also what strategies they used to impress their message on their hearers' ears. This reference to "hearers" rather than to readers is intentional, since the biblical texts were written to be heard. Not only were the Hebrew and Christian Scriptures composed to be heard in the public gathering of God's people but also before the invention of moveable type, and few would have had access to their own copies of the Scriptures. While the contributors to this series acknowledge with Paul that every Scripture—that is, every passage in the Hebrew Bible—is God-breathed, we also recognize that the inspired authors possessed a vast repertoire of rhetorical and literary strategies. These included not only the special use of words and figures of speech, but also the deliberate selection, arrangement, and shaping of ideas.

The primary goal of this commentary series is to help serious students of Scripture, as well as those charged with preaching and teaching the Word of God, to hear the messages of Scripture as biblical authors intended them to be heard. While we recognize the timelessness of the biblical message, the validity of our interpretation and the authority with which we teach the Scriptures are related directly to the extent to which we have grasped the message intended by the author in the first place. Accordingly, when dealing with specific texts, the authors of the commentaries in this series are concerned with three principal questions: (1) What are the principal theological points the biblical writers are making? (2) How do biblical writers make those points? (3) What significance does the message of the present text have for understanding the message of the biblical book within which it is embedded and the message of the Scriptures as a whole? The achievement of these goals requires careful attention to the way ideas are expressed in the OT, including the selection and arrangement of materials and the syntactical shaping of the text.

To most readers syntax operates primarily at the sentence level. But recent developments in biblical study, particularly advances in rhetorical and discourse analysis, have alerted us to the fact that syntax operates also at the levels of the paragraph, the literary unit being analyzed, and the composition as a whole. Discourse analysis, also called macrosyntax, studies the text beyond the level of the sentence (sentence syntax), where the paragraph serves as the basic unit of thought. Those contributing to this series recognize that this type of study may be pursued in a variety of ways. Some will prefer a more bottom-up approach, where clause connectors and transitional features play a dominant role in analysis. Others will pursue a more top-down approach, where genre or literary form begins the discussion. However, we all understand that both approaches are required to understand fully the method and the message of the text. For this reason, the ultimate value of discourse analysis is that it allows the text to set the agenda in biblical interpretation.

One of the distinctive goals for this series is to engage the biblical text using some form of discourse analysis to understand not only what the text says, but also how it says it. While attention to words or phrases is still essential, contributors to this commentary series will concentrate on the flow of thought in the biblical writings, both at the macroscopic level of entire compositions and at the microscopic level of individual text units. In so doing we hope to help other readers of Scripture grasp both the message and the rhetorical force of OT texts. When we hear the message of Scripture, we gain access to the mind of God.

Format of the Commentary

The format of this series is designed to achieve the goals summarized above. Accordingly, each volume in the series will begin with an introduction to the book being explored. In addition to answering the usual questions of date, authorship, and provenance of the composition, commentators will highlight what they consider to be the main theological themes of the book and then discuss broadly how the style and structure of the book develop those themes. This discussion will include a coherent outline of the contents of the book, demonstrating the contribution each part makes to the development of the principal themes.

The commentaries on individual text units that follow will repeat this process in greater detail. Although complex literary units will be broken down further, the commentators will address the following issues.

1. **The Main Idea of the Passage:** A one- or two-sentence summary of the key ideas the biblical author seeks to communicate.
2. **Literary Context:** A brief discussion of the relationship of the specific text to the book as a whole and to its place within the broader arguments.
3. **Translation and Exegetical Outline:** Commentators will provide their own translations of each text, formatted to highlight the discourse structure of the text and accompanied by a coherent outline that reflects the flow and argument of the text.
4. **Structure and Literary Form:** An introductory survey of the literary structure and rhetorical style adopted by the biblical author, highlighting how these features contribute to the communication of the main idea of the passage.
5. **Explanation of the Text:** A detailed commentary on the passage, paying particular attention to how the biblical authors select and arrange their materials and how they work with words, phrases, and syntax to communicate their messages. This will take up the bulk of most commentaries.
6. **Canonical and Theological Significance:** The commentary on each unit will conclude by building bridges between the world of the biblical author and other biblical authors and with reflections on the contribution made by this unit to the development of broader issues in biblical theology—particularly on how later OT and NT authors have adapted and reused the motifs in question. The discussion will also include brief reflections on the significance of the message of the passage for readers today.

The way this series treats biblical books will be uneven. Commentators on smaller books will have sufficient scope to answer fully each of the issues listed above on each unit of text. However, limitations of space preclude full treatment of every text for the larger books. Instead, commentators will guide readers through #1–4 and 6 for every literary unit, but Full Explanation of the Text (#5) will be selective, generally limited to twelve to fifteen literary units deemed most critical for hearing the message of the book.

In addition to these general introductory comments, we should alert readers of this series to several conventions that we follow. First, the divine name in the OT is presented as YHWH. The form of the name—represented by the Tetragrammaton, יהוה—is a particular problem for scholars. The practice of rendering the divine name in Greek as κύριος (=Heb. אֲדֹנָי, "Adonay") is carried over into English translations as "LORD," which represents Hebrew יהוה and distinguishes it from "Lord," which represents Hebrew אֲדֹנָי. But this creates interpretive problems, for the connotations and implications of referring to someone by name or by title are quite different. When rendering the word as a name, English translations have traditionally vocalized יהוה as "Jehovah," which seems to combine the consonants of יהוה with the vowels of אֲדֹנָי. However, today non-Jewish scholars often render the name as "Yahweh," recognizing that "Jehovah" is an artificial construct.

Second, frequently the verse numbers in the Hebrew Bible differ from those in our English translations. Since the commentaries in this series are based on the Hebrew text, the Hebrew numbers will be the default numbers. Where the English numbers differ, they will be provided in square brackets (e.g., Joel 4:12[3:12]).

Third, when discussing specific biblical words or phrases, these will be represented in Hebrew font and in translation, except where the transliterated form is used in place of an English term, either because no single English expression captures the Hebrew word's wide range meaning (e.g., *ḥesed* for חֶסֶד, rather than "lovingkindness"), or when it functions as a title or technical expression not readily captured in English (e.g., *gōʾēl* for גֹּאֵל, rather than "kinsman redeemer").

Daniel I. Block, general editor

Author's Preface and Acknowledgments

The writing of a commentary, even on a short book like Nahum, is a project that cannot be completed without help from many people. I thus have the happy opportunity to thank many individuals and institutions for their encouragement and support as I researched and wrote this volume. I should begin by thanking Dr. Miles Van Pelt, Alan Belcher Professor of Old Testament and Biblical Languages and Dean at Reformed Theological Seminary in Jackson, for the confidence in me that he demonstrated by inviting me to participate in this series. The writing of the commentary began while I was teaching at RTS, and I am thankful for the encouragement of my colleagues there and for the seminary's financial support of its faculty's research. Parts of the commentary were also written when I was teaching at the University of Sudbury, and I gratefully acknowledge the generous support of the Board of Regents Faculty Research and Publication Award that enabled research and conference participation. I express my gratitude to the Faculté de théologie évangélique in Montreal and to Puritan Reformed Theological Seminary in Grand Rapids for the varied forms of support and encouragement that they provided as I saw this volume through to completion. Students at RTS and the FTE also helped advance my understanding of Nahum as we made our way unit by unit through a book that is as challenging as it is concise. Finally, the Priscilla and Stanford Reid Trust also provided monies for conference travel and participation, and I am happy to express my gratitude to them.

I deeply appreciate the careful and constructive feedback I received from my series editors, Dr. Daniel I. Block and Dr. Kevin J. Youngblood. Both of these men helped improve the work substantially, and any remaining infelicities are my sole responsibility. I also thank Mrs. Katya Covrett, Executive Acquisitions Editor, and Dr. Nancy Erickson, Executive Production Editor, for shepherding the manuscript through the editing and production process in a timely and efficient manner. My gratitude is likewise due to Dr. Jean Revez, Professeur titulaire d'histoire at the Université de Québec à Montréal, for his expert help with some details on the archaeology of Thebes.

Last of all, I am thankful to God for the many blessings and opportunities that have flooded my life, and for which He alone deserves the praise. Chief among them are my wife of over fifteen years, Andreea, and our sons, Nathan and Felix. Our sons bring joy and much more into our lives, and Andreea brings more than I can say into all three of our lives. In appreciation for her unfailing love as wife and mother, her tenacity and strength in tasks and responsibilities without number, and her constant companionship, I gratefully dedicate this work to her. I pray that it will help believers, and the church as a whole, especially where it is persecuted, to know and trust the God whose righteousness and justice are our only solid hope. In an age when the world seems as chaotic, broken, and hopeless as ever, the triune God "is good, a stronghold in the day of trouble, and he knows those who take refuge in him" (Nah 1:7).

Daniel C. Timmer
Montreal, 2020

Abbreviations

Abbreviations for books of the Bible, pseudepigrapha, rabbinic works, papyri, classical works, and the like are readily available in sources such as the *SBL Handbook of Style* and are not included here.

AAA	Annals of Archaeology and Anthropology
AB	Anchor Bible
ABC	*Assyrian and Babylonian Chronicles*. Albert K. Grayson. TCS 5. Locust Valley, NY: Augustin, 1975
ABD	*Anchor Bible Dictionary*. Edited by David Noel Freedman. 6 vols. New York: Doubleday, 1992
ABG	Arbeiten zur Bible und ihrer Geschichte
AJA	*American Journal of Archaeology*
AKM	Abhandlungen für die Kunde des Morgenlandes
ANET	*Ancient Near Eastern Texts Relating to the Old Testament*. Edited by James B. Pritchard. 3rd ed. Princeton: Princeton University Press, 1969
AOAT	Alter Orient und Altes Testament
AOS	American Oriental Series
ARAB	*Ancient Records of Assyrian and Babylonia*. Daniel David Luckenbill. 2 vols. Chicago: University of Chicago Press, 1926–1927. Repr., New York: Greenwood, 1968
ARI	*Assyrian Royal Inscriptions*. Albert K. Grayson. 2 vols. Wiesbaden: Harrassowitz, 1972–1976
ARMT	Archives royales de Mari, transcrite et traduite
AS	Assyriological Studies
ASOR	American Schools of Oriental Research
ATD	Das Alte Testament Deutsch
ATJ	*Ashland Theological Journal*
AYBC	Anchor Yale Bible Commentary
BBR	*Bulletin for Biblical Research*
BCAW	*Blackwell Companions to the Ancient World*

BHQ	*Biblia Hebraica Quinta*. Edited by Adrian Schenker et al. Stuttgart: Deutsche Bibelgesellschaft, 2004–
BHS	*Biblia Hebraica Stuttgartensia*. Edited by Karl Elliger and Wilhelm Rudolph. Stuttgart: Deutsche Bibelgesellschaft, 1983
Bib	*Biblica*
BibInt	Biblical Interpretation Series
BibOr	Biblica et Orientalia
BSac	*Bibliotheca Sacra*
BSAH	*Blackwell Sourcebooks in Ancient History*
BWA(N)T	Beiträge zur Wissenschaft vom Alten (und Neuen) Testament
BZAW	Beihefte zur Zeitschrift für die alttestamentliche Wissenschaft
CAH	Cambridge Ancient History
CANE	*Civilizations of the Ancient Near East*. Edited by Jack M. Sasson. 4 vols. New York, 1995. Repr. in 2 vols. Peabody, MA: Hendrickson, 2006
CBC	Cambridge Bible Commentary
CBQ	*Catholic Biblical Quarterly*
CEB	Commentaire évangélique biblique
CHANE	Culture and History of the Ancient Near East
COS	*The Context of Scripture*. Edited by William W. Hallo and K. Lawson Younger, Jr. 4 vols. Leiden: Brill, 1997–2016.
DDD	*Dictionary of Deities and Demons in the Bible*. Edited by Karel van der Toorn, Bob Becking, and Pieter W. van der Horst. Leiden: Brill, 1995. 2nd rev. ed. Grand Rapids: Eerdmans, 1999
DTIS	*Dictionary for Theological Interpretation of Scripture*. Edited by Kevin J. Vanhoozer. Grand Rapids: Baker Academic, 2005
EBC	Expositor's Bible Commentary
EDB	*Eerdmans Dictionary of the Bible*. Edited by David Noel Freedman. Grand Rapids: Eerdmans, 2000
EHLL	*Encyclopedia of Hebrew Language and Linguistics*. Edited by G. Khan. 3 vols. Leiden: Brill, 2013
ETCSL	Electronic Text Corpus of Sumerian Literature
ExAud	*Ex Auditu*
FAT	Forschungen zum Alten Testament
FOTL	Forms of the Old Testament Literature
FRLANT	Forschungen zur Religion und Literatur des Alten und Neuen Testaments
GTJ	*Grace Theological Journal*
HALOT	*The Hebrew and Aramaic Lexicon of the Old Testament*. Ludwig Koehler and Walter Baumgartner. Revised by Walter Baumgartner and Johann J. Stamm. Translated by Mervyn E. J. Richardson. 2 vols. Leiden: Brill, 2001
HBAI	*Hebrew Bible and Ancient Israel*

HBS	Herders biblische Studien
HBT	*Horizons in Biblical Theology*
HCOT	Historical Commentary on the Old Testament
Historia	*Historia: Zeitschrift für alte Geschichte*
HMS	Hearing the Message of Scripture
HR	*History of Religions*
HSAT	*Die Heilige Schrift des Alten Testaments*. Edited by Emil Kautzsch and Alfred Bertholet. 4th ed. Tübingen: Mohr Siebeck, 1922–1923
HSM	Harvard Semitic Monographs
HThKAT	Herders Theologischer Kommentar zum Alten Testament
ICC	International Critical Commentary
IrAnt	*Iranica Antiqua*
JANES	*Journal of Ancient Near Eastern Studies*
JAOS	*Journal of the American Oriental Society*
JBL	*Journal of Biblical Literature*
JBLMS	Journal of Biblical Literature Monograph Series
JESHO	*Journal of the Economic and Social History of the Orient*
JESOT	*Journal for the Evangelical Study of the Old Testament*
JETS	*Journal of the Evangelical Theological Society*
JHebS	*Journal of Hebrew Scriptures*
J-M	*Joüon, Paul, and T. Muraoka. A Grammar of Biblical Hebrew.* Third reprint of the second edition, with corrections. Subsidia Biblica 27. Rome: Gregorian & Biblical, 2011
JNES	*Journal of Near Eastern Studies*
JSOT	*Journal for the Study of the Old Testament*
JSS	*Journal of Semitic Studies*
JTS	*Journal of Theological Studies*
KTU	*KTU: The Cuneiform Alphabetic Texts from Ugarit, Ras Ibn Hani, and Other Places*. Edited by Manfried Dietrich, Oswald Loretz, and Joaquin Sanmartin. Münster: Ugarit-Verlag, 1995 (= *CTU*)
LAI	Library of Ancient Israel
LHBOTS	The Library of Hebrew Bible/Old Testament Studies
LSAWS	*Linguistic Studies in Ancient West Semitic*
NDBT	*New Dictionary of Biblical Theology*. Edited by T. Desmond Alexander and Brian S. Rosner. Downers Grove: InterVarsity Press, 2000
NICOT	New International Commentary on the Old Testament
NIDOTTE	*New International Dictionary of Old Testament Theology and Exegesis*. Edited by Willem A. VanGemeren. 5 vols. Grand Rapids: Zondervan, 1997
NIGTC	New International Greek Testament Commentary
NSBT	New Studies in Biblical Theology

NTT	New Testament Theology
OBO	Orbis Biblicus et Orientalis
OEANE	*The Oxford Encyclopedia of Archaeology in the Near East.* Edited by Eric M. Meyers. 5 vols. New York: Oxford University Press, 1997
OIP	Oriental Institute Publications
OIUCAS	Oriental Institute of the University of Chicago Assyriological Studies
OTE	*Old Testament Essays*
OTL	Old Testament Library
OtSt	*Oudtestamentische Studiën*
PHSC	Perspectives on Hebrew Scriptures and Its Contexts
PIHANS	Publications de l'Institut historique-archéologique néerlandais de Stamboul
PTSDSSP	Princeton Theological Seminary Dead Sea Scrolls Project
RA	*Revue d'assyriologie et d'archéologie orientale*
RANE	Records of the Ancient Near East
RHR	*Revue de l'histoire des religions*
RIMA	The Royal Inscriptions of Mesopotamia, Assyrian Periods
RINAP	Royal Inscriptions of the Neo-Assyrian Period
SAA	State Archives of Assyria
SB	Sources bibliques
SBLMS	Society of Biblical Literature Monograph Series
SBLSym	SBL Symposium Series
ScrHier	Scripta Hierosolymitana
SSN	Studia Semitica Neerlandica
StOr	Studia Orientalia
TBei	*Theologische Beiträge*
TDOT	*Theological Dictionary of the Old Testament.* Edited by G. Johannes Botterweck and Helmer Ringgren. Translated by John T. Willis et al. 16 vols. Grand Rapids: Eerdmans, 1974–2018
TLOT	*Theological Lexicon of the Old Testament.* Edited by Ernst Jenni, with assistance from Claus Westermann. Translated by Mark E. Biddle. 3 vols. Peabody, MA: Hendrickson, 1997.
TynBul	*Tyndale Bulletin*
UCOP	University of Cambridge Oriental Publications
VTSup	Supplements to Vetus Testamentum
WAW	Writings from the Ancient World
WBC	Word Biblical Commentary
WMANT	Wissenschaftliche Monographien zum Alten und Neuen Testament
WTJ	*Westminster Theological Journal*
ZAW	*Zeitschrift für die alttestamentliche Wissenschaft*

Select Bibliography

Andersen, Francis I. *The Hebrew Verbless Clause in the Pentateuch*. JBLMS 14. Nashville: Abingdon, 1970.

Armerding, Carl E. "Nahum." Pages 447–89 in *Daniel and the Minor Prophets*. Edited by F. E. Gabelein. EBC 7. Grand Rapids: Zondervan, 1985.

Ataç, Mehmet-Ali. *The Mythology of Kingship in Neo-Assyrian Art*. Cambridge: Cambridge University Press, 2010.

Aufrère, Sydney H., Jean-Claude Golvin, and Jean-Claude Goyon. *Sites et temples de haute Égypte (1650 av. J.-C.—300 ap. J.-C.)*. Vol. 1 of *L'Égypte Restituée*. Paris: Errance, 1991.

Averbeck, Richard E. "Ancient Near Eastern Mythography as It Relates to Historiography in the Hebrew Bible: Genesis 3 and the Cosmic Battle." Pages 328–56 in *The Future of Biblical Archaeology: Reassessing Methodologies and Assumptions*. Edited by J. K. Hoffmeier and A. R. Millard. Grand Rapids: Baker, 2004.

Baker, David W. "The Mosaic Covenant against Its Environment." *ATJ* 20 (1988): 9–17.

Barnett, Richard D. *Sculptures from the North Palace of Ashurbanipal at Nineveh, 668–627 B.C.* London: British Museum, 1976.

Barr, James. *Comparative Philology and the Text of the Old Testament*. Oxford: Clarendon, 1968.

Baumann, Gerlinde. *Gottes Gewalt im Wandel: Traditionsgeschichtliche und intertextuelle Studien zu Nahum 1,2–8*. WMANT 108. Neukirchen-Vluyn: Neukirchener, 2005.

Beaulieu, Paul-Alain. "Mesopotamia." Pages 165–72 in *Religions of the Ancient World: A Guide*. Edited by S. I. Johnston. Harvard University Press Reference Library. Cambridge: Belknap Press of Harvard University Press, 2004.

Becking, Bob. "Passion, Power and Protection: Interpreting the God of Nahum." Pages 1–20 in *On Reading Prophetic Texts: Gender-Specific and Related Studies in Memory of Fokkelien van Dijk-Hemmes*. Edited by B. Becking and M. Dijkstra. BibInt 18. Leiden: Brill, 1996.

Ben Zvi, Ehud, and James D. Nogalski. *Two Sides of a Coin: Juxtaposing Views on Interpreting the Book of the Twelve / the Twelve Prophetic Books*. Edited by T. Römer. Analecta Gorgiana 201. Piscataway, NJ: Gorgias, 2009.

Berlejung, Angelika. "Erinnerungen an Assyrien in Nahum 2,4–3,19." Pages 323–56 in *Die unwiderstehliche Wahrheit: Studien zur alttestamentlichen Prophetie: Festschrift für Arndt Meinhold*. Edited by R. Lux and E.-J. Waschke. ABG 23. Berlin: Evangelische Verlagsanstalt, 2006.

Bussmann, Hadumod. *Routledge Dictionary of Language and Linguistics*. Translated and edited by G. Trauth and K. Kazzazi. London: Routledge, 1996.

Buth, Randall. "Word Order in the Verbless Clause." Pages 79–108 in *The Verbless Clause in Biblical Hebrew: Linguistic Approaches*. Edited by C. L. Miller. *LSAWS* 1. Winona Lake, IN: Eisenbrauns, 1999.

Butler, Judith. *Excitable Speech: A Politics of the Performative*. New York: Routledge, 1997.

Cassin, Elena. "Le roi et le lion." *RHR* 198 (1981): 355–401.

Cathcart, Kevin J. "Nahum, Book of." *ABD* 4:998–1000.

Charles, J. Daryl. "Plundering the Lion's Den: A Portrait of Divine Fury (Nahum 2:3–11)." *GTJ* 10.2 (1989): 183–201.

Chavalas, Marc, ed. *The Ancient Near East: Historical Sources in Translation*. *BSAH*. Oxford: Blackwell, 2006.

Christensen, Duane L. *Nahum: A New Translation with Introduction and Commentary*. AYBC 24F. New Haven: Yale University Press, 2009.

Cifarelli, Megan. "Gesture and Alterity in the Art of Ashurnasirpal II of Assyria." *The Art Bulletin* 80 (1998): 210–28.

Cogan, Mordechai. *Imperialism and Religion: Assyria, Judah and Israel in the Eighth and Seventh Centuries B.C.E.* SBLMS. Missoula, MT: Scholars Press, 1974.

———. "Into Exile: From the Assyrian Conquest of Israel to the Fall of Babylon." Pages 242–75 in *The Oxford History of the Biblical World*. Edited by M. Cogan. Oxford: Oxford University Press, 1998.

Cogan, Mordechai, and Hayim Tadmor. *II Kings*. AB 11. New York: Doubleday, 1988.

Cook, John A. "The Finite Verbal Forms in Biblical Hebrew Do Express Aspect." *JANES* 30 (2006): 21–35.

Crouch, Carly. *War and Ethics in the Ancient Near East: Military Violence in Light of Cosmology and History*. BZAW 407. Berlin: de Gruyter, 2009.

Curtis, John. "The Dying Lion." *Iraq* 54 (1992): 113–17.

Davies, Philip R., and John W. Rogerson. *The Old Testament World*. 2nd ed. Louisville: Westminster John Knox, 2005.

Day, John. *God's Conflict with the Dragon and the Sea: Echoes of a Canaanite Myth in the Old Testament*. UCOP 35. Cambridge: Cambridge University Press, 1985.

De Backer, Fabrice. "Notes on the Neo-Assyrian Siege-Shield and Chariot." Pages 69–78 in *Time and History in the Ancient Near East: Proceedings of the 56th Rencontre Assyriologique Internationale at Barcelona, 26–30 July 2010*. Edited by L. Feliu et al. Winona Lake, IN: Eisenbrauns, 2013.

De Backer, Fabrice, and Evelyne Dehenin. *The Neo-Assyrian Shield: Evolution, Heraldry, and Tactics*. Material Culture of the Ancient Near East 1. London: Lockwood, 2012.

Delcor, Mathias. "Allusions à la déesse Istar en Nahum 2,8?" *Bib* 58 (1977): 73–83.

Desjarlais, Robert R. *Counterplay: An Anthropologist at the Chessboard*. Berkeley: University of California Press, 2011.

Dick, Michael B. "The Neo-Assyrian Royal Lion Hunt and YHWH's Answer to Job." *CBQ* 125 (2006): 243–70.

Dozeman, Thomas. "Inner-Biblical Interpretation of YHWH's Gracious and Compassionate Character." *JBL* 108 (1989): 207–23.

Duff, R. Antony. "Punishment." Pages 331–57 in *Oxford Handbook of Practical Ethics*. Edited by H. LaFollette. Oxford: Oxford University Press, 2003.

Elat, Moshe. "Phoenician Overland Trade within the Mesopotamian Empires." Pages 21–35 in *Ah, Assyria! Studies in Assyrian History and Ancient Near Eastern Historiography Presented to Hayim Tadmor*. Edited by M. Cogan and I. Eph'al. ScrHier 33. Jerusalem: Magnes, 1991.

Emerton, J. A. "The Meaning of the Verb *ḥāmas* in Jeremiah 13,22." Pages 19–28 in *Prophet und Prophetenbuch: Festschrift für Otto Kaiser zum 65. Geburtstag*. Edited by V. Fritz et al. BZAW 185. Berlin: de Gruyter, 1989.

Fabry, Heinz-Josef. *Nahum*. HThKAT. Freiburg im Breisgau: Herder, 2006.

Fales, Frederick M. *Guerre et paix en Assyrie: Religion et impérialisme*. Les conférences de l'École Pratique des Hautes Études. Paris: Cerf, 2010.

———. "On *Pax Assyriaca* in the Eighth-Seventh Centuries BCE and Its Implications." Pages 17–35 in *Isaiah's Vision of Peace in Biblical and Modern International Relations: Swords into Plowshares*. Edited by R. Cohen and R. Westbrook. Culture and Religion in International Relations. New York: Palgrave Macmillan, 2008.

Faust, Avraham. "The Interests of the Assyrian Empire in the West: Olive Oil Production as a Test-Case." *JESHO* 54 (2011): 62–86.

Floyd, Michael H. *Minor Prophets Part 2*. FOTL 22. Grand Rapids: Eerdmans, 2000.

Fokkelman, Jan P. *Major Poems of the Hebrew Bible: At the Interface of Hermeneutics and Structural Analysis*. Vol. 1, *Ex. 15, Deut. 32, and Job 3*. SSN. Assen: Van Gorcum, 1998.

Follingstad, Carl M. *Deictic Viewpoint in Biblical Hebrew: A Syntagmatic and Paradigmatic Analysis of the Particle* כי. Dallas: SIL International, 2001.

Fox, Nili. "Clapping Hands as a Gesture of Anguish and Anger in Mesopotamia and in Israel." *JANES* 23 (1995): 49–60.

Frame, Grant. *Babylonia, 689–627: A Political History*. Leiden: Nederlands Historisch-Archaeologisch Instituut te Istanbul, 1992.

Fuchs, Andreas. "Assyria at War: Strategy and Conduct." Pages 380–401 in *The Oxford Handbook of Cuneiform Culture*. Edited by K. Radner and E. Robson. Oxford: Oxford University Press, 2011.

Gelston, Anthony. *The Twelve Minor Prophets*. *BHQ* 13. Stuttgart: Deutsche Bibelgesellschaft, 2010.

Gese, Hartmut. "Jona ben Amittai und das Jonabuch." *TBei* 16 (1985): 256–72.

Gitin, Seymour. "The Neo-Assyrian Empire and Its Western Periphery: The Levant, with a Focus on Philistine Ekron." Pages 77–103 in *Assyria 1995*. Edited by S. Parpola and R. Whiting. Helsinki: Neo-Assyrian Text Corpus Project, 1997.

Goering, Greg S. "Proleptic Fulfillment of the Prophetic Word: Ezekiel's Dirges over Tyre and Its Ruler." *JSOT* 36.4 (2012): 483–505.

Goldsworthy, Graeme. "'Thus Says the Lord!'—The Dogmatic Basis of Biblical Theology." Pages 25–40 in *God Who Is Rich in Mercy: Essays Presented to D. B. Knox*. Edited by P. T. O'Brien and D. G. Peterson. Homebush West, NSW: Lancer; Grand Rapids: Baker, 1986.

Gordon, Robert P. "Prophecy in the Mari and Nineveh Archives." Pages 37–58 in *"Thus Speaks Ishtar of Arbela": Prophecy in Israel, Assyria, and Egypt in the Neo-Assyrian Period*. Edited by R. P. Gordon and H. M. Barstad. Winona Lake, IN: Eisenbrauns, 2013.

Grayson, A. Kirk. "Assyria, Assyrians." Pages 97–105 in *Dictionary of the Old Testament: Historical Books*. Edited by B. T. Arnold and H. G. M. Williamson. Downers Grove, IL: InterVarsity Press, 2005.

———. *Assyrian and Babylonian Chronicles*. Winona Lake, IN: Eisenbrauns, 2000.

———. "Assyrian Civilization." Pages 194–228 in CAH III:2: *The Assyrian and Babylonian Empires and Other States of the Near East, from the Eighth to the Sixth Centuries B.C.* Edited by J. Boardman et al. Cambridge: Cambridge University Press, 1991.

———. *Assyrian Royal Inscriptions. Part 2: From Tiglath-Pileser I to Ashur-nasir-apli II*. RANE 2. Weisbaden: Harrassowitz, 1976.

———. *Assyrian Rulers of the Early First Millennium B.C. I (1114–859 BC)*. RIMA 2. Toronto: University of Toronto Press, 1991.

Harris, Rivkah. "Inanna-Ishtar as Paradox and a Coincidence of Opposites." *HR* 30 (1991): 261–78.

Hillers, Delbert R. "*Hôy* and *Hôy*-Oracles: A Neglected Syntactic Aspect." Pages 185–88 in *The Word of the Lord Shall Go Forth: Essays in Honor of David Noel Freedman in Celebration of His Sixtieth Birthday*. Edited by C. L. Meyers and M. O'Connor. ASOR Special Volume Series. Winona Lake, IN: Eisenbrauns, 1983.

Holloway, Steven W. *Aššur is King! Aššur is King! Religion in the Exercise of Power in the Neo-Assyrian Empire*. CHANE 10. Leiden: Brill, 2001.

Holmstedt, Robert D. "Hypotaxis." Pages 220–22 in vol. 2 of *EHLL*. Edited by G. Khan. Leiden: Brill, 2013.

Horowitz, Wayne. *Mesopotamian Cosmic Geography*. Winona Lake, IN: Eisenbrauns, 1998.

Huddleston, John R. "Nahum, Nineveh, and the Nile." *JNES* 62 (2003): 97–110.

Isaksson, Bo. "An Outline of Comparative Arabic and Hebrew Textlinguistics." Pages 36–150 in *Circumstantial Qualifiers in Semitic: The case of Arabic and Hebrew*. Edited by B. Isaksson. AKM 70. Wiesbaden: Harrassowitz, 2009.

———. "The Textlinguistics of the Suffering Servant: Subordinate Structures in Isaiah 52,13–53,12." Pages 173–212 in *En pāsē grammatikē kai sophiā: Saggi di linguistica ebraica in onore di Alviero Niccacci, ofm*. Edited by G. Geiger. Milan: Franciscan, 2011.

Jacobsen, Thorkild, and Seton Lloyd. *Sennacherib's Aqueduct at Jerwan*. OIP 24. Chicago: Oriental Institute of the University of Chicago, 1935.

Jahnow, Hedwig. *Das hebräische Leichenlied im Rahmen der Völkerdichtung*. BZAW 36. Giessen: Töpelmann, 1923.

Johnston, Gordon H. "Nahum's Rhetorical Allusions to Neo-Assyrian Conquest Metaphors." *BSac* 159 (2002): 21–45.

———. "Nahum's Rhetorical Allusions to Neo-Assyrian Treaty Curses." *BSac* 158 (2001): 287–307, 415–36.

Kalami, Isaac, and Seth Richardson, eds. *Sennacherib at the Gates of Jerusalem: Story, History and Historiography*. CHANE 71. Leiden: Brill, 2014.

Kessler, Karlheinz. "'Royal Roads' and Other Questions of the Neo-Assyrian Communication System." Pages 129–36 in *Assyria 1995*. Edited by S. Parpola and R. Whiting. Helsinki: Neo-Assyrian Text Corpus Project, 1997.

Knowles, Murray, and Rosamund Moon. *Introducing Metaphor*. New York: Routledge, 2006.

Kuhrt, Amélie. *The Ancient Near East c. 3000–330 BC*. Routledge History of the Ancient World. 2 vols. London: Routledge, 1995.

Leichty, Erle. *The Royal Inscriptions of Esarhaddon, King of Assyria (680–669 BC)*. RINAP 4. Winona Lake, IN: Eisenbrauns, 2011.

Lerner, Gerda. "The Origins of Prostitution in Ancient Mesopotamia." *Journal of Women in Culture and Society* 11 (1986): 236–54.

Liverani, Mario. "The Ideology of the Assyrian Empire." Pages 297–317 in *Power and Propaganda. A Symposium on Ancient Empires*. Edited by M. T. Larsen. Copenhagen Studies in Assyriology 7. Copenhagen: Akademisk Forlag, 1979.

Longman, Tremper III. "Nahum." Pages 765–829 in *Obadiah, Jonah, Micah, Nahum, Habakkuk*. Vol. 2 of *The Minor Prophets: An Exegetical and Expository Commentary*. Edited by T. McComisky. 3 vols. Grand Rapids: Baker, 1993.

Longman, Tremper III, and Daniel G. Reid. *God Is a Warrior*. Studies in Old Testament Biblical Theology. Grand Rapids: Zondervan, 1995.

Luckenbill, Daniel D. *The Annals of Sennacherib*. Chicago: University of Chicago Press, 1924.

———. *Historical Records from Assyria from the Earliest Times to Sargon*. *ARAB* 1. Chicago: University of Chicago Press, 1926.

———. *Historical Records from Assyria from Sargon to the End*. *ARAB* 2. Chicago: University of Chicago Press, 1927.

Lumsden, Stephen. "Narrative Art and Empire: The Throneroom of Assurnasirpal II." Pages 359–85 in *Assyria and Beyond: Studies Presented to Mogens Trolle Larsen*. Edited by J. G. Dercksen. PIHANS 100. Leiden: Netherlands Institute for the Near East, 2004.

Machinist, Peter. "Assyria and Its Image in First Isaiah." *JAOS* 103 (1983): 719–37.

———. "The Fall of Assyria in Comparative Ancient Perspective." Pages 179–95 in *Assyria 1995*. Edited by S. Parpola and R. Whiting. Helsinki: Neo-Assyrian Text Corpus Project, 1997.

Mack, Russell. *Neo-Assyrian Prophecy and the Hebrew Bible: Nahum, Habakkuk, and Zephaniah*. PHSC 14. Piscataway, NJ: Gorgias, 2011.

Marrow, William. "Neo-Assyrian Influences in Manasseh's Temple?" *CBQ* 75 (2013): 53–73.

May, Natalie N. "Triumph as an Aspect of the Neo-Assyrian Decorative Program." Pages 461–88 in *Organization, Representation, and Symbols of Power in the Ancient Near East*. Edited by G. Wilhelm. Winona Lake, IN: Eisenbrauns, 2008.

Meier, Samuel A. *Speaking of Speaking: Marking Direct Discourse in the Hebrew Bible*. VTSup 46. Leiden: Brill, 1992.

Merwe, Christo H. J. van der, Jackie A. Naudé, and Jan H. Kroeze. *A Biblical Hebrew Reference Grammar*. Biblical Languages 3. Sheffield: Sheffield Academic, 2000.

Millard, Alan. "For He Is Good." *TynBul* 17 (1966): 115–17.

Nissinen, Martti, with contributions by C. L. Seow and Robert K. Ritner. *Prophets and Prophecy in the Ancient Near East*. WAW. Atlanta: SBL Press, 2003.

Oates, Joan. "The Fall of Assyria." Pages 162–93 in CAH III:2: *The Assyrian and Babylonian Empires and Other States of the Near East, from the Eighth to the Sixth Centuries B.C.* Edited by J. Boardman et al. Cambridge: Cambridge University Press, 1991.

O'Brien, Julia M. *Nahum*. 2nd ed. Readings: A New Biblical Commentary. Sheffield: Sheffield Phoenix, 2009.

Oded, Bustenay. *War, Peace and Empire. Justifications for War in Assyrian Royal Inscriptions*. Wiesbaden: L. Reichert, 1992.

Oswalt, John. *The Book of Isaiah: Chapters 40–66*. NICOT. Grand Rapids: Eerdmans, 1998.

Parker, Bradley J. "Archaeological Manifestations of Empire: Assyria's Imprint on Southeastern Anatolia." *AJA* 107 (2003): 525–57.

———. "The Construction and Performance of Kingship in the Neo-Assyrian Empire." *Journal of Anthropological Research* 67 (2011): 357–86.

———. "The Northern Frontier of Assyria: An Archaeological Perspective." Pages 217–44 in *Assyria 1995*. Edited by S. Parpola and R. Whiting. Helsinki: Neo-Assyrian Text Corpus Project, 1997.

Parpola, Simo. *Assyrian Prophecies*. SAA 9. Helsinki: Helsinki University Press, 1997.

———. "Assyria's Expansion in the 8th and 7th Centuries BCE and Its Long-Term Repercussions in the West." Pages 99–111 in *Symbiosis, Symbolism and the Power of the Past: Canaan, Ancient Israel and Their Neighbors from the Late Bronze Age through Roman Palestine*. Edited by W. G. Dever and S. Gitin. Winona Lake, IN: Eisenbrauns, 2003.

———. *Letters from Assyrian Scholars to the Kings Esarhaddon and Assurbanipal*. Parts 1–2. AOAT 5. Neukirchen-Vluyn: Neukirchener Verlag, 1970–1971.

Parpola, Simo, and Kazuko Watanabe. *Neo-Assyrian Treaties and Loyalty Oaths*. SAA 2. Helsinki: University of Helsinki Press, 1988.

Peels, H. G. L. *The Vengeance of God: The Meaning of the Root NQM and the Function of the NQM-Texts in the Context of Divine Revelation in the Old Testament*. *OtSt* 31. Leiden: Brill, 1995.

Perlitt, Lothar. *Die Propheten Nahum, Habakuk, Zephanja*. ATD 25.1. Göttingen: Vandenhoeck & Ruprecht, 2005.

Piepkorn, Arthur Carl. *Historical Prism Inscriptions of Ashurbanipal*. AS 5. Chicago: University of Chicago Press, 1933.

Pinker, Aron. "Descent of the Goddess Ishtar to the Netherworld and Nahum II 8." *VT* 55 (2005): 89–100.

———. "Nahum and the Greek Tradition of Nineveh's Fall." *JHebS* 6 (2006): article 8. doi:10.5508/jhs.2006.v6.a8.

———. "Nineveh's Defensive Strategy and Nahum 2–3." *ZAW* 118 (2006): 618–25.

Polz, Daniel C. "Thebes (modern Luxor)." Pages 384–88 in vol. 3 of *Oxford Encyclopedia of Ancient Egypt*. Edited by D. B. Redford. 3 vols. Oxford: Oxford University Press, 2001.

Porter, Barbara N. "Ishtar of Nineveh and Her Collaborator, Ishtar of Arbela, in the Reign of Assurbanipal." *Iraq* 66 (2004): 41–44.

Purcell, William M., and David Snowball. "Style." Pages 698–703 in *Encyclopedia of Rhetoric*. Edited by T. O. Sloane. Oxford: Oxford University Press, 2001.

Raabe, Paul. "Why Prophetic Oracles against the Nations?" Pages 236–57 in *Fortunate the Eyes That See: Essays in Honor of David Noel Freedman in Celebration of His Seventieth Birthday*. Edited by A. Beck, A. Bartlett, C. Franke, and P. Raabe. Grand Rapids: Eerdmans, 1995.

Radner, Karen. "The Assyrian King and His Scholars: The Syro-Anatolian and the Egyptian Schools." Pages 221–38 in *Of God(s), Trees, Kings, and Scholars: Neo-Assyrian and Related Studies in Honour of Simo Parpola*. Edited by M. Luukko, S. Svärd, and R. Mattila. StOr 106. Helsinki: Finnish Exegetical Society, 2009.

Reade, Julian. "Assyrian Illustrations of Nineveh." *IrAnt* 33 (1998): 81–94.

———. "The Ishtar Temple at Nineveh." *Iraq* 67 (2005): 347–90.

———. "Religious Ritual in Assyrian Sculpture." Pages 7–61 in *Ritual and Politics in Ancient Mesopotamia*. Edited by B. N. Porter. AOS 88. New Haven: American Oriental Society, 2005.

———. "Studies in Assyrian Geography, Part 1: Sennacherib and the Waters of Nineveh." *RA* 72 (1978): 47–72.

Redford, Donald B. *Egypt, Canaan, and Israel in Ancient Times*. Princeton: Princeton University Press, 1992.

Renaud, Bernard. *Michée, Sophonie, Nahum*. SB. Paris: J. Gabalda, 1987.

Renz, Thomas. "Nahum, Book of." Pages 527–28 in *DTIS*. Edited by K. Vanhoozer. Grand Rapids: Baker Academic, 2006.

———. "A Perfectly Broken Acrostic in Nahum 1?" *JHebS* 9 (2009): article 23. doi:10.5508/jhs.2009.v9.a23.

Rivaroli, Marta. "Nineveh: From Ideology to Topography." *Iraq* 66 (2004): 199–205.

Roberts, J. J. M. *Nahum, Habakkuk, and Zephaniah: A Commentary*. OTL. Louisville: Westminster John Knox, 1991.

Roth, Martha T. *Law Collections from Mesopotamia and Asia Minor*. 2nd ed. WAW 6. Atlanta: Scholars Press, 1997.

Russell, John M. *Sennacherib's Palace without Rival at Nineveh*. Chicago: University of Chicago Press, 1991.

Saggs, H. W. F. *The Might That Was Assyria*. Sidgwick and Jackson Great Civilizations Series. London: Sidgwick and Jackson, 1984.

Schart, Aaron. "Twelve, Book of the: History of Interpretation." Pages 806–17 in *Dictionary of the Old Testament: Prophets*. Edited by M. J. Boda and G. J. McConville. Downers Grove, IL: InterVarsity Press, 2012.

Scoralick, Ruth. *Gottes Güte und Gottes Zorn: die Gottesprädikationen in Exodus 34,6f und ihre intertextuellen Beziehungen zum Zwölfprophetenbuch*. HBS 33. Freiburg im Breisgau: Herder, 2002.

Scurlock, Joann. "The Euphrates Flood and the Ashes of Nineveh (Diod. II 27.1–28.7)." *Historia* 39 (1990): 382–84.

Sherwin, Simon. "'I Am against You': YHWH's Judgment on the Nations and Its Ancient Near Eastern Context." *TynBul* 54.2 (2003): 149–60.

Spieckermann, Hermann. "Barmherzig and gnädig ist der Herr . . ." *ZAW* 102 (1990): 1–18.

Spronk, Klaas. "Jonah, Nahum, and the Book of the Twelve: A Response to Jakob Wöhrle." *JHebS* 9 (2009): article 8. doi:10.5508/jhs.2009.v9.a8.

———. *Nahum*. HCOT. Kampen: Kok Pharos, 1997.

Strawn, Brent A. *What Is Stronger than a Lion? Leonine Image and Metaphor in the Hebrew Bible and the Ancient Near East*. OBO 212. Göttingen: Vandenhoeck & Ruprecht, 2005.

Stronach, David, and Kim Codella. "Nineveh." Pages 144–48 in vol. 4 of *OEANE*. Edited by E. Meyers. 5 vols. New York: Oxford University Press, 1999.

Stuart, Douglas. *Hosea–Jonah*. WBC 31. Waco, TX: Word, 1987.

Sweeney, Marvin A. "Twelve, Book of the." Pages 788–806 in *Dictionary of the Old Testament: Prophets*. Edited by M. J. Boda and G. J. McConville. Downers Grove, IL: InterVarsity Press, 2012.

Tadmor, Hayim. *The Inscriptions of Tiglath-Pileser III, King of Assyria: Critical Edition with Introductions, Translations, and Commentary*. Jerusalem: Publications of the Israel Academy of Sciences and Humanities, 1994.

Tadmor, Hayim, and Shigeo Yamada. *The Royal Inscriptions of Tiglath-Pileser III (744–727 BC) and Shalmaneser V (726–722 BC), Kings of Assyria*. RINAP 1. Winona Lake, IN: Eisenbrauns, 2011.

Talmon, Shemaryahu. "The 'Comparative Method' in Biblical Interpretation—Principles and Problems." Pages 320–56 in *Congress Volume: Göttingen, 1977*. Edited by J. A. Emerton. VTSup 29. Leiden: Brill, 1978.

Thompson, R. Campbell, and R. W. Hamilton. "The British Museum Excavations at the Temple of Ishtar at Nineveh, 1930–1931." AAA 19 (1932): 55–116.

Tidiman, Brian. *Nahoum, Habaquq, Sophonie*. CEB. Vaux-sur-Seine: Edifac, 2009.

Timmer, Daniel C. "Boundaries without Judah, Boundaries within Judah: Hybridity and Identity in Nahum." *HBT* 34 (2012): 173–89.

———. *A Gracious and Compassionate God: Mission, Salvation, and Spirituality in Jonah*. NSBT 26. Leicester: Apollos, 2011.

———. "Nahum." Pages 79–86 in *The Lion Has Roared: Theological Themes in the Prophetic Literature of the Old Testament*. Edited by H. G. L. Peels and S. D. Snyman. Eugene, OR: Pickwick, 2012.

———. "Nahum's Representation of and Response to Neo-Assyria: Imperialism as a Multifaceted Point of Contact in Nahum." *BBR* 24 (2014): 349–62.

———. *The Non-Israelite Nations in the Book of the Twelve: Thematic Coherence and the Diachronic-Synchronic Relationship in the Minor Prophets*. BibInt 135. Leiden: Brill, 2015.

Tucker, Gene M. "The Law in the Eighth-Century Prophets." Pages 201–16 in *Canon, Theology, and Old Testament Interpretation: Essays in Honor of Brevard S. Childs*. Edited by G. M. Tucker, D. L. Peterson, and R. R. Wilson. Philadelphia: Fortress, 1988.

Van De Mieroop, Marc. "Revenge, Assyrian Style." *Past and Present* 179 (May 2003): 3–23.

———. "A Tale of Two Cities: Nineveh and Babylon." *Iraq* 66 (2004): 1–5.

Vanhoozer, Kevin J. "Exegesis and Hermeneutics." Pages 52–64 in *NDBT*. Edited by T. D. Alexander and B. S. Rosner. Downers Grove, IL: InterVarsity Press, 2000.

———. "Language, Literature, Hermeneutics, and Biblical Theology: What's Theological about a Theological Dictionary." Pages 15–50 in vol. 1 of *NIDOTTE*. Edited by Willem A. Van Gemeren. 5 vols. Grand Rapids: Zondervan, 1997.

Van Til, Cornelius. *The Defense of the Faith*. Phillipsburg, NJ: P&R, 1955.

Verderame, Lorenzo. "Astronomy, Divination, and Politics in the Neo-Assyrian Empire." Pages 1847–53 in *Handbook of Archaeoastronomy and Ethnoastronomy*. Edited by C. L. N. Ruggles. Springer, 2014.

Waltke, Bruce K. "The Phenomenon of Conditionality within Unconditional Covenants." Pages 123–39 in *Israel's Apostasy and Restoration: Essays in Honor of Roland K. Harrison*. Edited by A. Gileadi. Grand Rapids: Baker, 1988.

Waltke, Bruce K., and M. O'Connor. *An Introduction to Biblical Hebrew Syntax*. Winona Lake, IN: Eisenbrauns, 1990.

Walton, John H. "The Object Lesson of Jonah 4:5–7 and the Purpose of the Book of Jonah." *BBR* 2 (1992): 47–57.

Watts, J. D. W. *The Books of Joel, Obadiah, Jonah, Nahum, Habakkuk and Zephaniah*. CBC. New York: Cambridge University Press, 1975.

Weissert, Elnathan. "Creating a Political Climate: Literary Allusions to *Enūma Eliš* in Sennacherib's Account of the Battle of Hulale." Pages 191–202 in *Assyrien im Wandel der Zeiten*. Edited by H. Hauptmann and H. Waetzold. *HSAT*. Heidelberg: Heidelberger Orientverlag, 1997.

———. "Royal Hunt and Royal Triumph in a Prism Fragment of Ashurbanipal." Pages 339–58 in *Assyria 1995*. Edited by S. Parpola and R. Whiting. Helsinki: Neo-Assyrian Text Corpus Project, 1997.

Wendland, Ernst R. "What's the 'Good News'—Check Out 'the Feet'! Prophetic Rhetoric and the Salvific Centre of Nahum's 'Vision.'" *OTE* 11 (1998): 154–81.

Westermann, Claus. *Basic Forms of Prophetic Speech*. Translated by H. C. White; foreword by G. M. Tucker. London: Lutterworth; Louisville: Westminster John Knox, 1991.

Winter, Irene J. "Art in Empire: The Royal Image and the Visual Dimensions of Assyrian Ideology." Pages 359–81 in *Assyria 1995*. Edited by S. Parpola and R. Whiting. Helsinki: Neo-Assyrian Text Corpus Project, 1997.

Wiseman, Donald J. *Chronicles of Chaldean Kings (626–556 B.C.) in the British Museum*. London: British Museum, 1961.

Wolters, Al. "The Text of the Old Testament." Pages 19–37 in *The Face of Old Testament Studies: A Survey of Contemporary Approaches*. Edited by D. W. Baker and B. T. Arnold. Grand Rapids: Baker, 1999.

Yee, Gale A. "The Anatomy of Biblical Parody: The Dirge Form in 2 Samuel 1 and Isaiah 14." *CBQ* 50 (1988): 565–86.

Youngblood, Kevin J. *Jonah: God's Scandalous Mercy*. HMS. Grand Rapids: Zondervan, 2013.

Younger, K. Lawson, Jr. "Assyrian Involvement in the Southern Levant at the End of the Eighth Century B.C.E." Pages 235–63 in *Jerusalem in Bible and Archaeology: The First Temple Period*. Edited by A. Vaughn and A. Killebrew. SBLSym 18. Atlanta: Society of Biblical Literature, 2003.

Zehnder, Markus. "Building on Stone? Deuteronomy and Esarhaddon's Loyalty Oaths (Part 2): Some Additional Observations." *BBR* 19.4 (2009): 511–35.

———. *Umgang mit Fremden in Israel und Assyrien: Ein Beitrag zur Anthropologie des 'Fremden' im Licht antiker Quellen*. BWA(N)T 168. Stuttgart: Kohlhammer, 2005.

Zewi, Tamar. "Syntax: Biblical Hebrew." Pages 688–99 in vol. 3 of *EHLL*. Edited by G. Khan. 3 vols. Leiden: Brill, 2013.

Translation of Nahum

Nahum 1

1The Oracle of Nineveh. The Book of the Vision of Nahum the Elkoshite.

2A zealous and avenging God is YHWH. Avenging is YHWH and wrathful. Aveng-
ing is YHWH against his adversaries, and he stores up wrath against his enemies.
3YHWH is slow to anger and of great power; he will by no means acquit the guilty.

In whirlwind and storm is his way, and the clouds are the dust of his feet. 4He
rebukes the sea and makes it dry, all the rivers he dries up. Bashan and Carmel wither,
the blossom of Lebanon withers. 5Mountains shake before him, and the hills melt;
the earth heaves before him, the world and all who dwell in it.

6Before his wrath who can stand? Who can resist his burning anger? His rage is
poured out like fire, and the rocks are broken up by him. 7YHWH is good, a refuge
in the day of trouble, and he knows those who seek refuge in him; 8but with an
overflowing flood, a complete end he will make of its place, and his enemies he will
pursue into darkness.

9Whatever you plot against YHWH, he is making a complete end; an adversary
will not arise twice! 10Surely, like thorns are tangled, and like drunkards' drink is
drunk, they will be consumed like fully dried chaff!

11From you has gone out one plotting evil against YHWH, one planning wick-
edness. 12Thus says YHWH: "Even if they are at full strength and just as numerous,
even so they will be mowed down and removed! I have afflicted you, but I will afflict
you no longer. 13Now I will break his yoke bar off you and will break off your cords."

14YHWH has ordained thus concerning you: "Your name will no longer be sown;
from the house of your gods I will eliminate sculpted image and cast image; I will
prepare your grave, for you are despicable!"

Nahum 2

1Look on the mountains! The feet of a messenger of good news, one who an-
nounces peace! "Celebrate your feasts, Judah! Pay your vows! For never again will
the wicked one invade you—he is completely eliminated!"

2"One who scatters has come up against you! Guard the ramparts! Watch the road! Get ready to stand firm! Summon all your strength!" 3Truly, YHWH restores the majesty of Jacob like the majesty of Israel, although wasters have wasted them, and they have ruined their branches.

4The shield of his mighty ones is reddened, (his) heroes are dressed in scarlet, the chariot is (made) of fiery steel. On the day of his preparation, the spears are brandished. 5In the streets the chariots race madly; they rush madly through the squares. Their appearance is like torches; like lightning they dash. 6He remembers his officers. They stumble as they come forward. They rush to the wall, where the mantlet is already set up. 7The river gates are opened; the palace sways. 8Her statue is set up; she is stripped; she is carried away, her maidens lamenting with the voice of doves, beating their breasts. 9Nineveh was like a pool of water throughout her days, but now they flee. "Halt! Halt!" There is no one who turns back. 10"Plunder the silver! Plunder the gold!" There is no end to the treasure! Wealth from every kind of precious thing! 11Desolation, emptiness, devastation! Hearts melt, knees knock, trembling is in every loin, all their faces gather redness.

12Where is the lair of the lion, and the territory of the young lions, where the lion and lioness go? There the lion dwells, and there is nothing that startles (them). 13The lion has torn enough for his cub, and strangled (enough) for his lionesses. He has filled his den with prey, his den (he has filled with) torn flesh. 14"Know that I am against you!" Utterance of YHWH of Hosts: "I will burn in the fire her chariots; your young lions the sword will devour, and I will cut off from the earth your taking of prey. The voice of your envoys will no longer be heard."

Nahum 3

1Woe to the bloody city! (It is) utterly deceitful! Of plunder (it is) full! No one takes away (its) prey. 2(There is) the sound of the whip. (There is) the sound of the rattling wheel and (of) the rushing horse and (of) the bounding chariot! 3Horsemen charging, the blade of the sword, the flash of the spear, multitudes of slain, piles of corpses! There is no end to the dead bodies; they stumble over their dead bodies. 4Because of the many debaucheries of the prostitute, gracefully alluring, mistress of sorceries, who sells nations through her debaucheries and tribes through her sorceries, 5"Know that I am against you!" Utterance of YHWH of Hosts: "I will uncover your skirts over your head, and I will show nations your nakedness and kingdoms your shame! 6I will throw filth on you, I will declare you contemptible, I will make you a spectacle! 7Then all who see you will shrink back from you and will say, 'Devastated is Nineveh! Who will lament her?' Where can I seek comforters for you?

8"Will it go better for you than for Thebes, that sat by the Nile's waters, with water surrounding her? Whose strength was a sea, her rampart water? 9Cush was her strength, Egypt too, and without limit; Put and Lybia were her helpers. 10Yet even she became an exile, she went into captivity; moreover, her infants were dashed in pieces at the head of every street; lots were cast for her nobles and all her prominent citizens were bound with fetters. 11You too will be drunk, you will be incapacitated, you too will seek refuge from the enemy!

12"All your fortified cities are fig trees with first-ripe figs; if they are shaken, they will fall into the mouth of the eater! 13Look! Your troops are women in your midst! The gates of your land are wide open to your enemy! Fire devours your gate-bars! 14Draw for yourself water for the siege! Fortify the stronghold! Go into the clay, tread the mortar, grab the brick mold! 15There the fire will devour you! The sword will cut you down! It will devour you like the creeping locust!"

"Multiply yourself like the creeping locust! Multiply yourself like migratory locusts! 16You multiplied your merchants more than the stars of the heavens! The creeping locust sheds its skin and flies away! 17Your courtiers are like migratory locusts! Your scribes are like locust swarms settling on the walls on a cold day. When the sun rises they flee; their whereabouts are unknown. Where are they?

18"Your shepherds doze, King of Assyria! Your nobles sit still! Your people are scattered over the mountains, and there is none to gather (them). 19There is no healing for your fracture! Your wound is severe! All who hear the news of you will clap their hands over you, for over whom has your evil not passed ceaselessly?"

Introduction to Nahum

The Divine Warrior as Avenger and Deliverer

The Message of Nahum

In Nahum, God as the Divine Warrior and only deliverer announces a global "day" in which he will pour out his righteous vengeance on the powers of evil that oppose him. This climactic divine intervention also entails the deliverance of those who seek refuge in him (1:2–8). The destruction of Assyria described in the rest of the book is a prelude to this larger, final intervention, and simultaneously delivers and restores Judah (2:3[2]), putting an end to God's previous covenantal discipline (1:12b). Judah's deliverance will also bring with it the liberation of other nations from the crushing domination of the Assyrian Empire (3:19).

Nahum's message has rich significance for contemporary audiences in light of its ongoing fulfillment in the person and work of Jesus Christ. First, it offers a trenchant analysis of the characteristics that distinguish those who are reconciled to God from those who are not. Second, it analyzes features of Assyrian imperialism that are rampant in human behavior across the centuries and in all cultures, including human autonomy, the abuse of power, and the pursuit of happiness and significance through materialism. Finally, Nahum's message challenges its readers to adopt a radically theocentric understanding of themselves and of their world that puts Christ and his work as king, deliverer, and judge at the center.

The Historical Background to Nahum's Prophecies

Historical Context: Judah in the Assyrian Empire

The book of Nahum is situated between the conquest of Thebes by Assyria in 663 BCE, to which Nahum refers as past (3:8), and the fall of Nineveh (Assyria's capital city at the time) that Nahum anticipates in 3:5–7, which came about in 612.[1] Together these two events establish the historical context in which the book was written, and

1. Assurbanipal's account of the fall of Thebes can be found in "Babylonian and Assyrian Historical Texts," trans. A. Leo Oppenheim (*ANET*, 295). The Babylonian "Fall of Nineveh Chronicle" gives Babylon's perspective on the fall of Nineveh; see A. Kirk Grayson, *ABC* (Winona Lake, IN: Eisenbrauns, 2000), 90–96.

the contrast between the Assyrian Empire's strength and the prediction of its fall accurately sketches the book's main dynamic.[2]

Assyria as a Militarily Established Empire

Judah had already been deeply affected by Assyria in the decades before Nahum, a period during which the empire was at the height of its power (cf. 1:12). Since its resurgence near the end of the tenth century BCE, Assyria was able to expand significantly, adding to its heartland on the Tigris River territory to the south and especially to the west, in the direction of Israel and Judah. This push toward the west was begun by Shalmaneser III (858–824 BCE), who had to confront repeatedly a coalition of states in the Levant that opposed Assyrian expansion in 853, 849, 848, and 845. Shalmaneser was eventually successful in subordinating Israel,[3] which became a vassal state, and its king (Jehu) or his emissary is portrayed on the Black Obelisk of Shalmaneser III bowing before the king.[4]

During this time Assyria's reputation for violence developed most clearly. Because Assyria's expansion did not always involve outright conquest of another state but rather bringing that state under its control as a vassal (a status that involved paying tribute and fulfilling military and other obligations toward the empire), Assyria first had to convince states that such submission was the only rational choice. It did so by pursuing its expansion through increasingly regular (even annual) military campaigns focused on subjugating new territory and by developing a reputation as a brutal and unstoppable opponent.

The strategy in pursuing this policy was very intentional and well organized. Numbering some tens of thousands if deployed as a single force,[5] the Assyrian army would assemble at the border fortress nearest the campaign's target, and once outside friendly territory would advance with considerable circumspection, building fortified camps at every stage.[6] The military strategy employed depended on the nature of the target: raids focused on depriving the enemy of its livelihood by destroying food stores and other necessities, conquests in general pursued the neutralization or destruction of an enemy, and sieges were laid against objectives when a direct attack would prove too costly.[7] In combat, Assyria exploited the combination of the bow and

2. Klaas Spronk, *Nahum*, HCOT (Kampen: Kok Pharos, 1997), 13, is probably correct when he suggests a date shortly after the fall of Thebes, since Egypt's recovery shortly afterward would lessen the impact of the comparison.

3. A. Kirk Grayson, "Assyria, Assyrians," *Dictionary of the Old Testament: Historical Books*, ed. B. T. Arnold and H. G. M. Williamson (Downers Grove, IL: InterVarsity Press, 2005), 100–101.

4. The 2-meter-high (6.5 ft.) monolith was made around the year 827 BCE and is currently in the British Museum. See the public domain photo by Steven G. Johnson, http://commons.wikimedia.org/wiki/File:Jehu-Obelisk-cropped.jpg.

5. See the estimates of partial and full forces in Frederick M. Fales, *Guerre et paix en Assyrie: Religion et impérialisme*, Les conférences de l'École Pratique des Hautes Études (Paris: Cerf, 2010), 97.

6. Andreas Fuchs, "Assyria at War: Strategy and Conduct," in *The Oxford Handbook of Cuneiform Culture*, ed. K. Radner and E. Robson (Oxford: Oxford University Press, 2011), 390.

7. Ibid., 390–91. On siege strategies, see Israel Eph'al, "Ways and Means to Conquer a City, Based on Assyrian Queries to the Sungod," in *Assyria 1995*, ed. S. Parpola and R. Whiting (Helsinki: Neo-Assyrian Text Corpus Project, 1997), 49–53.

the chariot, although foot soldiers also carried bows, slings, and spears.[8] Assyrian war chariots increased in size, armor, and sophistication over time, and proved extremely effective weapons.[9] Assyrian cavalry kept pace with this development, and often functioned alongside the chariots. The significant and often rapid expansion of the empire, which increased in size roughly fivefold from the early ninth century to the early seventh century (especially under Assurnasirpal II in the early ninth century and Tiglath-pileser III in the mid–late eighth century) bears poignant witness to the effectiveness of its army.

Assyrian Military Violence as a Strategy of Empire

Assyria's reputation for violence was very effectively developed and transmitted both on the battlefield by committing acts of spectacular violence and brutality and at home by means of propaganda of various sorts. On the battlefield, Assyrian troops would pile up their defeated enemies' severed heads, or mutilate captives by cutting off their noses, lips, ears, hands, or feet. In the case of rebellious vassals, even more brutal means were sometimes employed, including impalement, flaying, or evisceration. In his official description of his campaign against the rebellious Yau-biʾdi of Hamath, Sargon II (721–705 BCE) reports, "I mustered the masses of Aššur's troops and at Qarqar, together with his warriors, I burned Qarqar. Him I flayed. I killed the rebels in the midst of those cities."[10] Similar violence could also be brought home to the Assyrian populace, as when Esarhaddon had two rebellious kings beheaded and "to show the people the might of the god Assur, my lord, I hung (the heads) around the necks of their nobles and I paraded in the squares of Nineveh with singer(s) and lyre(s)."[11]

Numerous and extensive reliefs displayed in royal palaces served as more permanent representations of Assyria's brutality. These reliefs presented Assyrian power and violence to the eyes of the royal court and of visiting emissaries alike. Reliefs from Sennacherib's southwest palace at Nineveh that depict the siege and capture of the Judean city of Lachish in 701 BCE are typical of this kind of propaganda. At 2.69 meters (9 feet) high and 18.9 meters (62 feet) long in total, this series of reliefs covered entirely the walls of a room in the palace.[12] The panels portray various aspects of the Assyrian assault, beginning with the march to Lachish and continuing through the battle to the final deportation of the survivors to Assyria. One panel that is part

8. Fales, *Guerre et paix*, 109–17.

9. Fuchs, "Assyria at War," 393–94.

10. "The Great 'Summary' Inscription," trans. K. Lawson Younger, Jr. (*COS* 2.118E:296).

11. Erle Leichty, *The Royal Inscriptions of Esarhaddon, King of Assyria (680–669 BC)*, RINAP 4 (Winona Lake, IN: Eisenbrauns, 2011), 17, from Nineveh prism A.

12. See John M. Russell, *Sennacherib's Palace without Rival at Nineveh* (Chicago: University of Chicago Press, 1991). An idea of their visual power can be gained from a fly-through of a virtual reconstruction of the palace of Assurnasirpal II at Calah, online at http://www.aina.org/ata/20141010181255.htm.

of this series of reliefs represents parts of various phases of the battle and illustrates several elements of Assyrian warfare mentioned earlier. Inclined panels on the left depict foot soldiers and siege machinery attacking the city; the large central section depicts the transport of spoils by helmeted soldiers and the deportation of Judean women and children carrying what are presumably a few of their belongings; and the lower right corner depicts the flaying of two Judeans by pairs of soldiers.[13]

Royal records of these military campaigns also reflect the importance of violence for the ideology of the Assyrian king and empire. Sennacherib's account of his 701 BCE campaign against a number of nations and city-states in the Levant (including Lachish) states: "I advanced to Ekron and slew its officials and nobles who had stirred up rebellion and hung their bodies on watchtowers all about the city."[14] A few decades later, Assurbanipal (668–627 BCE), most likely the Assyrian king during Nahum's ministry, recounts how he punished by killing, impaling, and flaying not only unfaithful rulers but their subjects as well, "small and great."[15]

The purpose of surveying some representative Assyrian depictions of the empire's violence is not to portray them as more depraved or inhumane than other groups in the ancient Near East. Frederick Fales points out that while Assyria was capable of shocking violence, it was not an empire driven by bloodlust, nor was its religion focused on making all other peoples submit to Assur in some kind of religious conversion.[16] Rather, Assyria sought to extend its gods' rule (especially Assur's) through the most expedient means possible. This nexus of warfare and religion explains why Nahum treats Assyria as it does. Rather than condemning the Assyrians for being ethnically or politically Assyrian, the book evaluates Assyrians, and especially the Assyrian king and elite, on the basis of their behavior as an expression of their religion. Both condemnation and deliverance in the book of Nahum are primarily connected to this spiritual evaluation, while political or ethnic identity plays only a secondary role. This is clearest in the opening hymn, where individuals' ultimate fates are decided only on the basis of their relationship with YHWH, leaving aside all other facets of their identity.

13. For an image (photograph by Mike Peel, www.mikepeel.net) in the public domain, see http://upload.wikimedia.org/wikipedia/commons/7/7c/Lachish_Relief%2C_British_Museum_5.jpg. The relief was created shortly after the fall of Lachish and is presently in the British Museum. The aesthetics and ideology of these and similar reliefs are helpfully explored by Julian Reade, "Religious Ritual in Assyrian Sculpture," in *Ritual and Politics in Ancient Mesopotamia*, AOS 88, ed. B. N. Porter (New Haven: American Oriental Society, 2005), 7–61; Irene J. Winter, "Art in Empire: The Royal Image and the Visual Dimensions of Assyrian Ideology," in *Assyria 1995*, ed. S. Parpola and R. M. Whiting (Helsinki: Neo-Assyrian Text Corpus Project, 1997), 359–81; Stephen Lumsden, "Narrative Art and Empire: The Throneroom of Assurnasirpal II," in *Assyria and Beyond: Studies Presented to Mogens Trolle Larsen*, ed. J. G. Dercksen, PIHANS 100 (Leiden: Netherlands Institute for the Near East, 2004), 359–85.

14. "Sennacherib's Siege of Jerusalem," trans. Mordechai Cogan (*COS* 2.119B:302–3).

15. Sarah C. Melville, "Apology and Egyptian Campaigns," in *The Ancient Near East: Historical Sources in Translation*, ed. M. Chavalas, *BSAR* (Oxford: Blackwell, 2006), 364.

16. Fales, *Guerre et paix*, 9–25. This is not to say that Assyrian ideology did not develop in response to this long-lived

The Religious Facets of Assyria's Military Imperialism

Assyrian royal inscriptions from the seventh century make use of nearly all possible justifications for military action against the empire's enemies, notably rebellion against Assyria's gods, misplaced trust in other powers, and lack of fidelity and submission to the Assyrian monarch.[17] Esarhaddon takes up arms against those who have "sinned against the god Assur,"

and in another context justifies action against Abdi-Milkuti, king of Sidon, by asserting that he "did not fear my lordship (and) did not listen to the words of my lips, . . . trusted in the rolling sea and threw off the yoke of the god Assur."[19] Similarly, Sanda-uarri, king of the cities Kundi and Sissu, is presented as "a dangerous enemy, who did not fear my lordship (and) abandoned the gods, trusted in the impregnable mountains." He and an ally "swore an oath by their gods with one another, and trusted in their own strength," while Esarhaddon "trusted in the gods Assur, Sin."[20] A final example, drawn from Assurbanipal's description of his campaign that quelled a rebellion in Egypt and also destroyed Thebes in 663 BCE, explains that the rebellious vassal king Taharqa "forgot the might of Ashur and Ishtar and the great gods, my lords, and trusted in his own strength."[21] In response, Assurbanipal first prays to Assur and Ishtar, then gathers his troops, takes Thebes, and installs vassal kings in Taharqa's stead. But these vassals later "sinned against my oath. They did not preserve the oath of the great gods, forgot the good deeds I did for them and their hearts plotted evil," eventually establishing a coalition against Assyria. As a result, "The curse of Ashur, king of the gods, came over them for they sinned against the oath of the great gods."[22]

Complementing this emphasis on the failure of Assyria's enemies to recognize the legitimate claims of its gods on their lands was the positive assertion that Assur in particular was supremely powerful. As his earthly agent, the Assyrian king was both obliged and able to extend Assur's claims across the globe. This is evident in the appropriation, most clearly by Sennacherib, of material from Enuma Elish, which in its standard form recounts how Marduk created an orderly cosmos through violent

tradition of violence. Markus Zehnder (*Umgang mit Fremden in Israel und Assyrien: Ein Beitrag zur Anthropologie des 'Fremden' im Licht antiker Quellen*, BWANT 168 [Stuttgart: Kohlhammer, 2005], 546, 554) suggests that Neo-Assyria viewed the "other" as less than human and therefore was proportionately more likely to execute acts of cruelty than it would have been had it viewed the "other" as fully human.

17. See esp. Bustenay Oded, *War, Peace and Empire: Justifications for War in Assyrian Royal Inscriptions* (Wiesbaden: L. Reichert, 1992). Here I draw with permission on Daniel C. Timmer, "Nahum's Representation of and Response to Neo-Assyria: Imperialism as a Multifaceted Point of Contact in Nahum," *BBR* 24 (2014): 349–62.

18. Leichty, *The Royal Inscriptions of Esarhaddon*, 15.

19. Ibid., 16.

20. Ibid., 17.

21. Melville, "Apology and Egyptian Campaigns," 364.

22. Ibid., 364. In the case of Babylon's rebellion, Shamash-shum-ukin "plots evil" and interrupts Assurbanipal's worship at Babylon's temples, so the gods destroyed him by fire. Assurbanipal's gruesome response to this rebellion "calmed the hearts of the great gods, my lords" (366–67).

single combat and so became king of the gods.[23] During the last century of Assyria's existence,[24] this understanding of divine activity as well as other factors gave rise to the most developed phase of Assyria's ideology of kingship, which posited a strong parallel between divine and royal behavior.[25] As war is inseparable from kingship as exercised by Marduk (or by Anshar-Assur, in a version of the myth produced during Sennacherib's reign), so too for the human king.[26] In a word, the Neo-Assyrian Empire's essence was "warfare, kingship, order."[27] With only minor variations, this royal ideology is consistent in Neo-Assyrian royal inscriptions and prophetic texts alike.[28]

The result of this ideology is a conception of empire that knows no geographical boundaries, and a view of the king as the unstoppable representative and agent of Assur. This is clear from an inscription of Assurnasirpal II, which begins in typical fashion by describing him as "king of the universe, unrivaled king, king of all the four quarters, . . . destructive weapon of the great gods." [29] Similarly, a royal hymn for Assurbanipal begins with the exclamation "Ashur is king! Ashur is king!"[30] The exclusive possession by the Assyrian monarch of this divine prerogative and power means that he "is the only one to legitimately exercise universal dominion," is without equal, and "is the only one endowed with those qualities that render legitimate the exercise of power."[31] As we turn to consider Judah's history in the seventh century, and as we later study Nahum's message, this highly charged religious-political background must be kept in mind.

It is hardly surprising that in the face of Assyrian imperialism, especially from the middle of the eighth century onward, the comparatively tiny state of Judah came more and more under Assyrian influence and control. After a period of relative

23. Elnathan Weissert, "Creating a Political Climate: Literary Allusions to *Enūma Eliš* in Sennacherib's Account of the Battle of Hulale," in *Assyrien im Wandel der Zeiten*, ed. H. Hauptmann and H. Waetzold, HSAT (Heidelberg: Heidelberger Orientverlag, 1997), 191–202; see more generally Carly Crouch, *War and Ethics in the Ancient Near East: Military Violence in Light of Cosmology and History*, BZAW 407 (Berlin: de Gruyter, 2009), 21–28.

24. Fales notes that during the last century of Assyria's existence the ideology of kingship reached its fullest expression, *Guerre et paix*, 70.

25. Crouch, *War and Ethics*, 24.

26. K. Lawson Younger, Jr., "Assyrian Involvement in the Southern Levant at the End of the Eighth Century B.C.E.," in *Jerusalem in Bible and Archaeology: The First Temple Period*, ed. A. Vaughn and A. Killebrew, SBLSym, 18 (Atlanta: Society of Biblical Literature, 2003), 255.

27. Crouch, *War and Ethics*, 27.

28. For an example drawn from the Assyrian royal inscriptions corpus, see Sarah C. Melville, "Neo-Assyrian Texts 1," in *The Ancient Near East: Historical Sources in Translation*, ed. M. Chavalas, *BSAH* (Oxford: Blackwell, 2006), 282. For an example drawn from a prophetic text, see Martti Nissinen, with contributions by C. L. Seow and Robert K. Ritner, *Prophets and Prophecy in the Ancient Near East*, WAW 12 (Atlanta: SBL Press, 2003), 104–5.

29. A. Kirk Grayson, *ARI*, vol. 2, *From Tiglath-Pileser I to Ashur-nasir-apli II* (Weisbaden: Harrassowitz, 1976), 119 (from the Ninurta temple at Kalach, i 9).

30. Alasdair Livingstone, *Court Poetry and Literary Miscellanea*, SAA 3 (Helsinki: Helsinki University Press, 1989), 26 (text 11). Paul Garelli discusses the circumstances of its use in "Le temple et le pouvoir royal en Assyrie du XIVe au VIIIe siècle," in *Le temple et le culte. Compte rendu de la XXe Rencontre Assyriologique Internationale* (Istanbul: Nederlands Historisch-Archeologisch Institut te Istanbul, 1975), 116–17.

31. Mario Liverani, "The Ideology of the Assyrian Empire," in *Power and Propaganda: A Symposium on Ancient Empires*, ed. M. T. Larsen, Copenhagen Studies in Assyriology 7 (Copenhagen: Akademisk Forlag, 1979), 310.

weakness lasting roughly 75 years, Assyria quickly regained strength during the reign of Tiglath-pileser III (744–727 BCE), followed by Shalmaneser V (726–722), Sargon II (721–705), Sennacherib (704–681), Esarhaddon (680–669), and Assurbanipal (668–627). During this period the empire reached its greatest size, expanding in all directions and reaching as far as modern-day Iran in the east, Iraq in the south, Turkey in the north and west, and the Levant and Egypt in the southwest. While Assyria promised potential vassals peace and well-being if they submitted (the so-called *Pax Assyriaca*, cf. 2 Kgs 18:29–35), it was also a terrible threat when ignored or dealt with dishonestly. Judah's waffling foreign policy would give it opportunity to experience both these sides of the vassal-suzerain relationship.[32]

Judah's Gradual Decline before and during the Seventh Century

Although originally an independent and unified nation under David and Solomon, and then a pair of nations formed by the division of the Israelite united monarchy around 930 BCE, Israel and Judah were both frequently affected by the political stratagems of neighboring kingdoms and empires. During the ninth century, Aram (Syria) was a frequent threat to the north, and Assyria was involved in (northern) Israel's politics as early as the battle of Qarqar in 853 BCE.[33] By the middle of the eighth century, Assyria's influence had reached the Southern Kingdom of Judah, which became its vassal in exchange for military help against a coalition of Israelite and Aramean troops (2 Kgs 16:7–10; Isa 7–8). For the next century or so, Assyria's role was determinative for these two nations.

It is in this final period of Assyrian expansion that the Northern Kingdom of Israel was conquered and became the Assyrian-administered province of Samerina in 722 BCE, losing most of its Israelite inhabitants and becoming home to deportees from elsewhere in the Assyrian Empire (2 Kgs 17:24, 30–31). A few decades later, the abortive siege of Jerusalem led by the Assyrian king Sennacherib in 701 BCE was part of a campaign that was hardly less traumatic. In addition to shutting up Hezekiah (715–686 BCE) and those in Jerusalem "like a bird in a cage," Sennacherib "besieged forty-six of his fortified towns and surrounding smaller towns, which were without number" (as Sennacherib's official description of his campaign puts it) and annexed significant portions of Judah's territory.[34] Manasseh's reign (686–642 BCE) saw Assyria's domination continue, and he was required to contribute both forced labor and soldiers to Assyrian endeavors as late as 669 BCE.[35]

32. See Frederick M. Fales, "On *Pax Assyriaca* in the Eighth–Seventh Centuries BCE and Its Implications," in *Isaiah's Vision of Peace in Biblical and Modern International Relations: Swords into Plowshares*, ed. R. Cohen and R. Westbrook, Culture and Religion in International Relations (New York: Palmgrave Macmillan, 2008), 17–35.

33. See "Kurkh Monolith," trans. K. Lawson Younger, Jr. (*COS* 2.113A:261–64).

34. "Sennacherib's Siege of Jerusalem," *COS* 2.119B:302–3.

35. "Babylonian and Assyrian Historical Texts," *ANET*, 291, 294.

Assyria's power would eventually wane, especially when Assurbanipal was confronted with the rebellion of the province of Babylon in 652–648 BCE and with unrest in the east in the 630s BCE.[36] Assyria overextended itself in suppressing the rebellion of Babylon and never recovered, but its decline and fall lie outside the historical context of the book of Nahum and constitute instead early confirmation of its veracity.[37]

The biblical sources portray Judah's religious life during the middle decades of the seventh century as quite lackluster. Some sources present Manasseh as the primary instigator of religious error (2 Kgs 21:1–18; cf. 2 Chr 33:1–17), making his role so prominent that God promised that as a result he would do to Jerusalem what he had done to Samaria (2 Kgs 21:13). This is certainly not the whole picture, and other biblical sources provide additional data, particularly on popular mores and behavior. Isaiah felt it necessary to critique the majority of the Judean population roughly a half-century before Nahum (Isa 1), with deliverance being possible only through judgment. Isaiah's contemporary Micah likewise critiqued Judean (and Israelite) society in general, and their leaders in particular, for having engaged in a number of sinful activities, including oppression of the vulnerable and perversion of justice (Mic 3). Slightly later than Nahum's setting, Habakkuk and Zephaniah sharply condemned Judah for worship of false gods (Zeph 1:4–5) and violence (Hab 1:2–4; Zeph 3:1–4).

The picture of Judah in the eighth and seventh centuries gives evidence of widespread disobedience and even apostasy, with some kings leading the way (e.g., Manasseh, 2 Kgs 21:9) and others resisting the decline, Josiah in particular (640–609 BCE). Josiah's reforms, prompted by the rediscovery of the book of Deuteronomy, were far reaching and earned him the highest commendation possible from the author of Kings (2 Kgs 23:25), while enabling him to escape the looming punishment of Manasseh's sins (2 Kgs 22:14–20). By the time of Josiah's death, Assyria had almost completely fallen to Babylon and its allies, partially fulfilling Nahum's prophecy. Given Judah's significant religious problems during this period, it is striking that Nahum gives them minimal attention and instead focuses on the guilt and punishment of Assyria. This choice is reflected in the subjects and literary genres chosen by the book's author and suggests that Judah's history is to be seen in a larger, global perspective.

36. H. W. F. Saggs, *The Might That Was Assyria*, Sidgwick & Jackson Great Civilizations Series (London: Sidgwick & Jackson, 1984), 118–21; Joan Oates, "The Fall of Assyria," in CAH III:2, ed. J. Boardman et al. (Cambridge: Cambridge University Press, 1991), 162–93.

37. The history is presented in detail in Grant Frame, *Babylonia, 689–627: A Political History* (Leiden: Nederlands Historisch-Archaeologisch Instituut te Istanbul, 1992), 102–201.

Nahum's Rhetorical Aims and Strategies

The Speaker

The book of Nahum as a whole is identified by its opening lines as an "oracle" and a "vision" of Nahum of Elkosh. Since no other Nahum is mentioned elsewhere in the OT, and Nahum of Elkosh appears only here, no biographical data whatsoever are available apart from the name of his hometown. Even at this point certainty eludes us since several locations have been proposed for this town. Least likely is al-Qush, north of Nineveh, and proposed locations in Capernaum of Galilee are also quite unlikely since Nahum wrote for a Judean audience. The precise location of Elkosh in Judah remains uncertain and therefore gives us no information about the prophet.[38]

Given this paucity of data, all that is to be known of the author/speaker must be derived from the book. Here again there is very little to go on, since the author never speaks of himself in the first person or makes reference to his experience. While some interpreters have suggested that he was a staunch nationalist,[39] various features of his message prevent us from labeling him so simplistically. If we assume that the prophet himself (rather than someone in his entourage) put his words in writing, it is necessary to infer that Nahum was well educated, probably connected in some way with the royal court (the primary locus of scribal and archival activity), and familiar with Assyrian military activity and propaganda.[40]

On the level of discourse, the book consists of third-person descriptions of YHWH (presumably made by the prophet; 1:2–8), second-person speech by the prophet to Assyria (1:9–11), and YHWH's first-person speech to Nineveh/Assyria (1:14; 2:13[12]; 3:5–7) and to Judah (1:12–13). While the rest of the book (2:1[1:15]–3:19) is addressed directly to Assyria, it is sometimes difficult to determine whether the prophet is the speaker, or whether he is quoting God (2:2–11[1–10]; 3:1–4, 8–19). The significance of Nahum's message for those who trust and revere YHWH's word is probably hinted at by the prophet's name, which is related to the Hebrew verb meaning "to comfort, console."

The Audience

The Real Audience: Judeans

Since Nahum was written in Hebrew, it is clear that the book's initial or real audience was Judeans of the seventh century and later. This raises two questions: how did the author expect Judah, a nation whose population was quite heterogeneous

38. Ronald A. Simkins, "Elkosh," *EDB*, 401; Y. Kobayashi, "Elkosh," *ABD* 2:476.

39. E.g., Georg Fohrer, *Introduction to the Old Testament* (Nashville: Abingdon, 1968), 451, thinks Nahum is simplistic and nationalistic.

40. See the similar reflections of Michael H. Floyd, *Minor Prophets Part 2*, FOTL 22 (Grand Rapids: Eerdmans, 2000), 19; Spronk, *Nahum*, 1.

in terms of their religion, to receive his message, and why does a book to a Judean audience contain discourse most often addressed to Assyria?

Apart from what we saw earlier regarding the lackluster religious condition of Judah in the seventh century, we have only a few clues as to how Nahum viewed his Judean audience. Most significant is the fact that the first time Nahum speaks of YHWH's deliverance from a coming global judgment, the book presents it not as the certain future of "Judah" but rather as the future of those who "take refuge in him" (1:7).[41] This detail may seem unimportant, but when placed at the beginning of a book dealing with God's reaction to evil, particularly (but not exclusively) in Assyria, it is significant that the book's portrayal of the theophany that will usher in the definitive judgment of all evil does not simply put YHWH on the side of Judah, over against Assyria.

In addition to this implicit recognition that being Judean does not guarantee safety in the coming global judgment, several references to the punishment of Israel and Judah confirm that neither nation is presented as sinless or guaranteed a cloudless future once YHWH intervenes. Carmel and Bashan, both in (northern) Israelite territory, are among the areas that will be affected by the future judgment mentioned in 1:2–5. Although largely transformed into the Assyrian provinces of Megiddo and Dor (Carmel) and Gilead/Karnaim (Bashan) by the time Nahum was composed, these areas had belonged to Israel in the past.[42] Not only had they been lost, according to the Bible, as a result of the Northern Kingdom's heterodox cult (1 Kgs 12:26–33) and lifestyle that ignored Torah (Hosea, Amos), but their population during the seventh century still included a number of Israelites. As a result, the desolation that Nahum announces would have been interpreted as directed at least partially against Israelites. Similarly, Judah has already been afflicted by Assyria (1:12–13), something the book of Kings and various prophets repeatedly interpret as punishment for the sins of the Judeans and their leaders.

The very real threat that Assyria posed to Judah in the seventh century, as well as the probability that the Judeans would hear second-hand reports of its military successes elsewhere (e.g., in Egypt, with Assyrian forces inevitably passing by or through Judah to reach their target), ensured that Nahum's audience was sensitive to the past and present judgments the book mentions. To this we must add Judah's current status as Assyria's vassal (after Hezekiah, only Josiah seems to have stopped vassal payments to Assyria during the seventh century, an inference from his resistance to the Egyptian-Assyrian coalition). Judah's vassal status entailed significant economic pressure in the form of vassal payments and forced labor,[43] and evidence

41. The idiom "trust in" (חסה + ב) with God as its object consistently denotes those (in Israel or outside it) who seek refuge in him from the threat of the wicked; cf. Pss 2:12; 5:12[11]; 31:20[19]; 37:40; 64:11[10]; etc.

42. Bashan changed hands frequently due to its role as a buffer zone between Israel and Aram; cf. 1 Kgs 22:3; 2 Kgs 8:28; 10:32–33; 14:25.

43. Cf. Paula McNutt, *Reconstructing the Society of Ancient Israel*, LAI (Louisville: Westminster John Knox, 1999), 162–63.

of widespread Assyrian influence is attested by the presence of Assyrian "religious and ideological motifs . . . on locally manufactured seals and cult objects" in seventh-century Judah[44] as well as by the enormous impact of Sennacherib's destruction of forty-six(!) fortified Judean cities in 701 BCE.[45] Taken together, these factors would have made at least some Judeans aware of their past shortcomings and less likely to interpret Nahum's announcement of Assyria's future fall in nationalistic terms.

Another important clue to the way that the book of Nahum views its Judean audience lies in the ramifications of the echo in 1:2–3 of Exod 20:5–7, which, rather than adding elements of patience and forgiveness to the description of God's character, adds instead a strong emphasis on God's wrath against his enemies. The division of Israel in Exod 20:5–7 into those who "hate" YHWH and those who "love him and keep his commands" would give pause to any Judean reader or hearer of Nahum who was looking for "smooth words." There may also be an oblique reference to Jacob's new name in 2:3[2], such that God will restore to "Jacob" (i.e., Judah in a lackluster spiritual condition) the excellence and blessing that were associated with Israel/Jacob after his struggle with God (cf. Gen 32:27–28).[46]

These points allow us to conclude that Nahum's opening hymn (1:2–8) includes a distinction between Judeans who have no interest in knowing or following YHWH and those who trust him even amid punishment for their nation's sin. Other data suggest that such a distinction would have been nearly unavoidable given the religious diversity in seventh-century Judah that probably made sincere YHWH-worshippers a minority during that period. The OT itself (e.g., Zeph 1) and archaeological evidence both clearly show that not all Judeans were faithful to the God who had called his name over them.[47] Even though future deliverance is promised to "Judah" (2:1[1:15]), this should not be understood as an absolute promise for all Judeans regardless of their spiritual and moral condition.[48]

A final point should be made concerning the audience. Although the book was evidently composed prior to Nineveh's fall, so that the initial audience would be Judeans still under the Assyrian scourge, it is self-evident that the book held continued significance for future generations. When other challenges and threats arose, later readers would have interpreted them in relation to the danger posed long ago by

44. Simo Parpola, "Assyria's Expansion in the 8th and 7th Centuries BCE and Its Long-Term Repercussions in the West," in *Symbiosis, Symbolism and the Power of the Past: Canaan, Ancient Israel and their Neighbors from the Late Bronze Age through Roman Palestine*, ed. W. G. Dever and S. Gitin (Winona Lake, IN: Eisenbrauns), 103–4.

45. The Assyrian version of events is given in "Sennacherib's Siege of Jerusalem," *COS* 2.119B:302–3.

46. Victor P. Hamilton, "Jacob/Israel (Person)," *NDBT*, 588.

47. Note, for example, the pillar figurines found in the southern Levant from roughly 715–586 BCE; see Richard Hess, *Israelite Religions: An Archaeological and Biblical Survey* (Grand Rapids: Baker Academic, 2007), 308–12.

48. Some of these points are developed further in Daniel C. Timmer, "Nahum," in *The Lion Has Roared: Theological Themes in the Prophetic Literature of the Old Testament*, ed. H. G. L. Peels and S. D. Snyman (Eugene, OR: Pickwick, 2012), 79–86. Floyd draws the similar conclusion that in Nahum, "both YHWH's people and other nations can become either his allies or his enemies; the status of any nation as an ally or enemy of YHWH can change over time" (*Minor Prophets*, 18).

Assyria, a legitimate hermeneutical move given the larger perspective established by 1:2–8.

The Rhetorical Audience: Nineveh/Assyria

The second question mentioned above regarding the book's audiences puts before us something of a paradox: why are oracles with Judah as their real audience most frequently addressed rhetorically to Assyria? While some biblical prophecies were occasionally transmitted to other nations, this was clearly exceptional, and apart from Jonah's brief ministry in Nineveh, these situations are mentioned almost in passing by biblical writers.[49] Paul Raabe summarizes the relevant passages by noting that Jer 18:7–8 "logically implies the notion of a prior hearing of the prophetic oracle by the targeted nation"; that prophetic excursions beyond Israel's borders are biblically attested (e.g., 2 Kgs 8:7–15); that Jeremiah transmitted his message to the envoys from Edom, Moab, Ammon, Tyre, and Sidon (Jer 27:1–11), as did Isaiah to envoys from Philistia (Isa 14:32), Seir (Isa 21:11–12), and perhaps Cush (Isa 18:2); and that Nebuchadnezzar and his general Nebuzaradan knew of Jeremiah and his message (Jer 39–40).[50]

The biblical data mention perhaps six such incidents in the span of 300 years, suggesting that the phenomenon was indeed rare. More to the point, unlike Jonah, Nahum never introduces the possibility that Assyria, or even Nineveh alone, would repent. Finally, there is no evidence that Nahum's message was ever transmitted to Assyria. As a result, a book (and probably a relatively public prophetic ministry prior to its composition) which frequently addresses itself to Assyria was probably heard only by Judean ears.

This strange reality is not beyond explanation. Some of the oldest recorded prophecies from the ancient Near East are "oracles against foreign nations" that were pronounced by one side in a military conflict, presumably with the belief that such oracles would achieve their intended effect.[51] Similarly, some of the OT's earliest recorded prophecies against other nations were delivered on the battlefield and served to encourage Israel in combat (1 Sam 15:2–3; 1 Kgs 20:26–30; 2 Kgs 13:14–19) without being transmitted to their opponent at the same time. Nahum is akin to an oracle against a foreign nation that is *not* delivered in the context of military conflict with Assyria. Indeed, Judah and its king have no explicit role whatsoever in the conflict

49. For Jonah, see Bryan D. Estelle, *Salvation through Judgment and Mercy: The Gospel According to Jonah*, The Gospel According to the Old Testament (Phillipsburg, NJ: P&R, 2005); Daniel C. Timmer, *A Gracious and Compassionate God: Mission, Salvation, and Spirituality in Jonah*, NSBT 26 (Leicester: Apollos, 2011).

50. Cf. Paul Raabe, "Why Prophetic Oracles against the Nations?" in *Fortunate the Eyes That See: Essays in Honor of David Noel Freedman in Celebration of His Seventieth Birthday*, ed. A. Beck et al. (Grand Rapids: Eerdmans, 1995), 252–53; cf. Francis Andersen and David N. Freedman, *Amos*, AB 24A (New York: Doubleday, 1989), 232.

51. Paul M. Cook, "Nations," *Dictionary of the Old Testament: Prophets*, ed. M. J. Boda and G. J. McConville (Downers Grove, IL: InterVarsity Press, 2012), 565, with reference to the Sumerian "Curse of Agade" and Egyptian execration texts.

that YHWH announces with Assyria, precisely because the conflict belongs to YHWH (note his "I am against you" in 2:14[13]; 3:5).[52] As a result, Nahum is largely a transcript of a divine address to Assyria (the rhetorical audience) that is delivered to Judah (the real audience) for its benefit. A similar situation, also involving Judah under threat from Assyria, arises in 2 Kgs 18:13–19:37, where Hezekiah is informed of Sennacherib's impending defeat in a divine message transmitted by Isaiah. In that response, YHWH speaks directly to Sennacherib (the rhetorical audience) but only Hezekiah (the real audience) hears the message (2 Kgs 19:21–28).

The Rhetorical Strategy

In order to grasp Nahum's strategy for communicating his message, it is helpful to return to the overall (meta)genre of the book, that of an oracle against a foreign nation.[53] As we have seen, this kind of literature involves the deity letting the audience (Judah) hear what he is planning with respect to another group (Assyria). The choice of this genre allows the author to demonstrate very effectively to Judah that God is aware of Assyria's offenses, that it is within his prerogative and power to punish those offenses, that he will indeed do so, and that the outcome will be favorable for Judah. The book also sets this particular deliverance in a global context, assuring those who genuinely follow YHWH and those whose values reflect his that he will eventually bring a full end to all evil.

The hearing by the real audience (Judah) of what the rhetorical audience (Assyria) would have liked to know beforehand, but does not, makes such an oracle a very effective way of encouraging Judah. Since Judah knows what Assyria does not about its future, Judah could possess a confidence that allows calm, patient waiting prior to YHWH's intervention. A high level of confidence is further encouraged by the mocking tone of several passages. For Judeans who were to one degree or another familiar with Assyrian propaganda, this sardonic tone would have been a fitting antidote to the limitless confidence so evident in Assyrian correspondence, inscriptions, and verbal communications.[54] Finally, for a Judean audience that at least in some cases was familiar with the parts of the OT already written, the book's occasional reuse of earlier Scripture would encourage them to view the fall of Assyria in the context of God's overarching purposes for his people (e.g., the allusion to Isa 52:1, 7, in Nah 2:1[1:15]

52. See further Timmer, "Nahum's Representation of and Response to Neo-Assyria," 358–60. Judah's history during this time includes, as far as we know, no military resistance on the part of Judah to Assyria and its plans from the end of Hezekiah's reign (ca. 685 BCE) until the end of Josiah's (ca. 609). Assyrian records show that Manasseh in particular was a faithful vassal (cf. Esarhaddon's prisms in "Babylonian and Assyrian Historical Texts," *ANET*, 291–92, 294, 301).

53. I use the term "oracle" loosely and agree with Floyd that it is quite similar to the "prophetic historical exemplum" genre he assigns to the book as a whole (*Minor Prophets*, 15).

54. Peter Machinist, "Assyria and Its Image in First Isaiah," *JAOS* 103 (1983): 735–36, has identified a few cases in Nahum that likely reflect direct, verbal knowledge of Assyrian propaganda, including "flood" in 1:8, "yoke" in 1:13, and the lion imagery in 2:12–14[11–13].

With this general orientation, we can now look at the most prominent features of Nahum's communicative strategy. In many cases the very genres the author chose are part of this strategy, since the choice of literary genre is strongly influenced by what one wants to say and what one wants to accomplish by saying it.[55] But other factors play a role as well, including the way that the author characterizes Judah, Assyria, and the other nations; the order in which information is presented; and the choice to describe Assyria's destruction in the very terms with which it vaunted itself.

Global Context for Judah's Particular Situation

The enormous size and apparently unlimited power of the Assyrian Empire meant that Nahum's Judean audience needed to believe firmly that YHWH's power and control were truly unlimited. It is therefore not by chance that a book so focused on the Assyrian Empire should begin with the widest possible perspective. The middle section in the opening hymn (1:3c–5) includes a number of elements that affirm YHWH's power outside Israel and over the world in general (1:5c, d). Striding over the earth and raising dust that becomes the very clouds, he rebukes "the sea" and "all the rivers," demonstrating the extent of his power (1:4a, b). Territory currently under Assyrian control knows no protection. The regions of Carmel and Bashan, proverbially fertile due to rainfall and good soil, respectively, suddenly lose their agricultural productivity (1:4c, d). Lebanon, famous as a source of lumber, will similarly lose its valuable forest resources. The final optic through which Nahum prepares the reader to look at Assyria is emphatically global (1:5c, d). The upheaval of the earth, including the presumably permanent hills and mountains, demonstrates graphically that all that exists is under YHWH's control. The focus of YHWH's actions are human beings, of course, so the presentation of the theophany ends at the very point of contact between YHWH and every human being, including the book's Judean audience and their Assyrian oppressors.

YHWH's Character as Primary Ground and Cause for Judgment and Deliverance

The solution that Nahum presents to the terrifying problem of Assyria's apparently endless violence and exploitation of the weaker nations around it does not depend on some vague notion of justice, or worse, on a hateful nationalism. Rather, the book ties the announced judgment of Assyria, and the consequent deliverance of Judah and the other nations Assyria has abused, directly to YHWH's character (1:2–8).

Nahum does not present a full picture of YHWH's character, but chooses to highlight certain elements from Israel's past as recorded in Scripture. He begins with

55. See Kevin J. Vanhoozer, "Language, Literature, Hermeneutics, and Biblical Theology: What's Theological about a Theological Dictionary," in *NIDOTTE* 1:15–50, esp. 38–40.

God's self-description in Exod 20:5–6 (part of the second commandment), but rather than modifying it as God did in Exod 34:6–7 when he added "compassionate and gracious, slow to anger and abounding in covenant love and truth," Nahum elaborates on God's jealousy, i.e., on his passion for his own glory and honor. He puts particular stress on YHWH's "vengeance" or "punitive retribution" (נקם), a term that occurs three times in 1:2. This retribution has as its goal the preservation of God's holiness by demonstrating his commitment and ability to establish his justice.[56] Nahum also omits the mention of God's forgiveness (cf. Exod 20:6) in this context.

YHWH's role as the Divine Warrior flows directly out of these characteristics. YHWH's wrath, jealousy, and retribution are focused on his "enemies" and "adversaries" (1:2, 8), identified as the guilty (1:3). The role of Divine Warrior describes the way in which YHWH exercises his holy wrath against those who oppose him and refuse to find safety in him by trusting him for deliverance. This role appears first in Exod 14–15, where YHWH glorifies himself by destroying Israel's Egyptian pursuers and is glorified by his people as a result.[57] All the same, it was understood that YHWH as Divine Warrior could bring judgment on both non-Israelites and Israelites (against non-Israelites in Num 10:35–36, Josh 11:6; against Israelites in Josh 7, Jer 21:3–7, Lam 2:5).[58] Accordingly, the introductory section of Nahum is careful not to assign ultimate judgment and deliverance to particular nations without any nuance, while the remainder of the book makes clear that YHWH in this role will certainly do away with Assyria.

YHWH's combat with Assyria (the book does not make clear whether he will defeat the nation himself or through an unidentified intermediate means) implicitly denies to Judah any military role, and this prevents the Judean king in particular from taking center stage in the process. While there is nothing theologically problematic with the idea of a godly king accomplishing the divine will through military action (cf. Pss 2 and 110, and many of David's campaigns), the exclusive focus on God as the one who will deliver Judah and the other nations from Assyria creates a strong theocentric perspective in the mind of the reader/hearer. It is also a reminder of the foolish arrogance that the Assyrian king demonstrated in his claim of universal dominance (see the comments on 1:9 below).

Finally, just as judgment of those who oppose YHWH is grounded in his character, so too his deliverance of those who trust in him depends ultimately on his patience, his ability to deliver, and his goodness and willingness to enter a relationship with those who seek and find in him the only shelter from his punishment of evil.

56. Cf. H. G. L. Peels, "נקם," *NIDOTTE* 3:154–56.

57. Note the *niphal* of כבד, "I will gain glory," in Exod 14:17 and the profuse praise that the Israelites offer to YHWH in Exod 15; cf. William H. C. Propp, *Exodus 1–18*, AB 2 (New York: Doubleday, 1999), 36, 498.

58. See Tremper Longman III and Daniel G. Reid, *God Is a Warrior*, Studies in Old Testament Biblical Theology (Grand Rapids: Zondervan, 1995), esp. 31–60.

Much like God had delivered Israel from Egypt in a demonstration of his great power (Exod 32:11; Deut 4:37; 9:29; 2 Kgs 17:36; Neh 1:10) and spared them in his immense patience despite their frequent rebellion (Exod 34:6–7), his goodness makes him a refuge for those who trust in him.

These aspects of Nahum's message mean that despite the extremely palpable and dangerous nature of the relationship between Assyria and Judah, Judeans were not encouraged to interpret it primarily on a political level, nor were they to assume that they were in the right (after all, until recently God had seen fit to afflict them). Exclusive divine agency, the restriction of deliverance to those in a trusting relationship with YHWH, and an overwhelming focus on his glory and honor give the audience a carefully crafted lens through which to view the epoch-making fall of Assyria.

Binary Differences

Nahum's treatment of the Assyrian threat and its resolution involves a consistently binary approach, with most of the elements fitting into an "x or not-x" perspective. For example, God's character is described primarily in terms of wrath leading to vengeance or goodness leading to deliverance, and the groups associated with those two fates are very sharply distinguished from one another. Following the book's literary order, the first such distinction is between God's enemies or adversaries on the one hand, and those who take refuge in him on the other.

The second binary differentiation is more complex, identifying Assyria as YHWH's enemy and Judah (and the other nations Assyria exploited) as in some way trusting in him and/or benefiting from his deliverance. Some aspects of this difference were clear in the seventh century: Judah was a vassal state, while Assyria was the suzerain, and thus Judah was Assyria's victim. However, the clear distinction between the two also involves treating the two stereotypically, that is, as homogeneous groups that have sharply contrasting characteristics. When compared to Assyria, Judah appears in the book as implicitly or explicitly fair in trade (3:16), nonviolent in international relations (2:12–14[11–13]), firmly committed to YHWH in religion (1:9–11), and not guilty of idolatry in its worship (1:14).[59]

It is clear that the book of Nahum does not present these stereotypes as absolute—if that were the case, God's past judgment of Judah's sin would be inexplicable (1:12). If the mixed identity of seventh-century Judah as including some who trusted in YHWH and some who didn't is taken into account, however, the stereotype can be fully appreciated for the sharp contrast it establishes between Assyria and Judah even if that contrast remains relative. Judah's characterization is positive enough that it is not threatened by the same judgment that will bring down Assyria, and the division

59. These points are developed in more detail in Daniel C. Timmer, "Boundaries without Judah, Boundaries within Judah: Hybridity and Identity in Nahum," *HBT* 34 (2012): 173–89.

of the world into two groups in 1:2–8 also allows the author to present this particular divine judgment in the strongest possible colors in the rest of the book.

Ironic Reuse of Assyrian Propaganda

There are good reasons to conclude that the author of Nahum, whether the prophet himself or someone responsible for putting his message into writing, has intentionally reused some of Assyria's propaganda in his announcement of the empire's demise. This adds a strong note of irony to the book, as these elements of Assyrian propaganda were intended by their original (Assyrian) authors to promote the empire's glory and the submission of others to its will. Although many examples of this exist, here we will note two, leaving others for discussion in the commentary proper.

First, it is likely that Nahum uses Assyrian phraseology that originally described its military power to describe Nineveh's downfall amid a flood (cf. Nah 2:7[6]). The likelihood that Nahum is reusing an Assyrian motif arises from the fact that images of a flood or deluge appear occasionally in Assyrian royal inscriptions, always in the king's description of himself, but at the same time are quite rare in Biblical Hebrew.[60] For example, Assurnasirpal II (883–859 BCE) referred to himself as "fearless (in) combat, high flood-wave that has no opponent," while Shalmaneser III (858–824 BCE) said of himself that he "killed all his enemies and wiped (them) out like a flood."[61] Tiglath-pileser III (744–727 BCE) described himself as a "valiant man who, with the help of (the god) Assur, his lord, [smashed like pots] all [who were unsubmissive to him], swept over (them) like [the] Deluge."[62] Against this background, Nahum's proleptic description of the destruction of the king's palace in terms of a flood (cf. Nah 2:7[6]) ironically evokes this tradition of royal self-description in order to undermine the Assyrian king's claims.[63]

Nahum's deconstruction of the lion metaphor in 2:12–14[11–13] furnishes another example of the strategy of reusing Assyrian material created to serve the empire's interest in order to portray its downfall. "Standard phraseology, from Tiglath-pileser I onward, portrayed royal valor in the hunt," as when Tiglath-pileser I (1115–1077 BCE) boasted "I killed on foot 120 lions with my wildly outstanding

60. Machinist, "Assyria and Its Image in First Isaiah," 726–27, mentions Jer 46:7–8; 47:2; Dan 11:10, 40; 2 Sam 5:20 // 1 Chr 14:11; Nah 1:8.

61. Brent A. Strawn, "Ashurnasirpal II" and "Shalmaneser III," in *The Ancient Near East: Historical Sources in Translation*, ed. M. Chavalas, Blackwell Sourcebooks in Ancient History (Oxford: Blackwell, 2006), 287 and 289, respectively.

62. In a fragment from Calah, in Hayim Tadmor and Shigeo Yamada, *The Royal Inscriptions of Tiglath-Pileser III (744–727 BC) and Shalmaneser V (726–722 BC), Kings of Assyria*, RINAP 1 (Winona Lake, IN: Eisenbrauns, 2011), 116–18.

63. Note also the claims of Tiglath-pileser III that he "swept over [the people of Karzibra] like a downpour of the god Adad" (Kalhu Annals, slab 16), and of Assurbanipal that "like the onset of a furious storm I covered Elam completely" (Sarah C. Melville, "Civil War and Elamite Campaigns," in *The Ancient Near East: Historical Sources in Translation*, ed. M. Chavalas, Blackwell Sourcebooks in Ancient History [Oxford: Blackwell, 2006]), 365.

assault. In addition, 800 lions I felled from my light chariot."[64] Other Neo-Assyrian material develops the image of the king as a lion-like warrior, as when Esarhaddon described himself as "raging like a lion" against his enemies.[65] While Assyrian kings also described themselves as bulls, eagles, and other animals in military contexts, the image of the king killing a lion in hand-to-hand combat was particularly prominent as the royal seal from the time of Shalmaneser III onward (858–824 BCE),[66] and Assurbanipal adorned the eighteen entries of his capital city with lion figurines that represented the king as the city's protector par excellence.[67]

Interestingly, extant evidence suggests that "the most references to royal lion hunts in the [Assyrian] annals occur during the reign of Ashurbanipal," most likely king of Assyria during Nahum's ministry.[68] Favorable weather had evidently expanded the hunting grounds available to lions in parts of Assyria and the king was obliged to reduce their population by hunting them. The king judged this royal activity important enough to preserve a record of it in his annals.

> Since I took my seat upon the throne of the father who begot me, Adad has sent his rains. . . . The young of the lions thrive. . . . With their roaring the hills resound. . . . As if the plague had broken loose, there were heaped up corpses of dead men, cattle and sheep. . . . In the course of my campaign into [] their lairs I broke up. . . . [69]

Since Assurbanipal's lion hunts were part of his divinely authorized role as his people's protective shepherd, YHWH's announcement that he will do away with him in that role is doubly ironic. By destroying Assyria, the empire that had made other nations their prey, YHWH assumes the Assyrian monarch's role and eliminates him a threat to *his* people.[70]

Taunt, Mockery, Irony, Shaming

Nahum's ironic and subversive reuse of Assyrian imagery is part of a larger rhetorical strategy by which the book brings shame on Assyria. In several cases

64. Jeffrey J. Niehaus, *Ancient Near Eastern Themes in Biblical Theology* (Grand Rapids: Kregel, 2008), 49; A. Kirk Grayson, *Assyrian Rulers of the Early First Millennium BC I (1114–859 BC)*, RIMA 2 (Toronto: University of Toronto Press, 1991), 26 (A.0.87.1 vi 76–84).

65. Leichty, *The Royal Inscriptions of Esarhaddon*, 53.

66. This is also noted by Angelika Berlejung, "Erinnerungen an Assyrien in Nahum 2,4–3,19," in *Die unwiderstehliche Wahrheit: Studien zur alttestamentlichen Prophetie: Festschrift für Arndt Meinhold*, ed. R. Lux and E.-J. Waschke, ABG 23 (Leipzig: Evangelische Verlagsanstalt, 2006), 323–56 (here, 333). I agree with Heinz-Josef Fabry, *Nahum*, HThKAT (Freiburg im Breisgau: Herder, 2006), 37, that direct dependence cannot be proved, but contend that concept-based (rather than word-based) intertextuality is more important for the book's message and easier to show as probable given the evidence presently available.

67. Berlejung, "Erinnerungen," 334; see further the discussion of Nah 2:11–13 below.

68. Gordon H. Johnston, "Nahum's Rhetorical Allusions to the Neo-Assyrian Lion Motif," *BSac* 158 (2001): 287–307 (299).

69. Daniel D. Luckenbill, *Historical Records from Assyria from Sargon to the End, ARAB* 2 (Chicago: University of Chicago Press, 1927), 363, cited in Johnston, "Nahum's Rhetorical Allusions to the Neo-Assyrian Lion Motif," 300.

70. These and other uses of lion imagery in the ancient Near East are helpfully surveyed in Brent A. Strawn, *What Is Stronger than a Lion? Leonine Image and Metaphor in the Hebrew Bible and the Ancient Near East*, OBO 212 (Fribourg: Academic Press; Göttingen: Vandenhoeck & Ruprecht, 2005), 131–230.

this is apparent from the literary genre itself, as in the case of the taunts found in 2:12–14[11–13], 3:8–11, and elsewhere. In 2:12–14[11–13], for example, God asserts his superiority over the Assyrian king, adopting even his bombastic leonine personification.[71] The impressive and terrifying Assyrian army will be devoured, and the empire will crumble. In 3:8–11 the comparison turns to Nineveh's likeness to Thebes, a fortified city which nonetheless fell to enemy (Assyrian!) forces.

Irony (this time apart from the deconstructive reuse of Assyrian imagery) also appears in the description of Nineveh as a shamed prostitute (Nah 3:4–7). In this case there may be an allusion to Nineveh's worship of Ishtar, who was associated especially with sexual attraction, war, and prostitutes.[72] Regardless of whether this allusion is present, the irony is built on the image of an attractive prostitute who has had numerous clients who pay her (in the form of spoils and taxes collected by the empire) but who, ironically, gain nothing from their interaction with her. Rather, the client becomes the possession of the prostitute, who uses him for her own pleasure. This ironic turn is followed by another, as Nineveh is publicly stripped and shamed. Her shame contrasts sharply with her graceful and alluring appearance, and in a final irony her former victims witness the undoing of her pride and glory.

These and other images of unexpected or ironic outcomes in Nahum are part of a pattern in which Assyria's prestige is taken away and replaced with shame and destruction.[73] Against the background of an empire bent on self-aggrandizement and committed to creating and distributing hubristic self-representations, the repeated contrast between the supposedly unstoppable Assyrian army, the irresistible imperial network of commerce, religion, and warfare, and the glories of the king on the one hand, with the army's defeat, the empire's collapse, and the king's ignominious demise on the other, helped the book's Judean audience put the very real Assyrian threat in perspective. Most importantly, it reminded them that God had committed himself to defeating Assyria. This is emphasized by the repetition of "I am against you, declares YHWH of Hosts," in 2:14[13] (as part of a taunt) and in 3:5 (as part of a degrading metaphor).

Anticipated Fulfillment of the Foretold Judgment (Prolepsis)

While many biblical prophecies of the future include reflections on the new status quo that will follow their fulfillment, few such reflections are as detailed as the account of Nineveh's fall in 2:2–11[1–10]. The choice to devote such a large amount of text to Nineveh's fall, and especially to describe that fall in terms of its military defeat, is eminently appropriate in light of the militaristic nature of the Assyrian Empire. Further, detailed reflection on an event that had not yet taken place when this section

71. Floyd, *Minor Prophets*, defines a taunt functionally, as "a derisive utterance insinuating that one person, group, or thing is inferior to another" (649).

72. Tzvi Abusch, "Ishtar," *DDD*, 452–53.

73. Berlejung, "Erinnerungen," 340–41.

was written (cf. 3:8–11), known as prolepsis, goes beyond making such a military feat plausible to assuming its inevitability.[74] Building on the solid foundation of YHWH's certain justice in 1:2–8, prolepsis elsewhere in the book assures its readers and hearers that the Neo-Assyrian Empire cannot escape punishment.

The Force of Nahum's Communicative Strategies

Many have remarked that Nahum's poetry and imagery are concise, powerful, and compelling.[75] This is surely true, but the rhetorical elements noted in the preceding sections go far beyond the level of poetry to something like poetics, which refers to the aggregate contribution of these features to the literary composition.[76] Nahum uses a wide variety of literary features and strategies to present as forcefully as possible the most unlikely of future events on the basis of a most certain truth: the God of Israel will avenge himself on his enemies in order to establish cosmic justice, and this commitment entails the destruction of Assyria. Throughout the commentary we will note both the communicative strategies (e.g., irony) and the literary and syntactical features (e.g., word order) that lend beauty and power to Nahum's message.

Discourse Linguistics

Since our goal is to make sense of the whole text, including especially the rhetorical or pragmatic effect of how it says what it says, we must attend both to the parts and to their relation to each other. While trying to make sense of the whole is essentially a question of meaning or semantics, a text's semantics are inseparable from its grammar, structure, and so on.[77] In pursuing a holistic understanding of Nahum as a unified composition, this commentary will pay attention not only to the way that the meaning of one section relates to the rest of the book but also to the ways that the text's syntax and arrangement contribute to the formation and expression of that meaning.

To begin at the lowest level, syntax at the level of individual sentences or clauses refers to "the three basic relations, the attributive, the predicative, and the objective."[78] These relations, which readers identify almost unconsciously, govern the way that meaning is formed within a single expression. The fundamental classification of Biblical Hebrew clauses distinguishes between verbless (or nominal) clauses

74. Greg S. Goering, "Proleptic Fulfillment of the Prophetic Word: Ezekiel's Dirges over Tyre and Its Ruler," *JSOT* 36 (2012): 483–505: "Paired with a judgment oracle, the funeral dirge creates a certainty of judgment beyond that of a simple judgment oracle" (503).

75. See the opinions cited in Tremper Longman, III, "Nahum," in *Obadiah, Jonah, Micah, Nahum, Habakkuk* in *The Minor Prophets: An Exegetical and Expository Commentary*, ed. T. McComisky (Grand Rapids: Baker, 1993), 2:771–73; Richard D. Patterson and Michael E. Travers, "Nahum: Poet Laureate," *JETS* 33 (1990): 437–44.

76. This definition is drawn from Adele Berlin, *Poetics and Interpretation of Biblical Narrative* (Winona Lake, IN: Eisenbrauns, 1994), 18.

77. Hence Robert D. Holmstedt, "Hypotaxis," *EHLL*, 2:220–22, refers to hypotaxis (subordination in cases where it is indicated by "an overt function word") as expressing "the syntactic-semantic relationship" between phrases (220).

78. Tamar Zewi, "Syntax: Biblical Hebrew," *EHLL*, 3:688.

and verbal clauses, and this distinction will appear frequently in our discussion of the text.[79]

The next level is the relationship between clauses, usually expressed in terms of either coordination (clauses on the same level) or subordination (clauses that enhance, comment on, or otherwise serve a primary or "head" clause). While subordination in Biblical Hebrew is sometimes marked by a subordinating conjunction, it is more often indicated by a switch from one type of verbal syntax to another, or a change of subject, without the use of any subordinating conjunction.[80] In what follows, the Translation and Exegetical Outlines offer a graphic representation of coordinate and subordinate relationships in the text.

The Structure and Message of Nahum

The book of Nahum employs a number of genres and divides its message into various parts. Despite their variety in terms of genre, the book's sections exhibit clear semantic relationships with each other and are often linked on the verbal level by repetition, catchwords, and other features. The order in which information is presented in the book moves the reader from an awe-inspiring vision of YHWH's final arrival to judge (and deliver) on a global scale to a lengthy presentation of how and why YHWH as judge will soon punish Assyria. In the largest section of the book (1:9–3:19), condemnations of Assyria are consistently presented alongside descriptions of the punishment that will follow. However, more than once Nahum presumes Assyria's guilt in order to focus exclusively on the punishment that YHWH will mete out to it (e.g., 2:2–11[1–10] and the taunts in chapter 3). After impressing on the reader both Assyria's guilt and the certainty of its punishment, the book closes with a final reflection on the justice of YHWH's judgment and the joy it brings to many nations, forming a rough *inclusio* with the perspective of the opening hymn.

Nineveh, God, and Nahum (1:1)

The opening verse identifies Nineveh as the subject of the book and Nahum as the source of its content, whether he or a member of his circle put his oracles down in writing. The book, an "oracle" from YHWH, derives from the prophet's vision, but its historical setting is not elaborated on here.

79. See Zewi, "Syntax: Biblical Hebrew," 3:690, who recognizes that some clause types do not fit well into either of these two classes (693).

80. Bo Isaksson, "An Outline of Comparative Arabic and Hebrew Textlinguistics," in *Circumstantial Qualifiers in Semitic: The Case of Arabic and Hebrew*, ed. B. Isaksson, AKM 70 (Wiesbaden: Harrassowitz, 2009), 36–150; Holmstedt, "Hypotaxis," 2:220. While it is likely that subordination is fundamentally a function of clause structure even when so-called subordinating conjunctions are present, I will refer to such conjunctions as such and leave aside unnecessary theoretical detail.

The Threat of YHWH's Coming Global Judgment (1:2–8)

This section focuses on the expression of YHWH's vengeance against his enemies on a global scale and with definitive outcomes. It emphasizes the destructive nature of this vengeance when focused on YHWH's enemies but also stresses that *no one* is beyond danger. While early on, no group that benefits from YHWH's patience and saving power is identified, the poem eventually affirms that YHWH is in a personal relationship with, and saves, those who seek refuge in him.

The opening hymn carefully avoids all national and historical particulars and presents instead the quintessential, culminating divine intervention that will see evil and those practicing it destroyed, while those who trust in YHWH will be saved by his goodness. Several reuses of earlier Scripture focused on YHWH's covenantal relationship with Israel add force and richness to the section and press the reader to take YHWH's wrath and willingness to save with utmost seriousness so as to survive the "day of trouble."

Four Announcements of Assyria's Destruction and Judah's Deliverance (1:9–2:1[1:15])

This subunit leaves behind the general, global perspective of the opening hymn and discusses Assyria and the threat it poses to Judah in light of YHWH's commitment in 1:2–8 to destroy all who oppose him. It details Assyria's combative stance against YHWH before announcing in speeches to the empire and to the king that both will be destroyed by YHWH. The destruction of Assyria is inseparable from the deliverance of Judah from its oppressor, and the two speeches to Assyria are therefore interlaced with speeches assuring Judah that YHWH's punishment of their sin has ended and calling for them to renew their worship of him in light of this spectacular liberation.

The Prophetic Anticipation of Assyria's Fall (2:2–11[1–10])

This section undermines Assyria's image as an invincible military power by anticipating in very clear terms its defeat and destruction. The passage mentions in passing that Assyria's downfall is part of YHWH's larger plan to restore Judah but focuses on the fall of the Assyrian capital of Nineveh at the hands of the Medo-Babylonian army. Nineveh's capture is presented in progressively clearer and more emphatic ways as the text moves from the approach of the attacking army (2:2[1]) and its impressive appearance (2:4[3]) to aspects of its attack (2:5[4]). Attention then shifts to Nineveh's defenders, who are in disorder (2:6[5]), and then to several aspects of the city's fall (2:7–9[6–8]). Two final scenes present Nineveh after its defeat, with the attacker plundering its fabulous riches (2:10[9]) and the surviving Ninevites utterly defeated and undone. This clear anticipation of Nineveh's collapse puts the lie to Assyria's claims of invincibility and presents a clear (if anticipated) fulfillment of YHWH's commitment to destroy all his enemies, beginning with the Neo-Assyrian Empire.

The section that follows, 2:12–14[11–13], details the anticipation of Nineveh's fall with a taunt focused on the elimination of the Assyrian Empire and especially of its king. YHWH is the primary agent responsible for the as-good-as-accomplished destruction of Nineveh, and the king's bombastic, egotistic, and God-dishonoring claims to unlimited power and authority deriving from the Assyrian gods are shown to be false.

A Woe Oracle against Nineveh (3:1–7)

This woe oracle develops in equal measure Nineveh's guilt and YHWH's appropriate punishment of it. The condemnation that lies behind the woe focuses on Assyria's violence and the immense material wealth its abusive practices secured for the empire. Assyria's violence dehumanized its victims, while its rapacious practices in war and peace alike made whole people groups nothing more than a means to an end. Because Assyrian diplomacy involved deception and misuse of other nations while trumpeting the empire's glory and appeal, YHWH's punishment of the nation takes place on the same stage as Assyria's abuse. In this way the victims are witnesses to retribution that undoes Assyria's propagandistic image as powerful and well suited to rule the world. Assyria's punishment heaps shame on the once-great world power and brings about its end in a breathtaking way that causes no regret among its victims.

A Historical Taunt (3:8–11)

Drawing on the example of another fabulously wealthy city whose security was unquestioned, Nahum predicts that, despite its prowess and might, Nineveh will fare no better than Thebes, destroyed by Assyria only a few years before Nahum uttered his oracles. Infrastructure, military might, and capable allies were not enough to deliver Thebes from Assyria's attack, and Nineveh will fall to YHWH and his agent in spite of all that made it appear invincible.

A Military Taunt (3:12–15c)

This taunt undoes the belief that Assyria's military might would enable it to defend itself against any and all attacks. It focuses on the fortresses that directly served the army's operation, and announces the defeat of the army, as well as the destruction of its fortresses. The inevitability of this outcome allows the prophet to sarcastically encourage the still self-confident empire to prepare for an imminent attack, only to interrupt his instructions with another affirmation that before these preparations are completed, Assyria will have fallen to its enemies.

An Economic Taunt (3:15d–17)

Nahum's final taunt focuses on the Assyrian economic apparatus, which operated domestically and internationally. The taunt applies two prominent characteristics of locusts to the empire in order to contrast its present strength and its fate. Although as numerous as locusts now, the empire as an economic engine sustained by the goods and services of its subjects will disappear as swiftly as a swarm of locusts leaves one place for another. Whatever Assyria may do to prolong its dominance, YHWH's decision to punish it definitively ensures that it will disappear from the scene for good.

The Final Dirge for the Assyrian King (3:18–19)

This section is explicitly addressed to the king of Assyria (3:18b), referred to in every one of this section's lines (apart from the vocative in 3:18b and the denial of other helpers in 3:18e) by a second-person singular suffix on a noun "belonging to" the king.[81] Since the king represents the empire, when he falls, it falls with him. The end of the empire is presented in terms of its population (3:18) and of the king himself (3:19a–b), and it meets with applause on the part of all who hear the news. A strong note of theodicy is signaled by the affirmation that all this will come about because of the king's "evil" (רעה).

Nahum in the Book of the Twelve Minor Prophets

The past few decades have seen an explosion of interest in the formation of the Minor Prophets collection, usually referred to as the Book of the Twelve.[82] While some approaches to the issue have been consistent with the historical settings proposed in the superscriptions that begin most of these books, the majority of scholarly work on the subject has approached the collection as one that gradually grew not only through the inclusion of individual books (initially in their prefinal forms) but especially through redactions that span part or all of the collection.[83] In theory, the more place one gives to redactors that sewed the collection together without attention to the historical setting and unique perspective of each book, the more feasible it is to read the Twelve as one "book." On the other hand, the more seriously one takes the

81. In 3:18 the nouns that refer to various things that "belong to" the king are the second word of their respective lines (except for the vocative 3:18b); in 3:19a,b,c "your fracture," "your wound," and "news of you" are the second stress units,.

82. See Marvin A. Sweeney, "Twelve, Book of the," and Aaron Schart, "Twelve, Book of the: History of Interpretation," both in *Dictionary of the Old Testament: Prophets*, ed. M. J. Boda and G. J. McConville (Downers Grove, IL: InterVarsity Press, 2012), 788–806 (Sweeney), 806–17 (Schart).

83. Both approaches are concisely detailed in Ehud Ben Zvi and James D. Nogalski, *Two Sides of a Coin: Juxtaposing Views on Interpreting the Book of the Twelve / the Twelve Prophetic Books*, ed. T. Römer, Analecta Gorgiana 201 (Piscataway, NJ: Gorgias, 2009).

superscriptions, individual foci, unique emphases, and other features of each minor prophet as a book in its own right, the less feasible it is to ignore or downplay those features in a reading of one or more of the Twelve.[84]

This commentary understands Nahum to be a coherent book by itself and so pays significant attention to its unique features, historical setting, and complex perspective on Assyria.[85] Taking the same approach to the other books in the Twelve prohibits us from trying to make sense of the collection without first listening carefully to the twelve unique voices it contains and preserving their unique contributions in discussing the Twelve as a composite whole. On this view, the relationship between Jonah and Nahum, for example, should be approached in a way that preserves the different historical settings of each book and appreciates the very different ways that each book characterizes Assyria.[86]

The comparison between Nahum and Jonah is inevitable because they share the same subject (Assyria) but reach radically different conclusions as to its fate. Jonah asserts that the capital city of Nineveh turned from its "wicked way" and so escaped the judgment Jonah had threatened against it, while Nahum does not even mention the possibility that Assyria would repent and instead predicts with utter certainty its complete and final destruction. The historical settings of each book provide some initial orientation for a response to this diversity, since Nahum is set roughly one-hundred years later than Jonah. At the very least, therefore, Jonah and Nahum describe (part of) Assyria at very different times, with Jonah notably addressing Nineveh during a period of unusual unrest.[87] Nahum, by contrast, presents Assyria as it was near the middle of the seventh century, as strong as ever and so much less inclined to repent.

Other details confirm that the Jonah-Nahum relationship involves different presentations of Assyria. While Nineveh does "repent" (שׁוּב) in Jonah 3:10, there is no indication that this repentance was deep enough for Nineveh to jettison its trust in its gods, as was the case in the conversion of non-Israelites elsewhere in the OT (e.g., Ruth, Naaman).[88] It is logical to conclude, therefore, that after a significant but not

84. These questions are discussed in more detail in Daniel C. Timmer, *The Non-Israelite Nations in the Book of the Twelve: Thematic Coherence and the Diachronic-Synchronic Relationship in the Minor Prophets*, BibInt 135 (Leiden: Brill, 2015), 1–20, 221–44, and passim.

85. Kevin J. Vanhoozer, "Exegesis and Hermeneutics," *NDBT*, 52–64.

86. The varying placements of Jonah in the Twelve are sketched by Kevin J. Youngblood, *Jonah: God's Scandalous Mercy*, HMS (Grand Rapids: Zondervan, 2013), 27–28. In short, Jonah appears between Obadiah and Micah in the Masoretic tradition, between Obadiah and Nahum in the Greek (LXX) tradition, and perhaps at the end of the Twelve in 4QXII[a]. See Philippe Guillaume, "The Unlikely Malachi-Jonah Sequence (4QXII[a])," *JHebS* 7 (2007): article 15, 1–10, doi:10.5508/jhs.2007.v7.a15; George J. Brooke, "The Twelve Minor Prophets and the Dead Sea Scrolls," in *Congress Volume: Leiden 2004*, ed. A. Lemaire, VTSup 109 (Leiden: Brill, 2006), 19–43; Mika Pajunen and Hanne M. von Weissenberg, "The Book of Malachi, Manuscript 4Q76 (4QXII[a]), and the Formation of the 'Book of the Twelve,'" *JBL* 134 (2015): 731–51.

87. Timmer, *A Gracious and Compassionate God*, 91–94; Pajunen and Weissenberg, "The Book of Malachi," 731-51

88. John H. Walton, "The Object Lesson of Jonah 4:5–7 and the Purpose of the Book of Jonah," *BBR* 2 (1992): 54, mentions the contrasting examples of Ruth and Naaman, both of whom explicitly abandon their gods and attach themselves to YHWH (Ruth 1:16; 2 Kgs 5:17).

transforming repentance in the context of Jonah's ministry, Nineveh reverted to its earlier behavior. Assyria's hyperbolic assertions of its grandeur and ultimate security in Nahum show that the empire in the seventh century was far from where Nineveh had been a century earlier and that repentance was highly implausible.[89] In any case, the empire's time is up (1:12).

Ultimately, the question we are considering concerns not simply Nahum's place in the Twelve, but Nahum's place in the OT and in the Christian Bible as a whole. Accordingly, the commentary bypasses questions related to the Twelve as a collection in favor of biblical-theological reflection that reckons with the fundamental unity of the Bible as a whole.[90]

The Theological Message of Nahum

Nahum's theology appears quite simple at first glance, and indeed the number of theological themes it treats is relatively small: God, humanity, Israel/Judah and the nations, sin, justice, grace, deliverance, and perhaps a few others. However, these themes are developed differently in each of the two settings the book presents. Nahum's opening poem in 1:2–8 is a meditation on the final, global outpouring of God's vengeful wrath against sin, and makes no clear reference to Assyria or Judah, dealing instead with individuals who are identified only in terms of their relationship to YHWH. The rest of the book focuses exclusively on Assyria and Judah (with a few general references to other nations currently under Assyria's control), and the horizon of 1:9–3:19 does not go beyond the fall of Assyria and a rather vaguely described restoration of Judah once it is free from the empire's clutches.

The fact that the book's themes are presented and developed differently in these two sections of Nahum requires us to trace their development carefully. At the same time, the character of God that is foundational to the events foreseen in 1:2–8 is also at the heart of YHWH's judgment against Assyria as described in the rest of the book. In a very real sense, therefore, the book's theological coherence is guaranteed by the unity and harmony of YHWH's character.

89. This understanding is at least as old as Targum Pseudo-Jonathan (ca. sixth century CE), which prefaces Nahum with the following remark: "Earlier, Jonah the son of Amittai, the prophet from Gath-Hepher, prophesied against this city and she turned from her sins. When she later sinned again, Nahum from Beth-Koshi prophesied against her, as is recorded in this book" (noted by Fabry, *Nahum*, 118, author's translation).

90. Graeme Goldsworthy, "'Thus Says the Lord!'—The Dogmatic Basis of Biblical Theology," in *God Who Is Rich in Mercy: Essays Presented to D. B. Knox*, ed. P. T. O'Brien and D. G. Peterson (Homebush West, NSW: Lancer; Grand Rapids: Baker, 1986), 25–40.

God as Divine Warrior and Only Deliverer

It is not by accident that the first word of the Hebrew text of the main body of Nahum (1:2) is "God." His character and will are central to the book and determinative for the course of history. When seen against the grandiose pretensions of the Assyrian monarchs, this fact speaks volumes, for the heart of Assyria's mistreatment of Judah lies in Assyria's opposition to YHWH. This means that YHWH's vengeance against Assyria, described in detail in 1:9–3:19, is not exercised for ethnic or political reasons. Rather, 1:2–8 shows that YHWH's *eschatological*, *global* vengeance and deliverance are the background against which the fall of Assyria in the seventh century should be understood. As the Explanation sections will show, YHWH's vengeance is his wrathful reaction against all those who challenge or denigrate his uniqueness, glory, and supremacy and refuse to abandon their opposition to him. This means that even Assyria's mistreatment of Judah and other nations, while often involving culpable behavior against them (violence, exploitation, etc.), is to be evaluated above all as a violation of YHWH's will and a challenge to his character. In the context of 1:2–8, any human being (Assyrian, Judean, or other) who lives in such a way as to deny YHWH's identity as the only true God, king, and deliverer is threatened with inescapable judgment. At the same time, anyone who seeks refuge in YHWH will experience his full, gracious deliverance.

Judah and Assyria in Nahum

Once the global horizon of God's justice and deliverance has been sketched in the opening hymn, both Judah and Assyria come into focus, beginning in 1:9. Reflecting the book's interest in the fall of Assyria, most of 1:9–3:19 is given to descriptions of Assyria's fall, and only a few passages mention the significance of that event for Judah (and, more rarely, for other nations). The majority of this section catalogs Assyria's many sins and describes in detail the various punishments they merit. Nahum's condemnation of Assyria focuses on two main areas: its opposition to YHWH that mirrors that of YHWH's enemies in 1:2–8 and is manifested in pride and autonomy, and its violent exploitation of human beings for the empire's self-serving ends (2:13[12]; 3:1–4, etc.).

As clear and convincing as these condemnations are, they might lead the reader to conclude that all Assyrians are to be punished for the same reasons and that all were equally guilty of the offenses Nahum highlights. This, however, would be to miss an important facet of Nahum's theology. The author presents Assyria and Judah selectively in 1:9–3:19 in order to correlate the limited judgment of Assyria and limited deliverance of Judah described there with the absolute judgment and deliverance of the opening hymn. In the case of Assyria, this means that the "empire" (potentially including all Assyrians) consists especially of the king (1:14, etc.), the army and its officers (2:6[5], 3:1–4, etc.), and the administrative and economic elite (2:14[13]; 3:16–17, etc.), and only these parties are explicitly condemned. The general Assyrian population, by contrast, is effectively absent from Nahum's condemnation of the empire and so escapes (at least in the main) the charges the book levels against Assyria. Indeed, the destruction that Nahum announces will surely dismantle the empire and bring about the death of its leaders, but neither the book nor later history gives any reason to understand Nahum's message as entailing the wholesale eradication of each and every Assyrian. Once the empire fell to the Medo-Babylonian coalition, the majority of the Assyrian population, especially noncombatants, simply became Babylonians (note the survivors in Nineveh in 2:8[7], 11[10]), rather than being hunted down as the enemy.

Nahum's presentation of Judah follows similar lines. Despite the hint that not all was well with Judah in 1:12 (Why would God have punished them if they had not deviated from his will, something confirmed by numerous voices in the OT?), the book never develops that point, nor does it mention Judah's sins in the present. Moreover, Nahum presumes that its Judean audience has not lost faith in YHWH despite Assyria's dominance, was not involved in syncretistic or non-Yahwistic worship, and did not manifest the same defining characteristics as the Assyrian Empire (autonomy, abuse of power, pride, etc.).[91] Yet a moment's reflection will show that all of these sins were found in Judah by prophets earlier than and contemporaneous with Nahum (e.g., Amos 2:4–6; Isa 1–3, 5). This difference between "real" and "ideal" Judah means that Nahum promises good only to those Judeans who take YHWH at his word, revere him holistically, and follow his will wholeheartedly. The "real" Judah, as we saw earlier ("The Historical Background to Nahum's Prophecies"), was often quite far from YHWH's will, and this included most kings and presumably most of the general population. Just as the general population of Assyria fell outside Nahum's stereotype of that nation, so the general population of Judah fell outside Nahum's stereotype of the ideal for that nation and so would have failed to grasp Nahum's message or to experience fully the deliverance and restoration it promised (barring, of course, a fundamental spiritual change).

These two interrelated stereotypes present Judah and Assyria in the book of Nahum so that their characterization (good or bad) and the consequences that follow (blessing or woe) are intelligible in light of the opening poem.[92] It is important not to mistake Nahum's stereotypes in 1:9–3:19 for a sort of definitive spiritual-sociological census that includes every citizen of Judah and Assyria. Judah's very recent past saw it punished for its sin (1:12), and most Assyrians were not directly involved in royal,

91. Timmer, "Boundaries without Judah, Boundaries within Judah," 178–79.

92. L. V. Langenhove and R. Harré, "Cultural Stereotypes and Positioning Theory," *Journal for the Theory of Social Behaviour* 24 (1994): 363.

administrative, or economic governance. Keeping these qualifications in mind, we can understand why Assyria and Judah meet with only partial judgment and deliverance in 1:9–3:19 rather than with the ultimate fates spelled out for the two anonymous groups that include all humanity in 1:2–8. In other words, Nahum's stereotypes allow the easy correlation of the eschatological, cosmic judgment and deliverance of the opening hymn with the particular, geopolitically limited and partial judgment of Assyria and deliverance of Judah in the seventh century BCE. Like the avoidance of national or political identifiers in 1:2–8, these stereotypes or generalizations help prevent a xenophobic or self-righteous reading of the book that would mistakenly find in it a message of unconditional deliverance to all Judeans regardless of their relationship with YHWH. Individuals' relationships to God, even when they are part of a collective like Judah or Assyria, remain their most significant characteristic and take precedence over all else.

Judgment and Deliverance in Relation to God's Character

Given Nahum's focus on the judgment that loomed over Assyria in the seventh century, it is not surprising that his description of God's character gives more attention to divine vengeance, wrath, and justice than to deliverance. This emphasis is consistent across the book but also appears in specific passages, especially in 1:2–3. There the author draws selectively on the paradigmatic description of YHWH's character found Exod 34:6–7, leaving aside several elements that emphasize YHWH's patience and adding in their place further descriptions of YHWH's punishment of sinners in the exercise of his justice.

This two-sided representation of God's character is paired with a twofold division of humanity in 1:2–8. As already noted, there is no ethnic, national, or political description of any human being in the opening hymn. The author can therefore employ with great effect one of the binary differences noted above (see The Rhetorical Strategy) by dividing humanity into those who are YHWH's enemies and those who "seek refuge in YHWH" (1:7).

Finally, this division of humanity into two sharply contrasting groups works together with the opening hymn's strong accent on YHWH's vengeance to impress upon the reader the absolute necessity of escaping it. Indeed, the only mention of escape from the approaching judgment-theophany is withheld almost until the end of the poem, in 1:7. Even there it is sandwiched between the apparent impossibility of finding deliverance in 1:6 and a sobering affirmation that YHWH will absolutely destroy his enemies in 1:8. In addition to creating an unease in the reader that only trust in YHWH's goodness and saving power can assuage, this emphasis is probably also intended to prevent an overinterpretation of the rest of the book that would allow any and all Judeans to rest on their laurels rather than turning to YHWH in repentance and faith.

Judgment, Deliverance, and Doxology

It is fair to say that the purpose of the book of Nahum is to convince all who read or hear it to seek deliverance from YHWH's wrath in YHWH's goodness, manifested in his willingness to deliver all who trust in him. While Nahum's message would surely have strengthened the hearts of the faithful in Judah, it was equally well suited to challenge Judeans whose hope was focused on powers other than YHWH who, they believed, might deliver them from Assyria (e.g., Egypt).

Beyond this immediate purpose of deconstructing all other claims to provide justice, deliverance, and significance in the face of YHWH's uniqueness, Nahum's message finds its ultimate endpoint in the praise and glory of YHWH as expressed in the worship of his people. In many contexts in Nahum worship as a response to YHWH's saving or judging actions is inevitable but remains implicit (e.g., after 1:7, 13; 2:3[2], etc.). Similarly, the joy at Assyria's demise in 3:19 is clearly a response to YHWH's just destruction of the empire, yet the joy is not explicitly connected to him. The sole exception to this pattern appears in 2:1[1:15], where Nahum or the messenger calls Judah to celebrate their (thoroughly theocentric) feasts and pay their vows to YHWH. As Ernst Wendland argues, this is in some ways the "major thematic peak" of the book, not least because it looks beyond the fall of Assyria (on which most of the book focuses) to the period of deliverance and restoration that will follow.[93]

It is interesting that Nahum's only explicit command to celebrate YHWH occurs not after a description of Assyria's destruction *tout court*, but in response to YHWH's *deliverance of Judah* from an oppressor that took to itself divine powers in the face of YHWH's universal and absolute kingship. While inevitably involving knowledge of Assyria's fall, the worship called for in 2:1[1:15] involves holistic adoration of YHWH as the only righteous, all-powerful, gracious deliverer. The feasts Nahum calls Judeans to celebrate were focused on God's deliverance and provision, especially in the Passover and exodus from Egypt, and the fall of Assyria constitutes a similarly prodigious saving act of YHWH on behalf of his people. While the soteriological significance of the event lies partially concealed under the political trappings of the Assyrian Empire, the fall of Assyria is inseparable from God's ultimate victory in the redemption of his people and the final destruction of his enemies. The consummation of all things should evoke praise and petition even now (e.g., in the "YHWH reigns" psalms [Pss 93, 96–99; note also Pss 47, 146]), and that praise will continue forever (Eph 3:21; 1 Pet 5:10–11; perhaps most impressively in Rev 4–5, but note also Rev 14:3; 15:3–4; 16:5–7).

93. Ernst Wendland, "What's the 'Good News'—Check Out 'the Feet'! Prophetic Rhetoric and the Salvific Centre of Nahum's 'Vision,'" *OTE* 11 (1998): 154–81 (here, 169).

Outline of Nahum

Thanks in part to the modest length of the book of Nahum, its flow is not difficult to grasp. After a very short introduction, the first and largest stage is set with an impressive description of a definitive, eschatological theophany in which YHWH will destroy the wicked in vengeance but will also deliver all who seek refuge from that judgment in him. The main section of the book then considers, on a smaller stage, Assyria's fall from three perspectives. It first announces it, then emphasizes its certainty by anticipating it in detail, and finally reflects on it in a way that deconstructs Assyria's pride and self-sufficiency. The book closes on a note of moral resolution as the "evil" that Assyria has done is removed from the scene of history.

		Outline of the Book of Nahum Theme: The Divine Warrior as Avenger and Deliverer	
1		Introduction	A. Nineveh, God, and Nahum (1:1)
2		1. God's Character and His Enemies (1:2a–3b)	B. The Threat of YHWH's Coming Global Judgment (1:2–8)
3			
4		2. God's Intervention and the Natural Order (1:3c–5)	
5			
6		3. God's Intervention and Humanity (1:6–8)	
7			
8			
9		1. The First Address to Assyria (1:9–10)	C. Four Announcements of Assyria's Destruction and Judah's Deliverance (1:9–2:1[1:15])
10			
11		2. The First Address to Judah (1:11–13)	
12			
13			
14		3. The Second Address to Assyria (1:14)	
1		4. The Second Address to Judah (2:1[1:15])	
2		1. The Call to Prepare for YHWH's Attack (2:2[1])	D. The Prophetic Anticipation of Nineveh's Fall (2:2–14[1–13])
3		2. The Significance for Judah: Restoration (2:3[2])	
4		3. The Fall of Nineveh Anticipated (2:4–11[3–10])	
5			
6			
7			
8			
9			
10			
11			
12		4. The Fall of Assyria Anticipated (2:12–14[11–13])	
13			
14			
1		1. A Woe Oracle against Nineveh/Assyria (3:1–7)	E. The Deconstruction of Assyria's Pride (3:1–19)
2			
3			
4			
5			
6			
7			
8		2. A Historical Taunt (3:8–11)	
9			
10			
11			
12		3. A Military Taunt (3:12–15c)	
13			
14			
15			
16		4. An Economic Taunt (3:15d–17)	
17			
18		5. The Final Dirge for the Assyrian King (3:18–19)	
19			

CHAPTER 1

Nahum 1:1

A. Introduction: Nineveh, God, and Nahum

Main Idea of the Passage

The opening verse of Nahum not only specifies the author and his subject (Nineveh), but also identifies the book it introduces as visionary in nature and, in literary terms, as an "oracle."

Literary Context

Among the elements in the introduction, none is more central to the rest of the book than Nineveh. Although 1:2–8 provides a global context in which to understand YHWH's coming judgment of Nineveh/Assyria and so makes no mention of it, Assyria's fall is the horizon for almost every line of the book from 1:9 onward. Fittingly, at the end of the book Nineveh disappears, as it were, providing closure in the book's immediate historical context and leading the reader to consider once again the ramifications of the far-reaching vision described in 1:2–8.[1]

➡ **A. Introduction (1:1)**
- B. The Threat of YHWH's Coming Global Judgment (1:2–8)
  - 1. God's Character and His Enemies (1:2a–3b)
  - 2. God's Intervention and the Natural Order (1:3c–5)
  - 3. God's Intervention and Humanity (1:6–8)
- C. Four Announcements of Assyria's Destruction and Judah's Deliverance (1:9–2:1[1:15])
- D. The Prophetic Anticipation of Assyria's Fall (2:2–14[1–13])
- E. The Deconstruction of Assyria's Pride (3:1–19)

1. Spronk, *Nahum*, 28, and Duane L. Christensen, *Nahum: A New Translation with Introduction and Commentary*, AYBC 24F (New Haven: Yale University Press, 2009), 172, both argue that 1:1 is not only original but tightly integrated in the poetic structure of 1:1–10 (Christensen) or 1:1–11 (Spronk).

Translation and Exegetical Outline

Nahum 1:1

			A. Introduction (1:1)
1a	מַשָּׂא נִינְוֵה	The Oracle of Nineveh.	1. The Nature and Subject of the Composition (1:1a)
1b	סֵפֶר חֲזוֹן נַחוּם הָאֶלְקֹשִׁי	The Book/Scroll of the Vision of Nahum the Elkoshite.	2. The Speaker and Origin of the Oracles in the Composition (1:1b)

Structure and Literary Form

This short unit consists of two parts: the first specifies that what follows is an "oracle" focused on Nineveh, while the second ties the book's origins to the vision of Nahum from Elkosh.[2] As readers familiar with the biblical writing prophets soon realize, Nahum's double introduction is unusual. Still, diversity on this point is not surprising. While the titles of some prophetic books share a number of elements, of the eight features that Francis Andersen and David Freedman identify as potentially present in a book's superscription, no prophetic book in the OT uses all eight features.[3] The author of Nahum surely chose to include the elements he judged important while leaving aside others.

Explanation of the Text

The book's first line announces that its contents are "the oracle of Nineveh." The term "oracle" (מַשָּׂא) can refer to either the genre of a prophetic speech (i.e., a unit in a larger literary work) or to a prophetic book as a whole, as it does here.[4] This type of literature is composed of "citation of a previously communicated revelation either within the *maśśāʾ* itself or in the surrounding literary context" (most clearly 1:2–8), "additional prophetic discourse, including at least some oracular speech of YHWH" (the former throughout the book, the latter especially in YHWH's direct speech as highlighted in the Translation), "reports of past and/or present human acts" that demonstrate the relevance of YHWH's speech for the present and future (almost entirely Assyria's offenses, as outlined especially

2. There is no need to affirm that both parts of this introductory verse do not stem from the same hand, *pace* Lothar Perlitt, *Die Propheten Nahum, Habakuk, Zephanja*, ATD 25.1 (Göttingen: Vandenhoeck & Ruprecht, 2005), 5. Contrast the brief argument in favor of its literary integrity in Brian Tidiman, *Nahoum, Habaquq, Sophonie*, CEB (Vaux-sur-Seine: Edifac, 2009), 65.

3. Francis I. Andersen and David N. Freedman, *Hosea: A New Translation with Introduction and Commentary*, AB 24 (New York: Doubleday, 1980), 143–45.

4. Floyd, *Minor Prophets*, 631, argues that the genre typically consists of "(1) reports or announcements of YHWH's acts or intentions, combined in various ways with (2) description of human acts or events, so as to show that YHWH's involvement is manifest in the realm of human affairs, and (3) directives describing appropriate ways of thinking and/or acting in response to such divine activity." The suitability of the definition of the literary genre for the whole book, both the opening hymn (1:2–8) and what follows, argues against restricting its referent to only part of Nahum.

in 1:9–14; 2:12–14[11–13]; 3:1–7), and "directives addressed to the audience, describing appropriate ways of thinking and acting in view of how the previous revelation continues to take effect" (especially 2:1[1:15]).[5]

This oracle has to do above all, and almost exclusively (at least at first glance), with Nineveh, the capital of the Assyrian Empire from 704 BCE onward.[6] Synecdoche (mentioning the particular, Nineveh, in place of the broader term, Assyria) highlights the importance of this city for the Neo-Assyrian Empire while giving more focused elements (e.g., the fall of Nineveh in 2:4–11[3–10]) significance for the empire as a whole.[7] The book of Jonah's well-known statements about the city's size and importance (cf. Jonah 1:2; 3:3; 4:11) reflect partially but accurately the city's importance for the empire, and Nahum is clearly aware of its religious (cf. 1:14) and economic significance as well (cf. 2:10[9]; 3:1, 4). Nineveh was also an impressive example of a fortified city, boasting both massive walls and water defenses. Finally, as the primary center of government, Nineveh was the chief source of the ideology that Assyria consistently and effectively developed and disseminated. As will become clear, the author of Nahum seems to have heard or read a good deal of this ideology and offers several clear refutations of it in connection with YHWH's commitment to destroying Assyria. Nineveh is thus at the center of the book when we understand it as a מַשָּׂא, although the opening hymn reaches far beyond the borders of the Assyrian Empire and gives the whole a universal scope.

The second line of the introduction further specifies that what follows is the "book/scroll" of the "vision" of Nahum of Elkosh. It seems self-evident that the referent of "book/scroll" (סֵפֶר) is nothing other than what follows this introductory verse, thus a collection of Nahum's prophetic statements. Notably, it is something written, a sense for which there are numerous examples within the Hebrew Bible (e.g., a copy of the law, Deut 17:18; a letter, 1 Kgs 21:8–10; an inscription on a tablet, Isa 30:8, etc.) as well as outside it.[8] Although prophecies were occasionally recorded outside Israel/Judah (e.g., Mari in the eighteenth century and Assyria in the seventh century BCE), very few seem to have served any purpose after they reached their initial addressee (usually royalty) and were consequently filed away in archives.[9] Further, outside Israel and Judah there are almost no clear parallels of a prophetic text addressed to a general population rather than to a royal or distinguished recipient.[10] By contrast, Nahum's inclusive Judean audience situates his prophecy in the history of YHWH's relationship with Israel, past (1:12), present, and future (passim, esp. 1:12–13; 2:1[1:15]).

The final characteristic of the book before us is

5. Ibid., 632.

6. Russell, *Sennacherib's Palace*, 1.

7. Hadumod Bussmann, *Routledge Dictionary of Language and Linguistics*, trans. and ed. G. Trauth and K. Kazzazi (London: Routledge, 1996), 470.

8. The Balaam text found at Deir ʿAlla is perhaps the most apropos example, since it is introduced as "the misfortunes which constitute the Book [ספר] of Balaam," was composed in Israelite territory in the second half of the eighth century, and includes both an initial announcement of doom as well as prophetic discourse related to it. Cf. "The Deir ʿAlla Plaster Inscriptions," trans. Baruch A. Levine (*COS* 2.27:140–45).

9. For an overview, see Robert P. Gordon, "Prophecy in the Mari and Nineveh Archives," in *"Thus Speaks Ishtar of Arbela": Prophecy in Israel, Assyria, and Egypt in the Neo-Assyrian Period*, ed. R. P. Gordon and Hans M. Barstad (Winona Lake, IN: Eisenbrauns, 2013), 37–58. The Mari texts are presented in Jean-Marie Durand, *Archives épistolaires de Mari I/1*, ARMT 26 (Paris: Editions Recherche sur les Civilisations, 1988); the Assyrian texts in Simo Parpola, *Assyrian Prophecies*, SAA 9 (Helsinki: Helsinki University Press, 1997).

10. Cf. Seth L. Sanders, "Why Prophecy Became a Biblical Genre," *HBAI* 6 (2017): 26-52 (35). Note the exceptional address to the elders of Saggaratum in ARM 26 206, in Martti Nissinen, *Prophets and Prophecy in the Ancient Near East*, 2nd ed., with contributions from C. L. Seow, R. K. Ritner, and H. C. Melchert, WAW 41 (Atlanta: SBL Press, 2003), 38–39.

its nature as a "vision" (חָזוֹן). Whether this involves a specific visionary event, as when Isa 1:1 pairs the cognate terms "vision . . . which he saw," or a more general form of revelation of the divine word (note the parallel between vision and word in 1 Sam 3:1), the book presumes the divine origin of Nahum's vision (מַשָּׂא connotes the same[11]), which made clear predictions regarding the future and was soon confirmed by their realization (cf. Jer 23:16).[12]

The introduction ends by identifying "Nahum of Elkosh" as the source of what follows. Whether the prophet himself or someone who recognized that he spoke for YHWH assembled the book of Nahum as we now have it cannot be determined. What is essential is the confidence that the book as we have it faithfully transmits to us the words of the prophet, who clearly speaks for YHWH, most explicitly in 1:12–14, 2:14[13], and 3:5–7.

As we saw in the Introduction, the OT mentions no other Nahum, nor does it refer to the prophet outside the book that bears his name.[13] Knowing that he hailed from Elkosh is similarly of little help in terms of his life and setting, since there exist several possible locations for this village.[14] Despite this lack of precise information, there is no doubt that Nahum wrote to a Judean audience faced with the specter of domination and perhaps destruction by Assyria, and that he possessed more than a passing acquaintance with Neo-Assyrian ideology, history, and politics. Indeed, perhaps most relevant is what the name "Nahum" tells us, regardless of the historical specifics of the man whose it was. The name shares the same root as the verb נחם, "to comfort, console," and hence means "comfort" or "compassion."[15] Near the end of his prophecy Nahum will deny any "comforters" to Assyria (מְנַחֲ־מִים, 3:7), while throughout the book he announces "comfort" to Judah, calling them to celebrate their imminent deliverance from Assyria by YHWH (2:1[1:15]). Given their similar sounds, "Nahum" also probably anticipates נֹקֵם ("avenging"), much like "Elkosh" probably anticipates אֵל קַנּוֹא ("zealous God") in the following verse.

11. As suggested by J. J. M. Roberts, *Nahum, Habakkuk, and Zephaniah: A Commentary*, OTL (Louisville: Westminster John Knox, 1991), 40; cf. 2 Kgs 9:25; 2 Chr 24:27; Prov 30:1; 31:1; Isa 13:1 and passim; Jer 23:33, 34, 36, 38; Lam 2:14; Ezek 12:10; Hab 1:1; Zech 9:1; 12:1; Mal 1:1.

12. Bernard Renaud, *Michée, Sophonie, Nahum*, SB (Paris: J. Gabalda, 1987), 274–75, suggests that "vision" compensates for the absence of a more typical identification of the prophet or of his discourse.

13. Spronk, *Nahum*, 31, notes that the name "Nahum" appears on a seventh-century seal from Lachish, among other locations.

14. Spronk, *Nahum*, 32, suggests that אלקשי, *ʾelqošî*,, "the Elkoshite," should be broken into אל, *ʾēl*, "god," and קשי, *qāšî*, with קשי, *qāšî*, evoking קשה, *qāšâ*, "severe," much like Isa 19:4 announces that Egypt will be punished by "a severe lord."

15. Longman, "Nahum," 766, suggests "compassion."

CHAPTER 2

Nahum 1:2–8

B. The Threat of YHWH's Coming Global Judgment

Main Idea of the Passage

God's passion for his glory and justice will produce an unprecedented outpouring of his wrath and anger against his enemies on a global scale. Deliverance from this punishment is promised only to those who put their trust in him.

Literary Context

This hymn begins to unveil the nature and significance of the "Nineveh oracle" that Nahum has seen in a "vision" (1:1). The anonymity of the human subjects who either trust in or oppose YHWH, its use of comprehensive frames of reference (earth, world), and the note of finality tied to the ultimate outcomes of the "day of trouble" indicate that the hymn serves as the framework for the entire book. The increasingly detailed and specific descriptions from 1:9 onward of the future deliverance of Judah and the fall of Nineveh and Assyria are particular, limited realizations of the theophany described in 1:2–8.

A. Introduction (1:1)
➡ **B. The Threat of YHWH's Coming Global Judgment (1:2–8)**
  1. God's Character and His Enemies (1:2a–3b)
  2. God's Intervention and the Natural Order (1:3c–5)
  3. God's Intervention and Humanity (1:6–8)
C. Four Announcements of Assyria's Destruction and Judah's Deliverance (1:9–2:1[1:15])
D. The Prophetic Anticipation of Assyria's Fall (2:2–14[1–13])
E. The Deconstruction of Assyria's Pride (3:1–19)

Translation and Exegetical Outline

(See next page.)

Structure and Literary Form

This unit coheres by virtue of its consistent focus on God's coming to establish justice as the expression of his zeal and vengeance against human opposition to his character and will.[1] The shift from third-person descriptions of God in 1:2–8 to second-person addresses to various parties in 2:1[1:15] marks the end of the section.[2] The amount of text given to the punishment of God's enemies compared to the amount of text that describes deliverance, as well as the order in which information is presented and the *inclusio* formed by 1:2, 8, strongly emphasizes God's destruction of his enemies, although the possibility of deliverance for others is affirmed several times.

The hymn can be divided into three sections. First, in 1:2a–3b God's character is explored in relation to his vengeance against his enemies. The structure on the next page reflects Randall Buth's observation of a spectrum of markedness in the nonverbal clauses (1:2a–3a) and the semantic and syntactic contrasts between 1:3a and 1:3b.[3]

The intervention in world affairs that necessarily results from God's character as described in 1:2–3b is then presented in terms of its effect on the natural world in 1:3c–5, and in terms of its effects on human beings in 1:6–8. In 1:3c–5 the shift from a participle to a perfective finite verb in 1:4a–b corresponds to the subordination of 1:4b as the consequence of 1:4a. The parity of the following five clauses (1:4c–5b) in terms of verbal syntax makes them coordinate. Although not subordinate, 1:5d–e are indented to highlight the rhetorical weight of the tricolon (three closely interrelated poetic lines or cola) that shares the verb "heave" present in 1:5c.

The significance of YHWH's wrath for humanity is broached in 1:6a–b by two subordinate lines that anticipate the explicit mention of divine wrath in 1:6c (they surpass the effects on the created order presented in 1:2–5).[4] Before an answer is

1. Fabry, *Nahum*, 83, also argues for the coherence of the passage.

2. See Gerlinde Baumann, *Gottes Gewalt im Wandel: Traditionsgeschichtliche und intertextuelle Studien zu Nahum 1,2–8*, WMANT 108 (Neukirchen-Vluyn: Neukirchener, 2005), 46–49, for more arguments in favor of this structure; it is also adopted by Fabry, *Nahum*, 83.

3. Randall Buth, "Word Order in the Verbless Clause," in *The Verbless Clause in Biblical Hebrew: Linguistic Approaches*, ed. C. L. Miller, *LSAWS* 1 (Winona Lake, IN: Eisenbrauns, 1999), 79–108; cf. Christo H. J. van der Merwe, Jackie A. Naudé, and Jan H. Kroeze, *A Biblical Hebrew Reference Grammar*, Biblical Languages 3 (Sheffield: Sheffield Academic, 2000), 338.

4. Cf. Bo Isaksson, "The Textlinguistics of the Suffering Servant: Subordinate Structures in Isaiah 52,13–53,12," in *En pāsē grammatikē sophiā: Saggi di linguistica ebraica in onore di Alviero Niccacci, ofm*, ed. G. Geiger (Milan: Franciscan, 2011), 191, 201.

Nahum 1:2–8

			B. The Threat of YHWH's Coming Global Judgment (1:2–8)
			1. God's Character and His Enemies (1:2–3b)
2a	אֵל קַנּוֹא וְנֹקֵם יְהוָה	A zealous and avenging God is YHWH.	a. God's Character and Vengeance (1:2a–d)
2b	נֹקֵם יְהוָה וּבַעַל חֵמָה	Avenging is YHWH and wrathful.	
2c	נֹקֵם יְהוָה לְצָרָיו	Avenging is YHWH against his adversaries,	
2d	וְנוֹטֵר הוּא לְאֹיְבָיו	and he stores up wrath against his enemies.	
3a	יְהוָה אֶרֶךְ אַפַּיִם וּגְדוֹל־כֹּחַ	YHWH is slow to anger and of great power;	b. God's Character and Patience (1:3a)
3b	וְנַקֵּה לֹא יְנַקֶּה יְהוָה	he will by no means acquit the guilty.	c. God's Character and Punishment (1:3b)
			2. God's Intervention and the Natural Order (1:3c–5e)
3c	בְּסוּפָה וּבִשְׂעָרָה דַּרְכּוֹ	In whirlwind and storm is his way,	a. Heavenly Origins of God's Intervention (1:3c–d)
3d	וְעָנָן אֲבַק רַגְלָיו	and the clouds are the dust of his feet.	
4a	גּוֹעֵר בַּיָּם	He rebukes the sea	b. God's Intervention and Drying Up of Waters (1:4a–c)
4b	וַיַּבְּשֵׁהוּ	and makes it dry,	
4c	וְכָל־הַנְּהָרוֹת הֶחֱרִיב	all the rivers he dries up.	
4d	אֻמְלַל בָּשָׁן וְכַרְמֶל	Bashan and Carmel wither,	c. God's Intervention and Removal of Fecundity (1:4d–e)
4e	וּפֶרַח לְבָנוֹן אֻמְלָל	the blossom of Lebanon withers.	
5a	הָרִים רָעֲשׁוּ מִמֶּנּוּ	Mountains shake before him,	d. God's Intervention and Seismic Upheaval (1:5a–e)
5b	וְהַגְּבָעוֹת הִתְמֹגָגוּ	and the hills melt;	
5c	וַתִּשָּׂא הָאָרֶץ מִפָּנָיו	the earth heaves before him,	
5d	וְתֵבֵל	the world	
5e	וְכָל־יֹשְׁבֵי בָהּ	and all who dwell in it.	
			3. God's Intervention and Humanity (1:6–8)
6a	לִפְנֵי זַעְמוֹ מִי יַעֲמוֹד	Before his wrath who can stand?	a. God's Dreadful Wrath (1:6a–b)
6b	וּמִי יָקוּם בַּחֲרוֹן אַפּוֹ	Who can resist his burning anger?	
6c	חֲמָתוֹ נִתְּכָה כָאֵשׁ	His rage is poured out like fire,	b. God's Destructive Wrath (1:6c–d)
6d	וְהַצֻּרִים נִתְּצוּ מִמֶּנּוּ	and the rocks are broken up by him.	
7a	טוֹב יְהוָה	YHWH is good,	c. God's Deliverance of Those Who Trust in Him (1:7a–c)
7b	לְמָעוֹז בְּיוֹם צָרָה	a refuge in the day of trouble,	
7c	וְיֹדֵעַ חֹסֵי בוֹ	and he knows those who seek refuge in him;	
8a	וּבְשֶׁטֶף עֹבֵר	but with an overflowing flood,	d. God's Destruction of His Enemies (1:8a–b)
	כָּלָה יַעֲשֶׂה מְקוֹמָהּ	a complete end he will make of its place,	
8b	וְאֹיְבָיו יְרַדֶּף־חֹשֶׁךְ	and his enemies he will pursue into darkness.	

given to the questions they pose, the next two parallel lines front the object of divine wrath for additional emphasis (1:6c–d). The answer finally appears in the fronted predicate in 1:7a ("Good"), and the subordinate lines that follow elaborate on that assertion (1:7b–c). The section is closed by 1:8a–c with antithetical mainline assertions that YHWH will totally destroy his enemies.

The literary form (genre) of the passage is difficult to specify.[5] While parts of it correspond to well-known genres (e.g., 1:2–5 is a hymn of declarative praise, as are various psalms), other parts (e.g., the quasirhetorical questions in 1:6a, b) appear in other genres (e.g., Ps 106:2).[6] Further, the description of the theophany in terms of its effects on the natural world is something of a genre to itself (cf. Pss 18:8–16[7–15]; 114:4, 6; Isa 42:15; Jer 4:23–26; Hab 3:3–11).[7]

Although the passage itself seems to include a variety of genres, its thematic coherence is clear and is reinforced by the partial acrostic that spans 1:2–8. After the superscription in 1:1, ten of the first eleven letters of the Hebrew alphabet appear at the head of successive lines. Thus 1:2 begins with "A" (א), 1:3c begins with "B" (ב), and so on. While the absence of the fourth (missing from 1:4c) and perhaps the seventh letters (on the second rather than the first word of 1:6a) from the normal location makes the acrostic imperfect, the sequence is probably not unintentional. Furthermore, since the Hebrew alphabet consists of twenty-two letters, this partial acrostic (allowing for the imperfections just noted) covers exactly half of the Hebrew alphabet.[8] In the following table the Hebrew letters that form the acrostic and their corresponding English letters appear in gray print.

The opening lines of Nahum hide more literary artistry. Much like some Mesopotamian line acrostics, the first element in the acrostic (1:2a–3a, the "A" element) contains successive lines whose first letters form "I" (אֲנִי) while the final letters of 1:1b–3b form "YHWH."[9] This divine self-identification "I (am) YHWH" appears for the first time in the OT in Gen 15:7, and some 235 times thereafter (Exod 6:2; 29:46, etc.), characteristically in contexts which demonstrate that YHWH will deliver Israel or punish his enemies, and thus serves as a fitting introduction to the book.[10]

5. See especially Floyd, *Minor Prophets*, 40–41.

6. The role of the rhetorical question in 1:6 is not terribly prominent in the passage, making me doubt that Floyd is right to label the passage a "prophetic interrogation." (Floyd, *Minor Prophets*, 41.)

7. Perlitt, *Die Propheten* 8, with reference to Jorg Jeremias, *Theophanie*, WMANT 10, 2nd ed. (Neukirchen-Vluyn: Neukirchener Verlag, 1977).

8. Thomas Renz has argued convincingly for the presence of the broken acrostic here, "A Perfectly Broken Acrostic in Nahum 1?" *JHebS* 9 (2009): article 23, 1–26, doi:10.5508/jhs.2009.v9.a23.

9. Spronk, *Nahum*, 25.

10. Characteristically, that is, outside its frequent role as a motive in laws in Leviticus. See, for example, deliverance in Exod 6:2–8; 1 Kgs 20:13; Ezek 29:21 and passim; Joel 2:27; 3:17; destruction in Exod 7:5, 17, and throughout the plagues; also Exod 14:4, 18.

Table 2.1: The Broken Acrostic in Nahum 1:2–8

Verse	English	Hebrew	Hebrew letter
2	A God zealous . . .	*ʾēl qannôʾ* . . . אל קנוא	א
	Avenging . . .	*nōqēm* . . . נקם	
3	YHWH . . .	*YHWH* . . . יהוה	
	In whirlwind . . .	*bĕsūpâ* . . . בסופה	ב
4	Rebukes . . .	*gôʿēr* . . . גוער	ג
	Wither . . .	*ʾumlāl* . . . אמלל	(ד)
5	Mountains . . .	*hārîm* . . . הרים	ה
	And heaves . . .	*wattiśśāʾ* . . . ותשׂא	ו
6	Before his wrath . . .	*lipnê zaʿmô* . . . לפני זעמו	ז
	His rage . . .	*ḥĕmātô* . . . חמתו	ח
7	Good . . .	*ṭôb* . . . טוב	ט
	He knows . . .	*wĕyōdēaʿ* . . . וידע	י
8	A complete end . . .	*kālâ* . . . כלה	כ

Table 2.2: The Line Acrostic in Nahum 1:1–2

Verse	English text	End of line (Hebrew, English)	Beginning of line (Hebrew, English)
1b	. . . Elkoshite.	*hāʾelqōšî* . . . האלקשי (Y)	
2a, b	A God zealous . . . wrath	*ûbaʿal ḥēmâ* . . . ובעל חמה (H)	*ʾēl qannôʾ* . . . אל קנוא (A)
2c, d	Avenging . . . his enemies	*lĕʾōyĕbāyw* . . . לאיביו (W)	*nōqēm* . . . נקם (N)
3a, b	YHWH . . . YHWH	*YHWH* . . . יהוה (H)	*YHWH* . . . יהוה (Y)

In terms of literary genre, it is enough simply to title 1:2–8 a "hymn" in light of its emphasis on YHWH's character and actions.[11] In any case, even a passage that conforms very closely to a literary form must be viewed as a unique text composed of semantic elements and linguistic features and possessing a unique relation to a particular literary context. Here, the focus on YHWH's character as the explanation for the theophany it describes and the exploration of the divine-human relationship in terms of vengeance on YHWH's enemies and vindication of his devotees are sufficient to guide our interpretation of the passage.

11. While genres are on a continuum and do not possess absolute boundaries, the absence of a call to praise from 1:2–8 and its orientation toward the future rather than the past make it very difficult to see this passage as descriptive praise; see William Brown, *Psalms*, Interpreting Biblical Texts (Nashville: Abingdon, 2010), 41–55. Roberts, *Nahum, Habakkuk, and Zephaniah*, 48, is content to speak of a "hymnic text."

Explanation of the Text

1. God's Character and His Enemies (1:2–3b)

The five occurrences of "YHWH" as subject or predicate in these nominal clauses and the likely presence of the line acrostic "I (am) YHWH" in 1:1b–3b make clear that these clauses are focused on God's character.[12] The fundamental classification of Biblical Hebrew clauses distinguishes between verbless (or nominal) clauses and verbal clauses.[13] While the suggestion of Francis Andersen and Waltke-O'Connor that predicate-subject order classifies and subject-predicate order identifies the subject is appealingly simple, it leaves several questions unanswered, especially why verbal participles can reverse this relationship and how to classify phrases in which only part of the predicate occurs before the subject.[14] Randall Buth proposes a solution that accommodates the cases that pose problems for the analyses of Andersen and Waltke-O'Connor, taking the subject-predicate order as the "default order" but emphasizing the importance of any element placed before the subject-predicate pair, including a partial predicate in that position.[15] We will follow Buth's approach here, but will also make occasional reference to Andersen and Waltke-O'Connor's view.

The first characterization of YHWH, in 1:2a, is drawn in part from Exod 20:5: "A zealous and avenging God is YHWH."[16] The terms "zealous" (קַנּוֹא) and "avenging" (נֹקֵם) both modify the predicate "God," which precedes the subject, YHWH. Since the syntax of this clause is predicate-subject, the entire predicate is emphatic.[17] The adjective קַנּוֹא often expresses God's "fiery, angry reaction to the infringement of his rights vis-à-vis Israel" and to its violation of the covenant.[18] Whether this sense is appropriate must be determined from the context, however, since the term קַנּוֹא (or related forms) is used in a wide variety of circumstances when God's exclusive glory is infringed upon or obscured: Israel's idolatry (Exod 20:5; Deut 4:24; 5:9; Ps 78:58), its worship of other gods (Exod 34:14; Deut 6:15; 32:16, 21; 1 Kgs 14:22), egregious sin (Num 25:11), the abuse or denigration of Israel by other nations (Zech 1:14; Ezek 38:19), general opposition to his claims and purposes by Israel and/or other parties (Isa 42:13; 59:17; Ezek 36:5–6; Zeph 1:18; 3:8), or more complex situations (Ezek 39:25; Joel 2:18; Zech 8:1).

The situation most relevant to this passage, general opposition to YHWH's claims and purposes, is only indirectly related to Israel's covenant with God

12. Klaas Spronk, "Jonah, Nahum, and the Book of the Twelve: A Response to Jakob Wöhrle," *JHebS* 9 (2009): article 8, page 3, doi:10.5508/jhs.2009.v9.a8.

13. Zewi, "Syntax: Biblical Hebrew," 3:690. Zewi recognizes that some clause types do not fit well into either of these two classes (693).

14. Buth, "Word Order," 94–96. Classification answers the question, "What is the subject like?"; for example, "We are honest" (Gen 42:11). Identification answers the question, "Who or what is the subject?"; for example, "That is Moses" (Exod 6:27). See Bruce K. Waltke and Michael O'Connor, *An Introduction to Biblical Hebrew Syntax* (Winona Lake, IN: Eisenbrauns, 1990), 130, 132.

15. Buth, "Word Order," 96, 100–101. Cf. Francis I. Andersen, *The Hebrew Verbless Clause in the Pentateuch*, JBLMS 14 (Nashville: Abingdon, 1970); Waltke and O'Connor, *An Introduction to Biblical Hebrew Syntax*.

16. Ruth Scoralick, *Gottes Güte und Gottes Zorn: die Gottesprädikationen in Exodus 34,6f und ihre intertextuellen Beziehungen zum Zwölfprophetenbuch*, HBS 33 (Freiburg im Breisgau: Herder, 2002), 194, suggests that Josh 24:19 is in view, and indeed the only identical spelling of קַנּוֹא, *qannôʾ*, "zealous," occurs there (but note *ʾēl qannôʾ* in Exod 34:14; Deut 4:24; 5:9; 6:15). However, Exod 20 lies much closer to the center of the presentation of God that Nahum develops here than does Josh 24.

17. In Buth's terminology, it is a "focus constituent" ("Word Order," 81–83, 101).

18. H. G. L. Peels, "קנא," *NIDOTTE* 3:938.

and thus to the precise sense for קַנּוֹא noted above. Similarly, while aggression or abuse of Israel/Judah by the nations (quite relevant from 1:9 onward) may constitute an "external threat to the covenant" in other books, such a nuance is missing from the context here and from Nahum in general.[19] Indeed, the only time that Assyria's behavior toward Judah is cast in terms that bear on its covenant relationship with God, it is described as YHWH's affliction of Judah (1:12) rather than as Assyria's deformation of Judah's religious world or imposition of illicit religious practices.

These points lead us to conclude that here the term "zealous," קַנּוֹא, involves God's commitment to his glory, honor, and holiness in the face of direct opposition.[20] It is important to note that in Nahum YHWH will punish Assyria for its actions against Judah *and other nations alike* (3:19), something that clearly involves YHWH's character and reputation apart from any link to his covenant with Israel. The conclusion that the first trait of the divine character mentioned here has to do especially with God's commitment to his glory, honor, and holiness in the face of direct human opposition is corroborated by the use of binary language like "enemies" and "adversaries" in this unit (1:2, 8), the later reference to Assyria's anti-YHWH plot (1:9, 11), and YHWH's personal commitment to oppose his enemies (1:14; 2:14[13]; 3:5–7) at several other points in the book.

The second characteristic in 1:2a is "avenging." This aspect of the divine character has the same object as the zeal explored above: rebellious human beings (singly or together) seeking autonomy and the erasure of God's claims over them. Put in theological terms, the root נקם refers to "the punitive retribution of God, who, as the sovereign King . . . stands up for the vindication of his glorious name in a judging and fighting mode, while watching over the maintenance of his justice and acting to save his people."[21] This characteristic, here as in most other contexts in the OT, is exercised by God and directed against those who oppose him and usurp divine prerogatives.[22]

The close connection that this first line of Nahum's opening hymn establishes between God's character and his definitive, global intervention invites further reflection. In particular, a closer look at the relation of Nahum's description of God's character to similar texts in the OT is helpful. While various parts of the passage echo a wide range of biblical texts, the semantic contribution of the character element here and its significance throughout the book make its intertextual connections especially important.[23] We can assume that the foundational Decalogue text of Exod 20 and the equally influential divine self-characterization

19. Peels, *NIDOTTE* 3:939, suggests that this sense best fits the context of Nah 1:2. Bob Becking, "Passion, Power and Protection: Interpreting the God of Nahum," in *On Reading Prophetic Texts: Gender-Specific and Related Studies in Memory of Fokkelien van Dijk-Hemmes*, ed. B. Becking and M. Dijkstra, BibInt 18 (Leiden: Brill, 1996), 17, similarly suggests that YHWH's jealousy here is directed against "inimical powers who are injuring the Israelites." While that element is present, YHWH's jealousy for his glory in the face of Nineveh's opposition to him and worship of other gods predominates.

20. This mirrors the conclusion of E. Reuter, "קנא," *TDOT* 13:53–55, who argues well for the nuance of YHWH's unique glory over against the worship of other gods, with reference to Exod 20:5; 34:14; Deut 4:24; 5:9; 6:15.

21. Peels, *NIDOTTE* 3:154.

22. Peels, *NIDOTTE* 3:155, concludes that it is usually "turned against the nations because they attempt to reach out for world power in their unlimited lust for power." Édouard Lipiński, "נקם," *TDOT* 10:9, notes that it is sometimes turned against Jerusalem (Ezek 24:8), Saul (1 Sam 24:13), or groups within Israel (Ps 18:48; Jer 11:20).

23. On the relationship between Nahum and Isaiah, see Fabry, *Nahum*, 95–96; Carl E. Armerding, "Nahum," in *Daniel and the Minor Prophets*, ed. F. E. Gabelein, EBC 7 (Grand Rapids: Zondervan, 1985), 453–56.

in Exod 34:6–7 predated Nahum,[24] and the same is true for Micah. While these texts overlap significantly, there are also interesting differences between them that should be noticed.[25]

In the following table, text in italics identifies some of the prominent differences between the two Exodus texts, while elements unique to Nahum are underlined. Micah's adaptation of these materials largely reflects that of Exod 34, and so is not further analyzed. Similarly, the differences between Jonah's and Nahum's uses of the tradition are essentially a matter of omission or inclusion and so are self-evident. Finally, since Joel 2:13 echoes Exod 34 in much the same way as Jonah 4:2 (although only Jonah applies it to non-Israelites), it is not included here.[26]

Several important observations can be made on the basis of the similarities and differences that characterize the relationship among these texts. First, the modifications (or at least contrasts, if direct dependence does not obtain) to Exod 20 made in Exod 34 (and similarly in Mic 7, Jonah 4, and Joel 2) highlight God's gracious character, his patience, and his willingness to forgive.[27] Second, much to his chagrin, Jonah sees these same characteristics in God's sparing of Nineveh and adds that God is characteristically willing to relent. Nahum, written later than most if not all of these other books, includes only one of these positive elements in his presentation of the divine character (in 1:3a) and instead strengthens the emphasis on YHWH's wrath and focuses it on his enemies. When Nahum does follow Exod 34 (in 1:3b), it echoes the affirmation that YHWH will surely not let the guilty escape punishment (Exod 34:7b).[28] We will look at each of these elements individually below, but it is already evident that the author of Nahum, like other biblical authors who adapted the traditional descriptions of God's character in Exod 20 and Exod 34 to particular situations, has likewise chosen to emphasize certain aspects of God's character and actions while leaving aside others.

Nahum 1:2b adds to the traits already noted YHWH's vindictive wrath: "Avenging is YHWH and wrathful." "Characterization" is indeed the term for the affirmation made of God here (and in 1:2a, 2c, 2d), achieving what some have called description rather than simple identification in connection with the predicate-subject word order ("avenging is YHWH . . . ," quite awkward in English).[29] Unlike the forms that occur later in the hymn, the verbal forms here are mostly participles (many of which

24. On the antiquity of the Exod 34 expression which is linked in some way to Exod 20, see Hermann Spieckermann, "Barmherzig and gnädig ist der Herr . . . ," *ZAW* 102 (1990): 1–18. On the precedence of the law with respect to the prophets, note especially Gene M. Tucker, "The Law in the Eighth-Century Prophets," in *Canon, Theology, and Old Testament Interpretation: Essays in Honor of Brevard S. Childs*, ed. G. M. Tucker, D. L. Peterson, and R. R. Wilson (Philadelphia: Fortress, 1988), 201–16.

25. For an analysis of the related text in Num 14:17–18, see Greg Cook, "Power, Mercy, and Vengeance: The Thirteen Attributes in Nahum," *JESOT* 5.1 (2016): 27–37.

26. See Youngblood, *Jonah*, 154, and Thomas Dozeman, "Inner-Biblical Interpretation of YHWH's Gracious and Compassionate Character," *JBL* 108 (1989): 207–23. Jakob Wöhrle, "A Prophetic Reflection on Divine Forgiveness: The Integration of the Book of Jonah into the Book of the Twelve, *JHebS* 9 (2009): article 7, 1–17, doi:10.5508/jhs.2009.v9.a7, has argued that a "Grace-Redaction" involving Exod 34:6–7 was added to the Minor Prophets at a relatively late date. His arguments have been convincingly critiqued by Aaron Schart, "The Jonah-Narrative within the Book of the Twelve," in *Perspectives on the Formation of the Book of the Twelve. Methodological Foundations—Redactional Processes—Historical Insights*, ed. R. Albertz, J. D. Nogalski, and J. Wöhrle, BZAW 433 (Berlin: de Gruyter, 2012), 118–23.

27. Cf. Michael Widmer, *Moses, God, and the Dynamics of Intercessory Prayer: A Study of Exodus 32–34 and Numbers 13–14*, FAT 2/8 (Tübingen: Mohr Siebeck, 2004), 184–85.

28. The presence in 1:3b of an explicit subject and the interruption of the first two clauses' common syntax suggests that this clause is indeed independent and creates a contrasting characterization.

29. As suggested by Andersen, *The Hebrew Verbless Clause in the Pentateuch*, 39–50. As noted earlier, Buth, "Word Order," contends that this "characterization" is not the result of word

Table 2.3: The Relation of Nahum 1:2–3 to Other OT Texts

Exodus 20:5–7	Exodus 34:6–7	Jonah 4:2	Micah 7:18–20	Nahum 1:2–3
5b, c a jealous God, visiting the iniquity. . . . **7b** not leave unpunished the one who takes his name in vain	**7b** yet he will by no means leave the guilty unpunished, visiting the iniquity. . . .		**18a** Who is a God like you,	**2** a zealous and avenging God is YHWH, avenging is YHWH and wrathful, avenging is YHWH against his adversaries, and he stores up wrath against his enemies. . . . **3b** will by no means acquit the guilty
	6b *compassionate and gracious . . .*	**2f** gracious and compassionate	**19a** he will again have compassion on us	
	6c *slow to anger, and abounding in covenant love and truth . . .*	**2g** slow to anger and abundant in covenant love	**18d, e** he does not retain his anger forever, because he delights in covenant love.	**3a** Slow to anger and of great power
6 but showing lovingkindness to thousands of generations of those who love me and keep my commandments.	**7a** who keeps lovingkindness for thousands of generations, *who forgives iniquity, transgression and sin;*		**18b, c** who pardons iniquity and passes over the rebellion of the remnant of his possession . . . **19b, c** tread our iniquities under foot . . . cast all their sins into the depths . . .	
		2h who relents from punishment	**20a, b** you will give truth to Jacob, covenant love to Abraham	

do not function verbally), and speak of YHWH's character and related actions gnomically or generically, apart from specific historical manifestations.[30] The first portion of this clause repeats verbatim the characterization of YHWH in 1:2a, and "avenging is YHWH" will appear yet again in 1:2c, leaving no doubt that YHWH's vengeance is foundational to Nahum's presentation of God.

Like the preceding clause, a second adjective modifies YHWH here as well. While some have suggested that the expression "lord of wrath" expresses YHWH's full control of his wrath, in the same sense that in Biblical Hebrew an archer is the "lord" of his arrows, the only other collocations of בַּעַל with words in the semantic field of "anger/ rage" cannot be translated in this way (Prov 22:24;

order, which emphasizes part of the predicate ("Avenging . . .) by placing it in front of the subject, but of the variable relationship between "YHWH" (the more definite item) and the predicate, which is less definite (100).

30. While in Nah 1:2–3 none of the clauses exhibit the subject-verb (participle) order typical of verbal use of the participle, cases in which the participle takes an object (1:2c, d) are most likely verbal and so involve continuous action; cf. Merwe, Naudé, and Kroeze, *A Biblical Hebrew Reference Grammar*, 162–63.

29:22).[31] When used to describe human beings, as the relevant expressions in Proverbs are, they imply an inability to exercise self-control and thus a tendency to explosive expressions of anger.[32] When applied to YHWH here, the phrase strongly emphasizes YHWH's wrath (as does the context), but the consistent connection of this wrath with YHWH's enemies ensures that it is not unleashed arbitrarily.[33]

The third and final appearance of "avenging is YHWH . . ." begins 1:2c. This sole predicate is completed by the specification (for the first time) of the object of YHWH's vengeance: "his adversaries" (צָרָיו). Emphasis is again present on the first part of the predicate, "avenging," while its second part ("against his adversaries") follows the subject. Against the backdrop of the book's opening verse, it is striking that Nineveh or Assyria is not named, but as we have seen, this general, global approach is characteristic of the opening hymn as a whole. The 3ms possessive pronominal suffix that the Hebrew text attaches to "adversaries" is very important, since it shows the vertical or theological significance of this group's behavior. Rather than being primarily or ultimately directed against geopolitical or other humanly constructed entities, their behavior is fundamentally in opposition to YHWH himself.[34] While the rest of the book deals with Assyria, the description of God's enemies here means that Assyria is only one of a larger group that sets itself squarely against God and his claims.

The following phrase, "and he stores up wrath against his enemies" (1:2d), closely parallels 1:2c, including the common syntax in which part of the predicate is emphasized due to its appearance before the subject. The expression "stores up wrath" (נוֹטֵר) occurs only a few times in Biblical Hebrew (Ps 103:9; Jer 3:5, 12), and only here with the participle.[35] The expression occurs in parallel with divine discipline or correction of Israel and refers to the present reality of ongoing punishment. Not surprisingly, the three passages outside Nahum all express the wish or the determination that God's wrath not last "indefinitely" (לְעוֹלָם). It is unwarranted to infer on the basis of such a small number of uses that the divine wrath mentioned is always a present reality, and the general sense of the hymn also cautions us against concluding that YHWH has already begun to express his wrath against his enemies. The expression does, however, raise the real possibility that YHWH's wrath against some enemies would not be temporary or shortlived, and the next occurrence of "his enemies" in 1:8b finds divine vengeance pursuing them to the very end.

After four lines that describe YHWH's character in terms of vengeance against his enemies and of defense of his exclusive glory and honor, the first

31. H. G. L. Peels, *The Vengeance of God: The Meaning of the Root NQM and the Function of the NQM-Texts in the Context of Divine Revelation in the Old Testament*, *OtSt* 31 (Leiden: Brill, 1995), 204, thinks the phrase means "not a blind, impulsive aggression, but a[n] essential reaction to the evil of his enemies." William T. Koopmans, "בעל," *NIDOTTE* 1:682, concludes that God uses wrath as its lord much like archers are "lords" of their arrows (cf. Gen 49:23). Johannes C. de Moor, "בעל," *TDOT* 2:182, suggests only the general sense "owner of."

32. Bruce K. Waltke, *Proverbs 15–31*, NICOT (Grand Rapids: Eerdmans, 2005), 232, and note the phrase's apparent echoes of the Instruction of Amenemope. For some relevant excerpts from Amenemope, see Bill T. Arnold and Bryan E. Beyer, *Readings from the Ancient Near East: Primary Sources for Old Testament Study*, Encountering the Bible Series (Grand Rapids: Baker Academic, 2002), 187–89.

33. "God is finally and ultimately self-determinative." Cornelius Van Til, *The Defense of the Faith* (Phillipsburg, NJ: P&R, 1955), 77.

34. Scoralick, *Gottes Güte*, 195, suggests that Deut 32:41, 43 are particularly relevant. The term צַר involves mutual enmity and so excludes the possibility that God would act aggressively against those who are not (in his estimation, not theirs) opposed to him. Biblical Hebrew uses other expressions to describe unwarranted or one-sided aggression against another, e.g., Prov 1:11, 16, 18.

35. See Keith N. Schoville, "נטר," *NIDOTTE* 3:98–99.

line of 1:3 adds two new and contrasting elements that are part of the same divine character: "YHWH is slow to anger and of great power."[36] As noted above, 1:3a is the only case in which Nahum echoes a modification of Exod 20 that is not focused on judgment and vengeance. The first element of this facet of YHWH's character is drawn from Exod 34:6–7. Although the expression itself is anthropomorphic and metaphorical ("long of face/nostrils"), its meaning in Biblical Hebrew is consistently that YHWH is patient or slow to anger.[37]

This expression is the second time that the opening hymn mentions YHWH's wrath (cf. חֵמָה in 1:2b). In the context of 1:2b we noted that divine anger evidently bears an important relation to YHWH's zeal and vengeance against his enemies and saw that the following double references to his enemies in 1:2c–d revealed the personal or relational nature of his wrathful response to some human beings.[38] The hymn's repeated emphasis on opposition to YHWH identifies the reason behind that response, so that YHWH's anger can be seen as a personal or emotional response that also has objective grounds.[39]

By affirming that YHWH is "slow to anger," 1:3 adds complexity to what has been, until now, a monochrome description of YHWH. That YHWH is *slow* to anger finds classic expression in the context of Exod 32–34. Of the six instances in which God's "anger" (אַף) is mentioned in Exodus, one directs it against Moses (4:14), and one is part of a legal text that warns against abuse of widows and orphans (22:22–24). The remaining three (leaving aside 34:6) are clustered in Exod 32, which sees God nearly destroy Israel (except for Moses) as punishment for their idolatry and worship of other gods at Sinai. Following Moses's intercession, YHWH relents and agrees to continue his relationship with Israel, even though their sin is not without consequences (Exod 32:25–28, 33–35).[40] The conclusion of the rapprochement between YHWH and his people gives rise to the unparalleled description of his character in Exod 34:6–7.[41] Exodus 32–34 thus makes clear that YHWH's anger can threaten Israel but also that YHWH's patience can appear at the most unexpected moments. The hymn in Nah 1:2–8 generalizes these two truths. YHWH's wrath will inevitably strike his enemies who persist in opposition to him, while his patience can appear for the benefit of anyone else.

A second predicate, "of great power," closes this first clause.[42] The pair of Hebrew words behind this expression, one of Nahum's two additions to the Exodus texts compared above, occurs with reference to God about ten times in the OT, and has to do with either his creation of the universe (Ps 147:5; Jer 27:5; 32:17; cf. Job 26:12; Ps 65:7) or his deliverance of his people (Exod 32:11; Deut 4:37;

36. The fact that this clause uses subject-predicate order but is as concerned with characterization as were the predicate-subject clauses in 1:2a–d corroborates Buth's suggestion, "Word Order," 95, 101, 107, that word order in verbless clauses does not determine the precise semantic relationship between predicate and subject.

37. Gale B. Struthers, "אנף," *NIDOTTE* 1:464; Elsie Johnson, "אנף," *TDOT* 1:351.

38. Bruce Baloian, "Anger," *NIDOTTE* 4:382–83.

39. Donald Guthrie, *New Testament Theology* (Leicester and Downers Grove, IL: InterVarsity Press, 1981), 102, speaks of this "emotion" as "the revulsion of absolute holiness toward all that is unholy."

40. Daniel C. Timmer, *Creation, Tabernacle, and Sabbath: The Sabbath Frame of Exodus 31:12–17; 35:1–3 in Exegetical and Theological Perspective*, FRLANT 227 (Göttingen: Vandenhoeck & Ruprecht, 2009), 108–12.

41. Widmer, *Moses, God, and the Dynamics of Intercessory Prayer*, 183–203.

42. The line acrostic suggested by Spronk, *Nahum*, 24–25, may have given rise to the predicate-subject word order in 1:2 and may account for the subject-predicate order in 1:3a. If so, the emphasis on characterization above holds true because it depends mainly on predications that on the level of semantics have to do with character traits rather than simple identity.

9:29; 2 Kgs 17:36; cf. Isa 50:2; Neh 1:10).[43] Nahum's consistent interest in YHWH's relationship with human beings and in divine responses to human behavior focuses attention on the second group of texts, and their consistently positive nature underlines the contrast between 1:2 and 1:3a.[44] Although such deliverance also entails the destruction of God's enemies, as in Exod 15:6, the location of this phrase between two phrases from Exod 34 favors an emphasis on its positive aspect (deliverance). Thus while the first predicate in 1:3a merely allowed for the continued existence of an anonymous person or group in the event that God relents from or delays the expression of his anger against them, this expression speaks of his proactive intervention for their good.[45] Here again the Exodus passages present a striking parallel, since they combine many of these aspects of the divine character and its historical manifestations. At the same time, the hymn's nonspecific focus means that this divine ability to deliver cannot be limited to Israel's liberation from Egypt and allows the reader to imagine equal or greater deliverance from other threats.

The hymn's first section concludes by returning to a negative (i.e., nonsalvific) implication of YHWH's character when considered in the context of unforgiven sin. The passage thus has a chiastic structure (A-B-A′) that emphasizes judgment. With the assertion in 1:3b that YHWH "will by no means acquit the guilty," Nahum once again returns to an element of the divine character mentioned in Exod 34:7. Rather than simply stating that YHWH "will not" acquit the guilty, the expression consists of a two-part verbal construction that adds the emphasis reflected in "by no means."[46] The discontinuation of the first clause's subject-predicate-predicate syntax in favor of infinitive-negated verb-subject order here may reflect on the syntactic level the strong semantic contrast between 1:3b and 1:3a. The strong contrast between deliverance in 1:3a and condemnation and punishment in 1:3b means that the very flexible conjunction (ו) that begins 1:3b can be translated as "on the other hand."[47] Despite the surprising nature of YHWH's patience and his unlimited power to deliver, there is no final escape for the guilty—YHWH's commitment to justice will ensure they are punished. This too has been seen in Israel's history, including the recent destruction of the Northern Kingdom (2 Kgs 17), but even that judgment pales in comparison with what is presented here.

The *inclusio* of punishment that begins in 1:2a and ends in 1:3b not only brackets contrasting material on God's mercy but consistently accentuates punishment as an expression of divine zeal and vengeance. These nonsalvific elements receive eighteen words, while the mention of patience and

43. See Robin Wakely, "כח," *NIDOTTE* 2:621–31, esp. 624–25. Helmer Ringgren, "כח," *TDOT* 7:126, thinks that the term refers to power without any particular nuance.

44. Buth, "Word Order," 106, notes that 1:2–3a begins with a highly marked structure (two fronted constituents, i.e., predicates before the subject), followed by 1:2b (one fronted constituent and one after the subject), two clauses in which only part of the predicate is fronted (1:2c, d), and finally an unfronted subject-predicate order (1:3a) . His conclusion underlines the link between syntax and semantics: "The clauses with a Focus constituent describe the Lord with aggressive attributes, and they diminish in grammatical intensity until reaching the grammatically neutral closing clause, which describes the Lord with a conciliatory attribute."

45. The identical syntax of 1:3a, b (subject-adjective-noun-(ellipsis)-adjective-noun) also suggests that these two characteristics can be taken side by side as complementary or analogous: "on the one hand, YHWH is patient and has great power to deliver." Scoralick, *Gottes Güte*, 195, suggests that God's patience is completed or complemented by his saving power.

46. The lexical sense of נקה in the *piel* is clearly "to acquit." The verb is noncultic and appears nowhere in Leviticus; cf. J. P. J. Olivier, "נקה," *NIDOTTE* 3:152–54; Cornelis van Leeuwen, "נקה," *TLOT* 2:763–67 (here, 766); Georg Warmuth, "נקה," *TDOT* 9:556.

47. Merwe, Naudé, and Kroeze, *A Biblical Hebrew Reference Grammar*, 299.

deliverance in 1:3a consists of only five words. This, of course, is not the only or ultimate way to view this feature, since Assyria's destruction constitutes the deliverance of Judah and a number of other nations.

Intriguingly, the element that remains most ambiguous in the hymn is the nature or identity of those who will be delivered. Those who will be judged are clearly identified as YHWH's enemies and adversaries (in relational terms) and as guilty (in judicial terms). Those who might enjoy God's patience and benefit from his saving power, however, are never identified in the hymn's first section. This accounts for the questions left hanging in 1:6, and the reader must wait until 1:7 to discover who might escape God's wrath, and how.

By its resolute focus on impending judgment and by its echoes of earlier texts that record how such judgment has threatened Israel, the first section of the hymn creates a general unease in the reader by abruptly unveiling the specter of looming judgment for an unidentified group. This prevents the Judean reader from assuming that he or she is beyond the reach of that judgment. While YHWH's "great power" has delivered Israel from danger in the exodus and could do so again, the predominant tone here is foreboding. The fall of the Northern Kingdom to Assyria some seventy years before Nahum's ministry would certainly have been present in the memory of many Judeans, and Assyria's continued prowess made it quite possible that a similar fate threatened Judah. Further, Judah in the mid-seventh century BCE was not without reminders that it had often acted (even after 722) as Israel had (Isaiah; Hos 4:15; 5:10–15; 12:2; Micah), so that the same anger God had shown against Israel could break out against Judah (2 Kgs 17:11, 17–18). The text's ambiguity about the identity of those whom YHWH will deliver is probably intentional and calculated to prevent the reader's or hearer's automatic, reflexive identification with those who will be delivered.[48]

2. God's Intervention and the Natural Order (1:3c–5)

The second section of the book's opening hymn presents YHWH's theophanic arrival and its effects in terms of the natural world. It involves a general movement downward, from clouds to sea and land. As part of this movement, elevated land itself is brought downward (1:5). The closing lines stress the theophany's global reach (1:5c) and finally shift the focus back to human beings (1:5d). Not only YHWH's desiccation of the waters but also his effect on other aspects of the world develops further the negative, destructive tone set in 1:2–3b.

The imagery of whirlwind and storm in the OT is typical of theophanies which involve the judgment of the wicked, and this emphasis predominates in passages that use the first term found here, "whirlwind" (סוּפָה; Job 27:20; Ps 83:16; Isa 17:13; 29:6; 66:15; Jer 4:13; Amos 1:14; cf. Prov 1:27; 10:25).[49] YHWH's coming especially *for judgment* thus follows smoothly on the last element of the divine character noted in 1:3b, his commitment to ensure justice by punishing the guilty. The parallel line "and the clouds are the dust of his feet" carries more general theophanic connotations, without the additional nuance of judgment and indeed without

48. See also Floyd, *Minor Prophets*, 43.

49. Cf. Alex Luc, "Storm and the Message of Job," *JSOT* 87 (2000): 113–14. For punitive theophanies, see Isa 40:24; 41:16; Jer 23:19; 30:23. The term with which it appears, "storm" (שְׂעָרָה), occurs elsewhere only in Job 9:17. Other terms built on the same root share the negative connotation of judgment; see Manfred Dreytza, "שׂער," *NIDOTTE* 3:1264. It is unlikely that the Sinai theophany is in view, as suggested, for example, by Carl E. Armerding, "Nahum," 462, since lexical links between the passages are lacking and the purpose of the Sinai theophany is radically different.

the usual emphasis on stationary divine presence.[50] The apposition of "clouds" with "dust of his feet" portrays rather the dynamic image of the immensity and grandeur of the deity who approaches the world from outside it. Together, 1:3c, d, present the nature of God's intervention (primarily for judgment) and create suspense by portraying him as in motion, even walking on the earth, but not yet exercising his vengeance and wrath against human beings.

The first two lines of 1:4 (1:4a, b) begin to describe the effects of YHWH's arrival on the earthly scene. The first line echoes YHWH's splitting of the Reed Sea in the exodus as described in Ps 106 (cf. the pair גער + ים, which appears elsewhere only in Ps 106:9), although here the sea in general is the object rather than the specific sea through which Israel passed long ago.[51] The same historical link appears in the second line, whose verb (יבשׁ) is used in other texts to describe the opening of a passage for Israel through the Reed Sea (Josh 2:10) or the Jordan River (Josh 4:23; 5:1). These echoes of Israel's deliverance do not constitute a simple promise of its repetition, however. There is surely correspondence between these past events and the theophany of Nah 1, but there is no basis on which to assume that their natures or goals are identical. On the contrary, since these actions have a global rather than a limited focus, they potentially threaten all, not only some. In other words, the "rebuking" and "drying up" described here elicit the historical link to YHWH's saving intervention in the reader's or hearer's mind *in order to modify it*, turning what could be a simple reminder of Israel's past deliverance into the presentation of a future, global, and threatening event.

The parallel line in 1:4c emphasizes the extent of this divine rebuke by placing the verbal object (with כֹּל, "all") at the head of the clause. Although the focus shifts inland from the sea to "all the rivers," the theme does not change, and indeed is amplified: YHWH dries up all sources or bodies of water. This image appears once in a prophetic recollection of YHWH's deliverance of Israel at the Reed Sea (Isa 51:10) and more often in descriptions of YHWH's future punishment of Egypt or other powers as part of his deliverance of his people (Isa 19:5–7; 42:15; 44:27; Zech 10:11; cf. also Jer 51:36). While those texts refer to an aspect of YHWH's multifaceted and varied intervention against specific manifestations of evil, it would be unwarranted to import their specific focus on other nations here, as already seen in 1:4a.[52]

One important question remains to be asked of these references to water: what does water have to do with YHWH's intervention against his enemies on a global scale? Many have suggested that the OT, here and at various other points, is indebted to a Canaanite myth that presents a divine combat against watery opponents as part of the formation

50. Mark Futato, "ענן," *NIDOTTE* 3:465, notes that most uses of ענן speak of God's "theophanic presence" on Sinai, in the tent of meeting, in the temple, or elsewhere.

51. The collocation of the verb "rebuke" and "sea" occurs only in these two passages; other forms are used in Isa 50:2. Longman, "Nahum," 789–90, follows James M. Kennedy, "The Root *gʿr* in the Light of Semantic Analysis," *JBL* 106 (1987): 47–64, in translating *gāʿar* as "blast," but this sense has not persuaded a majority; cf. *HALOT*, 199–200.

52. Baumann, *Gottes Gewalt*, 121, argues that the lexemes based on יבשׁ (whether verbs or nouns) consistently denote acts of YHWH on Israel's behalf. Some past instances of YHWH's "drying up" vegetation or rivers are specific (Isa 19:5–7 is part of an oracle against Egypt), others are part of complex scenarios involving explicit judgment and salvation (Isa 42:15), and others are so gnomic that the sense of the expression remains difficult to elucidate (Isa 44:27). Some relevant uses of *hiphil* חרב include 2 Kgs 19:17, 24 // Isa 37:18, 25 (where Assyria is the verbal subject); Jer 51:36 (YHWH as subject; note also the semantic equivalent in Isa 50:2; 51:10). For YHWH drying up rivers (with a variety of verbs), see Isa 19:5–7; 42:15; 44:27; Zech 10:11.

of the cosmos.[53] This *Chaoskampf* (struggle against chaos) motif is indeed present in other passages of the OT (e.g., Ps 29:10), but its significance there, as here, must be determined in light of its context, which can connect the control or drying up of seas and rivers to creation (Pss 24:2; 89:9), the exodus (Pss 66:6; 77:16–19), or the present or future victory of YHWH over various groups (Ps 18:4, 15–19; Isa 11:15; 19:5).

It is helpful to recall that the passage's first mention of water, in 1:4a, was also the clearest allusion to the exodus, and thus is least susceptible to a *Chaoskampf* interpretation. While the other elements in 1:4a–c lack this clear tie to a foundational historical event, the complete absence of any opposition on the part of the waters (which are not personified) throughout these lines cautions us against importing a Canaanite conceptual matrix along with the imagery, even though that may be more evident elsewhere in the OT.[54] Since there is no hint that the cosmos has begun to fall into chaos in the present, the water imagery should probably be understood not as symbolizing the opposition that comes from YHWH's enemies but as illustrating literally YHWH's irresistible, overwhelming intervention in the created order. The drying up of the seas and rivers is like a shockwave that emanates outward from YHWH's arrival, reflecting indirectly the force of his attack on his enemies.[55]

The last two lines of 1:4 shift to a different motif, that of wilting nature, to continue the description of the effects of YHWH's coming on his inanimate creation. These two lines, closely tied to 1:4a–c by their continued focus on dryness, develop the negative (destructive or life-removing) aspect of the theophany by showing its deleterious effect on some of the most fertile regions Judah knew.[56] In 1:4d, two regions near the northern limits of Israel are said to "wither" (*pulal* of אמל). Bashan is a plateau east of Lake Galilee and was very fertile due

53. On the phenomenon in general, see John Day, *God's Conflict with the Dragon and the Sea: Echoes of a Canaanite Myth in the Old Testament*, UCOP 35 (Cambridge: Cambridge University Press, 1985). On this motif in Nah 1, see Crouch, *War and Ethics*, 158, 166–67.

54. A mythical nuance would jar with the swift transition to descriptions of Carmel and Bashan in 1:4d. Richard E. Averbeck, "Ancient Near Eastern Mythography as It Relates to Historiography in the Hebrew Bible: Genesis 3 and the Cosmic Battle," in *The Future of Biblical Archaeology: Reassessing Methodologies and Assumptions*, ed. J. K. Hoffmeier and A. R. Millard (Grand Rapids: Baker, 2004), 345, explains this phenomenon well: "The writers of the Hebrew Bible used the repertoire of ancient Near Eastern cosmic battle motifs and patterns to articulate certain aspects of faith and commitment to God/YHWH in ancient Israel. They used them precisely because these stories were powerful in the conceptual world of the ancient Israelites and, therefore, provided a set of motifs that could be used to speak powerfully about YHWH." Contrast Perlitt's comments on the "transmission" or "conversion" of myth into history in Isa 42:15; 51:10, and Ps 106:9 (*Die Propheten*, 10) with Fabry's more careful argument for a predominantly historical sense here (*Nahum*, 135–36).

55. An intriguing potential parallel appears in the summary of the Assyrian Rab-shakeh's speech in 2 Kgs 19 and Isa 37, where the king boasts through his spokesperson that he had, by his own might and that of his gods, "dried up all the rivers of Egypt" (2 Kgs 19:24; Isa 37:25). While a different word for rivers is used (יְאֹרֵי), it is possible that Nahum was aware of this element of recent Assyrian propaganda and attributed that ability to YHWH even more directly than do the accounts from 701 BCE (e.g., 2 Kgs 19:25) in order to refute Assyria's claims. See Marvin Sweeney, *I & II Kings*, OTL (Louisville: Westminster John Knox, 2007), 418; J. D. W. Watts, *Isaiah 34–66*, WBC 25 (Waco, TX: Word, 1987), 45; Mordechai Cogan and Hayim Tadmor, *II Kings*, AB 11 (New York: Doubleday, 1988), 237, and the Assyrian motifs of "traversing difficult passes, cutting mighty trees, and supplying the army with water" in the sources noted by Cogan and Tadmor, *II Kings*, 243.

56. Roberts, *Nahum, Habakkuk, and Zephaniah*, 51, with reference to Thomas W. Mann, *Divine Presence and Guidance in Israelite Traditions: The Typology of Exaltation* (Baltimore: Johns Hopkins University Press, 1977), 30. Mark F. Rooker, "Theophany," *Dictionary of the Old Testament: Pentateuch*, ed. T. D. Alexander and D. W. Baker (Downers Grove, IL: InterVarsity Press, 2003), 860, observes that "In contrast to both Mesopotamian and Canaanite traditions, in Israel God was not associated in theophany with beneficent phenomena of nature . . . but rather with those natural forces that terrify people."

to volcanic deposits there.[57] Carmel too, because it is high and near the coast, received significant annual rainfall and was thus a very productive region, which explains the use of "Carmel" for the region around the mountain range as a whole.[58] Nahum 1:4e adds a reference to Lebanon, which was never part of Israel's territory and, like Bashan and Carmel, refers to a region rather than to a political entity.[59] Biblical references to Lebanon make frequent mention of its cedars and other trees (Judg 9:15; 1 Kgs 4:33; 5:6; 2 Kgs 14:9; 19:23; Ezra 3:7; Ps 29:5; Isa 60:13), which explains why the region was an important source of building material for many states and empires, including Ugarit and Assyria.[60] This proverbially productive forest region "withers" in the same way (and with the same verb) as the agricultural regions of Bashan and Carmel.

In all three cases (Carmel, Bashan, and Lebanon), the destructive or sterilizing effect of YHWH on nature is emphasized by withering exceptionally productive regions.[61] It is difficult to argue that this divine judgment is primarily oriented against either Israel/Judah or Assyria, primarily because these regions had no politically aligned population and changed hands frequently. The global significance of the theophany in this section also argues against seeing their decimation as a divine response against a specific geopolitical opponent.[62] It is better to understand the destruction of these historically productive regions, the "point of contact" between part of the world and YHWH's theophany, as reinforcing the theophany's dominantly punitive-destructive aspect.[63] By ending plant and tree life in field and forest, the text conveys the threat that the theophany poses to *life* more effectively than the destruction of the inanimate elements before and after it (1:4a–c; 1:5a–c). The reader can almost see a change of colors in the text: YHWH's arrival turns these green, verdant regions into scorched, lifeless spaces.[64]

The description of YHWH's coming in terms of its effects on the material, inanimate world turns finally to topographical features. There is a general descent in 1:5 from the highest element ("mountains") to "hills" and finally to the "earth/land" and "world." The first two clauses put emphasis on the "mountains" and "hills" by placing them before their verbs, at least in part because these topographic features do not normally "shake" and "melt." While in other descriptions of theophanies

57. Randall W. Younker, "Bashan," *EDB*, 154–55.

58. Rick W. Byargeon, "Carmel," *EDB*, 224.

59. This makes Spronk's suggestion (*Nahum*, 41) that Bashan symbolizes pride less likely here than in its symbolic role in Isa 2:13 (where height and beauty are emphasized but productivity of natural resources is not). Although the verbal object is fronted in 1:4d, its pragmatic function is doubtful in light of the *inclusio* that the resultant syntax forms around 1:4d–e with אֻמְלַל, "it withers."

60. Robert H. Smith, "Lebanon," *ABD* 4:268–70. References to Lebanon's natural resources from the seventh century appear in Esarhaddon's royal inscriptions; see Leichty, *The Royal Inscriptions of Esarhaddon,* 23 (Nineveh A), 127 (Assur A); from slightly earlier, the royal inscriptions of Tiglath-pileser III, cf. Tadmor and Yamada, *The Royal Inscriptions of Tiglath-Pileser III and Shalmaneser V*, 124 (Summary Inscription 7). Ugaritic texts from the middle of the second millennium BCE mention Lebanon "for its wood" and as a source of "the strongest trees." Simon B. Parker, ed., *Ugaritic Narrative Poetry*, WAW 9 (Atlanta: Scholars Press, 1997), 60 ("Aqhat," *KTU* 1.17, vi 20–23), 133 ("The Baal Cycle," *KTU* 1.4, vi 18–19, 20–21).

61. Carmel, Bashan, and Lebanon are the first proper nouns (other than YHWH) to appear since 1:1.

62. Fabry, *Nahum*, 136–37, explores various possible connotations but is inconclusive. Notably, their use as positive elements in Israel's future includes explicit references to pasturing there (Mic 7:14).

63. If the drying up of the sea and rivers was the cause of a drought, one might interpret the resultant barrenness as a covenant punishment (Jer 14:1–7; Amos 4:7–8; cf. Deut 28:16, 22), as does Roberts, *Nahum, Habakkuk, and Zephaniah*, 51. However, not only were these areas not currently under Judah's control (and Lebanon never), but the drying up would presumably affect other nations in addition to Judah.

64. Longman, "Nahum," 790, sees here and elsewhere evidence of the Divine Warrior and specifically of his negation or displacement of Baal, but this element, if present, would be of secondary importance.

(e.g., Isa 2) mountains and hills symbolize pride and arrogance due to their height, here the verbs "shake" (רעשׁ) and "melt" (מוג) emphasize their transformation from permanent features into plastic, unstable ones.[65] In human experience generally, and so in the OT, mountains and hills are both ancient (Deut 33:15; Prov 8:25) and permanent, so their quaking and melting bear eloquent testimony to the supernatural and destructive nature of the theophany. The third element, "earth/land" (אֶרֶץ), often occurs in parallel with the fourth, "world/continents" (תֵּבֵל), and the pair characteristically expresses the comprehensive extent of YHWH's control over the world he created.[66] This is the case here too, as the two lines are parallel and share the verb "heave" (נשׂא). The shaking of the earth at the appearance of its Creator, despite the fact that it is not itself under his condemnation, captures YHWH's transcendence and his ability to devastate and undo it (cf. 1:6d) regardless of its apparent permanence.

The final element of 1:5e artfully brings the description of the theophany back to its human focus, established in 1:2–3b. Two points stand out: first, the term used for "world" here cannot (just like אֶרֶץ in 1:5c) refer to "land," and so denotes the earth in its entirety.[67] Consequently, Judah and every other nation will be affected by this theophany. Second, the verb "heaves" in 1:5c has as its subject not only the world in 1:5d but also "all who dwell in it" in 1:5e. Here the author explicitly mentions the effects of the theophany on his readers and hearers, who will experience profound upheaval at YHWH's coming.[68] This is elaborated upon in 1:6–8, but it is interesting that while 1:2–3b distinguished between YHWH's enemies and those whom he delivers, here *all* are overwhelmed and appear in all their human frailty before YHWH.

3. God's Intervention and Humanity (1:6–8)

After describing the secondary effects of YHWH's theophany on the inanimate creation, the text returns to its focus on humanity. This subunit stresses not so much God's *character* as the ground for his actions but rather his *actions* as the expression of his character and nature. These actions reach the reader by means of reflection (in 1:6) on God's wrath and burning anger that focuses on earth's inhabitants (cf. 1:5d–e). This then creates rhetorical space for a stronger emphasis on deliverance (in 1:7) than was evident in 1:2–3b. Together, the assertion that YHWH's arrival will make all humanity shake and the earlier distinction between his enemies and those whom he delivers hint that deliverance from the theophany *is* possible, but that possibility is developed very slowly. The gradual introduction of the possibility of deliverance impresses on the reader that it is not to be presumed or thought of as easily obtained.

In the first half of 1:6, two questions focus the reader's attention on this central existential question: if YHWH's coming in judgment leaves no one untouched, how can one hope to survive it? The first section (1:2–3b) made clear that it is YHWH's "enemies" and "adversaries" who would fall under his judgment, but nothing clear was said about if, and how, one might benefit from YHWH's patience and saving power (1:3a). The questions posed here are rhetorical if taken in the precise sense of being able to survive, by oneself, such an

65. The pair "mountains and hills" occurs a few dozen times in the OT, and of these a few instances involve theophanies (in connection with the exodus, Ps 114:4, 6; Isa 42:15; Jer 4:24; Hab 3:6).

66. 1 Sam 2:8; Job 34:13; Pss 24:1; 90:2; Isa 24:4; Jer 10:12; 51:15.

67. C. J. H. Wright, "תבל," *NIDOTTE* 4:272–73.

68. The same shift, with some shared terms, occurs in Isa 24:4.

event—of course no one can stand before YHWH's rage and burning anger! Following and building on the predominantly negative tone of 1:2–3b and the entirely negative tone of 1:3c–5e, these questions are intended to push the reader to the very brink of an existential dilemma while eliminating all easy solutions. Both questions presume the earlier reference to YHWH in 1:3a and simply refer to "his wrath" and "his burning anger." Both also include the interrogative "who?" as the subject of two verbs that express the elusive possibility of surviving the theophany.[69]

Despite the detailed survey of the theophany's effects on the creation in 1:3c–5, these verses remind the reader that YHWH's anger is not ultimately focused on the created order apart from humanity, but rather on human beings who have sinned against him. The terms that describe the threat in 1:6a–b make this clear, since when God exercises "his wrath" and "his burning anger" against human beings he invariably does so in response to sinful behavior.[70] The term "wrath" (זַעַם), leaving aside cases in which the sense "curse" is better, refers to God's wrath against those who sin, whether Israelites or not, individuals or groups, believers in YHWH (rarely) or not. The parallel expression "burning anger" (חֲרוֹן אַף) has more precise nuances. First, it is more intense than the "anger" to which YHWH is slow (1:3a), heightening the rhetoric of this section compared to 1:2–3b. Second, in terms of canonical order and in terms of Israel's history, it appears first in Exod 32:12 and afterward is most frequently used to express divine anger against Israel/Judah, again hinting that a Judean reader cannot easily evade it.[71]

This focus on the human target of divine wrath is given additional bite by placing it directly after the impressive imagery and sphere of reference seen in 1:3c–5. This is the first of two important developments in the rhetoric of this section. The first subunit (1:2–3b) spoke of God's wrathful character and the danger it posed to his enemies, with a short mention of deliverance. The second subunit (1:3c–5) developed a nearly overwhelming picture of YHWH's descent in wrath and the effects such an intervention will have on the created order, with a shift of focus to humanity at the very end of the subunit. The third subunit explicitly and emphatically connects that impressive picture of YHWH's destructive presence with his superlative display of wrath against humanity but broadens its potential scope (compared to 1:2–3b) to include not only YHWH's enemies, but all human beings. Immediately afterward, however, 1:7 clarifies that escape is indeed possible and finally identifies the group that will escape, as well as explaining how.

The following figure represents these dynamics by highlighting the varying severity of divine wrath

69. While זַעַם can also mean "curse," the juridical aspects that Longman ("Nahum," 791) sees here and which would favor such a sense seem to be implicit rather than explicit. Perlitt, *Die Propheten*, 10, concludes that the imagery of 1:3b–6 reflects a judgment-theophany, and the rest of the terms in this exceptional cluster are clearly in the semantic field of wrath; cf. Baumann, *Gottes Gewalt*, 136.

70. For זַעַם, leaving aside cases in which the sense "curse" is better, God's wrath is against those who sin (Pss 7:11; 38:3; Isa 26:21); against those who oppress God's followers (Ps 69:24); against Egypt (Ps 78:49); against Babylon (Jer 50:25); against non-Israelite nations (Isa 30:27; Jer 10:10); against YHWH's enemies (Isa 66:14); as punishment for sin (Ps 102:11); against Israel (Isa 10:5, 25; 13:5; Lam 2:6); etc. So also Bertil Wiklander, "זעם," *TDOT* 4:109, and on Ps 102:10, Willem VanGemeren, "Psalms, Proverbs, Ecclesiastes, Son" EBC 5, ed. F. Gaebelein (Grand Rapids: Zondervan, 1991), 646. As for "wrath" (חֵמָה), it can be directed against national sin (Jer 44:6; Ezek 5:13), against God's adversaries and enemies (Isa 59:18), or against "the nations" who reject YHWH's word (Mic 5:14).

71. "Burning anger" (חֲרוֹן אַף) can be directed against sin in Israel (Num 25:4–5; Josh 7:26), other nations (Ps 78:49), or against sinners everywhere (Isa 13:9–13). Of its 34 or so uses, the vast majority involves divine anger against Israel; on seven occasions non-Israelite groups are in view: Amalek (1 Sam 28:18); Babylon (Isa 13:9, 13; Jer 51:45); Elam (Jer 49:37); Nineveh (Jonah 3:9); "nations" (Zeph 3:8). Cf. Baumann, *Gottes Gewalt*, 136–42.

(dark when against YHWH's enemies, light when against humanity in general; white indicates the absence of wrath) and the progressive clarification of its targets (the binary contrast between enemies and devotees in 1:6–8 most clearly identifies those who will escape and those who won't, and removes the ambiguity that apparently included all humanity in 1:3c–5).

Figure 2.1: Accumulation and Specification of Divine Wrath and Those It Strikes in Nahum 1:2–8

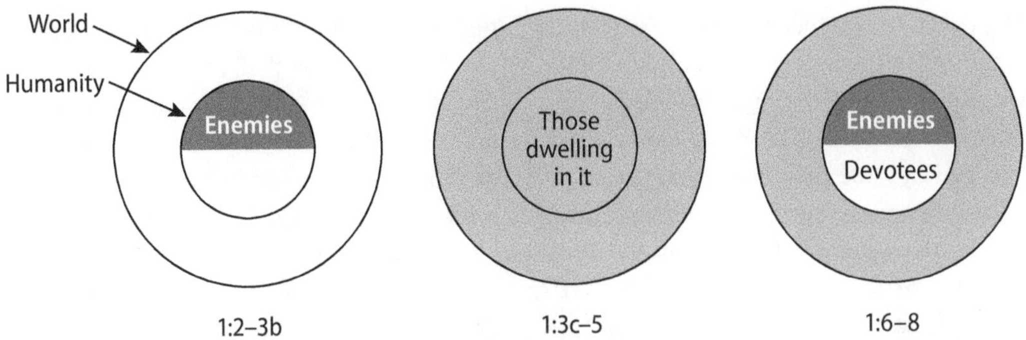

The simile in 1:6c emphasizes God's "rage" by placing an explicit subject before the verb and compares its pouring out to fire, commonly contained in a laver or tray (e.g., Lev 16:12).[72] The heat is evocative of God's burning anger (cf. 1:6b), while the "pouring out" implies uninterrupted or continuous judgment (Job 3:24; 10:10). The final description of God's wrath in physical terms in 1:6d portrays YHWH as breaking up rock cliffs (cf. the hills and mountains in 1:5a, b). The emphasis on the split cliffs as the verbal object (appearing before the verb here) gives the impression that YHWH's actions barely stop short of splitting the earth itself.[73]

In sum, 1:6 personalizes and potentially applies to all human beings the threat posed by YHWH's burning, destructive wrath—who could escape? Unlike the semantic fields present in 1:3c–5, which are only indirectly tied to divine wrath, those in 1:6 return the focus (already seen in 1:2–3b) to human behavior, specifically human sin.[74] The suspense created by the questions in 1:6a–b, fortified by the

72. The *qal* of נתך, "pour out," is used here; divine wrath is poured out with the same verb in 2 Chr 12:7; 34:21, 25; Jer 7:20; 42:18; 44:6; Ezek 22:22; note the "curse" poured out, Dan 9:11, and "destruction" poured out, Dan 9:27. The image seems to be that of a burning mass poured out on another surface. The heat element makes an association with divine anger natural (contrast the pouring out of water in Job 3:24 and of milk in Job 10:10), while the "pouring out" denotes a long-lasting or uninterrupted process regardless of what is poured (cf. the cries of Job 3:24). Other suggestions are less likely: volcanic activity is too specific for the imagery here (cf. Deut 32:22); links to theophanies associate the fire with God, not with his wrath, and not in a simile; fire describes lightning only in conjunction with other terms like "from heaven" or "of God;" and refining metal as a metaphor for purifying judgment always involves mention of various metals (Jer 6:29; Ezek 22:20; 24:12; Zech 13:9; Mal 3:2).

73. Roberts, *Nahum, Habakkuk, and Zephaniah*, 52, translates צור as "rock cliffs," and the plural (used here) often seems to denote cliffs or high rocks, not just boulders or rocks at ground level. In Num 23:9 they offer a vantage point and are in parallel with hills; in 1 Sam 24:3 and Isa 2:19, 21, they encompass caves, and in Job 28:10, channels.

74. Baumann, *Gottes Gewalt*, 136, notes that this is possibly the passage most densely filled with wrath-language, and that despite the fact that one of its four clauses has no such language (1:6d).

repeated emphasis on the terribly destructive effects of divine wrath, is intended to make the reader reflect on God and her or his relationship with him. Such reflection is guided not only by the material dealing with God's wrath and punishment of sin, but also by the brief mention of God's character in 1:2a–3b and especially by what follows in 1:7–8.

Whether the word order of verse 7 reflects the acrostic of 1:2–8 or a choice of word order focused on classification over identification, the reader who appreciates the danger that YHWH poses is struck, very agreeably, by the first word of 1:7—"Good" (טוֹב). The author seems to appreciate this contrast, for he shifts once again (but in the opposite direction) back to divine anger in 1:8. The logic of 1:7 is linear and makes three interconnected points on the basis of the threat that YHWH's wrath poses (cf. 1:6): YHWH is (also) good, specifically as a shelter to those threatened by his judgment, and it is by trusting in him that one comes under such shelter. The nearly rhetorical questions thus turn out to be, upon closer inspection, not purely rhetorical—there *is* a way to escape YHWH's wrath, but it is not through one's own efforts. Paradoxically, despite all that has been said earlier in the text about YHWH's awesome power, burning anger, and inescapable wrath, YHWH himself is the way to escape it.

YHWH's goodness often appears at the beginning or end of a hymn of praise (Ps 135:3; Jer 33:11) or is the only divine characteristic predicated of God in a larger context (Ps 34:8). Most strikingly, in Exod 33:19 God's "goodness" is shorthand for the display of the divine character that follows in Exodus 34.[75] That text, as we saw above, emphasizes YHWH's gracious and compassionate nature and his willingness to forgive, even in the face of Israel's worst apostasy. At the same time, YHWH's goodness coexists with his judgment of sin then (Exod 32:33, 35) and now. The shelter he offers is thus consistent with his justice—he is not harboring fugitives from justice or overlooking their sins.[76]

The affirmation that YHWH is a refuge in the day of trouble (1:7b) parallels and adds specificity to 1:7a by assigning a new role to YHWH—that of shelter.[77] The "day of trouble" is perhaps the tamest description of YHWH's arrival yet, although in context it simply summarizes the threat detailed in 1:2–6 that most other prophetic books call the day of YHWH (cf. Zeph 1:14–15). The only shelter from this threat that the text identifies is YHWH (1:7b), and the last clause of the verse provides the clearest identification yet of who will in fact escape YHWH's wrath and judgment—"Those who seek refuge in him."

YHWH's deliverance involves him on a personal level no less than it does the human beings who take refuge in him, since he "knows" them. YHWH "knowing" someone expresses a special, personal relationship with them.[78] Not only does YHWH's personal knowledge of those whom he delivers eliminate any possibility of arbitrariness from his saving and judging actions, his personal involvement also demonstrates that he is ready and willing to deliver all those who take refuge in him.[79]

The term that describes those whom YHWH knows, from the root חסה, can be translated either

75. This is noted by Robert P. Gordon, "טוֹב," *NIDOTTE* 2:355. Alan Millard, "For He Is Good," *TynBul* 17 (1966): 115–17, emphasizes the frequently covenantal context in which "YHWH is good" appears.

76. Fabry, *Nahum*, 139, observes that the "goodness" of YHWH is not automatically in Judah's favor.

77. Cf. the various categories for לְ on nouns in Merwe, Naudé, and Kroeze, *A Biblical Hebrew Reference Grammar*, 285, and note similar transitions with the same term and syntax in Ps 31:2; others suggest it is emphatic, e.g., Spronk, *Nahum*, 48. Assyria can find no refuge when the day of trouble falls upon it, Nah 3:11.

78. See Gen 18:19; Exod 33:12; Deut 34:10; Jer 1:5; Amos 3:2; and perhaps 2 Sam 7:20, all with God as the subject of ידע in the *qal*.

79. This is noted by Fabry, *Nahum*, 139.

literally as "seek refuge" or, as an extension of that sense, "trust in."[80] The mention of a "refuge" in 1:7b favors the more literal sense for חסה, but in any case the element of trust has already been elicited by the statement "YHWH is good" immediately following an extended meditation on the danger his theophanic appearance poses to humanity as a whole. While 1:3a keeps the reader from losing view of the possibility of deliverance, and more importantly connects that deliverance to YHWH in the midst of a much longer presentation of his zealous vengeance, here that same paradox appears more striking against the cataclysmic background of 1:3b–6. Amazingly, the God who comes in holy wrath against his enemies, and whose anger threatens all human beings, is simultaneously the only refuge from that danger.

The note on which this first section of Nahum closes is sobering, to say the least.[81] Both halves of 1:8 use a dynamic image (a rushing flood, a pursuing warrior) and terminal imagery ("[make] a complete end," "into darkness") to convey something of YHWH's relentless commitment to destroying those who oppose him. The verse begins with an adverbial phrase ("with an overflowing flood") that adds power to the assertion that YHWH will make "a complete end . . . of its place."[82]

There is no explicit element in the immediate context to which the 3fs suffix "her" can refer; most likely Nineveh or Assyria is in view.[83] If so, this constitutes the first historically specific reference to an object of YHWH's destruction since 1:1. Be that as it may, it is impossible to limit the hymn's horizon to Nineveh, here as elsewhere in 1:2–8, and it concludes with a focus on YHWH's generic "enemies," whom he will pursue into darkness.[84] Both clauses in 1:8 place the verbal object before the verb, emphasizing the result ("end," 1:8a) or object ("his enemies," 1:8b) of YHWH's actions.

The description of YHWH's judgment in terms of a flood is an example of the ironic reuse of language used to describe the Assyrian monarch's destruction of his enemies. Furthermore, the verb עבר is reused in 2:1[1:15], where the messenger of good news promises that Assyria will never again "pass through/over" Judah, and in 3:19, which

80. Andrew E. Hill, "חסה," *NIDOTTE* 2:218–20. Johann Gamberoni, "חסה," *TDOT* 5:70, argues that the participle consistently refers to "the devout worshipper in the best sense," and sometimes refers specifically to those who will escape eschatological wrath (Isa 57:13; Ps 2:12).

81. Note Thor Ramsey, "Where Is the Weeping in Your Sermon Notes," released June 3, 2014, http://thegospelcoalition.org/article/where-is-the-weeping-in-your-sermon-notes; and Jesus's response to the certainty of Jerusalem's judgment, Luke 13:34.

82. The LXX has "those who rise against him," reading a 3ms rather than a 3fs suffix on מְקוֹמָהּ. James Barr, *Comparative Philology and the Text of the Old Testament* (Oxford: Clarendon, 1968), 334, and G. R. Driver, "Vocabulary of the OT VIII," *JTS* 36 (1935), 300, take מָקוֹם to mean "opposition," though that is not attested in Biblical Hebrew; cf. *HALOT*, 626–27. For reasons of *lectio difficilior potior* and the general precedence of the MT, the MT reading represented in the translation offered here is preferable. Anthony Gelston, *The Twelve Minor Prophets*, *BHQ* 13 (Stuttgart: Deutsche Bibelgesellschaft, 2010), 84, similarly concludes that the Greek tradition's reading represents an assimilation from the context. On the general precedence of the MT, note the arguments of Al Wolters, "The Text of the Old Testament," in *The Face of Old Testament Studies: A Survey of Contemporary Approaches*, ed. D. W. Baker and B. T. Arnold (Grand Rapids: Baker, 1999), 19–37.

83. J. D. W. Watts, *The Books of Joel, Obadiah, Jonah, Nahum, Habakkuk and Zephaniah*, CBC (New York: Cambridge University Press, 1975), 105, suggests that it refers to Nineveh or to her patron goddess, Ishtar. Whatever the referent of "her," the parallelism between "her place" in 1:8a and "his enemies" in 1:8b argues strongly for an identical or analogous referent. Floyd, *Minor Prophets*, 36, sees it referring to the feminine noun "trouble" in 1:7b.

84. Spronk, *Nahum*, 49–50, notes a number of possible parallels between the images of flood and Neo-Assyrian royal annals and vassal treaties, while Gordon H. Johnston, "Nahum's Rhetorical Allusions to Neo-Assyrian Treaty Curses," *BSac* 158 (2001): 423–24, argues (perhaps less plausibly) that YHWH chasing his enemies into darkness echoes Neo-Assyrian sources.

summarizes Assyria's international violence in terms of "evil" passing over its victims. The flood of YHWH's just judgment will efface the flood of Assyrian violence.[85] Together, 1:7–8 constitute a second important development in this section's rhetoric, one that keeps pace with the broadening scope of the destruction which poses a danger to all human beings. This rhetorical shift, however, moves in a different direction than the one noted earlier and is evident from the amount of text given to the binary issue of one's fate in light of YHWH's coming. While on the one hand no one will be unaffected by that event, and all are indeed threatened by it, deliverance is still possible. In the first subunit (1:2–3b) deliverance receives only a short mention (1:3a) and is not connected with a particular group (unlike the "wrath" that will strike YHWH's "enemies"). In the second subunit (1:3c–5), the possibility of deliverance appears to vanish entirely, leading to the rhetorical peak in 1:6—"Who can stand?" Only at that crucial juncture does the passage apportion equal amounts of text to the binary fates of deliverance and destruction—1:7 uses eight words to announce the possibility of deliverance for one group, while 1:8 uses the same number of words to reaffirm the destruction of the other. These verses thus close off the unit in such a way that the reader, who has been awed by increasingly dark prospects for his or her future, is only presented with a clear way of escape at the end. The impression that literally no one will escape the destruction YHWH promises is thus corrected, but at the last possible moment. This encourages the reader to seek refuge in YHWH *before* the day of trouble arrives, while also preparing the reader for the next unit's message that Assyria will be destroyed while Judah will be delivered.

Figure 2.2: The Rhetoric of Wrath and Destruction to Promote a Faith Response in Nahum 1:2–8

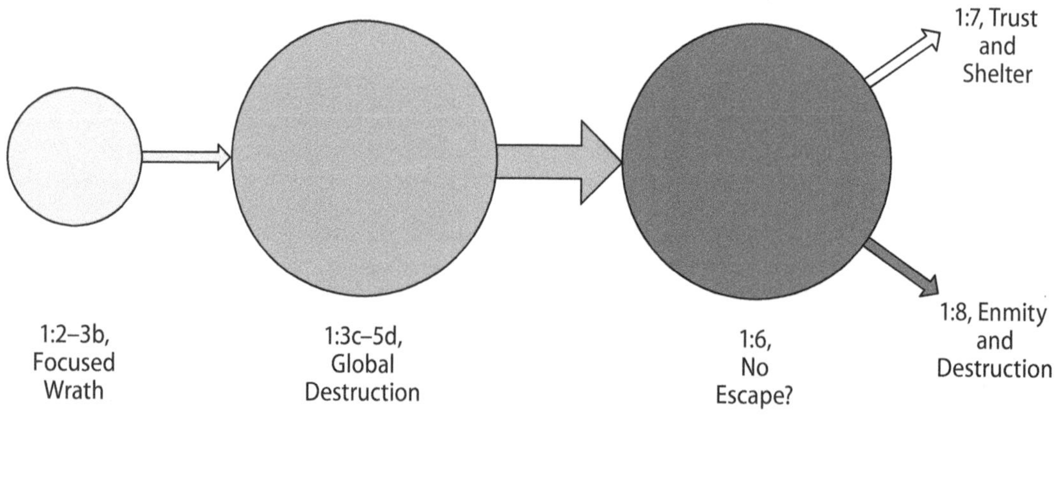

85. On this basis Michael J. Williams, "How Will God's Judgment Pass over You?" in *Devotions on the Hebrew Bible*, ed. Milton Eng and Lee M. Fields (Zondervan: Grand Rapids, 2015), 100–01, observes that the punishment fits the crime even on the level of grammar.

Canonical and Theological Significance

A Global, Ultimate Context for Assyria's Judgment

A key to understanding and appropriating Nahum's message outside the context of seventh-century Judah lies in the perspective offered by the opening hymn. Especially because the rest of the book is narrowly focused on Assyria and speaks of it and to it in very derogatory tones, it is important to appreciate this larger context so as to avoid facile nationalism, proud judgmentalism, and interpretations that fail to reckon with the complex connections between that specific situation and redemptive history.

Two important points of orientation appear in the hymn's global sphere of reference and its definitive outcomes. First, in terms of the sphere of reference, the hymn omits any connection to a particular, limited historical situation (the "day of trouble" is inherently flexible, much like the "day of YHWH"). Similarly, by focusing God's zealous vengeance on "his enemies," it presents the ultimate fate of those who oppose YHWH in spiritual, rather than national, terms. By the same token, those who "seek refuge" in YHWH are identified only in those terms, with no mention of their national or ethnic identity. Moreover, the whole world is affected by YHWH's coming, and "all who dwell in it" are in grave danger due to the pouring out of his burning wrath against sin.

Definitive or ultimate outcomes also prevent the reader from assuming that Assyria's judgment and the deliverance of Judah and other nations that judgment entails are more than a partial fulfillment of this final theophany. In the hymn YHWH offers full protection from his wrath, while being committed to the full destruction of those who resist his sovereign claims. When the day of trouble has run its course, only those who have sought refuge in YHWH remain, while all those who resist his sovereign will have been destroyed.

In light of these factors, interpretation of Nahum must begin and end with this universal context in which judgment and salvation are connected to the spiritual condition of individuals, apart from their belonging to any group, church, race, or nation. The hymn's assumption that all are threatened by YHWH's wrath further implies that all are to one degree or another guilty. Paradoxically and gloriously, however, the same God who is offended and whose glory is besmirched by human sin graciously offers shelter from sin's punishment, preserving his justice while offering amazing grace (Ps 85:10[9]; Rom 11:22). Nahum's focus on Assyria entails a corresponding focus on judgment rather than deliverance throughout the book, but it nonetheless clearly presents the justice and mercy of God together, especially by echoing classic expressions and demonstrations of God's character in Israel's past.

Finally, a solid grasp of Assyria's fall in the context of the ultimate divine intervention in 1:2–8 is the surest way to connect this book with the gospel. The gospel presents the endpoints of various trajectories that pass through Nahum. The same

God against whom human beings have sinned offers them salvation (already seen in Nahum), now revealed as coming through his punishment of their sin in his own Son and by his uniting them to him by his Spirit (1 Pet 2:24; 3:18). The destructive effects of his theophanic appearance, while purging the created order of sin, still usher in the new heavens and new earth rather than sundering all continuity with the created one sullied by sin (2 Pet 3:10–12; Rev 20:11; 21:1).[86] Perhaps most strikingly, the note of doxology that goes unuttered in 1:2–8 appears repeatedly in the NT in response to God's saving work in Christ. This suggests that the ultimate focus is not on the destruction of God's enemies, as clear and awe inspiring a demonstration of his justice as that is, but on his inexplicable mercy to former enemies whom he has drawn into a saving relationship with himself. Moreover, our joy is that of former enemies who have escaped the same destruction only because God's wrath has been exhausted in the sacrifice of his Son.[87] This response, coming from the very core of a redeemed person's being, reflects the text's focus on individuals as well as the canonical focus on the human being as an individual called to reflect the glory of God in every aspect of his or her being.[88]

YHWH's Gloriously Complex Character and His Interaction with Humanity

It may sound unorthodox to say that Nahum does not offer a balanced presentation of YHWH's character, but this is clearly the case, and the author's choices on this point are easily understood in light of his chosen subject. Here a comparison with Jonah is helpful. Jonah highlights the corrigibility of Nineveh in order to emphasize for Israel the dangers of a sense of earned grace, inherent worth, or innate superiority when compared with a nation that enjoyed no national covenant with YHWH. Jonah emphasizes that the same grace that Israel enjoyed in the past can be legitimately extended to Nineveh (Jonah 4:1–2).[89] In that case, the emphasis is nearly the inverse of Nahum's, since the plotline includes the deliverance of a foreign nation from judgment (cf. Jer 18:5–10).

In the case of Nahum, Assyria's perennial arrogance, violence, and autonomy have brought things to a head, and judgment is now inevitable. Consequently, it is impossible that a theology sketched within the boundaries of that specific situation

86. Douglas Moo, "Nature in the New Creation: New Testament Eschatology and the Environment," *JETS* 49 (2006): 449–88, who speaks of "radical transformation" of this created order rather than its complete annihilation; similarly, Al Wolters, "Worldview and Textual Criticism," *WTJ* 49 (1987): 405–13.

87. Note John Oswalt, *The Book of Isaiah: Chapters 40–66*, NICOT (Grand Rapids: Eerdmans, 1998), 693, on the interrelation of destruction and deliverance in the closing verse of Isaiah (Isa 66:24).

88. Cf. Eric L. Johnson, *Foundations for Soul Care: A Christian Psychology Proposal* (Downers Grove, IL: InterVarsity Press, 2007), 317: "God furthers his dramatic self-glorification by seeking and creating a new community of broken and sinful image-bearers who are being made increasingly capable of communion with the triune God by faith. . . ."

89. Timmer, *A Gracious and Compassionate God*, 119–23.

should include a dominant note of grace. As we have seen, grace and mercy are not absent from Nahum, but their presence is accounted for only by the inclusion of other nations, or (in terms of 1:2–8) by the inclusion of other groups whose relationship with YHWH is restored. Finally, the presentation of YHWH's vengeance and wrath includes several groupings of terms so dense and concentrated that they are essentially without parallel in the OT.

While Nahum's theology is asymmetrical, this poses no insurmountable obstacle to integrating Nahum in a larger canonical and theological discourse. Perhaps the most important contribution Nahum makes is to affirm of God that his character remains unchanged even in the context of historical circumstances that oblige him to act in predominantly one capacity (in Nahum, that of Divine Warrior) to establish justice.[90] Divine justice, however, is an element that is common to both the deliverance and punishment presented in 1:2–8, and exploring this will allow us to work out a little further the way the divine character functions there and across the canon. First, divine justice is taken for granted in Nahum. Both in the text and in the historical situations to which it alludes, YHWH's wrath and judgment are just and beyond critical examination (in the case of Assyria, they are, moreover, self-evident). Second, this means that the refuge he offers is consistent with his justice and so cannot consist of him simply overlooking human sin. This is reinforced by the emphasis in 1:8 on YHWH's pursuit of his enemies to the point of their extermination (1:8b) solely because they are guilty (cf. 1:3b). Third, universal sinfulness seems assumed by the universal danger that God's wrath poses (1:6), so we are warranted in concluding that this involves forgiveness as well, although the means are nowhere specified (however, as we will see, 1:12 involves the Sinai covenant). Fourth and finally, the book of Nahum is part of the Christian canon, and its connections to the rest of Scripture are not merely formal but organic, as the intertextual connections noted above show. The contexts in which YHWH's saving character is elaborated in the face of human inability and guilt (e.g., Exod 34; Rom 3) are most relevant here and help us situate Nahum in the larger context of *salvation* history. God's judgment of Assyria is an early point on this trajectory, Jesus's atoning death and resurrection constitute its glorious center, and the final judgment and consummation are its conclusion.

Nahum's Rhetoric and Appropriation of Its Message

The force and finesse with which Nahum's opening hymn collapses humanity into only two classes of people greatly helps the transmission and appropriation of its message. Other aspects of its rhetoric have been mentioned above, so here we

90. See further the brief reflections of Roberts, *Nahum, Habakkuk, and Zephaniah*, 52; Thomas Renz, "Nahum, Book of," in *DTIS*, 527–28.

will note only the dynamic element—that is, the movement from one perspective to another, the addition of new elements, and other changes that the text makes in the process of describing YHWH's final theophany and its implications.[91]

The opening lines focus the reader's attention on YHWH and are calculated to impress even the well-versed reader by focusing in an unparalleled way on his zealous vengeance. Repetition of the same word or words in the same semantic field hammers home YHWH's incalculable anger and the fact that it will affect human beings first and foremost.

The question then arises, Which human beings will be affected by this outpouring of divine vengeance? The initial answer is "God's enemies," and while the reader will almost surely have some idea of what sort of person would be in that category, it is still vague, and prompts the reader to ponder just that—*who* is an enemy of YHWH? Israel's history gives no simple answer, as the events in Exod 32–34 show. This distinction is a key element of the gospel, which distinguishes on the same grounds (even if in much clearer terms) between those who are currently reconciled to God and those who are not.

The shift in 1:3–5 to the natural world and the effects that YHWH's coming will have on it may seem an irrelevant excursus, but its contribution is important. Not only does it make clear that YHWH's vengeance will affect *all* human beings, but the vivid imagery of the destructive, almost annihilating effects that accompany his arrival (still focused on human beings) adds a significant emotional aspect to the text. Not just any field, but the most fertile regions become barren, the famous forests of Lebanon are suddenly deprived of life, and the very earth threatens to fall apart underfoot. The current focus on environmental sustainability, warranted in light of humanity's role as the steward of creation, exemplifies the disconcerting and disquieting nature of these phenomena for the survival of humanity on a much more limited scale that helps us, by comparison, grasp the unparalleled significance of Nahum's message.

The question of survival is then pursued in 1:6. Who could possibly escape unscathed from such a cataclysm? Surprisingly, there is one way to escape, and still more surprisingly it is found in the very God whose coming threatens all humanity. Here, finally, Nahum's presentation of God's character attains an equilibrium, with one verse focused on deliverance (1:7) and another (1:8) on punishment. All the same, the unit ends by returning to the opening emphasis on judgment and destruction, effectively insisting that the reader continue to reflect on and respond to its message so as to ensure his or her survival in YHWH's protection. The reciprocal relationship with YHWH, trusting him for deliverance from his just judgment and being known

91. Transition and climax are usually termed "structural" rhetorical devices; see William M. Purcell and David Snowball, "Style," in *Encyclopedia of Rhetoric*, ed. T. O. Sloane (Oxford: Oxford University Press, 2001), 698.

by him, transforms enemies into friends and promises a future in which his character and actions will continue to humble, amaze, and bring good to those who trust in him. It also constitutes a sure hope and confidence that will sustain his people in the face of trials and questions like those faced by the Judeans of Nahum's day.

The incomplete acrostic that spans 1:2–8 also strengthens the passage's emphasis on preparing for YHWH's theophanic arrival. The vast majority of biblical acrostics are complete, and use all 22 letters of the Hebrew alphabet to begin successive lines (e.g., Ps 25).[92] Psalm 119 takes this approach even further by beginning groups of eight verses with the same letter. These full acrostics invariably convey a sense of completeness, as the exhaustive meditation on Torah in Ps 119 demonstrates. The incomplete acrostic in Nah 1:2–8, by contrast, cannot have the same significance. Yet the high degree of artistry necessary for the construction of even a partial acrostic makes it nearly certain that there is indeed a rationale for this structure.[93]

What then might the acrostic of Nah 1 convey? Its incompleteness is emphatic given that it is limited to exactly half of the letters in the Hebrew alphabet. In light of the semantics of the passage, which focus on YHWH's intervention that will punish the wicked and resolve the moral disorder caused by sin, the half-formed acrostic most likely complements this presentation of unfinished business by adding controlled (because an acrostic) incompleteness (because partial). Just as the language of the poem foretells YHWH's theophanic arrival to judge and deliver fully and finally, its form emphasizes the presence of imperfect, incomplete order prior to that event. In the same vein as the question of 1:6 and the binary choices presented in 1:7–8, the incomplete acrostic's intimation that final resolution is still future also strengthens the rhetorical force that the poem exerts upon the reader in order to promote a response of faith and repentance toward YHWH.[94]

92. See C. J. Fantuzzo, "Acrostic," *Dictionary of the Old Testament: Wisdom, Poetry & Writings*, ed. Tremper Longman III and Peter Enns (Downers Grove, IL: InterVarsity Press, 2008), 1–4.

93. The acrostic of Nah 1:2–8 is clearly broken at only one place (the absent ד, "d," from the line in 1:4c). This makes it difficult to interpret its broken element, although Ronald Benun, "Evil and the Disruption of Order: A Structural Analysis of the Acrostics in the First Book of Psalms," *JHebS* 6 (2006): article 5, page 6, doi:10.5508/jhs.2006.v.6.a5, argues that most broken acrostics are created in order to express a clear message. Benun argues with respect to Pss 9–10 (the next most incomplete acrostic in the OT, using 15 letters) that the section at which that acrostic is most broken (six of the seven missing letters in Pss 9:14–15, 20–21; 10:1, 12–15) highlights the "breakdown in appropriate divine order" that corresponds with the "warped logic of the wicked." Gregory D. Cook explores the relationship between Nahum and Ps 9 in *Severe Compassion: The Gospel According to Nahum* (Phillipsburg, NJ: P&R, 2016), 47–59.

94. Renz's careful poetic analysis in "Perfectly Broken Acrostic," too detailed to include here, adds metrical and other considerations that corroborate the interpretation proposed here.

CHAPTER 3

Nahum 1:9–2:1[1:15]

C. Four Announcements of Assyria's Destruction and Judah's Deliverance

Main Idea of the Passage

YHWH speaks directly to Assyria and Judah, promising destruction to the one and deliverance to the other, in partial fulfillment of the theophanic judgment foretold in 1:2–8. The destruction is punishment for Assyria's opposition to God and its king's idolatrous claims, and is simultaneously Judah's liberation and the end of its covenant discipline.

Literary Context

The book's first main section (1:2–8) introduced a global, definitive judgment that will finally and fully annihilate evil and those who practice it in rebellion against YHWH. Amid this storm of wrath YHWH will also deliver from his judgment those who take refuge in him. The opening hymn based both destruction and deliverance on YHWH's character but remained general and global rather than specifying exactly who will be punished or delivered in Nahum's seventh-century context. It also exhibited a strong penchant for destruction in terms of its structure and the amount of text given to each topic.

This unit (1:9–2:1[1:15]) shifts the focus of this judgment to a particular enemy, to whom YHWH speaks in the second person.[1] Likewise, YHWH announces directly to Judah, also addressed in the second person, that it will no longer suffer at Assyria's hands. This historically specific perspective continues throughout the rest of the book. The present passage (1:9–2:1[1:15]) shares with the following section

1. Roberts, *Nahum, Habakkuk, and Zephaniah*, 52, also notes the "application" of 1:2–8 to the particular case introduced in 1:9.

(2:2–14[1–13]) its focus on the fall of Assyria but alternates between Assyria and Judah in a way that highlights the contrasting effects of God's intervention on the two nations. This macrounit, like the one that follows it, is an anticipated, partial fulfillment of the theophanic judgment (and deliverance) described in 1:2–8.

The final macrounit (3:1–19) unpacks the implications of Assyria's fall as anticipated here, with a focus on the empire's arrogance, violence, and autonomy. The mocking, taunting tone of this last unit is a focused attack on Assyria's arrogated glory, something that is highly offensive in YHWH's eyes. While remaining focused on the Assyrian Empire, the theocentric perspective of this final unit demonstrates the continuity of this specific punishment of a particular enemy of YHWH with the global, ultimate judgment announced in 1:2–8.

A. Introduction (1:1)
B. The Threat of YHWH's Coming Global Judgment (1:2–8)
➡ **C. Four Announcements of Assyria's Destruction and Judah's Deliverance (1:9–2:1[1:15])**
   1. The First Address to Assyria (1:9–10)
   2. The First Address to Judah (1:11–13)
   3. The Second Address to Assyria (1:14)
   4. The Second Address to Judah (2:1[1:15])
D. The Prophetic Anticipation of Assyria's Fall (2:2–14[1–13])
E. The Deconstruction of Assyria's Pride (3:1–19)

Translation and Exegetical Outline

(See next page.)

Structure and Literary Form

This unit consists of four succinct addresses, two each to Assyria and Judah, in alternating order. It is clearly separate from the opening hymn which precedes it, since the hymn uses exclusively third-person grammar and is focused on YHWH's character in connection with a global theophany. This unit's direct address in the second person creates a tone that is more directly confrontational (for Assyria) or comforting (for Judah), while also contributing to the shift from a general to a specific sphere of reference.

This unit is distinct from the following unit for the same reasons, since 2:2–11[1–10] is ostensibly addressed only to Assyria and shifts to a new scene, that of a battle. Furthermore, while 1:9–2:1[1:15] announces the destruction of Assyria and moves

Nahum 1:9–2:1 [1:15]

			C. Four Announcements of Assyria's Destruction and Judah's Deliverance (1:9–2:1)
			1. The First Address to Assyria (1:9a–10c)
9a	מַה־תְּחַשְּׁבוּן אֶל־יְהוָה	Whatever you plot against YHWH,	a. Assyria's Futile Plots (1:9a–c)
9b	כָּלָה הוּא עֹשֶׂה	he is making a complete end;	
9c	לֹא־תָקוּם פַּעֲמַיִם צָרָה	an adversary will not arise twice!	
10a	כִּי עַד־סִירִים סְבֻכִים	Surely, like thorns are tangled,	b. Assyria's Complete, Certain Destruction (1:10a–c)
10b	וּכְסָבְאָם סְבוּאִים	and like drunkards' drink is drunk,	
10c	אֻכְּלוּ כְּקַשׁ יָבֵשׁ מָלֵא	they will be consumed like fully dried chaff!	
			2. The First Address to Judah (1:11–13b)
11	מִמֵּךְ יָצָא חֹשֵׁב עַל־יְהוָה רָעָה יֹעֵץ בְּלִיָּעַל	From you has gone out one plotting evil against YHWH, one planning wickedness.	a. Assyria's Past Departure from Judah (1:11)
12a	כֹּה אָמַר יְהוָה	Thus says YHWH:	b. Assyria's Certain Destruction (1:12a–c)
12b	אִם־שְׁלֵמִים וְכֵן רַבִּים	"Even if they are at full strength and just as numerous,	
12c	וְכֵן נָגֹזּוּ וְעָבָר	even so they will be mowed down and removed!	
12d	וְעִנִּתִךְ	I have afflicted you,	c. Judah's Affliction Ended (1:12d–e)
12e	לֹא אֲעַנֵּךְ עוֹד	but I will afflict you no longer.	
13a	וְעַתָּה אֶשְׁבֹּר מֹטֵהוּ מֵעָלָיִךְ	Now I will break his yoke bar off you	d. Judah's Liberation Promised (1:13a–b)
13b	וּמוֹסְרֹתַיִךְ אֲנַתֵּק	and will break off your cords."	
			3. The Second Address to Assyria (1:14a–e)
14a	וְצִוָּה עָלֶיךָ יְהוָה	YHWH has ordained thus concerning you:	a. Elimination of the King's Name (1:14a–b)
14b	לֹא־יִזָּרַע מִשִּׁמְךָ עוֹד	"Your name will no longer be sown;	
14c	מִבֵּית אֱלֹהֶיךָ אַכְרִית פֶּסֶל וּמַסֵּכָה	from the house of your gods I will eliminate sculpted image and cast image;	b. Destruction of the King's Gods (1:14c)
14d	אָשִׂים קִבְרֶךָ	I will prepare your grave,	c. Preparation of the King's Grave (1:14d)
14e	כִּי קַלּוֹתָ	for you are despicable!"	d. YHWH's Destruction of Assyria's King Justified (1:14e)
			4. The Second Address to Judah (2:1a–f)
2:1a	הִנֵּה עַל־הֶהָרִים	Look on the mountains!	a. Arrival of a Messenger (2:1a–b)
1b	רַגְלֵי מְבַשֵּׂר מַשְׁמִיעַ שָׁלוֹם	The feet of a messenger of good news, one who announces peace!	
1c	חָגִּי יְהוּדָה חַגַּיִךְ	"Celebrate your feasts, Judah!	b. Celebrate YHWH, for Assyria Is No More! (2:1c–f)
1d	שַׁלְּמִי נְדָרָיִךְ	Pay your vows!	
1e	כִּי לֹא יוֹסִיף עוֹד (לַעֲבוֹר־) [לַעֲבָר־]בָּךְ בְּלִיַּעַל	For never again will the wicked one invade you—	
1f	כֻּלֹּה נִכְרָת	he is completely eliminated!"	

onward to contemplate its effects, 2:2–11[1–10] goes back in time to the beginning of the attack on Nineveh and then moves forward through its fall, plundering, and destruction (cf. the order and scope of events in the Assyrian bas-relief discussed in the Introduction).

The syntactic structure above reflects a number of points at which syntax or other considerations subordinate parts of the discourse. The distinct syntactic role of the fronted (prior to the verb) direct object in 1:9a and the shift in clause type that sets off 1:10a, b from their context, afford two clear instances of subordination in the first address to Assyria. The concessive "even if" that begins 1:12b is subordinate to the mainline assertion in 1:12c that the one plotting against YHWH will be destroyed, and the following direct speech (1:12d–2:1[1:15]f, with a few interruptions) is subordinate to the discourse that carries it. The causal role of 1:14e subordinates it to the preceding lines in 1:14b–d just as the reason for celebration in 2:1[1:15]e–f subordinates it to 2:1[1:15]c–d.

The four addresses in 1:9–2:1[1:15] employ diverse literary genres, and are further distinguished from one another by the grammar used for the addressee and by the radically different evaluations and fates assigned to these groups.[2] The first address to Assyria, 1:9–10, is a rhetorical question (although not clearly presented as YHWH's first-person speech) addressed to a masculine-plural party. The first words spoken to Judah (feminine singular) in 1:11–13 are a prophecy of deliverance uttered by YHWH, dismissing Assyria's might and affirming on the contrary that it will be easily destroyed. Assyria's destruction also entails the end of YHWH's affliction of Judah. The second address to Assyria in 1:14 reflects yet another genre, a prophecy of destruction focused on the Assyrian king (masculine singular). The final address, the second one made to Judah (2:1[1:15], again using the feminine singular), is presented as the message of a herald who brings good news. It consists of a command to Judah to celebrate its feasts and pay its vows in light of the anticipated complete elimination of the Assyrian threat.[3]

Table 3.1: Alternating Addressees in Nahum 1:9–2:1[1:15]

Reference	Addressee	Grammar of Addressee	Message
1:9–10	Assyria	Masculine plural	Destruction
1:11–13	*Judah*	*Feminine singular*	*Deliverance*
1:14	Assyria	Masculine singular	Destruction
2:1[1:15]	*Judah*	*Feminine singular*	*Rejoice!*

2. The characterization of Assyria in Nahum is explored further in Timmer, *The Non-Israelite Nations in the Book of the Twelve*, 116–35.

3. Fabry, *Nahum*, 147, also recognizes the importance of grammatical gender for distinguishing the addressees of these speeches.

Explanation of the Text

1. The First Address to Assyria (1:9–10)

The focus of this first speech is Assyria's opposition to YHWH and the certain truth that he will soon do away with that empire once and for all. Even if YHWH is not the speaker in this section, the speaker is at least addressing Assyria on YHWH's behalf. The explicit mention of Judah in 2:1[1:15] and the initial mention of Nineveh in 1:1 allow us, in the absence of a general scenario like that described in 1:2–8, to speak specifically of Judah and Assyria here. While the identities of Judah and Assyria are revealed only gradually in this section (and only partially, in the case of Assyria/Nineveh), there is less suspense than was the case in 1:2–8, since that passage spoke only of anonymous parties in the third person, avoiding all specifics.

The lexeme that begins 1:9 (מַה) can function as an interrogative ("What . . . ?") or as an indefinite pronoun ("Whatever . . ."').[4] There are thus two possible translations: "What do you plot against YHWH?" or "Whatever you plot against YHWH, . . ." The first option is clearly rhetorical. Since the enemy has been plotting against YHWH (cf. 1:11), the point of such a question is not to reveal exactly what plans have been laid, but rather to establish the irrelevance of any and all such plots. This is essentially the meaning of the second translation option as well, which makes the "whatever" explicit and follows it, in the same clause, with the affirmation that any and all plots will be ended by YHWH.

The "plotting" in which the subject of 1:9a is engaged makes it quite likely that it (here, masculine plural, although that can include any number of female individuals) is a particular manifestation of the generic "enemy" mentioned several times in the opening hymn.[5] At the same time, this element of conspiracy or plotting sheds new light on the enemy's disposition toward YHWH. While general opposition is necessitated by the use of the terms "adversary" and "enemy" in the previous unit (1:2c, d), here that enemy is alleged to have actively, intentionally made plans as a concrete expression of that antipathy against YHWH. While in 1:11 the terms "evil" and "wicked/worthless" add a strong negative evaluation of this activity, they merely reinforce what the semantics of this verse have already established.[6]

Regardless of the extent of the anti-YHWH plot and of the plotter's strength, the following clause (1:9b) affirms in a very matter of fact way that YHWH will put an end to it. The phrase is very similar to that in 1:8a, "a complete end he will make of its place," using the same verb (עָשָׂה), the same object (כָּלָה), and the same word order that emphatically places the verbal object first. While the context of 1:2–8 was the arrival of YHWH, with finite verbal forms used to describe its (future) effects, the use of a participle here avoids any precise chronological setting and probably conveys the idea that Assyria's schemes never caught YHWH by surprise.

When and where might the Assyrian Empire have plotted in this way? While Assyria occasionally acknowledges YHWH's "existence" in its propaganda against Judah (e.g., 2 Kgs 18:22), it is

4. Merwe, Naudé, and Kroeze, *A Biblical Hebrew Reference Grammar*, 262, 324–25.

5. So also Perlitt, *Die Propheten*, 13. The collocation of חָשַׁב, "plan, plot," with a preposition like אֶל, "to," especially when the wicked are the verbal subject, makes such a sense clear here. Cf. J. Hartley, "חשב," *NIDOTTE* 2:303–10.

6. Either אֶל, "to," or עַל, "on, concerning," marks the indirect object of חשב; cf. Jer 18:18; 49:20; 50:45.

condemned here for nothing less than conscious, proactive opposition to YHWH. The most notable example of such behavior, from a Judean point of view, would surely be Sennacherib's attack on Judah in 701 BCE, which was fresh in the Judeans' minds at the time of Nahum's ministry. Extant Assyrian records of the event include only partial parallels to the biblical material, which focuses on the religious facets of Sennacherib's attack.[7] While in the biblical accounts Assyria uses varied and sometimes contradictory arguments to convince Jerusalem to surrender, the central issue is Assyria's claim that YHWH, like the gods of other nations who have already fallen to Assyria, will not be able to deliver Jerusalem from Sennacherib's attack (Isa 36:18–20; 37:11–13). Hezekiah qualifies this as "mocking" YHWH (Isa 37:4, 17, חרף), while Isaiah calls it (quoting YHWH) "reviling/blaspheming" YHWH (Isa 37:6, גדף).

Perhaps the most striking aspect of the parallel accounts is how the Assyrian king pits himself (and not, in these texts, the Assyrian gods) against YHWH and the gods of the other nations (2 Kgs 18:33, 35 // Isa 36:18, 20). The outcome of the siege of Jerusalem is thus an indicator of the supremacy of one or the other of the contestants, and the biblical accounts never ignore the theological aspect of the Assyrian king's claims. By delivering Jerusalem, YHWH will show "all the kingdoms of the earth . . . that you, YHWH, are God alone" (2 Kgs 19:19 // Isa 37:20). Claims like those made by Assyria, whether tied explicitly to the supremacy of gods other than YHWH or not, are objectionable primarily because they reject YHWH's absolute and unique supremacy.

The biblical accounts just noted probably presume the reader's awareness that the Neo-Assyrian Empire, as represented by its own media and administrators, consistently presented itself and its expansion as in accord with the will of its gods and made possible by their active intervention in history.[8] On the one hand, the Assyrian king took titles that legitimized his project of world domination. Early in the seventh century, Esarhaddon authored numerous royal inscriptions that described him as

> great king, mighty king, king of the world, king of Assyria, governor of Babylon, king of Sumer and Akkad, king of the four quarters [of the world], true shepherd, favorite of the great gods, whom from his childhood the gods Aššur, Šamaš, Bēl, and Nabû, Ištar of Nineveh, (and) Ištar of Arbela named for the kingship of Assyria.[9]

Several decades earlier, Tiglath-pileser III, who had aided Ahaz against the joint threat of Aram and the Northern Kingdom of Israel (2 Kgs 16:5–10; Isa 7–8), had royal scribes portray him in these terms:

> Precious scion of Baltil (Assur), beloved of the god(dess) . . . creation of the goddess Ninmena, who [(. . .)] for the dominion of the lands . . . the one who overwhelms his foes, valiant man, the one who destroys [(. . .)] enemies.[10]

Given this royal ideology, when states refused to come under or stay under the "yoke" of vassalship to Assyria, they were (from the Assyrian point of view) illegitimately, arrogantly, and culpably refusing the will of the gods, and of Assur

7. See Mordechai Cogan, "Into Exile: From the Assyrian Conquest of Israel to the Fall of Babylon," in *The Oxford History of the Biblical World*, ed. M. Cogan (Oxford: Oxford University Press, 1998), 242–75, and in much more detail, Isaac Kalami and Seth Richardson, ed., *Sennacherib at the Gates of Jerusalem: Story, History and Historiography*, CHANE 71 (Leiden: Brill, 2014).

8. In this and the following paragraphs I draw on Timmer, "Nahum's Representation of and Response to Neo-Assyria," 349–62.

9. Leichty, *The Royal Inscriptions of Esarhaddon*, 11. Similar titles were used by numerous Assyrian kings before him.

10. Tadmor and Yamada, *The Royal Inscriptions of Tiglath-Pileser III and Shalmaneser V*, 22.

in particular.[11] Assyrian royal inscriptions from the seventh century regularly describe the insubordination of smaller states that Assyria had subjugated as rebellion against Assyria's gods.[12] As a result, Esarhaddon promised retribution against those who have "sinned against the god Assur," including Nabu-zer-kitti-lisir, "governor of the sea-land, . . . [who] did not keep his treaty nor remember the agreement of Assyria, forgot the good relations of my father . . ." and resisted Assyria on the battlefield. Similarly, Esarhaddon condemned Abdi-Milkuti, king of Sidon, who "did not fear my lordship (and) did not listen to the words of my lips, . . . trusted in the rolling sea and threw off the yoke of the god Assur." Esarhaddon also considered Sanda-uarri, king of the cities Kundi and Sissu, to be "a dangerous enemy, who did not fear my lordship (and) abandoned the gods," as he and an ally "swore an oath by their gods with one another, and trusted in their own strength."[13]

In light of these specific aspects of Assyria's interaction with Judah and other nations, and with an eye to the prior context in Nahum, we are able to answer the question, How can Nahum assert that Assyria is plotting against YHWH when examples of such opposition appear very infrequently in the OT? First, as the opening hymn emphasizes, YHWH is (whether acknowledged or not, cf. Rom 1:18) the sole creator and judge of all human beings. His power and prerogative are thus unlimited and absolute. When Assyria (or any other empire or entity) presents itself as the supreme or only power, YHWH's claims are rejected and his honor and glory are attacked.

Second, in this section we have seen how Assyria, like empires before and after it, characteristically asserted its unique claim to authority, power, and legitimacy. The royal titles mentioned above presuppose that "it was the Assyrian monarch's sacred obligation to explore, overcome, and incorporate [all non-Assyrian territories] into the realm of Ashur."[14] As noted in the Introduction, it is quite likely that the author of Nahum was aware of such inflated descriptions of the Assyrian Empire and its ruler, whether from biblical or extrabiblical sources (or, most likely, both). The author of Nahum saw such claims as flagrantly anthropocentric and idolatrous, and so directly opposed to YHWH's glory as unique creator, judge, and deliverer. These conflicting claims to global supremacy explain YHWH's "zeal" and his commitment to undertake "vengeance" for his own glory. This same reality lies behind YHWH's responses, in the first person, to Assyria in 1:14, 2:14[13], and 3:5, with the last two of these references including the confrontational challenge "I am against you!" (note the shaded portions in the relevant Translation and Exegetical Outlines).

The end result of YHWH's "making a complete end" of any and all plots against him (now with an imperfective form) will be that "an adversary" will not arise a second time. In light of the more specific focus of 1:9 on a particular adversary that is addressed directly, it is possible to translate צָרָה as "adversary" (concrete) rather than "adversity/trouble" (abstract).[15] Understood in this way, the clause expresses the logical outcome of YHWH's putting an end to *all* (Assyrian) plots against him

11. These characterizations are among those identified by Zehnder, *Umgang mit Fremden*, 66–69, and Oded, *War, Peace and Empire*, 56–57.

12. See Younger, "Assyrian Involvement in the Southern Levant," 235–63, esp. 242, 250–52, and Mario Liverani, "*Kitru, Katâru*," *Mesopotamia* 17 (1982): 43–66.

13. Leichty, *The Royal Inscriptions of Esarhaddon*, 15, 17.

14. Bradley J. Parker, "The Construction and Performance of Kingship in the Neo-Assyrian Empire," *Journal of Anthropological Research* 67 (2011): 363.

15. Cf. *HALOT*, 1054.

by putting an end to Assyria itself. Alternatively, the use of the term that makes up part of the title for YHWH's intervention ("day of trouble," 1:7) makes it possible that "adversity" here refers to that intervention, which will be once and for all. In that case, the "adversity will not arise twice" conveys the finality of YHWH's judgment on its own terms, rather than in terms of the enemy or plot it does away with.[16] Given the focus on Assyria in 1:9–10, a reference to Assyrian plots is more likely here.

The first two lines of 1:10 are among the most challenging in the OT.[17] Before we consider the details, it is important to remember that whatever 1:10a, b mean, they fit into their context. Specifically, they are illustrations of, or reflections on, what the preceding (1:9c) and following (1:10c) lines clearly affirm: that YHWH's opponents will be definitively and completely destroyed. Both lines (1:10a, b) involve wordplay: each one uses a subject and a modifier beginning with the letter *s*, and the second line uses the same root (סבא) twice (rendered by most translations as "drunk . . . drunkards"). The two lines are introduced by the particle כִּי, which when it appears first in its clause can be causal ("for/because") or, as is more likely here, asseverative ("surely . . ."').[18] The second word in 1:10a, עַד, is a common preposition that usually positions something in time ("until") or space ("as far as, to").[19] Neither of those meanings works here, but עַד can also function comparatively ("like/as"), and that meaning fits the context well and is also paralleled by the comparative כ in 1:10b.[20]

This leaves us with the two phrases, both similes for the destruction of those who plot against YHWH. But how are tangled thorns and a drink that is consumed like dry chaff that will (when exposed to fire) be completely burned? Once again, the clear sense of 1:10c helps, since the image of fully dried chaff being consumed by fire implies inevitability and irreversibility—how could it not all go up in a puff of smoke? The two troublesome clauses thus should probably be understood as follows: as thorns inevitably grow together and become entangled, and as a drink is drunk, so the end of those who craft schemes against YHWH is irreversible and sure.[21] The final line, as noted, is a clear affirmation that Assyria will be totally destroyed by God's response to its schemes.[22]

16. The versions usually amend the text to read צָרָיו, "his enemies," but as Longman notes ("Nahum," 795), not only is the expression intelligible as it stands but צָרָה is one of several roots that appear both in 1:7 and in 1:9. The collocation צָרָה with קום does not occur elsewhere in the OT.

17. See the discussions in Spronk, *Nahum*, 54–56; Kevin J. Cathcart, *Nahum in the Light of Northwest Semitic*, BibOr 26 (Rome: Biblical Institute Press, 1973), 60–62; Roberts, *Nahum, Habakkuk, and Zephaniah*, 46; Fabry, *Nahum*, 144. While the MT is not without difficulties, mainly because the images of thorns and drunkards are presented very succinctly, the versions offer little help and seem to have occasionally misread the Hebrew, which is preserved in the proto-Masoretic manuscript 88 from Wadi Murabbaʿat (second century CE); cf. Gelston, *The Twelve Minor Prophets*, 84.

18. Carl M. Follingstad, *Deictic Viewpoint in Biblical Hebrew: A Syntagmatic and Paradigmatic Analysis of the Particle* כִּי (Dallas: SIL, 2001), 52. Merwe, Naudé, and Kroeze, *A Biblical Hebrew Reference Grammar*, 300, properly recognize the importance of the term's syntactical position but do not suggest this meaning. For an overview of the discussion concerning the legitimacy of assigning asseverative force to כִּי, see Grace J. Park, "Stand-Alone Nominalizations Formed with *ʾăšer* and *kî* in Biblical Hebrew," *JSS* 61 (2016): 41–65.

19. Merwe, Naudé, and Kroeze, *A Biblical Hebrew Reference Grammar*, 291.

20. See Samuel E. Loewenstamm, *Comparative Studies in Biblical and Oriental Literatures*, AOAT 204 (Kevelaer: Butzon & Bercker and Neukirchener-Vluyn: Neukirchener Verlag, 1980), 88; *HALOT*, 787, which notes an identical usage in 1 Chr 4:27 and a similar usage (with the verb בוא, "come, go") in 2 Sam 23:19.

21. Drunkenness is often connected with judgment, but that connection is not apparent here; cf. 3:11; Isa 19:14; 51:17–23; Jer 25:15–19; 49:7–12; Lam 4:21; Ezek 23:31–34; Obad 16. The same is true for thorns (cf. Isa 10:17). Spronk, *Nahum*, 54, notes that some Assyrian sources compare enemies to "thorns and thistles."

22. The image of chaff as highly flammable material to be consumed in judgment appears elsewhere in Exod 15:7; Isa

2. The First Address to Judah (1:11–13)

The next unit begins by addressing a feminine-singular audience, a clear indicator that it is distinct from 1:9–10.[23] Furthermore, as we will see, the theme changes radically, from complete and irreversible destruction to unexpected deliverance. While at first an unidentified speaker addresses Judah (1:11), in 1:12–13 YHWH himself speaks to them directly ("I" and "you"). In terms of subject, the speech first takes up the departure from Judah of "one plotting evil against YHWH, one planning wickedness." The first line (1:11) uses the same verb as 1:9 (חשב) together with a nearly identical preposition to express this individual's scheming against YHWH. The expression here also includes the evaluative term "evil" (רָעָה) to underline the morally unacceptable nature of such actions.[24] The second expression, "one planning wickedness," combines a common activity of planning or advising with a rather rare term, בְּלִיַּעַל, "worthlessness/wickedness." This term refers to a specific kind of wickedness that is subversive of proper, God-established order, as in the rape-murder of the concubine at Gibeon by "men of sons of בְּלִיַּעַל" or the "sons of בְּלִיַּעַל" who give false testimony against Naboth (1 Kgs 21:10, 13).[25]

It is clear from 1:9a and 1:11 that this person's activities constitute focused opposition to YHWH, so we are warranted in asking who this might be. We have already seen, in considering 1:9, that the OT presents parts of the speech by Sennacherib's "Rab-shakeh" (chief cupbearer, including a diplomatic role in this case[26]) to Jerusalem and to Hezekiah as highly objectionable since they dismiss YHWH as a potentially successful opponent against the Assyrian king. That episode is the classic confrontation between YHWH and Assyria in Judah's history, being recorded in the books of Kings, Chronicles, and Isaiah. The "going out" mentioned in Nah 1:11 thus most likely refers to Sennacherib's departure from Jerusalem, which the OT sees as the result of YHWH's direct intervention.[27] After promising Hezekiah that Sennacherib

5:24; 33:11; 47:14; Joel 2:5; Mal 4:1[3:19]. The term is part of expressions that refer to the ease with which dry chaff is blown away by the wind in Job 13:25; 21:18; Pss 1:4; 35:5; 83:13; Isa 17:13; 29:5; 40:24; 41:2; Dan 2:35; Hos 13:3; Zeph 2:2. The use of a perfective verb here, in first position and with no conjunction, could suggest a past event, but the context's emphasis on the certainty of a future outcome favors a present-tense translation to underline the perfective aspect of the destruction. The present (tense) or perfective (aspect) focus of perfective verbs is advanced by John A. Cook, "The Finite Verbal Forms in Biblical Hebrew Do Express Aspect," *JANES* 30 (2006): 21–35, esp. 32–33. A number of commentators favor the future (tense) and imperfect (aspect) translation "will be consumed" (Fabry, *Nahum*, 148–49; Roberts, *Nahum, Habakkuk, and Zephaniah*, 53; Longman, "Nahum," 794; Spronk, *Nahum*, 54), but do not give reasons for doing so.

23. It is possible that the 2fs grammar in 1:11 refers to Nineveh and not to Jerusalem, and many Bible versions favor that view and so include 1:11 in the first address. In that case, the event referred to is Sennacherib's departure from Nineveh en route to Jerusalem, rather than the somewhat later departure of his army from Jerusalem after YHWH's decimation of it. The view presented in the commentary maintains the grammatical distinction between the addresses that are otherwise harder to delimit, but since the two options merely focus on the beginning or end of Sennacherib's campaign against Judah, the interpretative difference between them is limited.

24. For the same activity perpetrated by Israel, see Hos 7:15. Wendland, "What's the 'Good News,'" 168, concludes that 1:11 "summarizes the deliberate, rebellious sort of attitude and impious behaviour that moves a 'jealous' God to 'take righteous vengenace'" on Nineveh.

25. Theodore J. Lewis, "Belial," *ABD* 1:654–66. The term's construct relationship with "one planning" here means that the word בְּלִיַּעַל by itself does not refer to a person, i.e., to "Belial;" cf. Floyd, *Minor Prophets*, 46–48.

26. Cf. Stefan Jakob, "Economy, Society, and Daily Life in the Middle Assyrian Period," in *A Companion to Assyria*, ed. E. Frahm, *BCAW* (Chichester: John Wiley & Sons, 2017), 152.

27. So also Perlitt, *Die Propheten*, 13; Fabry, *Nahum*, 150–151; recall Nahum's close links to Isaiah and thus to the crisis of 701. Perlitt, *Die Propheten*, 14, sees Belial in 1:11 as closely related in sense to Deut 13:14[13] and context, which focuses on those in Israel who would lead the faithful into apostasy, and as further elucidated by the religious focus of Nah 1:14.

"shall not come into this city nor shoot an arrow there, nor come before it with a shield nor build a siege mound against it" (2 Kgs 19:32), YHWH's angel struck down 185,000 Assyrians in the camp outside Jerusalem, after which the Assyrian army returned to Assyria (2 Kgs 19:35–36). Nahum 1:11 likely refers to this ignominious departure in the context of this prophecy, intended to reassure Judah precisely because it reminds the Judean audience of YHWH's protection a few decades earlier. In this context such a reminder would serve as a foretaste of the more complete deliverance from Assyria that God now promises.

It is probably for this reason that 1:12 introduces YHWH as the speaker. The formula "Thus says YHWH" signals that the following are YHWH's words, directly from his mouth and without any intermediary. Not only that, but YHWH is the explicit or implicit subject of the verbs (in the first person, thus "I . . .") throughout the rest of the section. Whatever evil plans were laid against YHWH in the past and whatever opposition to him continues to foment in the present, the reader's focus is now fixed on him and no longer on the one who plotted against him, as in 1:11. This emphasis becomes increasingly apparent as 1:12 unfolds.

For the moment, YHWH speaks of, but not to, Assyria. The choice of subject is ironically deconstructive, however: YHWH mentions Assyria only in order to deny that it can resist his judgment. "Even if" Assyria is currently at the height of its powers, and "so" (כֵּן) numerous, "even so" (conjunction ו plus כֵּן) it will be "mowed down" and so "removed."[28]

The central idea that despite its prodigious might Assyria will be done away with by YHWH is then reinforced by the presentation of this same divine action from another angle, that of deliverance for Judah, in 1:12d–13. For the first time in the book, YHWH addresses Judah in the second person, a form of address which, since it is more direct than merely speaking *about* Judah in the third person, underlines the importance and closeness of his covenantal relationship with it. The meaning of 1:12d–e is straightforward: YHWH has (especially by means of Assyria) "afflicted" Judah in the past but will no longer do so. This simple decision on YHWH's part to put an end to this affliction is part of the all-important covenantal relationship that he has with Judah.

While covenants with Abraham and his descendants (Gen 15, 17) and with David and his successors (2 Sam 7) also see God involve himself in Israel's life, the covenant in view here is the one initiated at Sinai, at the very beginning of the nation's existence. That conditional covenant obliged Israel to holistic obedience and fidelity to YHWH, and the nation affirmed their acceptance of these terms even before the covenant was elaborated (Exod 19:5–8).[29] While the consequences of disobedience appear at various points in the Pentateuch (e.g., Exod 23:33, in the context of the

28. The repetition of "so" to describe both Assyria's strength *and* the state in which it will be mowed down adds irony to the recognition of her full strength here. This is the only instance in Nahum in which "pass over" (עבר) means "leave the scene" (contrast 1:8; 2:1[1:15]; 3:19), although similar uses appear elsewhere in the OT (Spronk, *Nahum*, 71, draws attention to Jer 13:24). Various proposals have been made to account for the MT's use of both plural and singular verbs in 1:12c; see Spronk, *Nahum*, 71; Fabry, *Nahum*, 145. It is not impossible that the plural and singular are original and reflect the similar shift from a singular subject (the "one" who plans, 1:11a, b) to the plural subject "they" who are at full strength (1:12b). The rare use of a verb-first perfect for a future tense or imperfective aspect here has parallels, including Jer 31:33.

29. Frank Polak, "The Covenant at Mount Sinai in the Light of Texts from Mari," in *Sefer Moshe*, ed. C. Cohen, A. Hurvitz, and S. M. Paul (Winona Lake, IN: Eisenbrauns, 2004), 119–34. Bruce K. Waltke, "The Phenomenon of Conditionality within Unconditional Covenants," in *Israel's Apostasy and Restoration: Essays in Honor of Roland K. Harrison*, ed. A. Gileadi (Grand Rapids: Baker, 1988), 123–39, helpfully avoids a simple un/conditional dichotomy in understanding the Sinai covenant.

"book of the covenant" received at Sinai, Exod 34:7; in much greater detail in Lev 26:14–39), they are laid out definitively in Deut 28:15–68.

This covenantal dynamic lies behind YHWH's punishment or "affliction" of Judah for its sin (1:12d).[30] A reading of these covenantal curses without attention to their context gives the impression that the Sinai covenant would be definitively broken if Israel failed to comply with its requirements. Indeed, something like this happened in Israel's history with the destruction and exile of the Northern Kingdom (from which no clear return is recorded) and with the destruction and exile of the Southern Kingdom (from which roughly 50,000 Judeans returned between 538 BCE and the middle of the fifth century). But Deut 28 is not the end of Deuteronomy, and Deut 30 anticipates a scenario in which, even though Israel is in exile and the covenant curses are in full force, YHWH commits to "circumcising the heart" of Israel in connection with their repentance. This enables them to "love YHWH your God with all your heart and with all your soul, so that you may live" (Deut 30:6). In a similar way, the curses outlined in detail in Lev 26 are immediately followed by God's commitment to accept Israel's repentance and to maintain the Sinai covenant on the basis of his earlier promise to Abraham (Lev 26:40–45).

While it was possible for a normal suzerain-vassal treaty in the ancient Near East to be broken (in which case the vassal would be liable to punishment), what sets apart YHWH's covenant with Israel is that, while it shares the same form (blessings and curses upon obedience and disobedience, respectively), YHWH is able to uphold the covenant even when Israel fails to fulfill its obligations.[31] In a word, this is a covenant maintained by grace.

Returning to 1:12d, YHWH's affirmation that he has been punishing Judah complicates Nahum's presentation of Judah. On the one hand, the book presumes that God has been just to afflict Judah by means of Assyria, and on the other it contrasts Judah with Assyria so sharply that Judah might be thought to be nearly sinless. The book's overall perspective on Judah, at least the Judah of the present and the future, might be called an idealization for this reason, whereas the Judah of the past, whose sins have brought it to this point, is the book's point of departure. The Introduction noted that most of Judah's kings, like most of its population, were often disobedient to the moral and religious guidelines set out in Israel's Scriptures. This explains why from the eighth century onward Israel's prophets shifted their focus from the kings to the populace as a whole (still including the king), emphasizing their guilt due to covenant disobedience and encouraging repentance in order to escape the threatened covenant curses.[32]

The disobedience of Israel and Judah provides the background to YHWH's confirmation here that

30. For God as subject of ענה (*piel*) with the sense of punish/afflict, see 1 Kgs 11:39 (limited punishment of the Davidic line); Pss 88:7 (punishment // wrath); 90:15 (punishment // experience evil); 107:17 (punishment for iniquities, *hithpael*); Isa 64:12 (punishment defined as exile and destruction of Jerusalem). The *qal* and *pual* appear in Ps 119:67, 71. Erhard S. Gerstenberger, "ענה," *TDOT* 11:237, asserts that affliction (*piel* ענה) is "contrary to the demands of justice and sees Nah 1:12 and Deut 8:2–3, 16; Exod 1:11–12; Isa 64:11 as "temporarily repudiating Israel's elect status." Both assertions seem overstated.

31. Daniel C. Lane, "The Meaning and Use of *berith* in the Old Testament," PhD diss., Trinity International University, 2001), 311, notes that suzerain-vassal treaties are formulated so that if the vassal proves unfaithful, the covenant ceases to operate. David W. Baker, "The Mosaic Covenant against Its Environment," *ATJ* 20 (1988): 9–17, notes that the Sinai covenant shares some formal features with suzerain-vassal treaties but is distinct on the possibility of repentance and restoration (among other things).

32. Patrick D. Miller, "The Prophetic Critique of Kings," *ExAud* 2 (1986): 82–95.

he has indeed punished Judah. What is surprising is that he also announces that he will put an end to it! If we ask why, it is remarkable that Judah's repentance is not given as a reason. This does not rule out the existence of repentant Judeans during Nahum's ministry but instead puts enormous emphasis on YHWH's grace in deciding to liberate (1:13) and renew (2:3[2]) Judah. Although Judah's deliverance is connected to its renewal (cf. Deut 30), Nahum does not elaborate on the nature of that connection.

This shift from past to future brings us back again to 1:12d–e, which uses the term "punish/afflict" first in a past tense ("I have afflicted you"), then in a future tense with negation ("but I will not afflict you") followed by an adverb (עוֹד, "any longer") to emphasize that when God's imminent intervention destroys Assyria, Judah's affliction at its hands will finally come to an end.[33] While "now" (1:13) may seem to be inconsistent with the promises that YHWH "will break" Judah's yoke and "will tear off" Judah's shackles (i.e., in the future), the term עַתָּה, which appears here with the conjunction ו, often functions as a discourse marker, indicating a "logical conclusion" or progression rather than the present moment.[34] The term in Nah 1:13 thus does not specify that at this very moment YHWH will act but rather that his coming fulfillment of his promise to end Judah's punishment at the hands of Assyria will inevitably entail its liberation from the empire's clutches.

The hold that Assyria had on Judah appears in two images that immediately follow YHWH's promise to end Judah's covenant punishment. Both images convey graphically the idea of subjugation and forced servitude. The first image, a yoke bar, is part of a yoke placed over the head of cattle to allow them to pull a wagon, a plow, or other implement.[35] The second image is that of "cords," either fetters attached to a prisoner's hands or feet or (as is more likely here) straps holding the upper and lower yoke bars together around the carrier's neck.[36] The yoke is a common metaphor for the subjugation and servitude of one group to another in the OT and in Assyrian royal sources alike.[37] Assyrian kings used the fixed expression "impose the heavy yoke of my lordship" to describe their imposition of vassal relationships on subjugated states, while rebellious vassals almost by definition "throw off the yoke of my lordship."[38] Regardless of whether Judeans knew that Assyrian discourse used the same metaphor, Judah's recent history

33. Spronk, *Nahum*, 72, also stresses the importance of the contrast between past and future.

34. Merwe, Naudé, and Kroeze, *A Biblical Hebrew Reference Grammar*, 308–9, 333.

35. Saggs, *The Might That Was Assyria*, 163–64.

36. When the context of מוֹסֵרָה does not mention a yoke (Pss 2:3; 107:14), "fetters" is appropriate (cf. *HALOT*; the use in Job 39:5 is figurative). In the other cases, all in Jeremiah, the yoke is apparently composed of the bars held together by cords; such an assembly is rather clear in Jer 27:2, and this sense is favored by Perlitt, *Die Propheten*, 14; Longman, "Nahum," 799. Since contexts that mention a "yoke bar" also mention "cords," it is most likely that the two together constitute the yoke itself. Note the same collocation of "yoke" and "harness" several times in Jeremiah. The collocation appears in Jer 2:20; 5:5; 27:2; 30:8. Jeremiah 2:20 and 5:5 share the same verbs and the noun מוֹסֵרָה but substitute עֹל for Nahum's מוֹט. Leslie C. Allen translates מוֹסֵרָה as "harness" when the imagery is literal, *Jeremiah*, OTL (Louisville: Westminster John Knox, 2008), 44, 71. Compare different images of a yoke and burden, Isa 10:27; 14:25.

37. John E. Harvey, "עֹל," *NIDOTTE* 3:400–402.

38. See, for example, the imposition of the yoke by Esarhaddon (Leichty, *The Royal Inscriptions of Esarhaddon*, 18, from Nineveh A) and by Sargon (from Egypt in the southwest to Urartu in the north and Gutian territory in the east) in Sarah C. Melville, "The Display Inscription from the Palace of Sargon at Dur-Sharrukin (Khorsabad)," in *The Ancient Near East: Historical Sources in Translation*, ed. M. Chavalas, 340. A description of rebellion as throwing off the yoke can be found in Sarah C. Melville, "Sargon's Letter to Ashur," in *The Ancient Near East: Historical Sources in Translation*, ed. M. Chavalas, 339. This sense of "yoke" fits the context better than the simple neck-yoke worn by prisoners of war; see Saggs, *The Might That Was Assyria*, 84–85, plate 13A.

would have convinced every Judean that Judah was indeed habitually subjugated by, and subservient to, Assyria. The same reality was present in Judah's everyday life in visible, tangible ways, and the presence of Assyrian "religious and ideological motifs . . . on locally manufactured [Judean] seals and cult objects" in seventh-century Judah give evidence that Assyrian influence there grew with time and was not restricted to the upper echelons of society.[39]

This reality would have touched with particular force those Judeans in royal or administrative capacities, since they were more likely to have received communiques from, or interacted directly with, Assyrian diplomats (cf. the "messengers" or "envoys" in 2:14[13]). Manasseh, king of Judah during the most likely dates for Nahum's ministry and the composition of his book, was obliged to send "large beams, tall columns, (and) very long planks of cedar (and) cypress" to Esarhaddon for the expansion of his armory in Nineveh, which Esarhaddon says "had become too small for me to have horses show their mettle (and) to train with chariots."[40] Manasseh was also compelled to supply troops to accompany Assurbanipal's army on a campaign to Egypt, in addition to bringing the usual "heavy gifts" of tribute.[41] YHWH's coming deliverance, which will "break" this onerous yoke and free Judah from oppressive servitude to Assyria, would surely be wonderful news to all Judeans.

3. The Second Address to Assyria (1:14)

This short unit is an address to a masculine-singular subject. After a brief introduction of YHWH's edict or ruling, the rest of 1:14 is presented as YHWH's direct speech (in the first person) to the addressee (in the second person; note the shaded text in the Translation, above). While YHWH's direct speech to Judah emphasized his relationship with his people and thus drew the two parties together, here the same phenomenon emphasizes his solemn commitment to eliminate, directly and personally, his opponent. The use of first-person and second-person grammar here expresses the intensity of the conflict between the two parties, culminating in the elimination of the one and the demonstration of the other's exclusive supremacy.

The unit's opening line presents what follows as a ruling or edict (*piel* of צוה) of YHWH "concerning" the Assyrian king. Compared with the more common "Thus says YHWH," this formula "has the connotation of greater authority attributed to the speaker."[42] Although the command itself is not addressed to anyone in particular, it surely involved agents on the human scene. At the same time, it preserves a focus on YHWH's role in what follows, regardless of the means by which his will is to be accomplished.[43]

The earlier part of this unit has provided good reason to suggest that the following lines are addressed to the Assyrian king. First, the alternating

39. Parpola, "Assyria's Expansion," 103–4.

40. Leichty, *The Royal Inscriptions of Esarhaddon*, 22–23, from Nineveh A. The semantic parallelism makes this parallel far more certain than one based on imprisonment, although Assyrian kings did occasionally put rebellious kings in fetters. Assurbanipal states that "my officers . . . arrested these kings and put their hands and feet in iron cuffs and fetters" ("Babylonian and Assyrian Historical Texts," *ANET*, 294 [from the Rassam Cylinder, i 24–46]).

41. Leo Oppenheim, "Babylonian and Assyrian Historical Texts," *ANET*, 294 (from the Rassam Cylinder, i 24–46).

42. So Spronk, *Nahum*, 74, following Samuel A. Meier, *Speaking of Speaking: Marking Direct Discourse in the Hebrew Bible*, VTSup 46 (Leiden: Brill, 1992), 197–201.

43. The collocation צוה + על occurs a few dozen times in the OT, and about half of these have syntax identical or similar to that here (Gen 2:16; 12:20; 28:6; Num 8:22; 2 Sam 14:8; 1 Kgs 2:43; 11:10, 11; 1 Chr 16:40; Esth 2:10, 20; 4:5, 8, 17; Job 36:32). Only here, however, is the recipient of the command unidentified.

addressees (feminine and masculine) and their contrasting fates (deliverance or destruction) presuppose two parties, one of whom is explicitly addressed as "Judah" (2:1[1:15]). Second, the general reference to an opponent "at full strength" (1:12) and the detailed description of that opponent as one who plots against YHWH and who left Jerusalem, makes Assyria the undoubted referent of the masculine grammar, and thus of the speeches in 1:9–10, 14. It remains only to account for the difference between the masculine-plural grammar in 1:9–10 and the masculine-singular grammar of 1:14, a difference readily explained by a focus that shifts from Assyria considered as a unity in the first case to its king in the second. An examination of the next four clauses (1:14b–e) will bring to light additional reasons for concluding that these words are indeed addressed to the Assyrian king.[44]

YHWH's first statement, "Your name will no longer be sown," means that a name, presently significant (the metaphorical seed), will not continue to be so into the future. The metaphor of "sowing a name" as formulated here (the verb זרע paired with the noun שֵׁם) has no exact parallel within the OT and is apparently not attested in other ancient Near Eastern sources either. However, Klaas Spronk notes the parallelism between "seed" (זֶרַע, the nominal form of the root for "sow") and "name" in Isa 66:22, and the same pair occurs elsewhere in the OT (1 Sam 24:21; Isa 48:19). The general idea of posterity (or none) is of course not bound to these few constructions: the OT frequently speaks of serious offenders being "cut off" from Israel (Lev 20:3; Ps 37:28), of one's name "perishing" (Deut 7:24; Ps 41:5), and so on. The various expressions that convey the same idea are a reminder of the importance of the semantic element in intertextuality. This, in conjunction with the working hypothesis that 1:14 addresses the Assyrian king, leads us to several Neo-Assyrian parallels that are semantically equivalent but not linguistically identical.[45]

To begin with a glance at the royal traditions in the ancient Near East in the millennium before Nahum, Dadusha, king of Eshnunna (ca. 1800 BCE), protected a stela bearing his name and image by threatening anyone who might efface his image or "erase my inscribed name" with the wrath of the great gods:

> "May the Annunaku (gods), those of heaven and earth, angrily swear to destroy his descendants—he himself and all of his family! May Ninurta, the caretaker of Ekur (temple) not allow him to acquire offspring that will mention his name!"[46]

From roughly the same time comes an inscription of Yahdun-Lim, king of Mari (ca. 1800 BCE), who threatens at length anyone who would desecrate a temple he built for Shamash. His threat ends, "May Bunene, the great vizier of Shamash, cut . . . his throat, pluck his seed and may his offspring and his name not escape Shamash!"[47] Dadusha's stela also includes, both in its description of the punishable action and in its curse, the idea that the king's image and name were sacrosanct, and both examples pair "name," "seed," and other expressions for descendants. Both texts show that "To deface or destroy an image of the king, in the conceptual world of ancient Mesopotamia,

44. This is widely agreed upon. See Fabry, *Nahum*, 155; Perlitt, *Die Propheten*, 14; Floyd, *Minor Prophets*, 48–49.

45. Spronk, *Nahum*, 75, and Johnston, "Nahum's Rhetorical Allusions to Neo-Assyrian Treaty Curses," 424–25, assemble a sizable list of examples, which I supplement here.

46. Frans van Koppen, "Dadusha Stele," in *The Ancient Near East: Historical Sources in Translation*, ed. M. Chavalas, *BSAH* (Oxford: Blackwell, 2006), 101.

47. Frans van Koppen, "Inscription of Yahdun-Lim, King of Mari," in *The Ancient Near East: Historical Sources in Translation*, ed. M. Chavalas, *BSAH* (Oxford: Blackwell, 2006), 97.

represented a genuine attempt on the living—or the afterlife of the dead—ruler."[48]

Various Assyrian kings in the centuries before Nahum also threatened those who might desecrate temples with the destruction of their "name and progeny,"[49] and those who might remove the name of a god or the king from a royal stele with the destruction of their progeny "as long as there is a heaven and an earth."[50] Adad-nirari II (ca. 900 BCE) authored an inscription in honor of his accomplishments that ends with these lines: "The one who erases my inscription and my name, may Ashur and Gula overthrow his kingship (and) make his name and his seed disappear from the land."[51] An example from the century in which Nahum is set appears in Esarhaddon's "succession treaty," which stipulated the transfer of power to his son Assurbanipal. Should anyone usurp the throne in his place, Assyrians "shall abolish his name and seed from the land."[52]

While biblical parallels should receive preference, the fact that the expression in 1:14 is unique gives more weight than usual to parallels found outside the OT.[53] Furthermore, although the concept and several common lexemes appear in both biblical and extra-biblical sources, Nahum's strong interest in Assyria in general, and in a masculine singular Assyrian figure in particular here, make it legitimate to understand the phrase "your name will no longer be sown" primarily in light of the threats of Assyrian kings against those who might efface their name from royal monuments and inscriptions or otherwise jeopardize their dynasty.[54]

YHWH's promise to eradicate the name of the Assyrian king is thus highly charged rhetoric in an idiom drawn from, or at least very similar to, the Mesopotamian royal tradition. Not only did Assyrian kings threaten to eradicate the names of those who opposed them, they also vaunted the glory and longevity of their own names. Assurbanipal, no less than his predecessors, presented his name (in connection with his gods) as glorious and of lasting significance. When he restored a storehouse-palace that Sennacherib had built, Assurbanipal added the following:

> A memorial inscribed with my name and the praise of my heroism—(how) with the help of Ashur, Sîn, Šamaš, Bêl, Nabû, Ishtar of Nineveh, Ishtar of Arbela, Ninurta, Nusku, (and) Nergal I walked back and forth in the lands, established (my) power and authority—I wrote and left (it)

48. Steven W. Holloway, *Aššur is King! Aššur is King! Religion in the Exercise of Power in the Neo-Assyrian Empire*, CHANE 10 (Leiden: Brill, 2001), 73.

49. Tikulti-Ninurta I (ca. 1240–1200 BCE), in Christopher Morgan, "The Construction of a New Capital," in *The Ancient Near East: Historical Sources in Translation*, ed. M. Chavalas, *BSAH* (Oxford: Blackwell, 2006), 156.

50. Nebuchadnezzar I (ca. 1126–1103 BCE), as translated by Jeff Cooley, "The Shitti-Marduk Stele," in *The Ancient Near East: Historical Sources in Translation*, ed. M. Chavalas, *BSAH* (Oxford: Blackwell, 2006), 163.

51. Sarah C. Melville, "Adad-Nirari," in *The Ancient Near East: Historical Sources in Translation*, ed. M. Chavalas, *BSAH* (Oxford: Blackwell, 2006), 285.

52. Sarah C. Melville, "The Succession Treaty of Esarhaddon," in *The Ancient Near East: Historical Sources in Translation*, ed. M. Chavalas, *BSAH* (Oxford: Blackwell, 2006), 356; Simo Parpola and Kazuko Watanabe, *Neo-Assyrian Treaties and Loyalty Oaths*, SAA 2 (Helsinki: University of Helsinki Press, 1988), 35. Numerous examples of the threat to destroy a rebellious vassal's "seed" and "name" also appear in the vassal treaties of Esarhaddon; they are conveniently listed in Johnston, "Nahum's Rhetorical Allusions to Neo-Assyrian Treaty Curses," 425. The full treaty appears in Parpola and Watanabe, *Neo-Assyrian Treaties*, 28–58.

53. William W. Hallo, "Ancient Near Eastern Texts and Their Relevance for Biblical Exegesis," in *COS* 1.xxiii–xxviii; Shemaryahu Talmon, "The 'Comparative Method' in Biblical Interpretation—Principles and Problems," in *Congress Volume: Göttingen, 1977*, ed. J. A. Emerton, VTSup 29 (Leiden: Brill, 1978), 320–56.

54. The presence of the preposition מִן on "name" is attested elsewhere in Biblical Hebrew (Exod 28:10; comparative uses such as 1 Kgs 1:47 are not relevant), and both cases are partitive; cf. Merwe, Naudé, and Kroeze, *A Biblical Hebrew Reference Grammar*, 289. "One of your name" thus conveys the idea of "one bearing your name, a (dynastic) successor."

> for the days to come. Let a later prince . . . among my royal descendants . . . restore its ruins. The memorial inscribed with my name let him behold, anoint (it) with oil, offer sacrifice. . . . Whoso destroys (this) memorial inscribed with my name . . . may the great gods of heaven and earth curse him in wrath, smite down his kingship, eradicate his name (and) his seed out of the land.[55]

The consistent use of name-centered self-glorification by Neo-Assyrian monarchs, including Assurbanipal, strengthens the warrant for reading 1:14 in light of such attempts at self-exaltation and legacy creation. Klaas Spronk is therefore right to highlight the irony in YHWH's promise to eradicate the Assyrian king: "The message of Nahum is that YHWH takes the place of the 'great gods' and that the heavenly wrath is now turned against the famous Assyrian kings who shall be hit by his curse."[56]

If the first element of YHWH's promise to put an end to the Assyrian king/dynasty (1:14b) can be said to have a royal focus, the prominence of religious elements in the Neo-Assyrian sources cited above reminds us that such an action is not without religious significance in Assyrian and Judean thought alike.[57] This religious facet is central in the next element of YHWH's promise (1:14c): "from the house of your gods I will eliminate sculpted image and cast image." Nineveh had housed a royal residence since the time of Shalmaneser I (1273–1244 BCE), and had become Assyria's capital city in 704, when Sennacherib (704–681 BCE) shifted the capital from the ill-omened Dar-Sharrukin built by his father Sargon II before Sargon was assassinated in a plot led by several of his sons.[58] This makes a temple at Nineveh the most likely, or at least most prominent, target of YHWH's destruction. Nineveh was especially famous for its temple of Ishtar, which had stood in Nineveh since the third millennium. Ishtar was important for royal interests as a goddess of war, and Assurbanipal also referred to her as the one who had nursed him, "the mother who bore me, endowed me with unparalleled kingship."[59] His esteem for her is demonstrated by his beautification of Ishtar's temples in Nineveh and Arbela.[60]

Other gods were important for Assyrian monarchs as well. Of primordial importance was the national god Assur, whose rule of the other gods made his role analogous to that of the Assyrian king.[61] Sennacherib's reforms further elevated Assur to new heights of power and prowess in the early seventh century.[62] Ninurta, firstborn son of Assur in the Assyrian pantheon and god of warfare and hunting,[63] would also have been significant for the expansion-oriented monarch, and two temples

55. Arthur Carl Piepkorn, *Historical Prism Inscriptions of Ashurbanipal*, OIUCAS 5 (Chicago: University of Chicago Press, 1933), 87, 89.

56. Spronk, *Nahum*, 75.

57. Cf. Fales, *Guerre et paix*, 71: "The actions of the king, himself the symbol of the empire, were controlled, guided, and favored by the divinity. The monarch was the vice-regent on earth of the national god Assur, and, as such, always acted in the name of and on behalf of the divinity" (author's translation).

58. David Stronach and Kim Codella, "Nineveh," *OEANE* 4:146.

59. Barbara N. Porter, "Ishtar of Nineveh and Her Collaborator, Ishtar of Arbela, in the Reign of Assurbanipal," *Iraq* 66 (2004): 41–42, citing K. 1285 and K. 1290.

60. Prism T, in Nissinen, *Prophets and Prophecy*, 143. "Ishtar" had several cult centers, and Assyrians may have distinguished these local manifestations from one another, at least prior to the seventh century. Some think that during the seventh century Ishtar was a unified personality (Nissinen, *Prophets and Prophecy*, 99), but contrast Porter, "Ishtar of Nineveh," 44.

61. A. Kirk Grayson, "Assyrian Civilization," *CAH* III:2, 222.

62. Paul-Alain Beaulieu, "Mesopotamia," in *Religions of the Ancient World: A Guide*, ed. S. I. Johnston, Harvard University Press Reference Library (Cambridge: Belknap Press of Harvard University Press, 2004), 171. See the texts that express Assur's support of the king cited by Alasdair Livingstone, "Assur," *DDD*, 108–9.

63. Assur's place in the Assyrian pantheon was modeled on the Mesopotamian Enlil, hence Ninurta was reckoned as one of his sons. Ibid., 108–9.

to Nabu (god of writing or, better, of "letters" in the sense of education) had been built in Nineveh in 788–787 BCE.[64] These multiple religious affiliations make it unnecessary to specify which gods YHWH's promise has in view. Indeed, there is probably no "short list" of gods in view. *All* the important Assyrian gods (routinely mentioned in royal inscriptions as the king's sponsors) are, despite their distinct characteristics, united in their efforts to support and equip the king, enabling his continual expansion of the Assyrian Empire.[65]

While 1:14c does not identify particular Assyrian gods for destruction, it does provide some details related to that destruction: YHWH will "eliminate" (*hiphil* כרת) the פֶּסֶל ("sculpted image"[66]) and מַסֵּכָה ("cast image"[67]). These two terms correspond precisely to Saggs's description of the typical Assyrian temple and the images housed there:

> Customarily the gods were represented by statues, which might be either wood or stone overlaid with gold, or images cast in copper or precious metals; normally each statue would stand on a pedestal or dais.[68]

Given the representative function of the god's statue, "the god and the statue were identical" for the purposes of ritual.[69] This fact and the related understanding of divine presence bear directly on the sense of Nah 1:14. First, the removal of a statue from a temple, except if undertaken as part of normal cultic or other purposes, was understood as proof of the god's displeasure with some aspect of his worshippers' behavior. Second, removal, rather than destruction, of another people's gods (i.e., of their statues) was the norm in cases of military conquest. Even Assyria, which characteristically used excessive violence against rebellious vassals in other spheres in order to discourage further rebellion, typically took the statues of the gods of conquered peoples to new temple-homes rather than destroying them.[70] Since the god's "absence" from his people was a sign of his displeasure with them, in Assyria's view a foreign statue's repatriation in an Assyrian shrine would serve as further proof that the conquered people's god was in agreement with Assyria's punishment or subjugation of them.[71] This means that when Nahum affirms that the Assyrian gods' statues would be "eliminated," meaning "destroyed" rather than simply "removed,"[72] he almost certainly envisions something rarely seen in the ancient Near East, the superlative nature of which emphasized YHWH's unique supremacy by doing away completely with the gods of the Assyrian king.

This is not all. In YHWH's assertion of his unique glory and sovereignty over history, not only the

64. Grayson, "Assyrian Civilization," 223. "Precedence amongst Assyrian deities, and questions of their interrelationship, clearly remained a problem until nearly the end of the empire," Saggs, *The Might That Was Assyria*, 202. On Nabu, see Alan Millard, "Nabu," *DDD*, 607–10.

65. Saggs, *The Might That Was Assyria*, 201–2, notes that while there were thousands of deities in Mesopotamia and Assyria, the number of those in the popular consciousness, and more certainly in the royal consciousness, was much smaller.

66. *HALOT*, 949.

67. *HALOT*, 605; cf. Zech 13:2.

68. Saggs, *The Might That Was Assyria*, 205.

69. F. A. M. Wiggermann, "Theologies, Priests, and Worship in Ancient Mesopotamia," *CANE*, 1862.

70. Holloway (*Aššur is King!*, 118–22) identifies fifty-five cases, from Tiglath-pileser I (1114–1076 BCE) to Assurbanipal (645 BCE or later), in which Assyria brought captured gods to Assyria and demonstrates that on rare occasions Assyrian kings would destroy the cult statues of gods whose people they conquered.

71. Mordechai Cogan, *Imperialism and Religion: Assyria, Judah and Israel in the Eighth and Seventh Centuries B.C.E.*, SBLMS (Missoula: Scholars Press, 1974), 22–41. Bob Becking, "'The Gods, in Whom They Trusted . . .' Assyrian Evidence for Iconic Polytheism in Ancient Israel?," in *Only One God? Monotheism in Ancient Israel and the Veneration of the Goddess Asherah*, ed. B. Becking et al. (London: Sheffield Academic, 2001), 151–63, discusses the claim of Sargon II that he "counted as spoil" the cult statues of the temple in Samaria, taken in 722.

72. Ernst Kutsch, "כרת," *TLOT* 2:636.

gods of the Assyrian monarch but the king himself will be done away with. While 1:14b focused on the elimination of his posterity, 1:14d shifts the reader's focus to the death of the one who embodied the essence of Assyria and its ideology. YHWH announces that the king will die godless and (for the purposes of dynasty and legacy) childless, despite his claimed invincibility, despite his efforts to ensure an endless legacy and dynasty, and despite his purportedly favored status with the many gods who supported and legitimized him.

While Assyrian kings, including Assurbanipal, accorded importance to a proper royal burial, there is no indication here that YHWH intends to dishonor the Assyrian king in the very act of burial.[73] Rather, the emphasis falls on YHWH's role in preparing the grave for, and presumably dispatching, the king without further ado.[74] This third and final divine action thus overlaps the first two as a means of rebuffing the king's claims to dynasty, divine support, and preeminence. The verbal syntax, in which the three actions in 1:14b–d are expressed with imperfective forms while the evaluation conclusion in 1:14e is in the perfective form, allows us to connect the Assyrian king's being despicable to all three threats.

The last clause in this verse, 1:14e, is presented as the reason for the foregoing and is introduced with כִּי. The thought is expressed in one word, using the *qal* of קלל. The four pertinent uses of the *qal* of קלל elsewhere in the OT lie within the semantic field of "to be despised; to be reckoned insignificant; to be small,"[75] and this sense is appropriate here. To appreciate the rhetorical sting of this divine edict, it suffices to remember the bombastic, hyperbolic, and autonomous (from a biblical point of view) nature of the Assyrian king and the ideology that defined his role. We have already seen examples of this ideology in the Assyrian kings' self-descriptions (especially the elements of divine sponsorship and global dominion) and their concerted effort to preserve their legacy and dynasty. These and other elements of Assyrian ideology too extensive to survey here present a king who enacts the will of his gods with the help of his gods for the glory of his gods: "The Assyrian kingship is the only one to legitimately exercise universal dominion," is without equal, and "is the only one endowed with those qualities which render legitimate the exercise of power."[76] It is *this* king—unrivaled, unstoppable, unique—that YHWH will dispatch along with his divine sponsors! Bombastic propaganda is of no avail, and much like Nineveh/Ishtar will be stripped of her glory in Nah 3, the Assyrian king is in truth despicable and of no account before YHWH.[77]

This particular threat was fulfilled by the gradual destruction of the Assyrian Empire. Assur and other cities fell in 614 BCE, Nineveh in 612, and the remainder of Assyria's forces was defeated at Carchemish in 605. This process included the

73. Saggs, *The Might That Was Assyria*, 113–15; constrast Assurbanipal's violation of Elamite royal tombs in response to persistent unrest there, 114.

74. Roberts, *Nahum, Habakkuk, and Zephaniah*, 54, suggests that it may also mean that no one else had survived to do so, implying the death of the king's sons in particular.

75. These are the contempt of Hagar for Sarah after Hagar conceived (Gen 16:4, 5), God's low esteem of those who despise him (1 Sam 2:30; there קלל is in parallel with בזה and an antonym of the *piel* of כבד), and Job's negative self-evaluation (Job 40:4). 1 Samuel 2:30 is the only other case in which the verb's subject is under the critical eye of YHWH, and Eli's household comes to an end for scorning YHWH (בזה). Cf., similarly, Josef Scharbert, "קלל," *TDOT* 13:38, who concludes that the meaning of the word is the antithesis of being important.

76. Liverani, "Ideology of the Assyrian Empire," 310.

77. Saggs, *The Might That Was Assyria*, 116, notes that, in contrast to all other Neo-Assyrian monarchs, "only Ashurbanipal put vindictiveness on display; only he slashed the face of a dead enemy, desecrated tombs of the dead he had not been able to punish when living, spared the lives of captive kings that he might humiliate them better living than dead. . . . Malice as a driving force behind the later Ashurbanipal is a fact of history."

deaths of Assurbanipal in 627 BCE, Sin-shar-ishkun (a son of Assurbanipal who had rapidly displaced the designated successor, his son Assur-etillu-ili) in 612, and Assur-uballit, the final ruler of Assyria, not long thereafter.[78]

4. The Second Address to Judah (2:1[1:15])

In 2:1[1:15] the addressee changes for the last time in this unit, back to Judah. While not moving entirely beyond the *process* of liberation and deliverance described in 1:11–12, this brief unit emphasizes the subjective reflex that Judah should have in response to the content of the unit thus far. As was the case in 1:9–10, it is not explicitly affirmed that YHWH is the speaker here, but he alone is responsible for the deliverance to be celebrated just as he is the exclusive focus of the "feasts" and "vows" that constitute that celebration.

The first phrase (2:1[1:15]a), which begins with the focus particle "Look!" (הִנֵּה), abruptly shifts the reader's attention to "the mountains." The phrase (similar to Isa 52:7) describes the messenger before the text reveals his message. If a generalization can be made on the basis of the few comparable uses of the motif of arrival over the mountains in the OT, such arrivals are welcome (Song 2:8; Isa 52:7). The image also conveys the idea that the one arriving has come from a significant distance and that his message has been awaited with much anticipation.[79]

The positive nature of the messenger's news is made clear in the parallel second line (2:1[1:15]b), which characterizes the message as "peace" (שָׁלוֹם). The term שָׁלוֹם is quite flexible and can refer to or include political stability (Jer 14:13), the absence of war (Judg 4:17), or holistic well-being in connection with the maintenance or restoration of one's relationship with God (Num 6:26; Isa 32:15–17). The context here requires that the term refer to the effects of Judah's liberation as described here, and the fact that the context limits itself to that (as do the last lines of this verse) cautions against seeing further nuances in it, such as Judah's spiritual renewal. This is also suggested by the relationship between this verse and the immediately preceding comment that Neo-Assyria's king is doomed (1:14).

The next two clauses (2:1[1:15]c, d) are commands uttered by the now-arrived messenger, urging Judah to celebrate "your feasts" and pay "your vows." The term "feast" (חַג) can refer to any one of the three pilgrimage festivals (Passover, Feast of Weeks, and Feast of Booths), all of which have reference to God's provision and deliverance in the past or present.[80] Among these, both Passover and Booths involve commemoration of aspects of God's preeminent saving act in the OT to this point, the exodus from Egypt and preservation *en route* to Canaan.[81] No reason is given for why these feasts were not celebrated under Assyrian oppression, and it is not even clear that they have not been celebrated.[82] The point seems to be, rather, that

78. Saggs, *The Might That Was Assyria*, 117–20; Oates, "The Fall of Assyria," 172–84.

79. The mountains can also be the scene for mourning (Judg 11:37–38) or destruction (Ezek 32:5; Nah 3:18).

80. Hendrik L. Bosman, "חגג," *NIDOTTE* 2:20–21; Carl E. Armerding, "Festivals and Feasts," *Dictionary of the Old Testament: Pentateuch*, ed. T. D. Alexander and D. W. Baker (Downers Grove, IL: InterVarsity Press, 2003), 300–13.

81. Roberts, *Nahum, Habakkuk, and Zephaniah*, 54, notes that, once free of Assyrian oversight, Josiah celebrated Passover, 2 Kgs 23:21–25.

82. If they were not celebrated, this was not due to religious oppression on the part of Assyria, which is never known to have prohibited the celebration of indigenous religious cults on the part of subjugated groups. Cf. Cogan, *Imperialism and Religion*, 88. The relevant OT legal passages make no provision for noncelebration (Exod 23:14–17; 34:18, 22; Deut 16:1–17), so apart from extreme duress, failure to celebrate these feasts would have been culpable.

this celebration of one or more of them will take account of God's prodigious deliverance of Judah from Assyria.

The second response to the news of deliverance is the payment of Judah's vows. Nothing is said of the nature of the vows to be paid, so context alone can provide plausible, but not certain, specificity. It is reasonable to assume that these vows were made in the context of the Assyrian threat and thus perhaps on behalf of the whole nation.[83] The plural "vows" reveals that many vows are in view here, again presumably on the part of numerous Judeans. What precisely would be paid to YHWH by honoring these vows is also uncertain: biblical examples include self-dedication (Lev 27:2–8), an animal (Lev 27:9–13), and worship (Gen 28:20–22), among other things. As was the case with the celebration of festivals, payment of these vows would have taken account of, and was contingent upon, YHWH's deliverance of Judah, as the following lines make clear.

The last two lines of the verse (2:1[1:15]e, f) provide the reason (with the causal כִּי) for these commands to celebrate Israel's historic feasts: YHWH will eliminate the "wicked" one. As we saw above in the context of 1:11, the term בְּלִיָּעַל refers to a specific kind of wickedness that is subversive of proper, God-established order, which here must include not the oppression of Judah per se (otherwise God could be thought guilty of the same, 1:12d) but oppression with means and motives like Assyria's. It is unnecessary to review here all that has been said above on these points, and the text itself concentrates not on the characterization of the worthless one but rather on the absolute cessation of his activities and his complete destruction. The first aspect is conveyed in 2:1[1:15]e, where instead of merely stating that this will not happen again, the addition of the preposition עוֹד yields the more emphatic "never again will . . ." (cf. the same preposition in 1:12e, 1:14b). The construction (negation + *hiphil* יסף + ל + infinitive) adds further emphasis to its claim (compare the more concise formulation in 1:12e). The activity that is ended is referred to by עבר, often "cross over" or "pass by" but here "invade" in light of Assyria's significant incursions into and annexation of Judean territory.[84]

The second aspect, the death of the "wicked one," uses the same verb seen earlier in YHWH's promise to "eliminate" carved and molten images alike from the king's temple (כרת, 1:14 [*hiphil*], also used in 2:14[13]; 3:15). Although the *niphal* form used here can mean simply "cut off," the addition of the noun כֹּל, "all," with a 3ms suffix gives the expression the same finality as in 1:12—the "wicked one" who had invaded and harassed Judah will never do so again and will in fact cease to exist.[85]

The unit thus ends on a strong note of finality: Assyria's complete destruction (king, gods, empire) spells the end of Judah's punishment, and Judah's consequent liberation from its clutches is to be followed by a celebration of God's redemptive character (in the feasts' historic referents as well as in this most recent deliverance, in addition to the payment of vows). The imminent arrival of the messenger, like the imminent arrival of YHWH in judgment in 1:2–8, encourages the reader/hearer to prepare for responsive worship of YHWH, much as in 1:2–8 the reader was to prepare for judgment by taking shelter in YHWH. The shift from shelter amid

83. Robin Wakely, "נדר," *NIDOTTE* 3:37, and cf. Ps 76:12[11].

84. Note the similar semantics of Joel 4:17, which also uses עבר; in that context Douglas Stuart, *Hosea–Jonah*, WBC 31 (Waco, TX: Word, 1987), 270, speaks of the exclusion of "foreign invaders."

85. If the form נִכְרָת at the end of 2:1[1:15] is a finite verb and not a participle (something its being in pause makes uncertain), the perfective form of the verb would most likely express the complete destruction of the enemy.

destruction (1:2–8) to deliverance and celebration as the result of judgment (1:9–2:1[1:15]) captures an important dynamic here, while the concrete scenario of 1:9–2:1[1:15] makes its perspective one that confidently foresees the partial fulfillment of the general, global vision of 1:2–8. This same dynamic appears once more in the book, reaching its peak in the celebration of Nineveh's demise in 3:19. Ernst Wendland identifies this correspondence between 2:1[1:15] and 3:19 as "conceptual epiphoria," meaning that both units close on a note of celebration due to the destruction of the oppressor.[86]

Canonical and Theological Significance

The Progressive Fulfillment of the Prophecy

The fulfillment of Nahum's prediction of Assyria's downfall was not long in coming. Nahum prophesied near the middle of the seventh century BCE, before Assyria entered its final period of instability, and within a half-century the seemingly irresistible empire had come to a sudden (and quite unforeseen) end. As J. J. M. Roberts notes, it is striking "how thoroughly this judgment was carried out in the collapse of the Assyrian Empire, when Nineveh was permanently destroyed, the gods of Assyria desecrated, and the Assyrian monarchy brought to an end."[87] In the same time frame, the deliverance of Judah that accompanied the collapse of Assyria became reality as well. This demonstrated God's patience with his covenant people and his commitment to do them good, even through judgment (of both Judah and Assyria), and was indeed cause for rejoicing.

We have observed that Assyria's fall, anticipated in 1:9–2:1[1:15] and described in more detail in the rest of the book, is a specific application of the book's opening vision in 1:2–8. Assyria's fall, however, is clearly an incomplete and preliminary application or "fulfillment" of the theophanic hymn, especially because in it Assyria is stereotyped and Judah is idealized. Not only is Assyria's population not divided into more and less guilty subgroups, but it no longer possesses the power to change, and YHWH's promise to judge Assyria is unqualified and inescapable.[88] Judah, for its part, is not divided into guilty and innocent either and seems to be on the cusp of renewal (cf. 2:3[2]). At the same time, the judgment that YHWH brings on Assyria falls far short of the ultimate destruction at the core of 1:2–8, and Judah's "deliverance" here is stated in almost entirely negative terms: it will no longer have to suffer at Assyria's hands, and Assyria will come to an end. This is hardly insignificant, but this

86. Wendland, "What's the 'Good News,'" 161. It is significant that the root שמע appears (without being negated, as it is in 2:14[13]) only in 2:1[1:15] and 3:19, both cases in which the message concerns Assyria's demise.

87. Roberts, *Nahum, Habakkuk, and Zephaniah*, 54.

88. We must appreciate this stereotypical perspective in order to properly understand the ethical validity of Nahum's rejoicing in the downfall of Assyria as a whole, including large numbers of individuals who played no direct role in the empire's plots and violence. C. S. Lewis helpfully explores this question in *The Problem of Pain* (San Francisco: HarperSanFrancisco, 2000), 416–20.

section says nothing of any means by which Judah's population would be transformed so as to avoid future covenant discipline, and even 2:3[2] has a very measured tone.

While the fall of Assyria thus confirms the reliability of YHWH's word and so directs the later reader to live in light of 1:2–8, the global, final perspective of that section requires the reader to understand it in light of redemptive history beyond the end of Assyria. The "good news" of Assyria's fall is organically related to God's triumph over evil, but the progress of God's work of redemption since the seventh century BCE has seen a number of actors leave the stage (including ethnic-national Israel as his only chosen people) and other categories undergo radical changes (especially the shift in the identity of YHWH's opponents, from the non-Israelite "nations" to any and all who resist his will and claims). The church of Jesus Christ, under the new covenant, is composed of believers from every nation and race, and it is in and through the church that God builds his (spiritual) kingdom.[89] Its enemies, as the NT repeatedly states, are not "flesh and blood" (John 18:36; Eph 6:10–20), even though they make use of earthly power in many different ways (cf. Rev 12–13). For the church today, confronted in its many settings with an enormous variety of opposition, complacency, and internal weakness, Assyria's fall as interpreted in Nahum confirms that God's justice is both vigorous and invincible, even though he may choose to exercise it only when opposition seems to have reached its peak (cf. 1:12).

This truth is sure thanks to Christ's victory over the spiritual powers that oppose God and his people (Eph 4:8–10; Col 2:15), itself a vindication of Christ's redemptive work on behalf of his people (Eph 1:19–23). God's victory ensures that no spiritual opposition can endanger his people (1 Pet 3:14–16), that they are complete in Christ (Col 2:16–23), alive to God (Col 3), and will inherit the immortality of which Christ's resurrection is the guarantee (2 Tim 1:12). Paul's frequent reminders that our peace with God is possible only on the basis of Christ's atoning death (Rom 5:8–11; 2 Cor 5:18–21; Eph 2:14–17; Col 1:20–22) highlight the two-sided nature of this peace, which, once established between the believer and God, comes to color the whole of the believer's life (cf. the salutations of all of Paul's letters).[90] The nearly monochrome message of Nahum, when viewed through the prism of redemptive history, thus displays an amazing spectrum of color. God's victory over evil, already won in principle, becomes the ground for confidence, hope, and progressive conformity to the image of his Son, all with a view toward the end of the age and the consummation of all things. For all believers confronted with evil and suffering, and for the persecuted church in particular, Nahum's message directs their faith and guides their emotions toward a resolute confidence and firm hope in God, both of which will be fulfilled by the revelation of the only empire that cannot be shaken (Heb 12:27).

89. Cf. Graeme Goldsworthy, "Kingdom of God," *NDBT*, 620.

90. Cf. Stanley Porter, "Peace," *NDBT*, 682–83.

CHAPTER 4

Nahum 2:2–14[1–13]

D. The Prophetic Anticipation of Assyria's Fall

Main Idea of the Passage

Despite its prowess and self-idolizing propaganda, Assyria (represented in 2:2–11[1–10] by Nineveh) is no match for YHWH or for the impressive army he will send against it. Nineveh's fall is so certain that it can be considered a fait accompli, confirming that YHWH is progressively restoring Judah (2:3[2]) and exercising his punitive justice against an empire that incarnates opposition to him.

Literary Context

This section is closely linked to the one immediately preceding it (1:9–2:1[1:15]), in which YHWH announces that Assyria's plans against him and his people will amount to nothing and that, on the contrary, he will put an end to Assyria, its king, and its gods. That section ended with an initial call to Judah to respond in joy to the message of deliverance through the complete destruction of its primary oppressor. This section focuses primarily on the fall of Assyria but includes a brief reflection (2:3[2]) on its implications for Judah.

However, we cannot ignore the larger context of the book established by 1:2–8. There YHWH announces his plan to punish not simply Assyria but all his enemies, defined as those who oppose him. That group is contrasted with those who take refuge in him as the only one able to deliver them from that worldwide judgment. This section, like the ones before and after it, is indebted to that perspective. In much the same way that in 1:9–2:1[1:15] Judah's sins were only hinted at while Assyria was treated under the images of its anti-YHWH imperial project and royal ideology, Nahum here speaks of Assyria as a historical manifestation of the "enemy" in the eschatological context of 1:2–8. While the previous section focused on exposing Assyria's guilt, 2:2[1], 4–14[3–13] move on to contemplate its final destruction without so much as a tear. In relation to 1:2–8, then, this section presents another, incomplete and very partial fulfillment of the final intervention of judgment and deliverance announced there, spelling out the effects of YHWH's vengeance on an empire that revels in and abuses its power. The initial vision of 1:2–8 is like the proverbial rock that, thrown into a lake, creates distinct but nearly identical ripples that emanate outward from the point of impact (1:9–2:1[1:15], 2:2–11[1–10], 12–14[11–13], etc.).

A. Introduction (1:1)
B. The Threat of YHWH's Coming Global Judgment (1:2–8)
C. Four Announcements of Assyria's Destruction and Judah's Deliverance (1:9–2:1[1:15])
➡ **D. The Prophetic Anticipation of Assyria's Fall (2:2–14[1–13])**
   1. The Call to Prepare for YHWH's Attack (2:2[1])
   2. The Significance for Judah: Restoration (2:3[2])
   3. The Fall of Nineveh Anticipated (2:4–11[3–10])
   4. The Fall of Assyria Anticipated (2:12–14[11–13])
E. The Deconstruction of Assyria's Pride (3:1–19)

Translation and Exegetical Outline

(See pages 120–21.)

Structure and Literary Form

This section falls neatly into four parts. After an initial call to Nineveh to prepare for the coming onslaught (2:2[1]) and a parallel affirmation that this event is linked to YHWH's restoration of Jacob (2:3[2]), the next two sections present Assyria's downfall in detail. In 2:4–11[3–10] this is done through partial prolepsis, meaning that the description of the early stages of the attack in the first few verses gives way to a description of Nineveh's fall *after* the attack has succeeded in the following verses. A prophecy of destruction uttered by YHWH himself and motivated by the Assyrian monarch's leonine self-image concludes this unit (2:12–14[11–13]).

The structure of the unit invites the reader's reflection in a number of ways. First, it quickly becomes clear that the opening call for Assyria to prepare for battle is ironic, since the rest of the unit shows that the outcome is a foregone conclusion. Second, although the book says very little about Judah, a pregnant statement about the ramifications of Assyria's fall for "Jacob" appears in 2:3[2], reinforced by the concession that "although" Judah has been "wasted" and "ruined" by Assyria, YHWH *will* restore it (the subordination of 2:3[2]b–c to 2:3[2]a is thus significant).

Nahum 2:2–14 [1–13]

			D. The Prophetic Anticipation of Nineveh's Fall (2:2–14)
2a	עָלָה מֵפִיץ עַל־פָּנַיִךְ	"One who scatters has come up against you!	1. The Call to Prepare for YHWH's Attack (2:2a–e)
2b	נָצוֹר מְצֻרָה	Guard the ramparts!	
2c	צַפֵּה־דֶרֶךְ	Watch the road!	
2d	חַזֵּק מָתְנַיִם	Get ready to stand firm!	
2e	אַמֵּץ כֹּחַ מְאֹד	Summon all your strength!"	
3a	כִּי שָׁב יְהוָה אֶת־גְּאוֹן יַעֲקֹב כִּגְאוֹן יִשְׂרָאֵל	Truly, YHWH restores the majesty of Jacob like the majesty of Israel,	2. The Significance for Judah: Restoration (2:3a–c)
3b	כִּי בְקָקוּם בֹּקְקִים	although wasters have wasted them,	
3c	וּזְמֹרֵיהֶם שִׁחֵתוּ	and they have ruined their branches.	
			3. The Fall of Nineveh Anticipated (2:4a–11e)
4a	מָגֵן גִּבֹּרֵיהוּ מְאָדָּם	The shield of his mighty ones is reddened	a. The Enemy Soldiers and Their Weapons (2:4a–e)
4b	אַנְשֵׁי־חַיִל מְתֻלָּעִים	(his) heroes are dressed in scarlet	
4c	בְּאֵשׁ־פְּלָדוֹת הָרֶכֶב	the chariot is (made) of fiery steel.	
4d	בְּיוֹם הֲכִינוֹ	On the day of his preparation,	
4e	וְהַבְּרֹשִׁים הָרְעָלוּ	the spears are brandished.	
5a	בַּחוּצוֹת יִתְהוֹלְלוּ הָרֶכֶב	In the streets the chariots race madly;	b. The Enemy Chariots Attack (2:5a–d)
5b	יִשְׁתַּקְשְׁקוּן בָּרְחֹבוֹת	they rush madly through the squares.	
5c	מַרְאֵיהֶן כַּלַּפִּידִם	Their appearance is like torches;	
5d	כַּבְּרָקִים יְרוֹצֵצוּ׃	like lightning they dash.	
6a	יִזְכֹּר אַדִּירָיו	He remembers his officers.	c. The Assyrians in Disorder (2:6a–d)
6b	יִכָּשְׁלוּ (בַּהֲלִכוֹתָם) [בַּהֲלִיכָתָם]	They stumble as they come forward.	
6c	יְמַהֲרוּ חוֹמָתָהּ	They rush to the wall,	
6d	וְהֻכַן הַסֹּכֵךְ׃	where the mantlet is already set up.	
7a	שַׁעֲרֵי הַנְּהָרוֹת נִפְתָּחוּ	The river gates are opened;	d. The Fall of the Palace (2:7a–b)
7b	וְהַהֵיכָל נָמוֹג׃	the palace sways.	
8a	וְהֻצַּב	Her statue is set up;	e. Ishtar's Image Stripped and Taken (2:8a–e)
8b	גֻּלְּתָה	she is stripped;	
8c	הֹעֲלָתָה	she is carried away,	
8d	וְאַמְהֹתֶיהָ מְנַהֲגוֹת כְּקוֹל יוֹנִים	her maidens lamenting with the voice of doves,	
8e	מְתֹפְפֹת עַל־לִבְבֵהֶן׃	beating their breasts.	

9a	וְנִינְוֵה כִבְרֵכַת־מַיִם מִימֵי הִיא	Nineveh was like a pool of water throughout her days,	f. Nineveh's Defenders Flee (2:9a–e)
9b	וְהֵמָּה נָסִים	but now they flee.	
9c	עִמְדוּ	"Halt!	
9d	עֲמֹדוּ	Halt!"	
9e	וְאֵין מַפְנֶה	There is no one who turns back.	
10a	בֹּזּוּ כֶסֶף	"Plunder the silver!	g. Nineveh Plundered (2:10a–d)
10b	בֹּזּוּ זָהָב	Plunder the gold!"	
10c	וְאֵין קֵצֶה לַתְּכוּנָה	There is no end to the treasure!	
10d	כָּבֹד מִכֹּל כְּלִי חֶמְדָּה	Wealth from every kind of precious thing!	
11a	בּוּקָה וּמְבוּקָה וּמְבֻלָּקָה	Desolation, emptiness, devastation!	h. Nineveh Desolated, Its Population Defeated (2:11a–e)
11b	וְלֵב נָמֵס	Hearts melt,	
11c	וּפַק בִּרְכַּיִם	knees knock,	
11d	וְחַלְחָלָה בְּכָל־מָתְנַיִם	trembling is in every loin,	
11e	וּפְנֵי כֻלָּם קִבְּצוּ פָארוּר	all their faces gather redness.	
			4. The Fall of Assyria Anticipated (2:12a–14f)
12a	אַיֵּה מְעוֹן אֲרָיוֹת	Where is the lair of the lion,	a. Anticipation of Assyria's Demise (2:12a–e)
12b	וּמִרְעֶה הוּא לַכְּפִרִים	and the territory of the young lions,	
12c	אֲשֶׁר הָלַךְ אַרְיֵה לָבִיא ↑	↑ where the lion and lioness go?	
12d	שָׁם גּוּר אַרְיֵה	There the lion dwells,	
12e	וְאֵין מַחֲרִיד	and there is nothing that startles (them).	
13a	אַרְיֵה טֹרֵף בְּדֵי גֹרוֹתָיו	The lion has torn enough for his cubs	b. The Lion, his Pride, and his Prey (2:13a–d)
13b	וּמְחַנֵּק לְלִבְאֹתָיו	and strangled (enough) for his lionesses.	
13c	וַיְמַלֵּא־טֶרֶף חֹרָיו	He has filled his den with prey,	
13d	וּמְעֹנֹתָיו טְרֵפָה	his den (he has filled) with torn flesh.	
14a	הִנְנִי אֵלַיִךְ	"Know that I am against you!"	c. YHWH Commits to Destroying Assyria (2:14a–f)
14b	נְאֻם יְהוָה צְבָאוֹת	Utterance of YHWH of Hosts:	
14c	וְהִבְעַרְתִּי בֶעָשָׁן רִכְבָּהּ	"I will burn in the fire her chariots;	
14d	וּכְפִירַיִךְ תֹּאכַל חָרֶב	your young lions the sword will devor,	
14e	וְהִכְרַתִּי מֵאֶרֶץ טַרְפֵּךְ	and I will cut off from the earth your taking of prey.	
14f	וְלֹא־יִשָּׁמַע עוֹד קוֹל מַלְאָכֵכֵה	The voice of your envoys will no longer will be heard."	

The third and longest section (2:4–11[3–10]) details in compressed but logical order the fall of Nineveh, from the initial assault, through the fall of the palace, to several outcomes for the city and its population: the forced relocation of some (2:8[7]), the plundering of the city's wealth (2:10[9]), and the Ninevites' realization of their utter defeat (2:11[10]). The interjection of direct speech at two points (2:9[8]c–d; 2:10[9]a–b) contrasts the voices of the Assyrian defenders and the attackers, and both add poignancy through repetition. Apart from those interruptions, the predominance of coordinate syntactical structures in 2:4–11[3–10] creates a rapid, almost breathless account of various facets of the battle and the subsequent fall of the city. Series of three or more parallel lines are indented to highlight the rhetorical effect of their parallelism (2:5[4]a–d; 2:11[10]b–e; 2:12[11]b–e).

The final subunit, 2:12–14[11–13], reinforces the focus of YHWH's wrath on the empire as a violent oppressor. In much the same way that the prolepsis of 2:2–11[1–10] moves from warning Nineveh of its danger through the unfolding battle to the spoiling of the city and the elimination of all its power, this short, mocking prophecy also mixes anticipation of Assyria's end with visions of its destruction as a fait accompli. The three subordinate lines that describe the lion's territory (2:12[11]c–e) convey its size, and the four parallel lines in 2:13[12] emphasize the lion's efficiency as a hunter. The signatory formula of 2:14[13]b that identifies this section as an "utterance of YHWH" adds power and solemnity to the subunit's closing lines by "placing the divine imprimatur" upon the prophet's message.[1]

Explanation of the Text

1. The Call to Prepare for YHWH's Attack (2:2[1])

The opening verb of this short subunit, regardless of whether perfective forms express aspect (a complete action) rather than tense (an event in the past), is clearly the basis for the four commands that the speaker issues afterward.[2] The expression "come up against" habitually expresses military opposition (among dozens of references, see Josh 22:12, 22:33; Judg 6:3; 15:10; Isa 8:7; 36:10; Joel 1:6), but who has arrived to threaten Assyria? The preceding context makes this person inseparable from YHWH himself, whose commitment to destroying his enemies everywhere is the driving motive for the whole book (1:2–8) and who has already presented himself as Assyria's opponent in the first person (1:14). At the same time, Nahum's depiction of the "scatterer" and the ensuing battle that destroys Nineveh involves no supernatural actions on the part of this entity, who should therefore be seen as a means in YHWH's hands. The instrumentality rather than the autonomy of the attacker can also be contrasted with YHWH's second direct confrontation with Assyria in the mocking divine announcement of Assyria's fall that closes this section (esp. 2:14[13]).[3]

Because the book of Nahum as a whole foretells

1. Daniel I. Block, *The Book of Ezekiel: Chapters 1–24*, NICOT (Grand Rapids: Eerdmans, 1997), 33.

2. See Cook, "Finite Verbal Forms," 21–35.

3. It is also notable that unlike YHWH in Nahum, the

the fall of Nineveh, 2:2[1] could be, first, an affirmation that YHWH has already begun his attack on Assyria (without that attack having brought about the city's demise). Second, 2:2[1] could be the first example in the book of prolepsis, in which a future state of affairs is presented as if it has already taken place. Third, it could be the presentation of a future event using a verbal form that looks at the attack as one, undifferentiated event (regardless of tense). Since 2:4–11[3–10] goes on to describe the fall of the city proleptically, since several commands to prepare for battle follow immediately in 2:2[1], and since Nahum's historical setting seems much closer to 650 than to 612 BCE, it is best to understand 2:2[1] as the first step of YHWH's campaign against Nineveh, and thus as prolepsis.

This understanding of 2:2[1] puts the reader within sight of Nineveh shortly before the decisive battle begins. As the army that YHWH will use to punish Assyria approaches the city, the prophet uses a series of four commands to exhort the Assyrian forces to prepare for battle (we soon learn that this is sarcasm or mockery): "Guard the ramparts! Watch the road! Get ready to stand firm! Summon all your strength!" The initial statement that the attacking army is on its way seems addressed to the city, since it uses a singular feminine pronominal suffix ("*your* face," 2fs). By contrast, the addressee of these four commands is a masculine singular entity, probably referring to the Assyrian army collectively. The four commands are connected in a number of ways: consonance (the repetition of sibilant consonant sounds [*ṣ* or *z*]),[4] syntax (command followed by the object), and a focus on activities and attitudes requisite to the defense of a city. The very fact that there are four commands that address both strategy and readiness might suggest that the city is currently unprepared, but in context these commands ironically reveal that even extensive preparation will be of no avail against YHWH.

This subunit clearly moves, in both time and space, from just before the attack on Nineveh through its fall and looting. Where appropriate, a figure like the one immediately below locates each verse's geographical perspective with respect to Nineveh. The progression is generally toward the geographic center of the city, but (especially since the royal citadel was the heart of Nineveh) the fact that this section ends with a slightly broader focus on the city and its inhabitants puts the anthropological or social aspect of Nineveh's collapse at the center of the reader's perspective. This is reinforced by the amount of text given to each focus, with one verse each for the various stages of the battle (2:2[1], 4–6[3–5]), two verses for the fall of the citadel (2:7–8[6–7]), and three verses for the city as a whole (2:9–11[8–10], with an emphasis on the hopeless plight of its inhabitants.

Figure 4.1a: Geographical Perspective with Respect to Nineveh (2:2[1])

<table>
<tr><td rowspan="2">Outside Nineveh (far) (2:2[1])</td><td rowspan="2">Outside Nineveh (near) (2:4[3])</td><td rowspan="2">Suburbs and/or wall (2:5[4])</td><td rowspan="2">Wall (2:6[5])</td><td>Citadel: palace (2:7[6])</td><td>City: defenders (2:9[8])</td></tr>
<tr><td>Citadel: temple (2:8[7])</td><td>City: treasuries (2:10[9])</td></tr>
<tr><td></td><td></td><td></td><td></td><td></td><td>City: inhabitants (2:11[10])</td></tr>
</table>

"scatterer" is not characterized in any way, nor does it receive any praise or recognition. Gordon H. Johnston, "Nahum's Rhetorical Allusions to Neo-Assyrian Conquest Metaphors," *BSac* 159 (2002): 40–42, suggests that instead of מֵפִיץ, "scatterer," one should read מַפֵּץ, "mace," and correlates that expression with the claims of Neo-Assyrian kings to be a "mighty weapon" of their gods, but the textual evidence for this reading is insufficient.

4. *J-M*, 24 (§5h).

2. The Significance for Judah: Restoration (2:3[2])

The mocking call for Nineveh to prepare for YHWH's attack is complemented by a brief consideration of this event's significance for Judah. Unlike 1:12d–e, where YHWH promises only to afflict Judah no longer, here he promises something more positive, the restoration of "Jacob's" glory. Arriving at a clear sense for this line requires some effort, and a number of questions arise.

First, while some have suggested that the verb שָׁב here is a form of שׁבב, "cut off," rather than שׁוּב, "turn, return, restore," a negative statement in a context dealing with the ramifications for Judah of YHWH's destruction of Assyria and the precedent of 1:12 make such a sense unlikely.[5] No less importantly, there is no textual support for such a sense in the versions.[6]

Second, if "restore" is indeed the proper sense of שָׁב here, what is being restored? The phrase גְּאוֹן יַעֲקֹב, "majesty of Jacob," occurs only three times outside this text and can be good (Ps 47:5[4]) or bad (Amos 6:8) when applied to non-divine entities, or, can function as a self-given divine title (Amos 8:7). The parallel phrase "pride/majesty of Israel" occurs elsewhere only in Hos 5:5; 7:10, where it refers to morally culpable behavior.[7] While Longman understands "Jacob . . . Israel" as honorific titles of Judah and takes the כִּ as emphatic, the juxtaposition of the two names suggests that this verse should be related to the Jacob narrative, where Jacob's name is changed to Israel following his encounter with God.[8] The contrast in Gen 32 is between Jacob who habitually deceives and Israel who struggles successfully with God and is not only spared, but given the promise that he will prevail with divine aid.[9] The promise in Nahum would thus be that God will restore to Jacob (Judah in a lackluster spiritual condition) the "majesty" that was associated with Israel (i.e., Jacob) after his struggle with God and the blessing and new name he received at its end.[10] This makes good sense in context, and also develops smoothly from the mildly negative nuance in 1:12 regarding God's punishment of Judah for its prior sin and through the transitional 2:1[1:15], which strikes a slightly positive note.[11]

Alternatively, "the majesty of Jacob" could designate the full extent of Israelite territory, as it does in Ps 47:5[4],[12] so that the verse simply foresees that Judah will repossess Israel's historical territory once liberated from Assyria's domination (cf. Num 32; 36; Josh 17, etc.).[13] Either positive sense fits well with an asseverative sense for the כִּי that begins the verse: "Truly, YHWH restores . . ." The land-focused sense might be favored by the concession in 2:3[2]b–c related to Judah's territory (see immediately below), but a wider sense for restoration hardly excludes the idea that a restored Judah would possess its land (cf. Amos 9:11–15, although its context explicitly

5. Longman, "Nahum," 802, points to several cases in which the verb (usually intransitive) is transitive (Ps 85:5[4]; Isa 52:8); cf. *HALOT*, 1430.

6. Neither Gelston, *The Twelve Minor Prophets*, 86, nor *BHS* note any variants.

7. So J. Andrew Dearman, *Hosea*, NICOT (Grand Rapids: Eerdmans, 2010), 209; Andersen and Freedman, *Hosea*, 392, 468.

8. Longman, "Nahum," 802; Hamilton, "Jacob/Israel (Person)," *NDBT*, 588.

9. G. J. Wenham, *Genesis 16–50*, WBC 2 (Dallas: Word, 1994), 296–97.

10. Tidiman, *Nahoum, Habaquq, Sophonie*, 93, favors this option.

11. This is noted by Tidiman, *Nahoum, Habaquq, Sophonie*, 93; Perlitt, *Die Propheten*, 19.

12. Hans-Joachim Kraus, *Psalms 1–59*, CC, trans. H. C. Oswald (Minneapolis: Augsburg Fortress, 1993), 468.

13. This sense is favored by Christensen, *Nahum*, 266, even though he goes on to speak of God restoring "to his people the lofty eminence of their divine calling" in connection with the election of Jacob. The reference to "branches" in 2:2c may have in view individual tribes, which would favor a territorial sense for "glory of Jacob" (as in Ps 47:5).

eliminates sinners from Judah, 9:9–10). The second כִּי, by contrast, is certainly concessive: "although." The condition of Judah at present is grave, since its enemies have "wasted" (בְּקָקוּם) them and "ruined" (שִׁחֵתוּ) their branches, but this lamentable state of affairs poses no difficulty to YHWH's intention to restore Judah.[14]

3. The Fall of Nineveh Anticipated (2:4–11[3–10])

Although YHWH is the primary enemy of Assyria in Nahum, this section presents and probably presumes the city's fall at the hands of a human army that serves as YHWH's instrument for punishing Assyria.[15] The text moves in a generally chronological order from the appearance of the attacking army through their conquest of the city and culminates in the plundering of the city and the abject defeat of the Assyrian survivors.[16] Despite an initial focus on the military aspects of the conquest of Nineveh, the text focuses more on its effects on the city's population and defenders and so maintains a focus on the anthropological and religious significance of Nineveh's fall.

The Enemy Soldiers and Their Weapons (2:4[3])

The first glimpse Nahum affords the reader of the army that threatens Nineveh is of the "reddened" (מְאָדָּם) shields borne by its infantry. The *pual* of אדם means "rubbed with reddle," reddle being a clay-like soil containing elements that give it a strong red color and make it suitable for marking sheep, coloring walls, etc.[17] If the Babylonians' shields were reddened, they are presumably not metallic (since such a substance would not adhere to a metallic surface) but leather. If the shields were metallic, as were some Assyrian shields beginning in the seventh century, their color would presumably be dictated by their constituent metals, and these would not have been bright red.[18] Neo-Assyrian analogues are closest both culturally and chronologically, but it remains impossible to determine exactly what sort of shields are in view here.[19]

It should be noted that although the first glimpse at the "battle of Nineveh" is set near the city, the scenario presupposes a good deal of military activity beforehand (albeit less dramatic and so less suitable to a depiction of the empire's fall). Aron Pinker and others have documented Assyria's extensive military infrastructure and communication network, and one must assume that the enemy's advance prior to this point has dismantled the empire's defenses, leaving its capital city as the most strategic target.[20]

With an eye to the historical nature of Nineveh's fall (and because the root used here, תלע, for

14. Roberts, *Nahum, Habakkuk, and Zephaniah*, 64, also recognizes the connection between Judah's restoration and Assyria's destruction.

15. The tone of this section is consistently nonsupernatural in terms of the army and its combat. The cosmic aspect, meaning YHWH's combat against evil, is present instead by virtue of the overall perspective afforded by 1:2–8.

16. Aron Pinker, "Nineveh's Defensive Strategy and Nahum 2–3," *ZAW* 118 (2006): 618–25, and others have argued that 2:3–4[2–3] in particular refer not to the attacker but to Nineveh's defenders. While plausible on some points, the overall contrast between the attacker's preparedness and effectiveness, on the one hand, and Nineveh's inability to defend herself followed by her complete defeat, on the other hand, make that understanding less plausible than the one suggested here.

17. *HALOT*, 14.

18. Fales, *Guerre et paix*, 112. The analogy of the "flaming torches" in 1 Macc 6:39 is weak, since the shields there are clearly bronze and their color is accordingly that of a torch, not bright red.

19. Cf. Fales, *Guerre et paix*, 111–12; Fabrice De Backer and Evelyne Dehenin, *The Neo-Assyrian Shield: Evolution, Heraldry, and Tactics*, Material Culture of the Ancient Near East 1 (London: Lockwood, 2012), 4, note that Babylonian shields were often made of leather.

20. Pinker, "Nineveh's Defensive Strategy," 621, who notes that Nahum "denies Nineveh its primary defensive premise—strategic warning."

Figure 4.1b: Geographical Perspective with Respect to Nineveh (2:4[3])

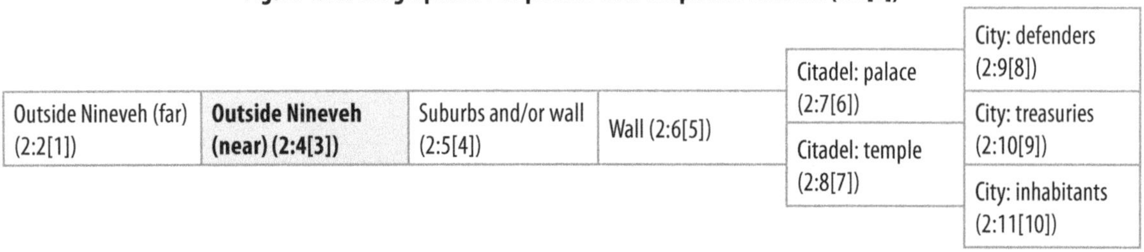

"dressed in scarlet," appears nowhere else in the OT), it is notable that the OT speaks elsewhere of Babylonian officials wearing red (Ezek 23:14). When worn by soldiers, many affirm that red in particular would evoke fear of bloodshed in the opposing army,[21] which is plausible even though this section most likely describes the opposing army before the assault begins ("on the day of his preparation," 2:4[3]d).[22] Such red uniforms were surely costly, and so probably were worn only by an elite group that led the assault.[23]

In 2:4[3]c the description shifts from the soldiers to the chariots. The author continues his practice of treating a military component and its color together (reddened shields, scarlet clothing) by adding that the steel of the chariots is "flashing" or "fiery" (בָּאֵשׁ) in appearance. The final element, the cypress spears, is the only item whose color is not mentioned; instead it is noted that these spears are "brandished" (הָרְעָלוּ). This is the only time in the description of the poised army that movement is perhaps present, and the rest of the information conveyed by 2:4[3] is akin to a photograph of the Medo-Babylonian force before it began its assault.[24] If Neo-Assyrian parallels are apt, the spearmen would have been a key element of the Babylonian army. Their engagement with the enemy would likely have been preceded by volleys of arrows launched by archers, and they may have been accompanied by soldiers wielding slings and other weapons as well as by teams of engineers tasked with destroying the foundations of the city's perimeter walls.[25]

The Enemy Chariots Attack (2:5[4])

The photo-like depiction of 2:4[3] gives way to an image bursting with movement and noise in 2:5[4]. While it may seem odd that an attack on a city would include chariots, the layout of Nineveh in the seventh century would have permitted chariots to circulate outside or on its main walls and perhaps even within the city.[26] Sennacherib boasted

21. Christensen, *Nahum*, 270–71, cites various ancient and classical examples. Fabry, *Nahum*, 170, concludes similarly, even though he thinks the soldiers in view are Nineveh's defenders. Renaud, *Michée, Sophonie, Nahum*, 300, following W. Rudolph, suggests that certain colors may have had an apotropaic function.

22. As noted by Renaud, *Michée, Sophonie, Nahum*, 299.

23. Tidiman, *Nahoum, Habaquq, Sophonie*, 95.

24. The Babylonians were aided by Median forces, "formalised by a treaty perhaps cemented by dynastic marriage," Amélie Kuhrt, *The Ancient Near East c. 3000–330 BC*, Routledge History of the Ancient World, 2 vols. (London: Routledge, 1995), 590.

25. Fales, *Guerre et paix*, 109–16.

26. Note the various suggestions of Renaud, *Michée, Sophonie, Nahum*, 300, which accord well with the fact that Assyrian chariots in the seventh century (and so presumably their Babylonian counterparts) carried archers who would be equally effective outside or inside the city; similarly Tidiman, *Nahoum, Habaquq, Sophonie*, 96; Christensen, *Nahum*, 276; Fabrice De Backer, "Notes on the Neo-Assyrian Siege-Shield and Chariot," in *Time and History in the Ancient Near East: Proceedings of the 56th Rencontre Assyriologique Internationale at Barcelona, 26–30 July 2010*, ed. L. Feliu et al. (Winona Lake, IN: Eisenbrauns, 2013), 69–78. Among other points, Pinker's protest in "Nineveh's Defensive Strategy," 622, that the fortified city's streets would not have been wide enough for chariots may be undercut by the width of the gates, some of which (e.g.,

Figure 4.1c: Geographical Perspective with Respect to Nineveh (2:5[4])

Outside Nineveh (far) (2:2[1])	Outside Nineveh (near) (2:4[3])	**Suburbs and/or wall (2:5[4])**	Wall (2:6[5])	Citadel: palace (2:7[6])	City: defenders (2:9[8])
					City: treasuries (2:10[9])
				Citadel: temple (2:8[7])	City: inhabitants (2:11[10])

of Nineveh, that in the course of his renovations, "I widened the squares, made bright the avenues and streets; . . . I made its market streets wide enough to run a royal road."[27] A closer look at the city will help us understand this and a number of related details.

The seventh-century BCE city of Nineveh proper consisted of a central walled area, roughly 5 kilometers (3 miles) long and averaging 1 kilometer (0.65 miles) in width.[28] The palace, other royal buildings, temples, and relatively wealthy residential areas were located within this area, which was surrounded by an immense stone wall, roughly 15 meters (50 feet) thick and 20 meters (65 feet) high. This main wall was pierced by at least fifteen gates (eighteen are attested in written sources, but not all have been positively located), some of which were 5–7 meters (16–23 feet) wide (before being narrowed in the years leading up to 612 BCE), and all were easily accessed by stone ramps.[29] Further, at two points the river Khosr ran under the city's wall and on its course through the city ran close enough to the royal palace that Sennacherib built a river wall to protect the citadel on which the palace was built from erosion.[30]

Figure 4.2: Nineveh in the Time of Sennacherib

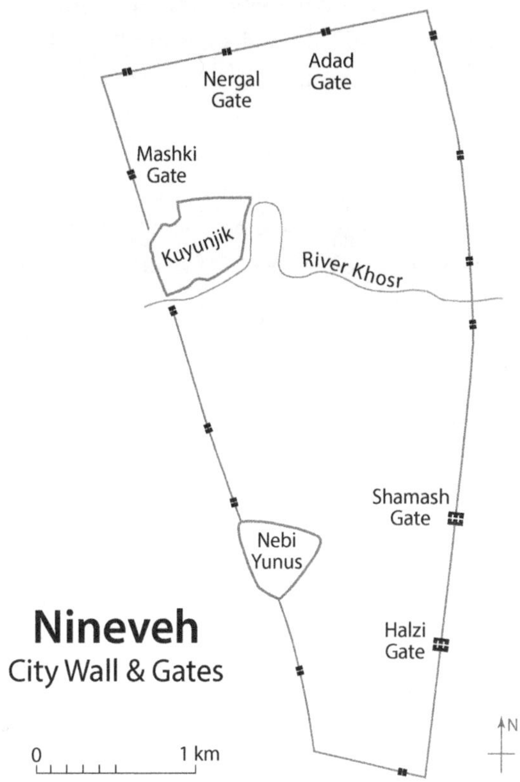

the Halzi gate) were (originally) between 5 and 7 meters wide; cf. David Stronach, "Notes on the Fall of Nineveh," in *Assyria 1995*, ed. S. Parpola and R. Whiting (Helsinki: Neo-Assyrian Text Corpus Project, 1997), 307–24, esp. 315–18. The width of at least some of these gates was reduced to approximately 2 meters in the years before Nineveh's fall, but that width would still most likely have allowed the entry of all but the largest chariots; cf. Fales, *Guerre et paix*, 126–30.

27. Daniel D. Luckenbill, *Historical Records from Assyria from Sargon to the End*, *ARAB* 2 (Chicago: University of Chicago Press, 1927), 162–63.

28. In this section, I follow Stronach, "Notes on the Fall of Nineveh," 311–13.

29. Julian Reade, "Studies in Assyrian Geography, Part 1: Sennacherib and the Waters of Nineveh," *RA* 72 (1978): 50–54; she proposes locations for eighteen gates in Julian Reade, "Assyrian Illustrations of Nineveh," *IrAnt* 33 (1998): 82.

30. Stronach, "Notes on the Fall of Nineveh," 319, 321.

In addition to this impressive main wall, Nineveh boasted a smaller, adjoining "curtain wall" that extended outward from the main wall, sometimes reaching more than 4 meters (13 feet) in width and 4–6 meters (13–20 feet) in height. This wall, like the gates, also had towers. A last defensive feature, begun in the late eighth century but never completed, was a large ditch intended to protect the city's longest, eastern wall. Archaeological explorations of several of Nineveh's gates reveal that they were not impregnable, and some are littered with the skeletons and weapons of those defending or attacking the gate when the city fell.

With a better grasp of the city's characteristics in the seventh century we can return to Nahum's description of the attack on the city, reminding ourselves that the nature of his vision (1:1) hardly requires that he foresee in every detail the city's final hours as realized in later history.[31] The fact that a verse of four lines focuses exclusively on chariots is striking, and its focus is emphasized by fronting nonverbal items twice, in 2:5[4]a ("in the streets") and 2:5[4]d ("like lightning"). This surely contributes to one of the passage's main points, the disorder and ineffectiveness of Nineveh's defenses in contrast to the power and effectiveness of its attacker. The description of the chariots in terms of speed and flashing appearance favors seeing them as part of the attacking force (note the similar description of the poised troops in 2:4[3]), and the difficulty of establishing exactly how they might have participated in the assault on Nineveh offers little impediment to including them among the attackers. Understanding the chariots as belonging to the attackers rather than to Nineveh's defenders also adds a note of irony, since Assyria's military had demonstrated over several centuries its mastery of the chariot, with dire consequences for its foes.[32]

The Assyrians in Disorder (2:6[5])

Once again we must decide to which group the text refers. Efforts to identify the referent by grammatical gender or number are frustrated by the text's vacillation between masculine and feminine as well as between singular and plural. As a result, we are forced to make a decision based on other considerations. While some have suggested that "his officers" (אַדִּירָיו) are military officers of the attacking army, the only other use in Nahum (3:18) clearly refers to high-ranking officials in the empire's administration and so slightly favors seeing them as Assyrians here too. Similarly, the fact that they stumble fits better the city's disheveled defenders than its attackers, whose assault apparently continues without interruption or signs of disorder.[33] This makes it possible to see the Assyrian king as the one who "remembers" his military officers, with the result that they hurry to defend the city from a vantage point on the wall.[34]

The arrival of those leading the city's defense at the wall is of little avail, however. The variation in verbal forms between the three imperfects with Assyrian subjects (remembers, stumble, rush) and the one perfective form ("set up," הֻכַן) used of the "mantlet" (a mobile protective shelter or large shield) suggests that the attackers are already in place next to the wall, continuing their assault.[35]

31. The point is duly noted with respect to 2:7[6] by Spronk, *Nahum*, 94–95: "The words of Nahum . . . are not a historical report but part of a prophetic vision."

32. Cf. Berlejung, "Erinnerungen," 329.

33. Fabry, *Nahum*, 171, notes the similarities in tone and subject between this verse and 2:2[1], where the Assyrian defenders are indisputably in view.

34. Perlitt, *Die Propheten*, 20, suggests that זכר here means "call (by name)" and so refers to the directions shouted out by the Medo-Babylonian attackers. See also Renaud, *Michée, Sophonie, Nahum*, 300–301; Roberts, *Nahum, Habakkuk, and Zephaniah*, 59, 65; cf. *HALOT*, 270.

35. See the illustrations of a typical Assyrian siege-shield in Christensen, *Nahum*, 282, who draws upon Yigael Yadin, *The*

Figure 4.1d: Geographical Perspective with Respect to Nineveh (2:6[5])

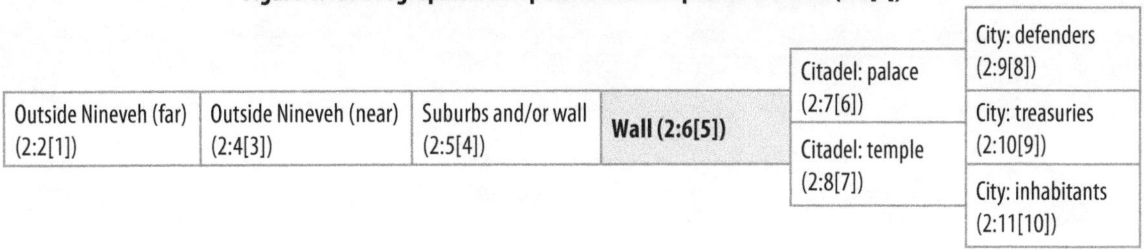

The arrival of the Assyrian commanders is thus too little, too late.

The Fall of the Palace (2:7[6])

Thanks to extensive waterworks projects undertaken by Sennacherib, a complex network of canals not yet fully understood brought water to, and into, the city of Nineveh. The first such project was the Kisiri canal, dug in order to bring water from the Khosr River at Kisiri (about 16km/10 miles from Nineveh) to the new capital city.[36] This canal irrigated the garden that Sennacherib built next to his new palace inside Nineveh, as well as gardens in other parts of the city, via a network of smaller canals. Sennacherib took obvious pride in the project:

> A great park like unto Mt. Amanus, wherein were set out all kinds of herbs and orchard fruits, trees such as grow on the mountains and in Chaldea, I planted by its (the palace's) side. . . . To make the orchards luxurious, from the border of the town of Kisiri to the plain of Nineveh, through mountain and lowland, with iron pickaxes I cut and directed a canal. For a distance of 1–1/2 bēru I caused to flow there . . . everlasting waters from the Khosr. Inside these orchards I made them flow in irrigation ditches.[37]

Later projects saw more canals dug in order to enrich the agricultural productivity of land outside the city as well as to beautify the region. Sennacherib again waxed eloquent:

> I greatly enlarged the site of Nineveh. . . . Its fields, which through lack of water had fallen into neglect . . . while its people, ignorant of artificial irrigation, turned their eyes heavenward for showers of rain—(these fields) I watered; and from the villages of Masiti, Banbarina . . . [fifteen other towns are named] . . . (and) the waters which were above the town of Hadabiti eighteen canals I dug (and) directed their course into the Khosr River.[38]

In addition to these canals, Sennacherib also began the construction of three moats which held significant amounts of water just outside Nineveh's walls, one each on the north, east, and south sides of the city.[39] Additionally, several dams were built upstream on the Khosr to prevent the flooding of the city.

Art of Warfare in Biblical Lands: In the Light of Archaeological Study, 2 vols. (New York: McGraw-Hill, 1963), 295. Fabry, *Nahum*, 171, sees the Assyrian commanders as the ones laboriously setting up a sheltered observation post on the wall, but it seems that observation of the battle is not the most pressing task for the defenders at this stage of the battle.

36. See the thorough description of the canals in and around Nineveh in Reade, "Studies in Assyrian Geography, Part 1," 61–72, whom I follow here.

37. Thorkild Jacobsen and Seton Lloyd, *Sennacherib's Aqueduct at Jerwan*, OIP 24 (Chicago: The Oriental Institute of the University of Chicago, 1935), 33, cited in Reade, "Studies in Assyrian Geography, Part 1," 61.

38. Jacobsen and Lloyd, *Sennacherib's Aqueduct at Jerwan*, 36, cited in Reade, "Studies in Assyrian Geography, Part 1," 71–72. A relief from Assurbanipal's North Palace at Nineveh depicts a monarch surveying a network of canals, more likely than not at Nineveh; see the relief (BM 124939,b) online at http://www.britishmuseum.org/research/collection_online/collection_object_details/collection_image_gallery.aspx?assetId=859647001&objectId=282174&partId=1.

39. Reade, "Studies in Assyrian Geography, Part 1," 68. It

Figure 4.1e: Geographical Perspective with Respect to Nineveh (2:7[6])

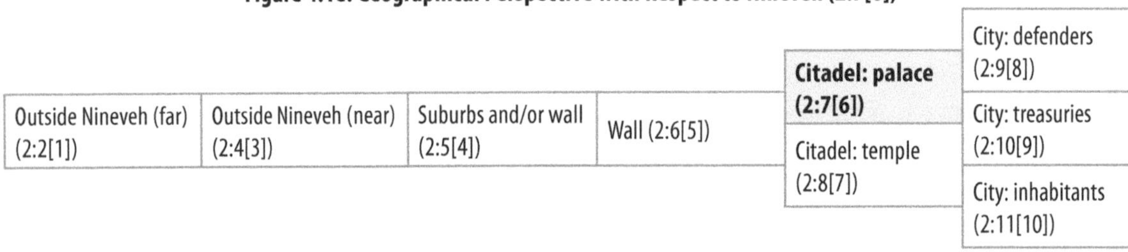

Reminding ourselves again that a prophetic vision of the city's fall need not predict by rote every detail of the later historical event, we turn to the laconic description of water's role in the city's fall in 2:7[6]. The text itself is straightforward and poses no text-critical problems. Although perhaps imperceptible in English translations, the placement of the verbal objects at the head of their clauses emphasizes this facet of Nineveh's fall: "the river gates are opened, the palace sways."[40] The rivers in question are the Khosr, the canals it fed, the Tigris, or the canal that ran through Nineveh. In light of the context's focus on the Assyrian king and his military leaders, "the palace/temple" (הֵיכָל) probably refers to the palace rather than to a temple, although several of each were located in the citadel next to which the canal ran.[41]

Given what is known of the water infrastructure in and around Nineveh, it is plausible to imagine that water played some role in the city's fall, remembering especially the proximity of the Khosr's canal to the citadel atop which Sennacherib's palace stood. Indeed, a number of prominent historians have affirmed as much, based in part on Xenophon (ca. 427–355 BCE) and Diodorus (ca. 90–30 BCE), two ancient Greek historians.[42] At the same time, the Babylonian record of the event, the oldest extant witness, makes no mention of a flood, whether natural or man-made.[43]

Given the height of the citadel above the plain (some 10 meters or 31 feet) and the vague sense of מוג, it is unwarranted to insist that water, and specifically the flow of the Khosr, played a key role in the fall of Nineveh. The use of similar imagery for the arrival of Assyrian forces in the Levant in Isa 8:7–8 should further caution the reader against forcing a literal sense on this pictorial description of part of Nineveh's fall.[44] The scenario in 2:7[6] could also be an ironic but nonliteral play on the

seems likely that these moats were also conceived of as part of Nineveh's defenses, and it appears they were intended to surround the city completely, even if that aspect of their construction was never realized.

40. Cf. *HALOT*, 555; Herbert M. Wolf and Robert D. Holmstedt, "מוג," *NIDOTTE* 2:863–65.

41. Aron Pinker also favors seeing the palace as the referent here; "Nahum and the Greek Tradition of Nineveh's Fall," *JHebS* 6 (2006): article 8, page 12, doi:10.5508/jhs.2006.v6.a8.

42. Among those who include some role for water in Nineveh's fall are Donald J. Wiseman, *Chronicles of Chaldean Kings (626–556 B.C.) in the British Museum* (London: British Museum, 1961), 17; Saggs, *The Might That Was Assyria*, 120; and Joann Scurlock, "The Euphrates Flood and the Ashes of Nineveh (Diod. II 27.1–28.7)," *Historia* 39 (1990): 382–84. The relevant sources are Xenephon, *Anabasis*, and Diodorus, *Bibliotheca historia*, II.

43. Although an argument from silence, this point is stressed by Pinker, "Nahum and the Greek Tradition," 16, who suggests that "the notion that Nineveh was captured through flooding . . . should be discarded." The Babylonian account is recorded on a tablet now in the British Museum (BM 21901).

44. The congruence and possible interrelation of these two texts are probed by Peter Machinist, "The Fall of Assyria in Comparative Ancient Perspective," in *Assyria 1995*, ed. S. Parpola and R. Whiting (Helsinki: Neo-Assyrian Text Corpus Project, 1997), 183.

water infrastructure originally intended to beautify and increase the productivity of Nineveh.[45]

At the same time, the fact that an extensive network of canals controlled by dams flowed near and even into the city, and that entities like these are specifically referred to by the text, not to mention the impossibility of completely neglecting the ancient sources that mention some sort of inundation, caution against equally blunt exclusions of some such scenario from Nineveh's fall.[46] Among other options, Peter Machinist suggests the possibility that after the city's fall the conquerors produced a relatively limited inundation of the city. On his view,

> It would thus have been a ritual act to seal the destruction of Nineveh, carried out especially by the Babylonian conquerors, a part of whom, the Babylonian Chronicle informs us, remained in Nineveh headed by their king, Nabopolassar, for a time after the capture.[47]

Machinist further suggests that such an inundation would have evoked memories of Sennacherib's destruction of Babylon some seventy years earlier, at which time the Assyrian king destroyed Babylon after a series of rebellions and related wars and sealed his victory by flooding the city.[48] Of that event Sennacherib said:

> Through the midst of the city I dug canals, I flooded its site (*lit.* ground) with water, and the very foundations thereof (*lit.* the structure of its foundation) I destroyed. I made its destruction more complete than that by a flood. That in days to come the site of that city, and (its) temples and gods, might not be remembered, I completely blotted it out with (floods) of water and made it like a meadow.[49]

This analogue confirms the historical plausibility of such a scenario at Nineveh in 612 BCE, even if it is difficult to determine conclusively whether Nahum's description of its destruction as involving water should be taken literally rather than figuratively.[50] It may be best to allow for more than one signification for the water in 2:7[6], as does Sennacherib's rationale for the construction of a new palace on a platform protected from the Tebiltu, a name for the canal that that flowed through Nineveh:[51]

> The Tebiltu River, a raging, destructive stream, which, at its high water, had destroyed the mausoleums inside and had exposed to the sun their tiers of coffins, and, from the days of old, had come close to the palace and with its floods at high water had worked havoc with its foundations and destroyed its platform.[52]

Discussing this passage, Marta Rivaroli suggests that Sennacherib's decision to build his palace on a

45. See the numerous examples in Johnston, "Conquest Metaphors," 32–34. Marc Van De Mieroop, "A Tale of Two Cities: Nineveh and Babylon," *Iraq* 66 (2004): 1–2, makes the parallel suggestion that Babylon's destruction by water is presented in terms that contrast it with Sennacherib's reconstruction of Nineveh (cited in part above), which emphasizes that he enlarged its wall and built an irrigation canal.

46. Cf. Fuchs, "Assyria at War," 380–401 (396), and Machinist, "Fall of Assyria," 191 and the notes there.

47. Machinist, "Fall of Assyria," 194.

48. See further Van De Mieroop, "A Tale of Two Cities," esp. 1–2; Van De Mieroop, "Revenge, Assyrian Style," *Past & Present* 179 (May 2003): 3–23.

49. Luckenbill, *Historical Records from Assyria from Sargon to the End*, 152 (the Bavian inscription).

50. Tidiman, *Nahoum, Habaquq, Sophonie*, 99, proposes that "gates of the river" refers to a set of doors on the royal palace, so that 2:7[6]a and 2:7[6]b are semantically parallel and both describe aspects of the palace's fall into enemy hands, but a sluicegate referent is much more plausible. Fabry, *Nahum*, 174, favors the sense of "panic in the palace" for 2:7[6]b ("the palace sways"), while Christensen, *Nahum*, 285–86, favors a symbolic rather than literal referent to "primordial floods."

51. Cf. Reade, "Studies in Neo-Assyrian Geography, Part 1," 61.

52. Luckenbill, *Historical Records from Assyria from Sargon to the End*, 163–64.

platform protected from the canal's eroding power attributes elements of mythical chaos to the river's "furious water," "high waves," and "washing away" of the previous palace's foundation.[53] This Assyrian understanding of the metaphorical or mythical connotation of streams may have prompted Nahum to include it in his description of the city's fall, adopting (as he clearly does elsewhere) Assyrian imagery and ideology for the purpose of ironically deconstructing it. The suggestion in the Introduction that 2:7[6] is an ironic inversion of the claims made by many Neo-Assyrian kings to be a raging flood that destroys their enemies, that role now belonging to YHWH, remains a plausible way to understand this verse and applies equally well to both literal and figurative roles for water in the city's fall.

Ishtar's Statue Is Stripped and Taken (2:8[7])

The beginning of this verse has long puzzled readers (3ms *hophal* perfect of נצב). The two other uses of the *hophal* in Biblical Hebrew refer to a physical object which is put in place (Gen 28:12; Judg 9:6, both participles), but here no physical object is mentioned.[54] Three of about twenty occurrences of the *hiphil* of נצב are clearly "decree, establish" (boundaries, Deut 32:8; Ps 74:17; rule, 1 Chr 18:3), so that the corresponding passive sense "decreed, established" is plausible per se for the *hophal*. However, the two uses of the *hophal* elsewhere may suggest that a physical object is the most natural subject, whereas when Nahum speaks of YHWH's decrees and decisions he emphasizes the related conflict between YHWH and the Assyrian element in question (e.g., 1:14).[55]

These points, together with the fact that no boundary (the other common object of the verb) is mentioned in view in 2:8[7]a, justify an attempt to understand the verb's subject as a physical object. Klaas Spronk takes the Assyrian king as the subject, with the sense of his being "put down" or cast aside as powerless.[56] However, the two following feminine verbs ("stripped," "carried away") could refer to the queen, although in both Assyrian ideology and in Nahum's description of Nineveh/Assyria she has no significant role. Third, all three verbs could refer to a cult statue, most likely that of Ishtar.

A host of textual and related issues complicate this question and unfortunately offer little ground for a confident conclusion. Not only does the first verb lack an explicit subject which cannot easily be supplied from context, but it also has a masculine-singular subject while the two following verbs have a feminine-singular subject. The second verb, the *pual* of גלה, expresses the uncovering or revealing of something that was previously covered or clothed (note Lev 20:18; Prov 27:5 has סתר, "hide," as the parallel antonym). The third verb (*hophal* of עלה) is used elsewhere only in Judg 6:28 (of a bull presented as offering) and 2 Chr 20:34 (of records written on a scroll),[57] and these few references do not allow us to draw any conclusions regarding the limits of the verb's use (e.g., of non-human subjects, etc.). That being the case, other factors merit consideration:

- Apart from the nebulous subject of the first part of this verse, the passage treats the following elements of Nineveh in describing its fall: outer defenses (2:2[1]), streets and squares

53. Marta Rivaroli, "Nineveh: From Ideology to Topography," *Iraq* 66 (2004): 199–205.

54. Cf. *HALOT*, 715, and see the extensive discussions of Fabry, *Nahum*, 161–62, who qualifies the state of the text as "hopeless," and of Christensen, *Nahum*, 287–91, who reviews numerous interpretative proposals.

55. It should not be overlooked that in most cases the *hiphil* of נצב refers to the setting up of altars and especially pillars, whether cultic or not.

56. Spronk, *Nahum*, 98.

57. Cf. *HALOT*, 830.

(2:5[4]), king, officers, and wall (2:6[5]), palace/temple (2:7–8[6–7]), fleeing soldiers (2:9[8]), plundering (2:10[9]), and defeated inhabitants (2:11[10]). The close association of the city with Ishtar makes it quite plausible to expect a mention of the city's principal patron deity here. Further, an appearance here would place her appropriately between the king (whose deities are mentioned in 1:14) and "her" city (cf. also 3:4–6).[58] These associations favor (if only slightly) a reference to her statue here.

- The Babylonian Chronicle explicitly mentions the spoiling of "the city and the temple." Although the royal citadel was the site of a temple of Nabu as well as the temple of Ishtar,[59] Ishtar's temple was complemented by a ziggurat that was "the pride of Nineveh."[60] The Ishtar temple itself included her throne and extensive alabaster wall panels portraying lion hunts and had been embellished with gold and silver by Assurbanipal.[61] It is thus hardly surprising that the Ishtar temple in Nineveh was burned, certainly after being despoiled, during the destruction of Nineveh in 612 BCE,[62] and this confirms the plausibility of including it among other facets of the city's fall in 2:2–11[1–10].
- The female servants mentioned in 2:8[7]d (with the noun אמה) are clearly associated with the feminine subject of the two preceding verbs, but again clarity eludes us. In Biblical Hebrew, the term refers to female servants or slaves in the service of any sort of person but, perhaps due to general disinterest in the details of foreign cults, is never used (unless here) of attendants of a deity.[63] Julian Reade notes that "a broken ninth-century glazed tile from the Ishtar Temple shows an armed female wearing a mural crown and plait, and followed by an attendant," but it is not clear whether the leading figure is the queen or Ishtar herself.[64] The rarity with which the queen figures in Neo-Assyrian art favors, however slightly, seeing this as a depiction of Ishtar.[65]

If the text is taken as it stands (and despite its difficulty the versions indicate no different original reading), the sense of 2:8[7] is thus most likely "Her statue is set up; she is stripped; she is carried away. . . ."[66] This requires, as Aron Pinker notes, that the gender of the first subject be taken as either a concession to Ishtar's variable gender (her androgyny was well-known) or as referring precisely to her statue (note the use of the masculine פֶּסֶל in 1:14, in parallel with the feminine מַסֵּכָה).[67]

58. Ishtar was often referred to as the "Lady of Nineveh" in the seventh century BCE (Porter, "Ishtar of Nineveh," 41), with Nineveh sometimes referred to as "the noble metropolis, the city beloved of Ishtar" (Luckenbill, *Historical Records from Assyria from Sargon to the End*, 160).

59. Julian Reade, "The Ishtar Temple at Nineveh," *Iraq* 67 (2005): 347–90 (348). A temple to Ishtar as Queen of Kidmuri may have stood on the site as well.

60. Ibid., 384; cf. Livingstone, *Court Poetry*, 18.

61. Reade, "The Ishtar Temple at Nineveh," 376–81.

62. R. Campbell Thompson and R. W. Hamilton, "The British Museum excavations at the Temple of Ishtar at Nineveh, 1930–1931," *Annals of Archaeology and Anthropology* 19 (1932): 70, cited in Reade, "The Ishtar Temple at Nineveh," 385.

63. Cf. *HALOT*, 61.

64. Reade, "The Ishtar Temple at Nineveh," 351.

65. Cf. Amy R. Gansell, "Images and Conceptions of Ideal Feminine Beauty in Neo-Assyrian Royal Context, c. 883–627 BCE," in *Critical Approaches to Ancient Near Eastern Art*, ed. M. Feldman and B. Brown (Boston: Walter de Gruyter, 2013), 393.

66. The only verb used of the temple's contents in the Babylonian Chronicle is "carried off;" see Grayson, *ABC*, 94 (line 45 of Chronicle 3).

67. Aron Pinker, "Descent of the Goddess Ishtar to the Netherworld and Nahum II 8," *VT* 55 (2005): 93. Rivkah Harris, "Inanna-Ishtar as Paradox and a Coincidence of Opposites," *HR* 30 (1991): 268–69, cites a number of sources that illustrate Ishtar's variable gender. Note, for example, "Though I am a woman I am a noble young man," and "When I sit in the alehouse, I am a woman (but) verily I am an exuberant man" (269). I disagree with Pinker's assertion that here the city has not yet fallen (especially 2:9[8]b–c seem to require that situation), so

Figure 4.1f: Geographical Perspective with Respect to Nineveh (2:8[7])

Outside Nineveh (far) (2:2[1])	Outside Nineveh (near) (2:4[3])	Suburbs and/or wall (2:5[4])	Wall (2:6[5])	Citadel: palace (2:7[6])	City: defenders (2:9[8])
				Citadel: temple (2:8[7])	City: treasuries (2:10[9])
					City: inhabitants (2:11[10])

Nineveh, directly personified or indirectly represented by the statue of its primary patron deity, is "stripped" of its cultic accoutrements and carried away, as deities of defeated peoples often were in the ancient Near East.

Seeing Nineveh's end, the maidens of its patron goddess sob or mourn "with the voice of doves" (cf. Isa 38:14; 59:11) and beat on their breasts (cf., in a distant parallel, Luke 18:13). As many have noted, this parallels depictions of gods or goddesses who lament the departure of their statue from a captured city.[68] This element rounds out the author's focus on the citadel.

Nineveh's Defenders Flee (2:9[8])

The text now explores the last moments of Nineveh's existence as the Assyrian capital (cf. 2:6[5]), describing first one of the Assyrian reactions to its fall. Even though this verse focuses on the fleeing troops (2:9[8]b–e), the image is inseparable from the city as a whole, and hence "Nineveh" is mentioned for the first time since 1:1.

While earlier water imagery (2:7[6]) probably had a literal and/or ideological basis, here the image of a pool is nothing more than a simile: Nineveh stood for decades, even centuries, untroubled and undisturbed (at least compared to the events of 612 BCE). Once a pool's integrity is fractured, however, it is impossible to retain the water it contained. The contrast between the first and second halves of the verse is made clear by the two ו conjunctions that appear at their head: "(ו) Nineveh was like a pool of water throughout her days, but now (ו) they flee. . . ."[69]

The two sections of the verse are further distinguished by a shift from the simile in the first part to a description of literal flight in the second. The command to halt is almost certainly directed to soldiers: there is no reason for the general population not to flee, while soldiers are expected to fight until the death or surrender. "Halt!" is the only Assyrian direct speech in the entire book, and it adds realism and conveys some of the alarm and chaos that accompanied the fall of the city. It also places the reader at a particular moment in the city's fall—the military leaders have not yet conceded defeat (cf. 2:6[5]), for it is they who prohibit the flight of their troops, but at least some of the rank-and-file are sufficiently unnerved to abandon their posts for safety.[70]

that her descent to the underworld is unnecessary. Longman, "Nahum," 806, and Delcor, among others, favor a reference to Ishtar or her cult statue here, achieved by emending MT's וְהֻצַּב, "it is set up/appointed," to צְבִי, "beauty." See Mathias Delcor, "Allusions à la déesse Istar en Nahum 2,8?," *Bib* 58 (1977): 73–83. If the referent is not Ishtar herself, a more general personification of the city is perhaps plausible, as suggested by Roberts, *Nahum, Habakkuk, and Zephaniah*, 66; David S. Vanderhooft, *The Neo-Babylonian Empire and Babylon in the Latter Prophets*, HSM 59 (Atlanta: Scholars Press, 1999), 182 n.225.

68. Note the frequent presence of this motif for numerous gods in "The Lament for Sumer and Urim," ETCSL translation: t.2.2.3, http://etcsl.orinst.ox.ac.uk/cgi-bin/etcsl.cgi?text=t.2.2.3#.

69. Cf. *J-M*, 602 and the analogous uses in discourse in Job 2:3; Isa 30:20; Ezek 28:2; Hos 7:15.

70. The masculine gender of the fleeing subject in 2:9[8]b could conceivably refer to the water of 2:9[8]a, which is also masculine. The simile seems to end after 2:9[8]a or after 2:9[8]b, since both the water and the fleeing soldiers are masculine. While

Figure 4.1g: Geographical Perspective with Respect to Nineveh (2:9[8])

Outside Nineveh (far)	Outside Nineveh (near)	Suburbs and/or wall	Wall	Citadel	City
					City: defenders (2:9[8])
Outside Nineveh (far) (2:2[1])	Outside Nineveh (near) (2:4[3])	Suburbs and/or wall (2:5[4])	Wall (2:6[5])	Citadel: palace (2:7[6])	City: treasuries (2:10[9])
				Citadel: temple (2:8[7])	City: inhabitants (2:11[10])

The calls apparently go unheeded, and the last of Nineveh's defenses dissipate like water.

Nineveh Plundered (2:10[9])

Without insisting on the chronological order of every scene in 2:2–11[1–10], it is clear that here the battle is over and the city has fallen. The verse divides naturally into two bicola, with two parallel lines each. The parallel commands to "plunder" in 2:10[9]a–b are addressed (whether by YHWH, the author, or Babylonian military personnel is not clear) to the conquering army and use the same verb (בזז) but have different objects: silver and gold. These two elements, and even their order, are the standard description of material wealth in Biblical Hebrew[71] and so should not be thought of as limiting the plunder to objects made of these two metals. Further, it is quite unlikely that the author thought of Nineveh as stocked with only two precious metals. Given his evident familiarity with the empire and the fact that Nineveh contained a dizzying variety of precious things, there are ample grounds for taking the phrase as a merism (in which several elements of a group or whole refer to the whole) in its widest sense.

As we saw earlier, the Babylonian Chronicle gives a very simplified account of the taking of Nineveh, and one of only five elements it mentions is the plunder: "They carried off the vast booty of the city and the temple."[72] Nineveh was the repository for vast and varied riches, the majority of which had come through conquest or vassal payment of subjugated states.[73] Esarhaddon (680–669 BCE) concludes a summary of many of his campaigns with the statement "I carried off their heaped-up possessions to Assyria (and) counted their gods, their helpers, as booty."[74] As another example from the same century in which Nineveh fell, Esarhaddon states that after defeating the rebellious vassal Abdi-Milkūti, he "carried off his wife, his sons, his daughters, his palace retainers, silver, gold, goods and property, precious stones, garments with trimming and linen(s), everything of value from his palace in huge quantities."[75] Still closer to the time of Nahum, Assurbanipal lists in detail the spoil he

waters do occasionally flee before YHWH when he comes in judgment (Pss 104:7; 114:3, 5; cf. also Nah 1:4), their personification here would be unexpected, and a call for them to halt would be without precedent in the OT (note, however, the announcement of its limits to a personified ocean in Job 38:11).

71. It occurs in descriptions of the patriarchs (Gen 13:2), in Israelite descriptions of Egyptian wealth (Gen 44:8), in descriptions of raw material for cult statues in the Decalogue (Exod 20:23), in Balaam's description of Balak's wealth (Num 22:18; 24:13), as part of an expanded list of spoils in the context of the conquest (Josh 6:24), as a description of David's wealth (2 Sam 8:11), and in later texts (Ezra 7:15; Hag 2:8) that refer to the contents of the Second Temple.

72. Grayson, *ABC*, 94 (Chronicle 3, line 45). In addition to the plundering, the Chronicle mentions "encamping" against the city, the following three-month siege, the defeat, and the destruction of the city.

73. J. Daryl Charles, "Plundering the Lion's Den: A Portrait of Divine Fury (Nahum 2:3–11)," *GTJ* 10.2 (1989): 183–201 (197–98).

74. Leichty, *The Royal Inscriptions of Esarhaddon*, 21 (Nineveh A, col. Iv).

75. Leichty, *The Royal Inscriptions of Esarhaddon*, 48, from Nineveh D = Nineveh S, col. 2′.

Figure 4.1h: Geographical Perspective with Respect to Nineveh (2:10[9])

					City: defenders (2:9[8])
Outside Nineveh (far) (2:2[1])	Outside Nineveh (near) (2:4[3])	Suburbs and/or wall (2:5[4])	Wall (2:6[5])	Citadel: palace (2:7[6])	**City: treasuries (2:10[9])**
				Citadel: temple (2:8[7])	City: inhabitants (2:11[10])

took from Thebes around 663 BCE: "Silver, gold, precious stones, the goods of his palace, . . . great horses, . . . two tall obelisks, fashioned of glittering electrum, whose weight was 2500 talents. . . . Booty, heavy and countless, I carried away from Thebes."[76] Scenes of tallying the spoils are likewise common on the bas-reliefs that decorated Assyrian palaces.[77]

The parallelism of the third and fourth lines makes it likely that "wealth" (כָּבֹד) is in apposition with the preceding "treasure/treasury" (תְּכוּנָה), and the Masoretic accents confirm that the break after "treasure/treasury" takes precedence over the following break (after "glory/riches").[78] The two lines reinforce the wide extent of the "silver . . . gold" merism in the first half of the verse while using more general terms.[79] The first clause emphasizes the endless extent of the city's repository (תְּכוּנָה) or treasury/storehouse, while the second underlines the variety of the treasures found there.[80]

By focusing its four lines on the despoiling of the empire, 2:10[9] brings into view Nineveh's wealth only to redistribute it. The conqueror becomes the conquered, and its inestimable riches are lost to the Babylonians. Whether or not it is correct to see Ishtar's image and temple in 2:8[7], the plundering mentioned here surely included stripping decorations from its temples.[81]

Nineveh Desolated, Its Population Defeated (2:11[10])

The final element in Nahum's proleptic description of Nineveh's fall focuses on the subjective effects of the city's fall on its population. While "all/every" appears twice later in the verse, the referent surely does not include the victor. The opening clause gives a global perspective and uses assonance (similar vowel sounds) and consonance (similar consonantal sounds) to emphasize the holistic nature of the city's fall. Each word is longer than the preceding one for added effect (בּוּקָה וּמְבוּקָה וּמְבֻלָּקָה, *bûqâ ûmĕbūqâ ûmĕbullāqâ*), and this progressive effect is felt by the reader in much the same way that Nineveh's fall must have gradually overwhelmed the psyche of the Assyrian populace.

76. Piepkorn, *Historical Prism Inscriptions of Ashurbanipal*, 38–41, cited in Spronk, *Nahum*, 101.

77. Mehmet-Ali Ataç, *The Mythology of Kingship in Neo-Assyrian Art* (Cambridge: Cambridge University Press, 2010), 63–64.

78. The *zaqeph qaton* that occurs with תְּכוּנָה is more disjunctive than the *zaqeph* that occurs with כָּבֹד; David Robinson and Elisabeth Levy, "The Masoretes and the Punctuation of Biblical Hebrew" (n.p., British & Foreign Bible Society Machine Assisted Translation Team, 2002), 15.

79. Longman, "Nahum," 807, draws attention to the same phenomenon in Isa 2:7.

80. See *HALOT*, 1731.While some suggest repointing כָּבֹד at the head of 2:10[9]d as a verb (cf. Gen 13:2), the nominal form is perfectly intelligible (cf. Gen 31:1; Isa 10:16; 22:24; 60:13; 66:12). Fabry, *Nahum*, 176, discusses the terminology for Nineveh's material wealth in detail.

81. Esarhaddon mentions that he used the spoils of vanquished foes to build and embellish "shrines of cult centers," including those of gods at Nineveh; Leichty, *The Royal Inscriptions of Esarhaddon*, 22 (Nineveh A, col. v).

Figure 4.1i: Geographical Perspective with Respect to Nineveh (2:10[9])

					City: defenders (2:9[8])
Outside Nineveh (far) (2:2[1])	Outside Nineveh (near) (2:4[3])	Suburbs and/or wall (2:5[4])	Wall (2:6[5])	Citadel: palace (2:7[6])	City: treasuries (2:10[9])
				Citadel: temple (2:8[7])	**City: inhabitants (2:11[10])**

This potent introduction is followed by four clauses, each of which is also longer (whether in terms of syllables or words) than the preceding one. Brian Tidiman suggests that 2:11[10]b, d refer to internal reactions while 2:11[10]c, e make reference to external physical phenomena, yielding an AB-AB structure.[82] By including both internal and external manifestations of fear and discomposure, this verse spans the spectrum of the whole human being, much as its last two lines explicitly include the whole (civilian) population. "Melting hearts" indicate a loss of courage in the face of imminent danger or disaster (cf. Deut 1:28; 20:8; Josh 2:11; 5:1; 7:5; 2 Sam 17:10; Ps 22:14; Ezek 21:12[7]; Isa 13:7; 19:1). "Knocking knees" (cf. similar expressions only in Isa 28:7; Jer 10:4; Ezek 7:17; 21:12[7]) in Biblical Hebrew can evidence either grief (cf. Ezek 7:17) or fear of impending disaster (Ezek 21:12[7]), and the use here can reflect both grief at the city's destruction as well as the emotional and physical discomposure felt by those who witnessed the carnage and mayhem of their city's fall.

"Trembling is in every loin" (cf. Isa 21:3) is captured idiomatically by John Oswalt as "abdominal pains,"[83] although the "loins" (מָתְנַיִם) are also the metaphorical location of "strength and vigor."[84] A literal rendering captures well the intensity of the Assyrians' emotional reaction to Nineveh's capture but is ultimately inseparable from the figurative sense. Exegetes debate whether the last line of 2:11[10] expresses the collection (קבץ, "gather") of color in the face, and thus redness or flushing, or whether the color normally in the face collects elsewhere, producing paleness.[85] Since the subject of the verb is "all their faces," the color is best seen as coming to those faces, which become red or dark.[86] This little puzzle aside, the image is clearly one of strong reaction, whether terror, uncertainty, shame, or simply emotional collapse in the face of the city's fall (cf. the same phrase in Joel 2:6, where it is a reaction to imminent disaster).[87]

Taken as a whole, 2:2–11[1–10] contributes in several ways to the book's unfolding vision of

82. Tidiman, *Nahoum, Habaquq, Sophonie*, 103.

83. John Oswalt, *The Book of Isaiah: Chapters 1–39*, NICOT (Grand Rapids: Eerdmans, 1986), 392.

84. Victor P. Hamilton, "מתנים," *NIDOTTE* 2:1150.

85. See *HALOT*, 909.

86. Commenting on a similar expression, Wildberger sensibly suggests that "growing pale when in terror and becoming red in the face when agitated are both reactions that can be described and used interchangeably and both can certainly serve as external indicators pointing to a deeply upsetting event." Hans Wildberger, *Isaiah 13–27*, CC, trans. T. H. Trapp (Minneapolis: Fortress, 1997), 24. Expressions similar to that in Nah 2:11[10] occur in Isa 13:7–8 and Jer 30:6.

87. Other possibilities are discussed by Christensen, *Nahum*, 301–33, and Spronk, *Nahum*, 103–4, who also notes a similar (but not metaphorical) description of "anxiety" in *KTU* 1.3, where Tiamat receives Baal's call to present herself before him as bad news: "her feet shake, behind, her back muscles snap, above, her face sweats, her vertebrae rattle, her spine goes weak" ("The Baʿlu Myth," trans. Dennis Pardee [*COS* 1.86:252]). Oswalt, *The Book of Isaiah: Chapters 1–39*, 305, correlates redness with shame and lack of color with fear. Johnston, "Nahum's Rhetorical Allusions to Neo-Assyrian Treaty Curses," 415–36, suggests that the closest parallel appears in the Vassal Treaty of Esarhaddon, which expresses the king's wish that the flesh of any unfaithful vassal and his entire family be "as black as [bitu]men, pitch and

Assyria's downfall. After four sarcastic commands to the Assyrians to prepare their defenses and a brief reflection on this event's relation to Judah's restoration, the text focuses on the attack, fall, and despoiling of Nineveh. Various scenes pass before the reader's eyes, alternating between the attackers and the defenders. First, the reader sees the impressive Medo-Babylonian army and witnesses the attack of its chariots (2:2[1], 4–5[3–4]). This is contrasted with the tardy and woefully inadequate response of the Assyrian defenders, chaos in the palace, the stripping and deportation of Ishtar's image, and the panicked flight of the Assyrian defenders (2:6–9[5–8]). A final pair of contrasting images see Nineveh's wealth transformed into the attacker's spoils (2:10[9]) and the city, and especially its surviving population, transformed into helpless, disheartened and impotent captives (2:11[10]).

The general order of the battle is clear, and the simplicity of the event in itself prompts the reader to wonder why so much attention is given to the attackers' formidable prowess and the defenders' inability to resist the Babylonian onslaught. The answer to that question is best sought against the background of an empire that routinely vaunted its own military prowess (and a great deal of attendant violence) in its prolific descriptions of its expansion across and control over the ancient Near East. Perhaps to avoid giving the impression that the Medo-Babylonian force was invincible, the text describes it in relatively restrained terms. Its focus on demonstrating Assyria's vulnerability or weakness (recalling that Nahum is a prophecy first transmitted when Assyria was at its height, 1:12) is best served by another strategy, one that details and fully exploits the anticipated failings of those defending the Neo-Assyrian Empire's last and most impressive capital city.

The proleptic depiction of Nineveh's fall is calculated to undercut several central elements that supported the Assyrian Empire's bombastic, self-glorifying propaganda as disseminated by royal inscriptions and bas-reliefs, military action, diplomatic affairs (including stela placed at the far reaches of the empire), and other modes of communication. It targets both the empire's functional heart (its military might, represented by Nineveh's defenders) and its administrative and ideological center (Nineveh itself, including its king, palaces, and temples). By anticipating in detail what Nineveh's fall could or would look like, the book rendered it more plausible (ideally, inevitable) than it would have seemed to Judeans in the seventh century BCE. By the same token it assured believing Judeans that Nineveh's fall was part of a far-reaching commitment on YHWH's part to restore Judah and reinforced their desire to see YHWH's word come to pass.

4. The Fall of Assyria Anticipated (2:12–14[11–13])

Rather like the prolepsis that moved from warning Nineveh of its danger through the unfolding attack on the city to its spoiling and the disappearance of all its power in 2:2–11[1–10], this sardonic prophecy also mixes anticipation of Assyria's end with visions of its destruction as a fait accompli.[88] In light of the Assyrian monarch's identity as a

naphtha" and, in a later curse, "altogether like the flesh of a chameleon" (585–87, 591–93, http://oracc.museum.upenn.edu/saao/saa02/P336598). The apparently inevitable difference in color between these two images cautions against drawing only on one and not the other in connection with Nahum, however, and the sense of 2:11[10] is clear apart from such possible parallels.

88. Some authors see a major unit ending at 2:11[10] and include 2:12–14[11–13] with 3:1–19 (e.g., Floyd, *Minor Prophets*, Renaud, *Michée, Sophonie, Nahum*). Christensen, *Nahum*, treats 2:12–14[11–13] separately from both 2:2–11[1–10] and 3:1–19, but many authors favor treating 2:2–14[1–13] as a unit, an approach I follow here (cf. Fabry, *Nahum*; Roberts,

lion-like figure who successfully protects his lair and his pride, its metaphorical presentation of the empire in leonine terms is particularly appropriate following the description of Nineveh's fall in 2:2–11[1–10]. Over against suggestions that Nahum is hateful, vengeful, or otherwise morally objectionable, we should remember that in this unit and throughout Nahum, Assyria is unrepentant and committed to its identity and role as YHWH's and Judah's opponent. The discourse of this subsection is illocutive speech, which "is itself the deed that it effects," dismissing Nineveh's power and accomplishments.[89]

Anticipation of Assyria's Demise (2:12[11])

The announcement of Assyria's fall begins with a rhetorical question regarding Nineveh's existence. The rhetorical nature of the question is apparent on the level of grammar as well as in the text's semantics. Taking the grammar first, in 2:12–13[11–12] the empire is the subject, and although verbal tense is ambiguous due to the prevalence of participles, the temporal setting still contrasts with the clearly future tense of 2:14[13].[90] This contrast in tense corresponds to a clear change in verbal subject, from Assyria in 2:12–13[11–12] to YHWH in 2:14[13]. Although all non-Assyrians knew only too well where Nineveh was, 2:12–13[11–12] speaks of it as if it is already gone, while 2:14[13] explains its unexpected disappearance.

Before considering this rhetorical question's semantics, we should first consider why the author has chosen to portray Nineveh as a lion's den and the empire as a pride of lions. In the Introduction we noted several ways that lion imagery was integrated in Neo-Assyrian royal ideology. Perhaps most notable in this context are the king's relish for killing lions on the one hand, and his self-description as a lion in his military role on the other.[91]

To begin with the king as a lion hunter, why should a monarch choose to hunt lions as opposed to any number of other, safer activities? While explanations tied to the demonstration of the king's physical prowess or courage are plausible per se, the activity is connected in specific ways to mythical and ideological strands.[92] One of the Assyrian king's primary roles was, as a shepherd, to protect his flock of citizens from the threat of savage beasts (literal or figurative), of which the lion was the clearest representative.[93] In more general terms,

Nahum, Habakkuk, and Zephaniah; Tidiman, *Nahoum, Habaquq, Sophonie*; Spronk, *Nahum*; Perlitt, *Die Propheten Nahum, Habakuk, Zephanja*).

89. Judith Butler, *Excitable Speech: A Politics of the Performative* (New York: Routledge, 1997), 3.

90. The only clause in 2:14[13] which has Assyria as its subject negates the significance of that grammar by eliminating the subject from the scene: "the voice of your envoys will no longer be heard."

91. Several rooms in Assurbanipal's North Palace at Nineveh were decorated with series of reliefs depicting royal lion hunts, with the king sometimes in his chariot and other times on foot. See John Curtis, "The Dying Lion," *Iraq* 54 (1992): 113–17 and plates. Elena Cassin, "Le roi et le lion," *RHR* 198 (1981): 369–70 (author's translation), summarizes the Assyrian kings' attitudes and self-descriptions (Neo-Assyrian and earlier) thus: "The royal inscriptions demonstrate the close relationship one perceives between the fury that inflames the king's heart because of his enemies and his attitude as a lion ready to do battle."

92. See Cassin, "Le roi et le lion," 357–60, 381 and passim; Michael B. Dick, "The Neo-Assyrian Royal Lion Hunt and YHWH's Answer to Job," *CBQ* 125 (2006): 243–70; Natalie N. May, "Triumph as an Aspect of the Neo-Assyrian Decorative Program," in *Organization, Representation, and Symbols of Power in the Ancient Near East*, ed. G. Wilhelm (Winona Lake, IN: Eisenbrauns, 2008), 461–88.

93. See the data surveyed by Cassin, "Le roi et le lion," 375–85. The lion hunt reliefs in Assurbanipal's North Palace at Nineveh spanned several rooms and hallways, and include scenes from Assurbanipal's victory over the Elamites as proof of his preservation of order and his ability to extend the kingdom; cf. Dick, "Neo-Assyrian Royal Lion Hunt," 246–47, 255; May, "Triumph," 477–80; Elnathan Weissert, "Royal Hunt and Royal Triumph in a Prism Fragment of Ashurbanipal," in *Assyria 1995*, ed. Simo Parpola and R. Whiting (Helsinki: Neo-Assyrian Text Corpus Project, 1997), 349.

the king was charged with keeping chaos at bay, and the royal Assyrian lion hunt was thus charged with religious significance evocative of Ninurta's defeat of leonine Anzû, who threatened cosmic order.[94] Indeed, the royal lion hunt in its entirety held religious meaning, and at its conclusion a libation offering would be poured out over the dead lion's body.

In some cases the mythical and literal aspects of the king's role as shepherd converged. Assurbanipal's Great Hunting Text (K 2867+) "describes at length how, prior to the arrival of the royal savior, prides of lions harassed people and animals living peaceably in the plains." The text recounts that "the shepherds and herdsmen had been complaining that lions were dev[ouring in the cattle-pen(s) and] sheep-fold(s)," and only a royal response could eliminate the problem.[95] Another of Assurbanipal's inscriptions depicts the problem in similar terms: "In the plai[n, a wide expanse]—[befo]re my arrival hug[e lions, a fier]ce [mountain breed, attacked] (there) the cattle-p[en(s)]."[96] Ample rainfall had apparently increased the territory on which lions in parts of Assyria could hunt, and the lions' arrival in new areas endangered the human and animal populations there. In such cases Assurbanipal's lion hunts were clearly essential to his divinely authorized role as his people's shepherd, preserving them from danger and keeping the forces of chaos and death at bay.

Assurbanipal also organized hunts in an arena near Nineveh, a localized exercise of his royal shepherd role that allowed him to demonstrate his importance for the protection of the capital city in an unprecedented way. Again attested by bas-reliefs from his North Palace at Nineveh (Room C), these hunts involved the release of "raging" lions from their cages within the arena.[97] The series of reliefs offers (from left to right) a panoramic overview of the event: some of Nineveh's residents as spectators on a hill outside the enclosure; a well-guarded perimeter maintained by spearmen and hunting dogs; in the arena eleven lions struck by arrows and in various stages of death, the king in an oversized chariot with his bow drawn, and seven more lions, six of whom are dead while the last is just emerging from his cage; and finally another perimeter on the far right of the image.[98] In the same context the king is said to have killed eighteen lions, each representing one of Nineveh's gates and so demonstrating his ability to defend the city from any attack.[99] Since Nahum is set during Assurbanipal's reign it is intriguing that despite the long history of this tradition in Assyrian royal ideology, one can still observe that Assurbanipal's court went

> out of their way to broaden this theme and to contribute to its content. Never before in Assyrian art has [*sic*] the relentless quarrel between man and beast been so dramatically portrayed as it was in the hunting reliefs of the North Palace of Nineveh; and none of the hunting accounts integrated into early Neo-Assyrian historical writings matches the literary qualities of Ashurbanipal's hunting texts.[100]

94. Dick, "The Neo-Assyrian Lion Hunt," 252.

95. Weissert, "Royal Hunt and Royal Triumph," 342.

96. As restored by Weissert, "Royal Hunt and Royal Triumph," 343.

97. Ibid., 351.

98. See Ibid., 354–55, figure 3, and in more detail Richard D. Barnett, *Sculptures from the North Palace of Ashurbanipal at Nineveh, 668–627 B.C.* (London: British Museum, 1976), plates VI–IX. See also the reliefs in a video with excellent commentary by Kahn Academy ("Ashurbanipal Hunting Lions") at https://www.khanacademy.org/humanities/ancient-art-civilizations/ancient-near-east1/assyrian/v/ashurbanipal-hunting-lions-assyrian.

99. Weissert, "Royal Hunt and Royal Triumph," 354. Assurbanipal adorned the eighteen entries of his capital city with lion figurines (Berlejung, "Erinnerungen," 334).

100. Weissert, "Royal Hunt and Royal Triumph," 339.

While lions as threats to the Assyrian king and his realm are manifestations of chaos and so must be eliminated, leonine imagery is used in a very different way when the king himself is portrayed as a lion when he attacks his enemies. In this capacity Adad-nirari II (911–891 BCE) self-identified as "a potent lion,"[101] Sargon II (721–705 BCE) said that he was like "a wild lion who is lordly with frightfulness" on the battlefield,[102] Sennacherib claimed that "like a lion I rampaged,"[103] and Esarhaddon recounted that he "raged like a lion" when he heard of his brothers' attempts to usurp his throne[104] and when he undertook his campaign to subdue Egypt in 671.[105] In a stela memorializing one of his victories (Zincerli), Esarhaddon (680–669 BCE) further described himself as a warrior king "whose advance is like a flood and whose attitude is like that of a terrible lion."[106] The king's violence against leonine threats to his people and the king's lion-like violence against his enemies express together his unparalleled ability to establish and preserve order throughout his empire against even the most imposing threats while defeating the chaos that predominates outside its boundaries.

With this background in mind, the rhetorical force of the question in 2:12[11] becomes apparent. Nineveh, the source of leonine violence against its lesser adversaries and the locus of order that opposes all anti-empire chaos, has essentially disappeared! To this 2:12[11] adds an emphasis on the size and territory of the lion's pride. In terms of the pride's numerical size, in addition to the "lion" (אַרְיֵה, three times) the text mentions the lionesses (לָבִיא) and a variety of juveniles (the "young lions," כְּפִיר, as well as the still younger "cubs" or whelps, גּוּר), painting a picture of a sizable pride of lions at the height of its power (cf. 1:12). Similarly, while Nineveh is primarily in view here (as it was in 2:2–11[1–10]), its organic relation to the rest of the empire probably lies behind the text's mention of both a lair (מְעוֹן, 2:12[11]a), presumably equivalent to the empire's homeland, and feeding grounds (מִרְעֶה, 2:12[11]b), most likely the far-flung peoples and territories brought under the empire's control.[107] In addition to all this, the reader is reminded that the empire dominated the ancient Near East so completely that until now there existed no foe who might pose a serious threat ("there is nothing that startles [them]," 2:12[11]e).

The Lion, His Pride, and His Prey (2:13[12])

The rhetorical question posed in 2:12[11]a seems to include all of 2:13[12] as well, which adds to the already extensive description of Assyria's size and power a vivid portrayal of its violence. In keeping with the link between leonine imagery and the Assyrian king, here the lion is the only actor, while his cubs and lionesses receive the prey he kills and brings to them.[108] While this may well diverge from

101. Sarah C. Melville, "Adad-Nirari II," in *The Ancient Near East: Historical Sources in Translation*, ed. M. Chavalas, *BSAH* (Oxford: Blackwell, 2006), 282.

102. Sarah C. Melville, "Sargon II," in *The Ancient Near East: Historical Sources in Translation*, ed. M. Chavalas, *BSAH* (Oxford: Blackwell, 2006), 340.

103. Sarah C. Melville, "Sennacherib," in *The Ancient Near East: Historical Sources in Translation*, ed. M. Chavalas, *BSAH* (Oxford: Blackwell, 2006), 348.

104. Nineveh Prism A (Leichty, *The Royal Inscriptions of Esarhaddon*, 13).

105. Nineveh Prism E = Prism S (Leichty, *The Royal Inscriptions of Esarhaddon*, 53).

106. Cited in Cassin, "Le roi et le lion," 371 (author's translation).

107. Similarly, the closing verse of the section (2:14[13]) broadens its perspective to include various aspects of the empire as a whole.

108. Gelston, *The Twelve Minor Prophets*, 112*, thinks that a *hiphil* infinitive construct (להביא) is most likely behind the MT's לָבִיא, and the versions seem to have understood some form of "go," from בוא. Readings of the relevant term in 4QpNah differ; contrast Florentino García-Martíntez and Eibert J. C. Tigchelaar, *The Dead Sea Scrolls Study Edition*, 2 vols. (Leiden: Brill; Grand Rapids: Eerdmans, 2000), 1:336, who reads לבוא in both the citation of the biblical text and the pesher, and John M.

(contemporary) zoological descriptions of the roles of various members of a lion pride, the text surely does not intend to offer a precise description but rather accommodates the leonine metaphor to the realities of the Assyrian monarch and the accompanying ideology, especially its focus on the king to the exclusion of all other actors (including his own army).[109] Moreover, Neo-Assyrian reliefs and royal inscriptions limit their representations of humans and animals alike almost exclusively to males,[110] most likely due to their creators' association of masculine gender with potency, vigor, authority, dominance, and rule.[111] The focus on the male that leads the pride is thus inevitable, given the ideology of (male) kingship in Neo-Assyria.

Continuing the focus on the lion that leads the pride, the descriptions of his aggressive activity, his victims, and his ability to provide for his pride are highly detailed. The lion "has torn" (טרף) enough prey for his cubs, "strangles" (*piel* participle of חנק) prey for his lionesses, and fills his lairs with prey (טֶרֶף) and his dens with torn flesh (טְרֵפָה). The three verbs and four objects, plus the emphasis on the ample supply of food provided by the lion (בְּדֵי, "enough;" *piel* of מלא, "filled"), perfectly adapt the metaphor of the lion pride to the ideological self-presentation of the Assyrian monarch, who routinely portrays himself (in the first-person singular) as the warrior who defeats his foes, with his army in tow.

YHWH Commits to Destroying Assyria (2:14[13])

This "challenge formula" appears approximately twenty times in oracles (usually against the nations) in which YHWH is the speaker (e.g., Jer 50:31; 51:25; Ezek 26:3; 28:22; Nah 3:5).[112] While it is true that the phrase "I am against you" excludes Judah from the role of avenger and that actions against Nineveh are consistently attributed to YHWH (1:9, 14; 2:14[13]; 3:5–6), this formula's greatest significance lies in its reaffirmation that the fall of Assyria is not merely a feat of the Medo-Babylonian army whose effectiveness is evident earlier in Nah 2. On the contrary, it is the result of YHWH's punishment of Assyria's self-serving violence, autonomy, and service of other gods (1:9–11, 14), and is a specific, partial fulfillment of his commitment to completely destroy those who oppose him (1:2–8).

YHWH's retribution is described in four parallel lines that form a chiasm. Its opening and closing lines (2:14[13]c, f) describe the literal destruction of its army and its diplomatic corps, while the middle of the chiasm consists of two metaphorical descriptions of Assyria's destruction as a lion. The verbal subject (italicized below) varies between YHWH (2:14[13]c, e) and a sword (2:14[13]d, active) and the passive Assyrian subject (2:14[13]f).

I will burn in the fire her chariots[113] (3fs);
your (2fs) young lions *the sword* will devour,

Allegro with the collaboration of Arnold A. Anderson, *Qumrân Cave 4: I (4Q158–4Q186)*, DJDJ V (Oxford: Clarendon, 1968), 38, 41, who read לביא in the biblical citation but לבוא in the pesher. In favor of retaining the MT, Joel 1:6 has in parallel אַרְיֵה and לָבִיא, which are asyndetic here, and the Masoretic tradition attests no variants for Nah 2:14[13]. Spronk, *Nahum*, 105, notes that Isa 5:29 collocates "lioness" (לָבִיא) with the term that precedes the word in question here, כְּפִירִים, and observes that Nah 2:13[12] includes lion, lioness, and cub.

109. Cf. Fuchs, "Assyria at War," 381: "Leading every single attack in person and from the front, omnipresent, throwing themselves happily into the very midst of battle, rushing on, yelling, shooting, killing, in breathtaking races to glorious victories: that is how Assyrian kings wanted to be remembered."

110. Ataç, *The Mythology of Kingship*, 58.

111. Irene J. Winter, "Sex, Rhetoric, and the Public Monument: The Alluring Body of Naram-Sin of Agade," in *Sexuality in Ancient Art: Near East, Egypt, Greece, and Italy*, ed. N. B. Kampen, Cambridge Studies in New Art History and Criticism (Cambridge: Cambridge University Press, 1996), 11.

112. See the full list of references in Christensen, *Nahum*, 318. Simon Sherwin, "'I Am against You': YHWH's Judgment on the Nations and Its Ancient Near Eastern Context," *TynBul* 54.2 (2003): 149–60, examines the phenomenon.

113. In favor of retaining the MT's 3fs "her" here, the singular form "chariot" (רֶכֶב) with a 3fs suffix is paralleled by the use of רֶכֶב with a 3ms suffix for a collective (Exod 14:6; Judg 5:28; 1 Sam 8:12, etc.). The motif of burning chariots as

and *I will* cut off from the earth your (2fs) taking
of prey.
The voice of your (2m/fs) envoys will no longer
be heard.

While the behavior described in 2:13[12] would not be unnatural or excessive for a literal lion, which according to 2:12[11] would need to provide a substantial and continuous supply of meat for his sizable pride,[114] the divine challenge "I am against you" in 2:14[13] triggers the application of the metaphor to the Assyrian ruler and his empire.[115] The transfer to the Assyrian king or empire of the violence and scope of the lion's "tearing" and "strangling" of its prey and "filling" of its caves with the same creates a picture of an empire whose treatment of other human beings is unacceptably destructive and whose material wealth is both excessive and the corrupt fruit of predatory violence.[116] While the lion's habit of preying on lesser animals is natural and without moral coloring (apart, that is, from Isa 11:6; 65:25; Rom 8:22, and a few similar texts), the metaphor depicts Assyria as preying *on other human beings* with the same raw violence and power.

YHWH's punishment of such behavior entails a range of grave consequences for Assyria. First, its chariots will be burned (cf. Josh 11:6 for the same motif). Assyrian combat strategies exploited the combination of the bow and the chariot, but even by itself, the armored Assyrian chariot, which had been refined over decades, was an extremely effective weapon.[117] In a related context, the king's chariot and a chariot associated with the Assyrian deity Nergal were involved in a victory ritual that saw Assyrian officials ride in one chariot and the king ride in his own in an imitation of the successfully concluded battle in which "the main protagonist is the king, who accompanied by his retinue, captures the enemy."[118] Whether Nahum has in view these particular chariots or the army's much larger chariot force, the semantics of the motif involve YHWH's complete destruction of the already neutralized enemy or his celebration of the same.

---

a sign of victory appears in biblical sources (Josh 11:6), and similar motifs are in the Succession Treaty of Esarhaddon: "[if you break this treaty] may all the gods who are called by name in this treaty tablet break your bow and subject you to your enemy; may they turn over the bow in your hands and make your chariots run backwards," SAA 02 006, lines 573–75; http://oracc.museum.upenn.edu/saao/saa02/corpus; "([If you should sin against] this [treaty] of Esarhaddon, king of Assyria, [and of] his sons and grandsons,) ditto; just as this chariot is drenched with blood up to its base-board, so may your chariots be drenched with your own blood in the midst of your enemy," SAA 02 006, lines 612A–15; http://oracc.museum.upenn.edu/saao/saa02/corpus.

However, in the Nahum pesher (4Q169) several of the pronominal suffixes in 2:14[13] are masculine (note also the mixed form of the suffix on the last word of the verse in MT, מַלְאָכֵכֵה); see Maurya P. Morgan, "Nahum Pesher," in *Pesharim, Other Commentaries, and Related Documents*, ed. J. H. Charlesworth, PTSDSSP 6B (Tübingen: Mohr Siebeck; Louisville: Westminster John Knox, 2002), 148–49. Pieter B. Hartog, "Nahum 2:14 Text-Critical Notes," *VT* 63 (2013): 546–54, and Gelston, *The Twelve Minor Prophets*, 88, 112*–13*, argue that the reading רובכה, "your host/multitude," is original (cf. *HALOT*, 1173). The apparent combination of masculine and feminine suffixes on the verse's last word suggests that those transmitting the Masoretic text were aware of this variety. The fact that the image of burning a host (of an army) would be without a parallel in the OT (cf. only Jer 5:14) makes any conclusion difficult, and because of the consistency of MT's feminine referent here, I retain the MT.

114. This is clear from the imperfect form of יְמַלֵּא, "filling" in 2:13[12], and should probably be inferred on that basis from the participles "tearing" and "strangling" as well. Cf. Spronk, *Nahum*, 106.

115. On leonine imagery and Neo-Assyrian royalty in general, see Ataç, *The Mythology of Kingship*, and for a case specific to Assurbanipal, see Weissert, "Royal Hunt and Royal Triumph." On the irony that may be present here, cf. Johnston, "Nahum's Rhetorical Allusions to the Neo-Assyrian Lion Motif," 287–307.

116. Note the boast of Assurbanipal: "The whole territory of my land in its entirety they filled (with them [= spoils]) to its farthest border," in Piepkorn, *Historical Prism Inscriptions of Ashurbanipal*, 83.

117. Fuchs, "Assyria at War," 393–94.

118. May, "Triumph," 462–63.

The next two lines draw on elements introduced in 2:12–13[11–12] that represent the empire on the one hand (the young lions) and its victims on the other (the prey). The sense of 2:14[13]d is immediately clear, emphasizing the young lions by placing them before the verb that announces their death, but 2:14[13]e (if read as it stands in the MT) affirms that YHWH will "cut off from the earth" those who have become the empire's prey. This is difficult to understand since "cut off" consistently involves elimination or destruction. Accordingly, Spronk suggests that the consonants be repointed to yield the infinitive "your taking of prey," which makes better sense.[119]

The final line announces the silencing of Assyria's envoys. These diplomats contributed to Assyria's self-image and imperialism as they "negotiated treaties, presented capitulation-documents, and delivered to a vassal-king the orders of his suzerain."[120] Karen Radner has argued that there may well have been an Assyrian official lodged in Jerusalem as a liason, a scenario that would add poignancy to Nahum's vision here.[121] Be that as it may, the section clearly affirms that both the empire's fearsome power and those who served to formalize it will be eliminated. Over against Assurbanipal's lion hunts that were part of his divinely authorized role as his people's protective shepherd, YHWH's announcement that he will end the Assyrian king's lion-like existence is doubly ironic. Not only will YHWH take the leonine role that the Assyrian monarch claimed, but in that role he will destroy the king as a threat to *his* people.

Canonical and Theological Significance

Knowing the End from the Beginning: Hope!

When viewed in the context of the book's opening hymn, Nahum's use of prolepsis to reinforce the certainty of Assyria's fall reinforces the book's claim that YHWH will surely conquer the forces of evil that oppose him and his people. Moreover, although the book of Nahum itself does not anticipate the final stages of redemptive history with the same anticipatory clarity, the rest of Scripture, and the NT in particular, are consistently oriented toward this endpoint, especially in the NT's emphasis on the resurrection of Jesus Christ from the dead as the "first begotten of the dead" and in its various descriptions of the consummation of all things in the new heavens and new earth.

Christ's resurrection is the undeniable confirmation of believers' justification (Rom 4:25) and thus of their fully restored relationship with God (Rom 5:1); the assurance that "as we have borne the image of the earthly man, we shall also bear the

119. Spronk, *Nahum*, 109. Alternatively, Christensen, *Nahum*, 320, argues that since Assyria is the verbal object in all four lines, one can simply supply the object here: "I will cut (you) off from the land of your prey."

120. Berlejung, "Erinnerungen," 335 (author's translation).

121. Karen Radner, "Assyrische *ṭuppi adê* als Vorbild für Deuteronomium 28,20–44?," in *Die deuteronomistischen Geschichtswerke: Redaktions-und religionsgeschichtliche Perspektiven zur "Deuteronomismus"-Diskussion in Tora und Vorderen Propheten*, ed. M. Witte et al., BZAW 365 (Berlin: de Gruyter, 2006), 351–78. I owe this reference to William Marrow, "Neo-Assyrian Influences in Manasseh's Temple?," *CBQ* 75 (2013): 55.

image of the heavenly" (1 Cor 15:49); and the divine pledge that death itself will be overcome (1 Cor 15:26). Yet "hope that is seen is no hope at all," and every Christian can expect trials of various sorts (2 Tim 3:12; Jas 1:2–4). In Pauline theology such suffering is the inevitable expression of the believer's union with Christ not only in his resurrection, but also in his death (2 Tim 2:12).

This two-fold reality also appears throughout the book of Revelation, which presents with equal clarity the suffering and persecution of the church prior to Christ's final victory and the glory of its consummated redemption. Yet it is significant that Revelation presents Christ's death and resurrection before it details the sufferings of the church in chapter 6. The book's first description of the Lord Jesus Christ presents him as "the faithful witness, the firstborn of the dead, and the ruler of kings on earth" (1:5 ESV), affirming both his sacrificial death and his ultimate victory over death, sin, and the devil. In the same way, the first presentation of Jesus Christ in the vision of the heavenly throne room (chapters 4–5) juxtaposes his title as "the Lion of the tribe of Judah" with its description of him as "a Lamb standing, as though it had been slain" (5:5–6 ESV). These images attest to the reality of suffering in believers' lives but at the same time fix our faith and hope on the one through whom we will be more than conquerers. Using a relevant image from Nahum, Rev 5:5 also affirms that whatever earthly powers militate lion-like against God's people, his rule and reign are already established, so that all that happens to them is under his control.

While having pride of place in terms of a focus on the consummation of all things, Revelation is hardly alone in turning believers' minds toward the end of the age. The Gospels contain glimpses of the coming of the kingdom (Matt 25:34–40), the eschatological banquet (Matt 8:11), and of course John's amazingly intimate, relational descriptions of our glorified state (John 14:1–3) that are in no way inferior to the Christocentric and Trinitarian focus of Revelation (John 17:24). At the same time they call all of Christ's followers to fidelity (Matt 10:32–33; 24:13).

The Christian hope is thus multifaceted and is built on the certitude that God's grace in Jesus Christ will sustain the believer through suffering and trial, that his or her adoption as a child of God will one day be consummated (Rom 8:17), and that the whole creation will finally be released from the futility to which it has been subjected (Rom 8:18–25). Hope of this magnitude cannot but transform us when we push aside our quotidian concerns and see ourselves, the church, the world, and the entire cosmos in light of what God has in store for those who love him.

CHAPTER 5

Nahum 3:1–19

E. The Deconstruction of Assyria's Pride

Main Idea of the Passage

This macrounit announces a variety of punishments against Nineveh, all of which are intended to bring shame on Assyria by contradicting its claims to glory, power, and inviolability. Regardless of what Assyria has done or might do to remain supreme, YHWH's punishment of its evil cannot be avoided or escaped.

Literary Context

The previous macrounit anticipated in detail the fall of Nineveh (2:2–11[1–10]) and of the Assyrian Empire (2:12–14[11–13]) in order to show that both were inevitable. This final macrounit takes for granted the inevitability of Assyria's fall, maintains the previous section's focus on the empire as a whole, and sharpens its rhetoric (especially in its taunts) in order to emphasize the ill-founded and idolatrous nature of its claims. Its closing focus on the "good news" of Assyria's fall connects the unit's theologically oriented critique of the empire to the "good news" of 2:1[1:15] that announces the liberation of Judah and other nations from its grasp.

A. Introduction: (1:1)
B. The Threat of YHWH's Coming Global Judgment (1:2–8)
C. Four Announcements of Assyria's Destruction and Judah's Deliverance (1:9–2:1[15])
D. The Prophetic Anticipation of Assyria's Fall (2:2–14[1–13])
➡ **E. The Deconstruction of Assyria's Pride (3:1–19)**
   1. A Woe Oracle against Nineveh/Assyria (3:1–7)
   2. A Historical Taunt (3:8–11)
   3. A Military Taunt (3:12–15c)
   4. An Economic Taunt (3:15d–17)
   5. The Final Dirge for the Assyrian King (3:18–19)

Translation and Exegetical Outline

(See pages 148–51.)

Structure and Literary Form

The macrounit consists of five subunits. After an initial woe oracle, three taunts dismiss with rhetorical flourish Nineveh's security, the empire's military preparedness and its impressive economic apparatus. The unit concludes with a dirge against the Assyrian king. The structure, literary form, and syntax of each subunit will be discussed in their respective sections below.

Explanation of the Text

1. Woe Oracle against Nineveh (3:1–7)

Woe and First Condemnation (3:1)

This subunit is the first of five in this unit, all of which undermine, ignore, or mock Assyria's grandiose claims to unlimited power, glory, and autonomy. While the preceding macrounit focused on the fall of Nineveh and Assyria in the context of military conflict, these subunits focus on deconstructing the empire's ideology and the worldview in which it and its gods are supreme. This first subunit announces the punishment of Nineveh for its abusive, materialistic, and idolatrous motivations and actions. YHWH will shame the Assyrian Empire on the international scene by exposing its weakness and ill-founded confidence.

A woe oracle typically consists of an opening pronouncement of woe, an accusation, and a pronouncement of judgment.[1] As such the oracle expresses "a threat or curse directed against the enemies of God" rather than a lament over the subject's demise.[2] After the initial "Woe!" this section dedicates similar amounts of text to condemnations of Nineveh and to a description of YHWH's punishment of its crimes.

Syntactic subordination is most evident in the grounds for Nineveh's shaming given in 3:4a, set off from the mainline by the preposition מִן, which indicates causation here.[3] That ground is reinforced by three parallel lines that are in apposition with 3:4a, all of which refer to the "prostitute" it introduces (3:4b–d). That emphatic condemnation is then followed by the description of punishment in 3:5–7. Nahum uses the emphasis created by three or more parallel lines to drive home his condemnation of Nineveh (3:1b–d), his description of carnage in battle (3:3a–g), and the empire's deceitful political strategies (3:4b–d).

1. Willem VanGemeren, *Interpreting the Prophetic Word: An Introduction to the Prophetic Literature of the Old Testament* (Grand Rapids: Zondervan, 1990), 404–5; similarly, Floyd, *Minor Prophets*, 649. Note especially the often explicit reason that links a concluding punishment to preceding condemnations in the woe oracles in Isa 10:5–19 (with כִּי at the head of 10:13 and לָכֵן, "therefore," at the head of 10:16); Amos 6:1–3, 4–7 (with לָכֵן at the head of 6:7); Mic 2:1–5 (with לָכֵן at the head of 2:3, 5); Zeph 3:1–8 (with לָכֵן at the head of 3:8).

2. Longman, "Nahum," 812.

3. Cf. Merwe, Naudé, and Kroeze, *A Biblical Hebrew Reference Grammar*, 289.

Nahum 3:1–19

			E. The Deconstruction of Assyria's Pride (3:1–19)
			1. A Woe Oracle against Nineveh/Assyria (3:1a–7e)
1a	הוֹי עִיר דָּמִים	Woe to the bloody city!	a. Woe and First Condemnation (3:1a–d)
1b	כֻּלָּהּ כַּחַשׁ	(It is) utterly deceitful!	
1c	פֶּרֶק מְלֵאָה	Of plunder (it is) full!	
1d	לֹא יָמִישׁ טָרֶף	No one takes away (its) prey.	
2a	קוֹל שׁוֹט	(There is) the sound of the whip.	b. Second Condemnation (3:2a–3g)
2b	וְקוֹל רַעַשׁ אוֹפָן	(There is) the sound (of) the rattling wheel,	
2c	וְסוּס דֹּהֵר	and (of) the rushing horse,	
2d	וּמֶרְכָּבָה מְרַקֵּדָה	and (of) the bounding chariot!	
3a	פָּרָשׁ מַעֲלֶה	Horsemen charging,	
3b	וְלַהַב חֶרֶב	the blade of the sword,	
3c	וּבְרַק חֲנִית	the flash of the spear,	
3d	וְרֹב חָלָל	multitudes of slain,	
3e	וְכֹבֶד פָּגֶר	piles of corpses!	
3f	וְאֵין קֵצֶה לַגְּוִיָּה	There is no end to the dead bodies;	
3g	יְכָשְׁלוּ בִּגְוִיָּתָם	they stumble over their dead bodies.	
4a	מֵרֹב זְנוּנֵי זוֹנָה	Because of the many debaucheries of the prostitute,	c. Third Condemnation (3:4a–d)
4b	טוֹבַת חֵן בַּעֲלַת כְּשָׁפִים	gracefully alluring, mistress of sorceries,	
4c	הַמֹּכֶרֶת גּוֹיִם בִּזְנוּנֶיהָ	who sells nations through her debaucheries	
4d	וּמִשְׁפָּחוֹת בִּכְשָׁפֶיהָ	and tribes through her sorceries,	
5a	הִנְנִי אֵלַיִךְ	"Know that I am against you!"	d. Punishment (3:5a–6c)
5b	נְאֻם יְהוָה צְבָאוֹת	Utterance of YHWH of Hosts:	
5c	וְגִלֵּיתִי שׁוּלַיִךְ עַל־פָּנָיִךְ	"I will uncover your skirts over your head,	
5d	וְהַרְאֵיתִי גוֹיִם מַעְרֵךְ	and I will show nations your nakedness	
5e	וּמַמְלָכוֹת קְלוֹנֵךְ	and kingdoms your shame!	
6a	וְהִשְׁלַכְתִּי עָלַיִךְ שִׁקֻּצִים	I will throw filth on you,	
6b	וְנִבַּלְתִּיךְ	I will declare you contemptible,	
6c	וְשַׂמְתִּיךְ כְּרֹאִי	I will make you a spectacle!	

7a	וְהָיָה כָל־רֹאַיִךְ יִדּוֹד מִמֵּךְ	Then all who see you will shrink back from you	e. Outcome (3:7a–e)
7b	וְאָמַר	and will say,	
7c	שָׁדְּדָה נִינְוֵה	'Devastated is Nineveh!	
7d	מִי יָנוּד לָהּ	Who will lament her?'	
7e	מֵאַיִן אֲבַקֵּשׁ מְנַחֲמִים לָךְ	Where can I seek comforters for you?"	
			2. A Historical Taunt (3:8a–11c)
8a	הֲתֵיטְבִי מִנֹּא אָמוֹן	"Will it go better for you than for Thebes,	a. No-Amon's Apparent Strength (3:8a–9c)
8b	הַיֹּשְׁבָה בַּיְאֹרִים	that sat by the Nile's waters,	
8c	מַיִם סָבִיב לָהּ	with water surrounding her?	
8d	אֲשֶׁר־חֵיל יָם	Whose strength was a sea,	
8e	מִיָּם חוֹמָתָהּ	her rampart water?	
9a	כּוּשׁ עָצְמָה	Cush was her strength,	
9b	וּמִצְרַיִם וְאֵין קֵצֶה	Egypt too, and without limit;	
9c	פּוּט וְלוּבִים הָיוּ בְּעֶזְרָתֵךְ	Put and Libya were her helpers.	
10a	גַּם־הִיא לַגֹּלָה	Yet even she became an exile,	b. No-Amon's Stunning Fall (3:10a–e)
10b	הָלְכָה בַשֶּׁבִי	she went into captivity;	
10c	גַּם עֹלָלֶיהָ יְרֻטְּשׁוּ בְּרֹאשׁ כָּל־חוּצוֹת	moreover, her infants were dashed in pieces at the head of every street;	
10d	וְעַל־נִכְבַּדֶּיהָ יַדּוּ גוֹרָל	lots were cast for her nobles	
10e	וְכָל־גְּדוֹלֶיהָ רֻתְּקוּ בַזִּקִּים	and all her prominent citizens were bound with fetters.	
11a	גַּם־אַתְּ תִּשְׁכְּרִי	You too will be drunk,	c. Nineveh's Similar Fate (3:11a–c)
11b	תְּהִי נַעֲלָמָה	you will be incapacitated,	
11c	גַּם־אַתְּ תְּבַקְשִׁי מָעוֹז מֵאוֹיֵב	you too will seek refuge from the enemy!"	

Continued on next page.

Continued from previous page.

12a	כָּל־מִבְצָרַיִךְ תְּאֵנִים עִם־בִּכּוּרִים	"All your fortified cities are fig trees with first-ripe figs;	3. A Military Taunt (3:12a–15c)
12b	▲ אִם־יִנּוֹעוּ	▲ if they are shaken,	a. Assyria's Vulnerability (3:12a–13d)
12c	▲ וְנָפְלוּ עַל־פִּי אוֹכֵל	▲ they will fall into the mouth of the eater!	
13a	הִנֵּה	Look!	
13b	עַמֵּךְ נָשִׁים בְּקִרְבֵּךְ	Your troops are women in your midst!	
13c	לְאֹיְבַיִךְ פָּתוֹחַ נִפְתְּחוּ שַׁעֲרֵי אַרְצֵךְ	The gates of your land are wide open to your enemy!	
13d	אָכְלָה אֵשׁ בְּרִיחָיִךְ	Fire devours your gate-bars!	
14a	מֵי מָצוֹר שַׁאֲבִי־לָךְ	Draw for yourself water for the siege!	b. A Sarcastic Call for Assyria to Prepare for Battle (3:14a–15c)
14b	חַזְּקִי מִבְצָרָיִךְ	Fortify the stronghold!	
14c	בֹּאִי בַטִּיט	Go into the clay,	
14d	וְרִמְסִי בַחֹמֶר	tread the mortar,	
14e	הַחֲזִיקִי מַלְבֵּן	grab the brick mold!	
15a	שָׁם תֹּאכְלֵךְ אֵשׁ	There the fire will devour you!	
15b	תַּכְרִיתֵךְ חֶרֶב	The sword will cut you down!	
15c	תֹּאכְלֵךְ כַּיָּלֶק	It will devour you like the creeping locust!"	
15d	הִתְכַּבֵּד כַּיֶּלֶק	"Multiply yourself like the creeping locust!	4. An Economic Taunt (3:15d–17h) a. A Sarcastic Call for Assyria to Multiply Its Personnel (3:15d–15e)
15e	הִתְכַּבְּדִי כָּאַרְבֶּה	Multiply yourself like migratory locusts!	
16a	הִרְבֵּית רֹכְלַיִךְ	You multiplied your merchants	b. The Number and Transience of Assyria's Economic Personnel (3:16a–16b)
	▲ מִכּוֹכְבֵי הַשָּׁמָיִם	▲ more than the stars of the heavens!	
16b	יֶלֶק פָּשַׁט וַיָּעֹף	The creeping locust sheds its skin and flies away!	
17a	מִנְּזָרַיִךְ כָּאַרְבֶּה	Your courtiers are like migratory locusts!	c. The Number and Transience of Assyria's Palace Personnel (3:17a–h)
17b	וְטַפְסְרַיִךְ כְּגוֹב גֹּבָי	Your scribes are like locust swarms	
17c	▲ הַחוֹנִים בַּגְּדֵרוֹת	▲ settling on the walls	
17d	▲ בְּיוֹם קָרָה	▲ on a cold day.	
17e	▼ שֶׁמֶשׁ זָרְחָה	▼ When the sun rises	
17f	וְנוֹדַד	they flee;	
17g	וְלֹא־נוֹדַע מְקוֹמוֹ	their whereabouts are unknown.	
17h	אַיָּם	Where are they?"	

18a	נָמוּ רֹעֶיךָ	"Your shepherds doze,	5. The Final Dirge for the Assyrian King (3:18a–19d) a. The Collapse of the State (3:18a–e)
18b	מֶלֶךְ אַשּׁוּר	King of Assyria!	
18c	יִשְׁכְּנוּ אַדִּירֶיךָ	Your nobles sit still!	
18d	נָפֹשׁוּ עַמְּךָ עַל־הֶהָרִים	Your people are scattered over the mountains,	
18e	וְאֵין מְקַבֵּץ	and there is none to gather (them)!	
19a	אֵין־כֵּהָה לְשִׁבְרֶךָ	There is no healing for your fracture!	b. The Prognosis: Death of the King (3:19a–b)
19b	נַחְלָה מַכָּתֶךָ	Your wound is severe!	
19c	כֹּל שֹׁמְעֵי שִׁמְעֲךָ תָּקְעוּ כַף עָלֶיךָ	All who hear the news of you will clap their hands over you,	c. The Reaction: Universal Joy (3:19c–d)
19d	▲ כִּי עַל־מִי לֹא־עָבְרָה רָעָתְךָ תָּמִיד	▲ for over whom has your evil not passed ceaselessly?"	

Chapter 3 opens with a woe against "the bloody city," a title that leaves little doubt as to the ground for YHWH's violence against it.[4] Neo-Assyria's violence has been referred to repeatedly in the book of Nahum and was arguably one of its defining characteristics. Similarly, the assertion that Nineveh was "full" of plunder can hardly be doubted, being presumed in the description of extensive plundering of 2:10[9] and noted in the Babylonian Chronicle that documents the city's fall and despoiling. As we saw above, Nineveh's treasuries were filled primarily by its vassals' substantial payments and its appropriation of other states' wealth by force. Both sources of wealth can thus be traced back to the empire's rapacious, violent use of its power. Despite the authentic nature of these historical descriptions, the reader now knows from 2:12–14[11–13] and other preceding passages that Assyria's plundering will come to an end (2:14[13]e) and that the material wealth it had amassed at others' expense will indeed be taken away (2:10[9]). The link between 3:1 and 2:12–14[11–13] is further strengthened by the reuse of "prey," טֶרֶף, and the root מלא.

The grounds for the pronouncement of woe are elaborated on in the parallel lines that follow in 3:1b–d. The emphasis on Nineveh's deceit (כַּחַשׁ) in 3:1b appears here for the first time in Nahum, and the assertion that "all of it" (כֹּל with a 3fs suffix) is deceitful elevates this accusation to the level of a defining characteristic.[5] The noun translated "deceitful" here appears only a handful of times in the OT, and carries no particular connotations, so our understanding of it in this context must be determined by relevant material elsewhere in Nahum and by our historical knowledge of Neo-Assyrian diplomacy and propaganda.[6] For the moment it is sufficient to note that even in Judah's relatively short history with Assyria there were already grounds for this charge (note especially the Assyrian propaganda in 2 Kgs 18 // Isa 36, discussed earlier). The prominence of a similar accusation in 3:4 favors a fuller treatment of it later.

Second Condemnation (3:2–3)

The second condemnation offered in support of the opening pronouncement of woe is a development of the epithet "bloody city" in 3:1a. Given what 2:12–13[11–12] has already said about the empire's use of violence, explicit condemnation is left aside here in favor of an extensive description of the human toll of Assyria's military action. While some see this section as referring to Nineveh's fall at the hands of its enemies (as in 2:4–5[3–4]), it is equally plausible to see it as expanding upon Nineveh's bloody violence as introduced in 3:1.[7] The following points support this latter approach: First, the vision of Nineveh's fall in 2:4–11[3–10], and even YHWH's promises to destroy it in 1:9–10, 12, 14, are quite restrained in their descriptions of Assyrian casualties and the violence they entail, whereas the book consistently (and especially in chapter 3) details Assyria's violence against others. An inversion of this pattern, while not impossible, is thus unlikely. Second, the semantic connection between 3:1 ("bloody city," 3:1a, "no one takes away (its) prey," 3:1d) and the battle scene in 3:2–3 is very

4. On the legitimacy of seeing the addressee as integral to the woe oracle, see Delbert R. Hillers, "*Hôy* and *Hôy*-Oracles: A Neglected Syntactic Aspect," in *The Word of the Lord Shall Go Forth: Essays in Honor of David Noel Freedman in Celebration of His Sixtieth Birthday*, ed. C. L. Meyers and M. O'Connor, ASOR Special Volume Series (Winona Lake, IN: Eisenbrauns, 1983), 185–88.

5. Reference has already been made to Assyria's plotting in Nah 1:9, but there the element of deceit was absent.

6. Cf. *HALOT*, 470. Fabry, *Nahum*, 188, suggests that propaganda in the context of diplomacy is in view. A focus on Assyrian diplomacy is also suggested by Longman, "Nahum," 812, who suggests the events of 2 Kgs 16 and Assyria's opportunistic exploitation of Judah's request for help. Spronk's reference to Isa 36 (*Nahum*, 118) is probably more persuasive, especially in light of the close relationship between Isaiah and Nahum.

7. Form-critical observations are not decisive here since in both cases the order of the elements of the woe oracle remains

close, suggesting that 3:2–3 refers to the violence with which Assyria killed its prey. Similarly, the connection between 3:2–3 and 3:4 is very natural if 3:2–3 refers to Assyria, whose imperialistic violence contributed directly to its massive wealth and exploitative diplomacy, and these same two features are interwoven in the preceding context (2:12–14[11–13]).[8] Finally, the deceit of 3:1b is elaborated upon in 3:4, suggesting that 3:2–4 is an orderly expansion on the elements introduced in 3:1, moving from Assyria's violence to its wealth gained through looting and diplomatic machination. These factors weigh in favor of seeing the graphic snapshot in 3:2–3 as describing Assyria's acts of war rather than its punishment at the hands of the Medo-Babylonian alliance.

The text gives two complementary perspectives on Assyria's attacks against its enemies.[9] The first, in 3:2, is aural, focusing on the sound (קוֹל, twice) of the whip, wheel ("rattling," רַעַשׁ), horse, and chariot. This audible facet is complemented by descriptions of visible movement of the "rushing" horse and the "bounding" chariot in particular. The overall effect portrays the rapid, nearly blurred motion of the army's chariotry. This breathless description of helter-skelter movement is given additional force through the use of noun phrases in 3:2c–d that lack an explicit grammatical subject (the "sound" of 3:2a–b) and are consequently subordinated.

The second perspective adopts a contrasting, exclusively human focus but mixes the living attacker and the dead opponent in a way grimly suited to the description of a battle. The description moves from the initial charge of the horsemen through hand-to-hand combat with sword and spear to a horrific focus on the results of the battle. No fewer than four lines are given to this outcome, with two nominal phrases (3:3d–e) followed by a verbless clause (3:3f) and finally by a verbal sentence (3:3g). Three of the four lines line use a different term for the dead, and the third and fourth lines vary between the singular and plural forms of a shared lexeme (something difficult to capture in English translation): "slain . . . corpses . . . dead bodies . . . dead bodies."[10] The last two lines further emphasize the carnage by using absolute terminology ("no end") and by involving the corpses in the action in a way that shows their number and the attacker's lack of any respect for them.[11] These rhetorical features accentuate the horrible human cost of Assyria's violence and put that macabre reality directly in the center of the reader's field of vision as a fitting end to the second accusation.

Third Condemnation (3:4)

The initial מִן of 3:4 explicitly identifies the following activities and descriptions of Assyria as additional reasons for the judgment that finally follows in 3:5–7.[12] While 3:4a by itself would have

(1) woe (3:1a); (2) condemnation (3:1a–d, 3:4 or 3:1a–4); (3) punishment (3:2–3, 5–7, or only 3:5–7). Nahum 3:2–3 is taken as a description of Nineveh's fall by Perlitt, *Die Propheten*, 27; Tidiman, *Nahoum, Habaquq, Sophonie*, 108; Renaud, *Michée, Sophonie, Nahum*, 311, and others. Floyd, *Minor Prophets*, 69–70, recognizes more ambiguity in the subject of 3:2–3.

8. The possibility that the "because" that begins 3:4 refers to Assyrian violence in 3:2–3 is considered below.

9. Each shares identical syntax, beginning with an asyndetic noun and followed by a string of clauses beginning with the conjunction ו.

10. Reading the plural בגוית, cf. *BHS*, LXX (which uses a plural), so also Dietrich, *Nahum, Habakuk, Zefanja*, 73, 75.

11. Nahum 3:3f, g also use alliteration, employing twice the same term for corpses that begins with "g" (ג). I follow the *ketiv* (*qal* imperfect of כשל).

12. For another such use, see Deut 7:7; cf. van Merwe, Naudé, and Kroeze, *A Biblical Hebrew Reference Grammar*, 289. It is possible that the "because" explains the violence of 3:2–3 as serving the purpose of Assyria's unjust and exploitative relationships with other states, in part since the "I am against you" of 2:14[13] is introduced without a causative particle. Even if the particle secondarily reflects the import of 3:1–3 for the activities of 3:4, the connection between 3:4 (and indeed 3:1–4) and the punishment of 3:5–7 is primary.

no metaphorical potential and so lead the reader to imagine a condemnation for literal sexual promiscuity, the preceding context and especially the rest of 3:4 make clear that Assyria's relations with other states are at issue. The metaphor of "many debaucheries" involves a "source domain" of illicit sexual activity and so characterizes the "target domain" of Assyria's relations with other states as similarly out-of-bounds.[13] This general appraisal is developed by three more specific condemnations, all articulated in subordinate clauses whose subject is in apposition with the prostitute of 3:1a.[14]

First, while being "gracefully alluring" is not objectionable in itself, the assertion in 3:1 that Nineveh is deceitful and its abusive treatment of the nations with which it has dealings both suggest that the benefits Assyria promised and sometimes gave to its vassals were outweighed by other, unstated costs. The phrase thus refers to an attraction that involves misrepresenting the costs and benefits of the relationship that Assyria offers, at the expense of the other.

Second, in the context of Assyria's international relations, "mistress of sorceries" (בַּעֲלַת כְּשָׁפִים) likely makes reference to the pervasive presence of Assyria's gods in its warfare and diplomacy (cf. Isa 47:9 and the earlier discussions of Assyrian royal ideology).[15] Paul-Alain Beaulieu corroborates this when he observes that Esarhaddon's reign provides "the most extensive evidence for the excessive popularity of divination, especially astrology, at the court."[16] Whether in diplomacy or in war, Assyria's interaction with other states was permeated by religious elements that the OT condemns as categorically wrong.

The final activity condemned in this section is presented in two lines in close parallelism: "who sells nations through her debaucheries, and tribes through her sorceries." The double appearance of the plural objects sold ("nations" [גּוֹיִם], "tribes" [מִשְׁפָּחוֹת][17]) expresses the number and variety of groups involved in the empire's expansion, while the mention of "debaucheries" and "sorceries" underlines the prominence and illicit nature of such dealings.[18] Further, there is a strong note of exploitation and abuse involved in the metaphor. As Thomas Renz notes, "Nineveh is not depicted as an ordinary prostitute making a living, let alone as a sexually liberated and self-confident woman. Rather, she is a source of ensnarement and thinks nothing of selling peoples for her pleasure."[19] Since there was only one winner in Assyria's imperial project, the metaphor represents Assyria as the only one profiting from her interaction with others. She effectively sells the nations to herself, while in the metaphor the client derives no benefit, and indeed only loss, from the relationship. In sum, this third condemnation alleges that on a large scale and through the use of propaganda in particular, deceit and exploitation characterized Assyria's diplomatic and military dealing with the states around her (cf. 3:1a).

13. See Murray Knowles and Rosamund Moon, *Introducing Metaphor* (New York: Routledge, 2006), 26. On the meaning and referents of זנה, see Seth Erlandsson, "זנה," *TDOT* 4:99–104; Gary H. Hall, "זנה," *NIDOTTE* 1:1122–25.

14. While there is no reason to read זְנוּנֵי זוֹנָה in 3:4 as an infinitive absolute/finite verb pair, emphasis is still present in the pairing of cognate nouns.

15. See Lorenzo Verderame, "Astronomy, Divination, and Politics in the Neo-Assyrian Empire," in *Handbook of Archaeoastronomy and Ethnoastronomy*, ed. C. L. N. Ruggles (New York: Springer, 2014), 1847–53. The lexical field of כשף is rather general; cf. *HALOT*, 503.

16. Beaulieu, "Mesopotamia," 171.

17. Philip R. Davies and John W. Rogerson, *The Old Testament World*, 2nd ed. (Louisville: Westminster John Knox, 2005), 33, note that the מִשְׁפָּחָה is a "descent group" not quite identical to a clan, since there was no surname and a מִשְׁפָּחָה could divide "to form new maximal lineages."

18. The use of the root זנה three times in 3:4 further emphasizes the illicit nature and profitability of Assyria's imperialism; cf. Tidiman, *Nahoum, Habaquq, Sophonie*, 110.

19. Thomas Renz, "Nahum, Book of," *DTIS*, 528.

Punishment (3:5–6)

After the three accusatory sections of the woe (3:1, 2–3, 4) follows the punishment (3:5–6). Given the detailed nature and sharp tone of the accusations, it is appropriate that the promised punishment is also described in detail. Before presenting the individual punishments, however, the text orients the reader by making YHWH the primary actor through the book's second challenge formula: "Know that I am against you!" As we saw in 2:14[13], this formula prevents the reader from interpreting Assyria's imminent fall in purely politico-military terms, emphasizing instead the religious significance of the empire's identity and activity. This section thus has an organic relation to the affirmation in 1:2–8 that YHWH will completely destroy those who oppose him.

YHWH's most direct response to Assyria's violence and autonomy is presented in six parallel lines (3:5c–6c), all of which are direct speech. In each line YHWH is the verbal subject, and Assyria, or an aspect of its feminine personification, is the object. With the exception of the elided verb in 3:5e, the lines share identical syntax, with a perfective form (*waw consecutive*) at the head of the clause. Personifying Nineveh as an exploitative, violent prostitute (3:4) makes it logical to present its punishment under the same personification. The first three lines of 5c–6c focus on the personified prostitute's public nudity as a source of shame, while the last three lines contemplate her humiliation in other ways. Both tricola are indented in the translation above to capture the pragmatic effect of their sustained parallelism. Assyria's humiliation is followed by a summary reaction on the part of the nations whom Assyria mistreated (3:7c–e) that moves from Nineveh's shame to its welcome demise.

The description of Nineveh's public denuding presents several challenges The syntagm גלה שׁול, "uncover (a) skirt" occurs elsewhere only in Jer 13:22, where it is in parallel with נֶחְמְסוּ עֲקֵבָיִךְ, "your heels suffered violence." While the parallel phrase there is apparently a euphemism for rape, it seems at least equally clear that גלה שׁול does not refer to sexual assault there.[20] As William McKane notes, the parallelism between גלה שׁול in Jer 13:22 and חשׂף שׁול in Jer 13:26 argues against understanding גלה שׁול in 13:22 in terms of rape and favors seeing it as an image of "judicial punishment."[21] Several other points also make it unlikely that גלה שׁול means "rape" in Nah 3:5. First, the phrase that follows "uncover your skirts" (עַל־פָּנָיִךְ, "over your head") requires that the object of the verb גלה be a skirt, not a person, so that the act is one of exposure and not of rape. This is confirmed by the connection that the subsequent phrases ("I will show nations your nakedness [מַעַר][22] and kingdoms your shame [קְלוֹן]," 3:5d, e) make between the lifting of the skirt and its result. Both phrases focus on the communicative aspect of this punishment as public exposure and the shame that denuding produces and give no hint of sexual violence. Finally, the literal public denuding of those guilty of certain crimes makes recourse to euphemism unnecessary and quite unlikely here.[23] Other biblical texts (Ezek 16:37–39;

20. So Georg Fischer, *Jeremia 1–25*, HThKAT (Freiburg im Breisgan: Herder, 2005), 460–61. J. A. Emerton, "The Meaning of the Verb *ḥāmas* in Jeremiah 13,22," in *Prophet und Prophetenbuch: Festschrift für Otto Kaiser zum 65. Geburtstag*, ed. V. Fritz et al., BZAW 185 (Berlin: de Gruyter, 1989), 19–28, argues that the verb חמס means "uncover" here and in Job 15:33; Lam 2:6. Cf. Peter C. Craigie, Page H. Kelley, and Joel F. Drinkard, *Jeremiah 1–25*, WBC 26 (Dallas: Word, 1991), 193; Allen, *Jeremiah*, 164.

21. William McKane, *A Critical and Exegetical Commentary on Jeremiah*, ICC, 2 vols. (Edinburgh: T&T Clark, 1986), 1:311.

22. Cf. *HALOT*, 615; the object "displayed" (*hiphil* ראה) is "nakedness," from ערה, "to uncover, expose" (*HALOT*, 881–82).

23. Unambiguous expressions for rape utilize terms other than those found in Nah 3:5: לקח with שׁכב and ענה (*piel*, Gen 34:2); תפשׂ with שׁכב (Deut 22:28); ענה (*piel*, 2 Sam 13:12, Tamar's description of Amnon's intention); ענה (*piel*) with שׁכב

Jer 13:26; Hos 2:5[3]) and several legal texts from the Middle Assyrian period call for both men and women to be stripped as punishment for inappropriate behavior related to sexual or social norms.[24] A code of conduct for the royal palace authored under Tiglath-pileser I called for the stripping of a male court attendant in the case of his inappropriate physical proximity to a "woman of the palace."[25] The Middle Assyrian Laws address the problem of prostitutes presenting themselves in public wearing a veil, something restricted to (and indeed required of) married women. A veiled prostitute was to be publicly stripped (after due process) at the entry to the palace, as was anyone who did not arrest her on the spot and gather witnesses against her.[26] While the relevant biblical passages punish illicit relationships as such and so suggest that Assyria's behavior is punishable as metaphorical sexual immorality, the Assyrian legal analogues just noted may hint that Nineveh's punishment is also due to her deceit (cf. 3:1, 4). It is therefore appropriate that the "nations" and "kingdoms" that have been deceived by her should witness her punishment, which ensures that she will no longer hold them in her thrall and that her schemes will be exposed for what they are.[27]

The focus then moves from the shame of public nudity in the tricolon of 3:5c–e to a different but equally forceful sequence of shaming acts in the tricolon of 3:6a–c, each of which again begins with a perfective verb with YHWH as the verbal subject. The discourse is again presented as YHWH's direct speech, so that the first-person actions are inseparable from the first-person challenge issued in 3:5a. The first action is the most striking: "I will throw filth (שִׁקֻּצִים) on you!" In cultic contexts שִׁקּוּץ refers to images of deities (e.g., 1 Kgs 11:5), to unclean food (e.g., Zech 9:7), or to a generically horrible thing. The use here is not cultic, but an appropriate sense is difficult to determine. It makes little sense to pelt personified Nineveh with idols, since that action is not attested in the OT or elsewhere and since this would not shame Nineveh in her own eyes or in the eyes of most other nations. The most common sense in noncultic contexts, "filth," is sufficient.[28] Lothar Perlitt's observation that being

אֶת (2 Sam 13:14, the narrator's description). See also Gregory D. Cook, "Nahum and the Question of Rape," *BBR* 26 (2016): 341–52.

24. Note also the Sefire treaty ("The Inscriptions of Bar-Ga'yah and Mati'el from Sefire," trans. Joseph A. Fitzmeyer [*COS* 2.82:214]), which threatens one of its parties as follows in the case of violation: "[And just as] a [har]lot is stripped naked], so may the wives of Mati'el be stripped naked . . ."

25. Martha T. Roth, *Law Collections from Mesopotamia and Asia Minor*, 2nd ed., WAW 6 (Atlanta: Scholars Press, 1997), 206.

26. Roth, *Law Collections*, 168–69. The same was to occur for slave women and those who failed to bring them to justice. Cf. Gerda Lerner, "The Origins of Prostitution in Ancient Mesopotamia," *Journal of Women in Culture and Society* 11 (1986): 250.

27. While Nineveh's shame is produced by the metaphorical exposure of her nakedness, the focus is not on her as a sexual object but as a prostitute who is shamed for deceiving, exploiting, and destroying others for her own satisfaction. Exposing the nudity of a culpable prostitute to shame her is no more sexist than is YHWH's promise to exterminate the (male) king in 1:14. Contrast Julia M. O'Brien, *Nahum*, Readings: A New Biblical Commentary, 2nd ed. (Sheffield: Sheffield Phoenix, 2009), 62, who thinks this metaphorical public humiliation characterizes "YHWH . . . as a man who sexually assaults Nineveh." In support of her argument she mentions Lev 8:18 [*sic*—18:8?], where גלה "is paralleled with taking a woman as rival to her sister; it is paralleled with the outpouring of lust in the description of Israel's whoring in Ezek 16.36; and in Jer 13.22 Judah is not only exposed but also 'violated'" (note the divergent opinions of commentaries on the latter text). From this she concludes that in 3:4–7 "YHWH is characterized as a man who sexually assaults Nineveh in return for her promiscuity, as other nations, characterized as men, gaze at her nakedness." However, Lev 18:8 has עֶרְוָה, "nakedness," as the object of גלה, "uncover," and refers euphemistically to consensual sexual union with one's mother(in-law); likewise Ezek 16:36 uses גלה, "uncover," with the object עֶרְוָה, "nakedness," to refer metaphorically to consensual sexual union. Jer 13:22 has been discussed above.

28. *HALOT*, 1640, suggest "filth" for שִׁקּוּץ in noncultic contexts; cf. Michael A. Grisanti, "שׁקץ," *NIDOTTE* 4:245.

covered with filth emphatically strips Nineveh of her beauty and seductive capacities captures well the text's semantics, in which Assyria goes from being an attractive harlot to a shamed and despised object of revulsion.[29]

The second shaming act is also public but is articulated in terms of a divine pronouncement concerning Nineveh: "I will declare you contemptible" (נִבַּלְתִּיךְ, *piel* of נבל).[30] This term is in the same semantic field as YHWH's evaluation of the Assyrian king in 1:14 (קַלּוֹתָ), whose hyperbolic claims to unlimited power, unfailing support from the gods, and unique status God emphatically rejects. Here the focus is on Nineveh as the personified incarnation of the empire, and the image of the prostitute facilitates the depiction of the empire's attractive power and duplicitous strategies. The context, in which an audience of nations watches YHWH's judgment of Assyria, makes it more likely that a declarative sense is best for נִבַּלְתִּיךְ. YHWH's declaration is witnessed by the nations and is clearly self-authenticating.

YHWH's final means of shaming Nineveh, "I will make you a spectacle," is the most general of the shaming acts in this passage. At the same time, it makes clear that Nineveh's humiliation in this section, which presents the only description in Nahum of nonretributive punishment, *communicates* something to those who witness it. While in other passages Assyria's pride, violence, and opposition to YHWH entail its destruction (e.g., 2:4–11[3–10]), here YHWH commits to shaming the empire so as to expose what it would rather keep hidden (unmasking its deceit) and to covering the personified empire with filth (obscuring its attraction) in order to make it contemptible (undoing its illegitimate claims to unique sovereignty and status). The communicative function of this sort of punishment involves both the offender and the public,[31] and the scene here has a strong social aspect due to the audience of nations who witness Assyria's shaming. Antony Duff helpfully analyzes the analogous human-to-human process as follows: "What makes punishment intrinsically appropriate as a response to crime, on communicative accounts, is that crimes are public wrongs that merit censure, and punishment communicates that censure."[32]

Transposed to the scenario in which YHWH punishes wrong committed by some of his creatures in the presence of those wronged, Duff's analysis helps us understand what is happening here. The empire has usurped prerogatives of deity and arrogated to itself a position far above the rest of humanity, often treating its fellow human beings as less than human.[33] YHWH's punishment therefore undoes its false standing (bringing it down to a "merely" human level) and simultaneously reasserts its victims' full humanity.[34]

29. Perlitt, *Die Propheten*, 29.

30. This sense is similar to that suggested by *HALOT*, 663; note especially the parallel terms in Jer 14:21; Deut 32:15. William McKane, *Micah: Introduction and Commentary* (Edinburgh: T&T Clark, 1998), 214, suggests "I will despise you."

31. R. Antony Duff, "Punishment," *Oxford Handbook of Practical Ethics*, ed. H. LaFollette (Oxford: Oxford University Press, 2003), 343.

32. Duff, "Punishment," 343.

33. Zehnder, *Umgang mit Fremden*, 63–74, 546, 554; Megan Cifarelli, "Gesture and Alterity in the Art of Ashurnasirpal II of Assyria, *The Art Bulletin* 80 (1998): 210–28, esp. 212–13. Clear examples include the portrayal of vassals as leashed animals on slab 7 from Nimrud's northwest palace, Court D (see Cifarelli, "Gesture and Alterity," 215); the comparison by Tiglath-pileser III of the king of Damascus to a mongoose when he took refuge in his city (Hayim Tadmor, *The Inscriptions of Tiglath-Pileser III, King of Assyria: Critical Edition with Introductions, Translations, and Commentary* [Jerusalem: Publications of the Israel Academy of Sciences and Humanities, 1994], 78f, cited in Zehnder, *Umgang mit Fremden*, 72); and Sennacherib's comparison of Babylonian troops with pigeons that flee when they are pursued (Daniel D. Luckenbill, *The Annals of Sennacherib* [Chicago: University of Chicago Press, 1924], 47, 27–31, cited in Zehnder, *Umgang mit Fremden*, 73).

34. Despite not being "retributive," this "communicative" punishment is not intended to deter or rehabilitate Nineveh or to reconcile her to Judah and her other victims.

Outcome (3:7)

The communicative aspect of Nineveh's humiliation is reinforced by the shared visual terminology that connects the end of 3:6 with the opening line of 3:7 (רֳאִי, "spectacle," 3:6; participle of ראה, "spectator, observer," 3:7). Nahum 3:7a makes clear that YHWH's punishment of Assyria, although perfectly just, is not a pretty sight: "All who see you will shrink back from you!" Nineveh's humiliation and fall have the same effect on all who see it, and their response will be to "flee" or "shrink back" from such a horrific sight.

While 3:5–6 focused on communicative punishment that vindicated those whom Assyria had oppressed while unmasking and undoing the empire's malevolent schemes, the perspective of 3:7 includes the retributive punishment that predominates elsewhere in the book. The first word of the nations' response in 3:7c puts this beyond doubt: "Devastated!" The use of direct speech on the part of non-Assyrians, a feature seen only one other time in Nahum in the call to plunder Nineveh (2:10[9]a–b), emphasizes the fearsomeness of the divine punishment of Nineveh's sin. The next line spells out the complex nature of YHWH's punishment of Nineveh and its results: while the carnage is shocking (3:7a), the devastation (3:7c) has a predominantly positive significance. Although there is no shortage of observers ("nations," "kingdoms," "all who see you"), they know of no one who will mourn Assyria (3:7d, with נוד), a point emphasized by their rhetorical question.[35] What is more, YHWH knows that not one among them is inclined to lament Assyria's fall and affirms with another rhetorical question that he himself is unable to find comforters (מְנַחֲמִים; note the joy of Assyrian's former victims in 3:19).[36] Bernard Renaud pointedly observes that this means God himself will not grieve for or comfort the empire, and the denial of "comforters" for Nineveh amounts to a pun on the name "Nahum"—while the prophet announces relief from the Assyrian scourge to the nations oppressed by the empire, God's intervention entails an antithetical fate for the empire, which although destroyed is mourned by no one.[37]

2. A Historical Taunt (3:8–11)

This subunit is the second of five in chapter 3, all of which undermine, ignore, or mock Assyria's grandiose claims to unlimited power and glory. Probably because of the detailed condemnation of Assyria in 3:1–4, this subunit pays no attention to Assyria's wrongs, and focuses exclusively on its downfall, as does the following section (3:12–15c).

This, the first taunt in the book, places a large question mark behind Nineveh's apparent inviolability by comparing it to Thebes, an illustrious Egyptian city deep within the heart of Egypt. Despite appearing to lie beyond the reach of its enemies, and despite its military strength built on numerous alliances, Thebes fell (ironically, to Assyria), was looted, and saw its inhabitants alternately killed or disgraced. Nineveh is no different, and will meet a similar fate.

The taunt consists of three interconnected parts. Nahum 3:8–9 begins with an interrogative particle (הֲ) that introduces the essential question, Will Nineveh fare better than Thebes? The lengthy first subsection then details in seven lines the various features that made Thebes appear beyond the reach of its foes. Thebes's *apparent* security is then shown to have been of no value in the face of

35. Cf. Job 2:11; 42:11; Ps 69:21[20]; Isa 51:19 for collocations of נוד and נחם. The audience here is initially emphasized due to its placement at the head of 3:7a, after the temporal indicator and before the verb.

36. Cf. 2 Sam 10:3 // 1 Chr 19:3.

37. Renaud, *Michée, Sophonie, Nahum*, 314.

its foes in 3:10, which begins with the concessive "even" (גַּם). That logic is then applied to Nineveh in 3:11, introduced with the same particle "too" (גַּם) that is repeated again at the head of 3:11c. Despite its grandeur and defensive capabilities, Assyria's capital will meet with a similar fate.

As shown in the translation above, syntactic subordination is evident in the circumstantial clauses that qualify Thebes in 3:8b–e. The coordination of the material dealing with Thebes in 3:8a, 9a–c and 3:10a–e and that concerning Nineveh (3:11) reinforces the relevance of Thebes as proof of Nineveh's vulnerability. Although no subordinating conjunctions are present, 3:9b–c, 3:10b–e, and 3:11b–c are indented to reflect the literary-rhetorical effect of successive parallel lines.[38] The whole section is indented from the mainline since it is direct discourse.

In terms of literary genre, this is the first clear example of a taunt in Nahum. This literary genre can be defined as "a derisive utterance insinuating that one person, group, or thing is inferior to another."[39] While most taunts are uttered for their effect on the other, the taunt in Nahum is (at least in its original setting) for Judean ears only.[40] The addressee is feminine singular throughout this section, surely a personification of the city of Nineveh. Its presentation as direct speech is part and parcel of its confrontational tone.

The taunt begins with a rhetorical questions. The *hiphil* imperfective form of יטב, "be good, do good" exhibits a reflexive component in a few cases (Ps 49:19[18]; Eccl 11:9; perhaps Prov 17:22; Gen 4:7).[41] By contrast, the simple contrastive formula "is not X better than Y" typically uses the nominal form טוֹב, "good" rather than the verbal (and especially imperfective) form of יטב.[42] These points suggest that the sense of the question here is probably not "Are you (presently) better than . . . ?" but "Will it go better with you than . . . ?" or "will you do better than?"[43] Further, a simple comparison between Nineveh and Thebes would be rhetorically self-negating since it was Assyria that had captured and looted Thebes, and since Nineveh was far better fortified. The comparison can still be made but is moot within the context of their shared fate as well-defended sites (each in its own way).

We noted in the Introduction that Assyria was increasingly present in the Levant from the time of Tiglath-pileser III onward (744 BCE and later). The empire's westward expansion eventually brought it to the borders of Egypt, which until then had not interfered in Assyria's affairs.[44] Assyria's unprecedented proximity to Egypt prompted a shift in Egyptian policies, and soon Egypt was actively resisting Assyrian presence in the Levant and lending support to vassal states that resisted the empire's claims, most notably against Sennacherib at Eltekeh.[45] In the face of such staunch opposition, Sennacherib withdrew from the Levant for

38. Cf. Jan P. Fokkelman, *Major Poems of the Hebrew Bible: At the Interface of Hermeneutics and Structural Analysis, Volume 1, Ex. 15, Deut. 32, and Job 3*, SSN (Assen: Van Gorcum, 1998), 54.

39. Floyd, *Minor Prophets*, 649.

40. Robert R. Desjarlais, *Counterplay: An Anthropologist at the Chessboard* (Berkeley: University of California Press, 2011), 20.

41. For uses of the *hiphil* imperfect, cf. Gen 4:7; 32:10[9], 13[12]; Num 10:32; Judg 17:13; 1 Sam 2:32; 1 Kgs 1:47; Job 24:21; Ps 49:19[18]; Prov 15:2, 13; 17:22; Eccl 11:9; Isa 41:23; Jer 2:23; 7:5; Mic 2:7; Zeph 1:12.

42. See, e.g., Gen 29:19, Exod 14:12, Amos 6:2, and approximately 70 other references. Exceptions include Ruth 3:10; 1 Kgs 1:47; Ps 69:32[31]; Song 4:10.

43. This latter sense is proposed by Christensen, *Nahum*, 354; Perlitt, *Die Propheten*, 30; Spronk, *Nahum*, 126; Fabry, *Nahum*, 200, 210.

44. See the concise overview of this period in Kuhrt, *The Ancient Near East*, 499–501.

45. See Donald B. Redford, *Egypt, Canaan, and Israel in Ancient Times* (Princeton: Princeton University Press, 1992), 351–53; I draw on Redford, 351–64, in the following summary.

the duration of his reign, and it fell to Esarhaddon to neutralize the threat posed by the Egyptian and Levantine states. In the meantime, Egyptian campaigns had reached as far north as Phoenicia in 684–683 and 682–681 BCE, and Egypt had renewed diplomatic ties with Tyre and Sidon as well. Esarhaddon moved swiftly against these threats, reasserting his sovereignty over Tyre and Sidon and pushing steadily into the Sinai. In 674 BCE he attempted an invasion of Egypt itself but suffered a rare defeat, only to attack again in 671, taking the delta city of Memphis in half a day and driving the Egyptian king Taharqa southward to safety. The next decade or so saw Egypt's delta repeatedly come under Assyrian control only to rebel afterward.

It was Assurbanipal who put an end to this oscillating state of affairs in 663 BCE, when he chased the Egyptian king Tanwetaman, Taharqa's successor, as far as Thebes to avenge the murder of the Assyrian regent in Egypt. "For the first time in a thousand years Thebes . . . was brutally sacked and its treasures carted off to Assyria, including silver, gold, gems, costumes, chattels, and even obelisks."[46] Assurbanipal's report of the fall of Thebes reads as follows:

> In my second campaign I marched directly against Egypt (*Muṣur*) and Nubia. Urdamane [= Tanwetaman] heard of the approach of my expedition (only when) I had (already) set foot on Egyptian territory. He left Memphis and fled into Thebes to save his life. The kings, governors, and regents whom I had installed in Egypt came to meet me and kissed my feet. I followed Urdamane (and) went as far as Thebes, his fortress. He saw my mighty battle array approaching, left Thebes and fled to Kipkipi. Upon a trust(-inspiring) oracle of Ashur and Ishtar I, myself, conquered this town completely. From Thebes I carried away booty, heavy and beyond counting: silver, gold, precious stones, his entire personal possessions, linen garments with multicolored trimmings, fine horses, (certain) inhabitants, male and female. I pulled two high obelisks, cast of shining *zaḫalû*-bronze, the weight of which was 2,500 talents, standing at the door of the temple, out of their bases and took (them) to Assyria. (Thus) I carried off from Thebes heavy booty, beyond counting. I made Egypt (*Muṣur*) and Nubia feel my weapons bitterly and celebrated my triumph. With full hands and safely, I returned to Nineveh, the city (where I exercise) my rule.[47]

This review of the events leading up to the fall of Thebes raises a pressing question regarding the section's rhetoric—why did Nahum choose to demonstrate Assyria's weakness by comparing it with a city that Assyria itself had destroyed only a few years before the prophet spoke? Does not the fact that Assyria was able to take such a significant city despite the forces that had kept it safe for a thousand years prove rather than disprove its power? What is more, Nineveh could boast that it possessed numerous defensive structures that Thebes did not, so that it was more secure than Thebes.

To reason along these lines, although logical, is to miss the point of the taunt. Yes, Assyria was able to take Thebes, and yes, Nineveh was better defended than its Egyptian counterpart. But the point of the taunt is not to compare the two cities on empirical grounds in order to establish that Nineveh is presently weaker, or at least not stronger, than Thebes. Rather, the taunt *affirms* that Nineveh will fare no better than Thebes, regardless of its comparative strength and security.

Thebe's Apparent Strength (3:8–9)

Noting again that the rhetorical question that begins the taunt dismisses whatever fortifications

46. Ibid., 364.

47. "Babylonian and Assyrian Historical Texts," *ANET*, 295.

Nineveh had as irrelevant in light of its coming fall, we turn to the taunt itself. The location of Thebes, a city which then and now straddles the Nile,[48] satisfies the sense of 3:8b, but it is less clear what is intended in the next three lines, which state that "water (מַיִם) (was) surrounding her," that "(her) strength" was a "sea" (יָם), and that her "rampart" (חוֹמָה) was water.[49] John Huddleston argues that "the success of the comparison with Nineveh—with its rivers, walls, and moats—hinges" upon the similarity between the two cities' use of water for defensive purposes, although he is reticent to demand "that one demonstrate correspondence for each feature."[50] As we have seen, however, the taunt requires no detailed comparison of the two cities' infrastructure or military alliances. While Huddleston's suggestion that Nahum's description of Thebes has been influenced by his knowledge of Nineveh is plausible, it is not directly relevant.

To begin with 3:8c, while the city was not surrounded by water, its situation was similar to that of Nineveh, which while not entirely surrounded by water had the Tigris immediately to its west and the Khosr farther off to its east and southeast. It is thus plausible to see this description as a reference to the fact that the Nile boxes in the western half of the city, which backs up against cliffs, and forms the western boundary of the city's eastern half at the same time. If we add to the Nile the various canals that ensured access to several of the more prominent temples, we have in Thebes a city with water at its very center.

To this second element of water in the description of Thebes, 3:8d adds a third: "whose rampart/strength is a sea." The term חֵל/חֵיל is often read (with different vowels) as חַיִל, "strength," although the parallel term חוֹמָה, "wall," in the following line may favor the sense "rampart" here (cf. 2 Sam 20:15; Isa 26:1; Lam 2:8).[51] How we translate חֵל/חֵיל is also connected to whether the sense of the clause is that Thebes's rampart/strength *was* a sea, meaning a body of water was its defense, or whether "sea" should be understood metaphorically as signifying its strength (or that of its rampart). Similarly, we must ask in 3:8e ("her rampart water") whether a literal wall was equivalent to a water defense, or if the Nile and the canals in Thebes offered some protection in lieu of a literal wall.[52]

Klaas Spronk helpfully notes that יְאֹר, "river," יָם, "sea," מַיִם, "water," and other terms are used in parallel in Isa 19:5–8 to describe Egypt's rivers, canals, and other water resources.[53] Since these terms are sometimes used interchangeably, even if a literal sense were best here, there is no need to insist that "sea" refers to a large body of water like the Mediterranean.[54] Rather, a literal sense here would mean that 3:8d–e present Thebes as being protected by the Nile. The difficulty with this understanding is

48. See Daniel C. Polz, "Thebes (modern Luxor)," *Oxford Encyclopedia of Ancient Egypt*, ed. D. B. Redford (Oxford: Oxford University Press, 2001), 3:384–88. The plural יְאֹרִים, "rivers, Niles" may refer to the branches which ran parallel to the Nile where it bisected Thebes, or may simply be an intensifying plural, perhaps in light of the Nile's seasonal flooding; cf. Ezek 29:3–5; 30:12. Polz, "Thebes," 385, clearly shows two branches of the ancient Nile in Thebes.

49. Following the Vulgate and other versions, which read "water" rather than "from the sea" (different vocalization of identical consonants).

50. John R. Huddleston, "Nahum, Nineveh, and the Nile," *JNES* 62 (2003): 101, 107.

51. Cf. *HALOT*, 311–12; see also Pss 48:14[13]; 122:7. The same sense may also be attested in Zech 9:4; Dan 11:7; 1 Kgs 21:23, and in the last case the LXX clearly understood "rampart."

52. MT reads מִיָּם, "from/of a sea," but some of the versions read מַיִם, "water," and the parallelism between these lines makes varying terminology more likely.

53. Spronk, *Nahum*, 129.

54. There is thus little ground to suppose, as some interpreters have, that the text refers not to Thebes but to a city in the Egyptian delta (and thus in proximity to the Mediterranean).

that the Nile offered no protection whatsoever to the city. If anything, it facilitated the attack of any enemy able to navigate the Nile.

For this reason it is more likely that the water elements in 3:8d–e are comparative, portraying the security offered by Thebes's walls and ramparts as equivalent to that offered by massive water defenses. While Thebes was not surrounded by a perimeter wall as was Nineveh, some of its very large royal temples were surrounded by sizable walls and were accessible only through fortified gates.[55] As odd as this may seem in comparison with Nineveh, given the absence of any nearby threat to Thebes, it was enough for some Egyptian monarchs to fortify their immense temples there to protect them from raiders. Hence Ramses III fortified Medina-Habou, a Theban temple complex that measured roughly 300 meters (1000 feet) in length and 200 meters (650 feet) in width, with a double perimeter wall several meters thick and perhaps 10 meters (31 feet) in height. Access to the complex was possible only through one of its two fortified gates.[56]

Moving to 3:9, the second source of Thebes's security and strength lay in Egypt's large population and, when that was not enough, in its use of mercenary soldiers. The battle at Eltekeh, mentioned above, saw Egypt assemble a force large enough to resist Sennacherib's army. In Sennacherib's own words, "The kings of Egypt, (and) the bowmen, chariot corps and cavalry of the kings of Ethiopia assembled a countless force and came to their (i.e., the Ekronites') aid."[57] Nahum's description of Egypt in the seventh century mentions Kush, Put, and Libya as its allies. At the time of the fall of Thebes some decades later, the Nubian Taharqa was recently deceased, but the reference to Kush may refer to the southern origins of Taharqa, to his recapture of the delta from Assyria in 667 BCE, or (more probably) to the location of Thebes itself, south of the first cataract.[58] Libya is associated with Egypt's military endeavors more than once in the OT (1 Kgs 14:25–28, in the mid-tenth century; 2 Chr 16:8, some decades later),[59] as is Put (Jer 46:9; Ezek 30:5). The cumulative effect of the various components of Egypt's army is one of "strength" (עָצְמָה) in numbers, the soldiers being "without limit" (אֵין קֵצֶה).[60]

Thebe's Surprising Fall (3:10)

Despite Thebes's alliances, defenses, armed forces, and distance from the Assyrian threat (Thebes was roughly 300 miles or 500 km south of the delta region that had suffered Assyrian aggression in the preceding decade), "even she" fell. The גַּם ("even") that begins 3:10 emphasizes the ultimate irrelevance of all that was in the city's favor, and the result is stated in two parallel lines: the personified city "became an exile" (גוֹלָה), and "went into captivity" (שְׁבִי).

The following three lines describe, sometimes in horrifying detail, the traumatic outcome of the city's fall for its population (cf. the similar focus on Nineveh's population in 2:9–11[8–10]). Another גַּם ("moreover") begins this section and makes clear that these lines intensify the comparatively benign description of deportation in 3:10a–b. The brutal murder of young children is portrayed as taking

55. Although the Amada Stela recounts that Amenhotep II hung the bodies of six dead rebels on the walls of Thebes, the absence of any wall surrounding the city means a temple or similar wall must be in view; see Anthony J. Spalinger, *War in Ancient Egypt*, Ancient World at War (London: Routledge, 2005), 78.

56. See Sydney H. Aufrère, Jean-Claude Golvin, and Jean-Claude Goyon, *Sites et temples de haute Égypte (1650 av. J.-C.—300 ap. J.-C.)*, vol. 1 of *L'Égypte Restituée* (Paris: Editions Errance, 1991), 171–84.

57. "Sennacherib's Siege of Jerusalem," *COS* 2.119B:302–3.

58. Donald B. Redford, "Kush," *ABD* 4:109.

59. Warren J. Heard, Jr., "Libya," *ABD* 4:324.

60. Nahum uses אֵין קֵצֶה, "without limit," elsewhere only in 2:10[9]; 3:3.

place all over the city,[61] the city's highest-placed or most esteemed citizens are traded like wares to be trafficked, and "all" her great men are fettered. In addition to depicting gruesome violence calculated to dissuade the population from any rebellion against the conqueror, 3:10c implies the partial eradication of the conquered population (no future generation), while 3:10d–e portray the profound shaming and disenfranchisement of the city's elite, typical in cases when the defeated population had persisted in rebellion.[62]

Nineveh's Similar Fate (3:11)

The clearest and most significant negative reply to the question of 3:8 appears in 3:11. It emphatically will *not* go better for Nineveh than it did for Thebes, despite the Assyrian capital's significant (and in many ways superior) defenses. While an Assyrian hearer would presumably be reminded of the triumph of Assyrian arms at Thebes (and, if consistent with Nahum's characterization of the empire, would also answer "Yes!" to the question of 3:8a), a more objective evaluation would recognize that substantial defenses and military partnerships can be overcome—in other words, that no city is invincible, be it Thebes or Nineveh. Assurbanipal himself seems to have recognized that surprise played an important role in his victory in Egypt, and his statement that the Egyptian king heard of the "approach of my expedition (only when) I had (already) set foot on Egyptian territory" proves that strategy and surprise can outweigh other factors.[63] More importantly, the certainty that Nineveh will not meet a better end than Thebes is guaranteed by YHWH's commitment to punishing the wicked (1:2–8) and to bringing Nineveh to justice (1:9–11, 12c, 14; 2:14[13]; 3:5).

The rhetoric of 3:11 drives this point home for its Judean audience. The first line, 3:11a, begins with a גַּם that makes explicit Nineveh's similarity to Thebes (this same construction appears again at the head of 3:11c): "You *too* will . . ." The first prediction regarding Nineveh is that she will "be drunk" (שׁכר). This metaphorical use of intoxication describes the application of YHWH's wrath to Judah (Isa 51:17–23) or, more frequently, to non-Israelite nations.[64] As Paul Raabe explains, this metaphor invites the reader to "see what it is like to receive divine wrath in light of and against the background of drinking wine."[65] Here, of course, it is Assyria that will drink from YHWH's cup, so the Judean reader is first to process the metaphor then apply it to YHWH's (and Judah's) most prominent enemy. While in some cases the metaphorical intoxication is fatal, here the progression of the verse favors seeing the results as stopping short of death (at least temporarily; cf. 3:10). YHWH's wrath causes Nineveh to seek concealment and shelter from its enemies, with the assumption that none will be found (cf. 1:7, where only YHWH constitutes shelter in the day of judgment).

The last two lines of this section contemplate Nineveh's eventual fall to its attackers (cf. 2:11[10]) by drawing on two related effects of being "drunk" with YHWH's cup of wrath. The first effect is

61. The OT explicitly attributes this horrible act only to nations other than Israel (2 Kgs 8:12; Ps 137:9; Isa 13:16; Hos 10:14; 14:1[13:16]). To date, it is mentioned in only one nonbiblical text, a hymn to Tiglath-pileser; cf. Mordechai Cogan, "'Ripping Open Pregnant Women' in Light of an Assyrian Analogue," *JAOS* 103 (1983): 755–57.

62. Esarhaddon recounted (Prism E) that when he quashed an earlier Egyptian rebellion he "appointed his servants to kingship (and) viceroyship," inevitably dismissing (or worse) the previous Egyptian rulers (Piepkorn, *Historical Prism Inscriptions of Ashurbanipal*, 11).

63. "Babylonian and Assyrian Historical Texts," *ANET*, 295.

64. Cf. also Job 21:19–20; Pss 60:5[3]; 75:9[8]; Isa 49:26; 63:6; Jer 25:15–29; 49:12; 51:7–8, 39, 57; Lam 4:21; Obad 16; Ezek 23:31–34; Hab 2:16; cf. Zech 12:2, and the exhaustive treatment of the metaphor in Paul Raabe, *Obadiah*, AB 24D (New York: Doubleday, 1996), 206–42.

65. Raabe, *Obadiah*, 207.

direct: Nineveh will be inebriated, that is, her capacities will be impaired.[66] The description of the subjective effects of Nineveh's fall on its inhabitants in 2:11[10] was literal yet captured the shock and bewilderment that would sweep over the survivors. Here the picture is similar, and 3:11c adds that the incapacitated Nineveh will (in vain) "seek refuge from the enemy." This may seem an anticlimactic conclusion to this section, but 3:11c is longer than the first two lines of this verse due to the emphatic "yes!" or "you too" (גַּם) with which it begins and the enemy element with which it ends. Further, the image of a personified Nineveh vainly seeking concealment while the enemy overruns it is hardly benign. Even though the terrible imagery used of the fall of Thebes is lacking here, the two cities are in fact mirror images. The assertion that it will *not* go better for Nineveh than for Thebes implies that an equally horrible fate awaits the Assyrian capital, although the worst is left to the reader's imagination.

3. A Military Taunt (3:12–15c)

This subunit is the third of five in this unit, and like the others it undermines and mocks Assyria's very real power as a military empire. Like the preceding and following subunits, it presumes Assyria's guilt on the basis of 3:1–4 and similar passages. It foresees fatal problems in every aspect of Assyria's military readiness and asserts that contrary to appearances Assyria is completely unable to defend itself against the unspecified threat that looms over it. This certitude prompts the speaker to sarcastically exhort the Assyrians to prepare for battle only to immediately add that all such efforts will be in vain. It closes with a catchword ("locust") that connects it to 3:15d–17.

The passage can be divided into two roughly equal halves based on semantic and grammatical features. The first half mocks the adequacy of Assyria's army, infrastructure, and preparedness, and consists of both verbal and verbless clauses. The second half consists of five sarcastic commands to prepare for war (all with imperatives) that are cut short by the assertion that these activities will themselves be interrupted by Assyria's destruction.

As the translation shows, syntactic subordination is evident in the protasis and apodosis that follow 3:12a. No subordinating conjunctions are present apart from the אִם that introduces the protasis, but 3:14b–e and 3:15b–c are indented to reflect the pragmatic or rhetorical effect of successive parallel lines.[67] The entire taunt is indented from the mainline since it is direct discourse.

In discussing 3:8–11 we defined a taunt as "a derisive utterance insinuating that one person, group, or thing is inferior to another,"[68] and this section too can be seen as a taunt even though the comparisons are scattered across the passage rather than framing it, as was the case in 3:8–11.[69] These comparisons are so radical (comparing Assyrian fortresses to figs ready to fall, 3:12, and Assyrian soldiers to women, 3:13a–b) that Angelika Berlejung is correct to see them as elements of a world

66. Because of the cognitive aspects of the verb, Clemens Locher, "עלם, תעלמה," *TDOT* 11:150–51, proposes "out of your senses," explaining the sense as follows: "Drunkenness and its consequences are a very common 'collective punishment' in the prophets. . . . The cognitive nuances of the word . . . suggest that it refers here to a lowered level of consciousness, which will manifest itself as helplessness in the face of the enemy (v. 11b)." See also Christensen, *Nahum*, 361–62.

67. Cf. Fokkelman, *Major Poems of the Hebrew Bible*, vol. 1, 54–55.

68. Floyd, *Minor Prophets*, 649.

69. The literary genre could more simply be that of "insult," but although insults function communicatively with both real and rhetorical audiences, their focus on degrading the other through association with a taboo (religious, moral, etc.) is generally lacking here; cf. José Mateo and Francisco Yus, "Insults: A Relevance-Theoretic Approach to Their Translation," *International Journal of Translation* 12 (2000): 1–2, 97–130. The equation of Assyria's fortresses with ripe fig trees, for example, implies that the fortresses will be conquered and is thus closer

turned upside down.[70] Nahum's taunt inverts the political-military realities of his day in the belief that they soon *will be* inverted by YHWH. Given Assyria's strength in the middle of the seventh century and the probability that many in his audience were quite skeptical regarding any such change, such taunts also contribute rhetorically to the book's message. Like the preceding taunt, this one is addressed to a Judean audience (the real audience), although grammatically the addressee is Assyria (the rhetorical audience, referred to in the feminine singular).[71]

As noted in the Introduction, Nahum delivered his oracles at a time when Assyria was near the zenith of its power (1:12b) and before it entered its final decline. The empire's decline thus cannot account for the confidence with which Nahum speaks. His message depends instead on YHWH's irrevocable decision to do away with all evil, starting with Assyria. The section moves logically from a presentation of the empire's vulnerability (3:12–13) to a sarcastic warning for Assyria to take measures to withstand YHWH's attack (3:14) to a strong affirmation that the empire's defeat is inevitable and will be devastating. The addressee is feminine singular throughout this section.

Assyria's Vulnerability (3:12–13)

Nahum presents Assyria's vulnerability to an implied Assyrian audience in four images. The first and most developed image is based on Assyria's expansive network of "fortresses," which were not dedicated, exclusively military installations but fortified cities that housed a military garrison. Expansion of the Assyrian Empire involved the establishment of new administrative centers at existing sites within its newly conquered territory, and these sites were then fortified and developed through the construction of the necessary buildings and infrastructure.[72] From these centers, usually situated near rivers or other transportation corridors, the empire was able to efficiently oversee the exploitation of the region's population and resources.[73] Further, these towns became the points of departure for new campaigns by means of which the empire continued its expansion. In the time between such campaigns, the towns would obtain "stores of food, oil, wine, and fodder from the surrounding countryside" for the sustenance of the troops based there.[74] Such fortresses existed within proximity to Judah in the seventh century, including in Edom, where among other purposes they served "to sustain and protect the north-south trade route."[75]

Nahum compares this concrete and visible manifestation of the Assyrian Empire's military power and domination with another widespread phenomenon of an agricultural nature: the fig tree.[76] Figs were a popular comestible in Mesopotamia as early

to a prophecy of disaster than to an insult. The same is true of comparing Assyria's soldiers to women; rather than being a sexist insult, the statement probably means that they will be too weak to defend themselves against their attacker.

70. Berlejung, "Erinnerungen," 341.

71. Desjarlais, *Counterplay*, 20.

72. The larger examples of Assyrian fortified cities were surrounded by sizeable walls. Cf. Bradley J. Parker, "The Northern Frontier of Assyria: An Archaeological Perspective," in *Assyria 1995*, ed. S. Parpola and R. Whiting (Helsinki: Neo-Assyrian Text Corpus Project, 1997), 233.

73. Bradley J. Parker, "Archaeological Manifestations of Empire: Assyria's Imprint on Southeastern Anatolia," *AJA* 107 (2003): 525–57; Karlheinz Kessler, "'Royal Roads' and other Questions of the Neo-Assyrian Communication System," in *Assyria 1995*, ed. S. Parpola and R. Whiting (Helsinki: Neo-Assyrian Text Corpus Project, 1997), 134–35.

74. Fuchs, "Assyria at War," 390–91.

75. Seymour Gitin, "The Neo-Assyrian Empire and Its Western Periphery: The Levant, with a Focus on Philistine Ekron," in *Assyria 1995*, ed. S. Parpola and R. Whiting (Helsinki: Neo-Assyrian Text Corpus Project, 1997), 81.

76. Margareta Tengberg, "Fruit-Growing," in *A Companion to the Archaeology of the Ancient Near East*, ed. D. T. Potts (London: Blackwell, 2012), 181–200, esp. 191–92.

as the Old Babylonian period[77] and a very common sight in any historical period.[78] Nahum uses the image of fig trees with first-ripe figs in a simple but eloquent metaphor for Assyrian fortresses.[79] In the event of an attack, these fortified cities would be the first to face the enemy, and in that situation the fortress (like a shaken fig tree) would fall (like a ripe fig) into the mouth of the attacker. The "eater," mouth open under the fig tree he is shaking, is a striking image of the power and appetite of the attacker, while the shaking conveys the abrupt end that awaits the Assyrians.[80] Already effective as a purely literary image, the image would perhaps have added irony for an audience familiar with Nineveh or with Neo-Assyrian propaganda, since Sennacherib had planted fig trees along major streets in Nineveh and encouraged its citizens to eat their fruit: "The area of Nineveh, my royal city, I enlarged. . . . All kinds of mountain vines, all the fruits of (all) lands (settlements), herbs and fruit-bearing trees I set out for my subjects.[81]

Following the image that equates Assyria's defenders with soon to be eaten figs is another (preceded by the focus particle הִנֵּה, 3:13a) that equates them with women (3:13b). This is the fourth and final use of הִנֵּה in Nahum, and each time it introduces something that is unexpected or climactic in the context.[82] Its use here may be due to the shift from the impersonal fortified cities to their human population, who will attempt to defend their cities in vain, but it also surely underlines how unexpected will be Assyria's weakness and consequent collapse.

The term translated "troops" (עַם) is most often translated "people," but the sense of "troops" is much more suitable here, since women were probably roughly half of the empire's population.[83] Not only is a military referent required by the context (cf. 1 Sam 11:11; 1 Kgs 20:10), but the comparison of (outmatched) troops with women is attested elsewhere in the OT (Isa 19:16; Jer 50:37; 51:30) and in Assyria's descriptions of its foes. Esarhaddon says that as he approached the enemy's "crack troops" who were preparing for battle, "Fear of the great gods, my lords, overwhelmed them, (and when) they saw my mighty battle array, they became like crazed women."[84] Similarly, his vassal treaty, composed to ensure a smooth transition of power to his son Assurbanipal, threatened those who violated its terms thus: "May all the gods who are called by name in this treaty tablet . . . make you like a woman before your enemy."[85] The comparison's apparently misogynist or sexist element evaporates when one

77. Frances Reynolds, "Food and Drink in Babylonia," in *The Babylonian World*, ed. G. Leick (London: Routledge, 2007), 178.

78. Lucia Mori, "Land and Land Use: The Middle Euphrates Valley," in *The Babylonian World*, ed. G. Leick (London: Routledge, 2007), 47.

79. The first crop of figs was typically harvested by merely shaking the tree, while later crops had to be harvested by hand (Christensen, *Nahum*, 364).

80. Cf. the less emphatic image in Isa 28:4. The image is surely more striking than the image of destroyed fruit trees so common in descriptions of sieges laid by Assyrians in their royal inscriptions and bas-reliefs; see Steven W. Cole, "The Destruction of Orchards in Assyrian Warfare," in *Assyria 1995*, ed. S. Parpola and R. Whiting (Helsinki: Neo-Assyrian Text Corpus Project, 1997), 29–40.

81. Luckenbill, *Historical Records from Assyria from Sargon to the End*, 171 (Rassam Cylinder, section 399). I owe this reference to Christensen, *Nahum*, 364.

82. Earlier in Nahum it was used in connection with the arrival of the messenger of good news (2:1[1:15]) and YHWH's statements that he is "against" Assyria and will destroy it completely (2:14[13]; 3:5).

83. Édouard Lipiński, "עם," *TDOT* 11:176.

84. Leichty, *The Royal Inscriptions of Esarhaddon*, 15 (Nineveh Prism A, column i).

85. Vassal Treaty of Esarhaddon, lines 616A–17, http://oracc.museum.upenn.edu/saao/saa02/P336598. Markus Zehnder, "Building on Stone? Deuteronomy and Esarhaddon's Loyalty Oaths (Part 2): Some Additional Observations," *BBR* 19 (2009): 519, notes this same motif in Hittite treaties.

remembers that physical size and strength were vastly more important than other considerations in ancient warfare. Similarly, the terror of the female population after their defeat by Assyria was not senseless dishevelment but a perfectly reasonable awareness of the frequency of rape as part of the plunder and exploitation of the vanquished.[86] Nahum's taunt implies that the enemy is of superior strength and that Assyria as a whole, and not only its women, will be unable to resist and should fear the coming destruction.

The third image that conveys Assyria's vulnerability makes reference to the "gates" of its cities and fortresses, normally closed with a cross-bar (בְּרִיחַ, 3:13d) when the population was under threat. The extreme danger posed by open gates is clearly emphasized by the unusual word order of this line, which places a prepositional phrase before the verb: "To your enemy are wide open the gates of your land." Further emphasis on this disastrous situation comes from the infinite-finite verb pair that describes the gates as not simply "open" but "wide open" (פָּתוֹחַ נִפְתְּחוּ). Finally, the widespread nature of this lack of preparation is made clear by locating the gates not at a particular city, but generally in "your land."[87] The order of the text presumes that these gates are eventually closed before the enemy's arrival but to no avail.[88]

The final image of fire burning (literally "consuming," אכל) gate-bars probably reflects the final stages of a siege, when the attackers have come near enough to the city's primary gate to set it on fire.[89] Given the urban focus of much warfare in the ancient Near East, this tactic was employed by many nations, including Assyria.[90] Here the burning of the gate-bars marks the end of Assyria's cities, confirming the evaluation made in 3:12 and bringing the taunt proper to a close. The certainty of Assyria's fall prepares the reader to interpret the warning that follows in 3:14 as sarcasm.

A Sarcastic Call for Assyria to Prepare for Battle (3:14–15c)

This call for Assyria to prepare for a siege takes the reader back to a point in time prior to the arrival of the enemy army. This temporal discontinuity with the perspective of 3:13d underlines the sarcastic nature of these commands, since instructions for preparing for the siege are given *after* (in terms of textual order) an announcement that the attack will succeed. Only two aspects of preparation are mentioned: the water that was most necessary to human survival, and how Assyria should fortify its fortresses (מִבְצָר, the same term as in 3:12a). The first element is self-explanatory, but the intensification evident across the four instructions for strengthening the fortresses' defenses and the larger sequence of five commands to prepare (in vain!) for YHWH's punishment strengthen the passage's sarcastic tone.

Following the command to draw water before the siege starts, the next four elements move from the general command ("fortify!" in 3:14b) to more specific commands to go into the clay (3:14c, for eventual use in the brick mold in 3:14e) and to tread mortar (3:14d, used to join the bricks that would eventually be completed[91]) to a final imperative,

86. Berlejung, "Erinnerungen," 337, and against the suggestion that this motif makes women (disparagingly) "emotional."

87. Craigie, Kelley, and Drinkard, *Jeremiah 1–25*, 204, understand the same phrase in Jer 15:7 similarly.

88. Alternatively, Fabry's suggestion of hendiadys is a plausible explanation for the sequence of open gates followed by burned gate-bars (*Nahum*, 217).

89. The root אכל occurs six times in Nahum (1:10; 2:14[13]; 3:12, 13, 15 [twice]), always with Assyria as the object that is eaten or consumed, whether in part or whole.

90. Fales, *Guerre et paix*, 191.

91. Although חֹמֶר can denote either clay (for bricks) or mortar used to join them, the parallels in Gen 11:3; Exod 1:14 suggest that חֹמֶר denotes mortar here; cf. *HALOT*, 330.

"grab the brick mold!" (3:14e).[92] The reinforcing of the city's walls with brick contrasts with attested Assyrian practice, which (when undertaken sufficiently in advance) reinforced Nineveh with cut stone.[93] The text probably implies that although these preparations are undertaken before the siege begins, the timeframe is so short that the laborious and time-consuming masonry required for the construction of more durable defenses is out of the question. Even more intriguingly, this detailed sequence is incomplete, since no bricks are formed with the brick mold "grabbed" in 3:14e, no formed bricks are baked, and no baked bricks are ever added to the defenses.

The explanation for this interrupted sequence is to be found in 3:15, which in terms of literary order literally interrupts the series of commands to prepare for a siege with the affirmation that *there*, in the very place of preparation for the assault, fire and sword will devour Assyria (the adverb "there," שָׁם is placed at the head of the verse for emphasis).[94] This adds still more sarcasm to these commands—not only are they futile in light of the inevitable fall of the empire (3:13d), but the preparations themselves will not be completed before the enemy overwhelms and kills the defenders. Like the preceding series, this one too evidences intensification over several lines (see Exegetical Outline). Two of the three clauses have identical syntax (verb with object suffix followed by subject) and all use imperfective verbal forms (imperfective). Further, the root אכל, "eat, consume," is repeated, appearing in 3:15a, c (it also closed the first subsection, 3:13d, which also uses אֵשׁ, likewise present in 3:15a).

The idea that Assyria would be consumed by fire has already appeared in the metaphor of 1:10 (implicitly, with אכל) and in the divine threat of 2:14[13] (with בער), where it consumes Assyria's chariots. Here the fire consumes Assyria itself (3:15a), as does the locust. The repetition of fire as a force that completely consumes of Assyria is reinforced by the middle line of the tricolon, where the sword "eliminates" Assyria (with *hiphil* כרת).[95] Finally, although the verbs אכל and כרת are shared with 2:14[13], here Nahum expands the extent of the "consuming" and "elimination" from the particular (chariots, young lions, and violence in 2:14[13]) to the general or global (the empire itself and as a whole: "you"). Even if defensive preparations are undertaken, the *complete* destruction of *all* of Assyria is certain.

4. An Economic Taunt (3:15d–17)

This is the third and last taunt in this unit. Like the two earlier taunts, it takes Assyria's guilt for granted (cf. 3:1–4) and explores its punishment in ways that undo the empire's self-confidence on the basis of its extensive and successful management and exploitation of subjugated territories and vassal states. It is closely connected to the preceding taunt by its genre and by the catchword "locust" that appears in the last line of the preceding taunt and the first line of this one. The taunt plays on two features of locusts, their number and their transience. Although the Assyrian Empire had spread over the ancient Near East like an immense swarm of locusts, visible among other ways in its

92. The *hiphil* of חזק means "grasp" and not "use, employ," so that here bricks are never actually made, although the necessary equipment and raw materials are in place; cf. *HALOT*, 304.

93. Cf. Stronach, "Notes on the Fall of Nineveh," 315–18.

94. While the bricks could be sun dried rather than baked in an oven (so Tidiman, *Nahoum, Habaquq, Sophonie*, 121), neither activity is mentioned here. Cf., however, Spronk, *Nahum*, 135–36, who thinks the brickmaking process is completed here.

95. In 2:14[13] the sword "consumes" Assyria's "young lions."

administrative and economic personnel, their departure will be sudden and complete.

This subunit begins with parallel sarcastic commands for the empire to multiply further its already numerous administrators. The following two subunits are distinguished by their use of one or the other of the two types of locusts mentioned in the opening lines and by dealing with distinct spheres of activity, economic in 3:16 and royal/administrative in 3:17. Each of these two subunits concludes with the anticipated departure and disappearance of the locusts, so that the empire (as represented by its personnel) disappears twice in the taunt, ironically complementing the double command to multiply those personnel.

Subordination is present in the adverbial phrase at the end of 3:16a and in the circumstantial clauses in 3:17c–e. The coordination in 3:15d–e corresponds to the repeated imperatives, much like the parallel equations of Assyrian administrative figures with locusts entail coordinate lines in 3:17a–b. The subordination in 3:17c–e ends abruptly as the locusts flee; the sunrise is subordinate to the following clause as the circumstances for the action it describes (note also the subject-verb order in 3:17e). The whole section is indented from the mainline since it is direct speech.

We can once again adapt our definition of a taunt to this section, since it explicitly compares Assyria's imperial personnel with locusts and presents them as identical in terms of the characteristics it focuses on. Unlike earlier taunts, this one offers no explanation for the departure of the metaphorical locusts. It resembles the military taunt, however, in its sarcastic call for Assyria to enlarge further its corps of personnel, only to affirm that, like locusts, this immense group representing the empire will disappear and never be seen again. This taunt also shares with the others the use of direct speech, addressing a rhetorical Assyrian audience (the empire, usually in the second-person feminine singular) but heard only by the real Judean audience.

A Sarcastic Call for Assyria to Multiply Its Personnel (3:15d–e)

The taunt begins with repeated commands for Assyria to multiply itself (*hithpael* of כבד) (3:15d, e).[96] Each command has a different term for "locust," the first more rare (יֶלֶק, "creeping locust") and the second more common (אַרְבֶּה, "migratory locust").[97] Both references evoke the extremely large populations of these insects, and while they could connote their capacity to consume food resources on which human life depends (cf. 3:15c), that aspect seems (surprisingly) absent from the text.

The choice of the locust as opposed to other entities that are characteristically numerous (e.g., sand on the seashore) may reveal Nahum's awareness of Neo-Assyrian military self-descriptions in terms of locusts.[98] For example, Sargon II (721–705 BCE) said of himself, "In the anger of my heart I overran these lands like a swarm of locusts,"[99] and Sennacherib (704–681) compared his military advance to "the onset of the locust swarms of the springtime."[100] If Nahum intentionally uses the

96. The masculine-singular form that begins 3:15c should be amended to a feminine-singular imperative, in keeping with the two following verbs. The sense of multiplication for the *hithpael* of כבד is attested only here, but is recognized by *HALOT*, 456. Its overlap with the sense of the *hiphil* is arguably indicated here by the *hiphil* form in 3:16a.

97. Cf. *HALOT*, 83.

98. The enemy's forces were occasionally compared to "a spring invasion of a swarm of locusts," Sennacherib 22, v 56 (http://oracc.museum.upenn.edu/rinap/pager).

99. Luckenbill, *Historical Records from Assyria from Sargon to the End*, 10, cited in Johnston, "Nahum's Rhetorical Allusions to Neo-Assyrian Conquest Metaphors," 38.

100. Luckenbill, *Historical Records from Assyria from Sargon to the End*, 252, cited in Johnston, "Nahum's Rhetorical Allusions to Neo-Assyrian Conquest Metaphors," 38.

same imagery, he modifies it by removing any menacing role from it so that Assyria's army is characterized primarily by transience, no more threatening than a locust swarm without appetite.

The Number and Transience of Assyria's Economic Personnel (3:16)

This subunit begins with the affirmation that Assyria did indeed develop its economic and administrative infrastructure, referred to with רֹכְלִים, "merchants" (3:16a). While this term is very general, Assyrian practice allows us to add at least two details. First, much of Assyria's wealth came in the form of vassal payments coerced from subjugated states and from spoils taken in war, as noted above. A similar source of wealth was the extraction of resources from territories it controlled, as was the case with the large-scale exploitation of the olive oil industry in Assyrian-controlled Ekron in the seventh century BCE.[101] The absence of military terminology in this section favors seeing this aspect as secondary, but probably not entirely absent. Second, Assyria also pursued international trade with states that were not under its control, and this sense seems to be required by רֹכְלִים.[102] As an example, apart from its brief domination by Assyria in the middle of the seventh century BCE, Egypt remained an independent power and consequently conducted its trade with Assyria on an entirely different basis than did vassal states.[103] This trade necessitated both personnel and administrative structures. In some cases Assyria established trade offices in various ports "where the king and his merchants were accorded special trading privileges," while in the case of Egypt, Assyria appointed a resident "warden" from a north Arabian tribe.[104] Yet despite Assyria's careful development of a sizable economic corps, both inside the empire's borders and especially beyond them, it will disappear without a trace.

The Number and Transience of Assyria's Palace Personnel (3:17)

This final subunit picks up on the second type of locust mentioned at the beginning of the taunt, the "migratory locust" (אַרְבֶּה). This insect is compared with the first of two Assyrian officials, the מִנְזָר. This word in Biblical Hebrew occurs only here, with a proposed sense of "courtier."[105] The second term for an Assyrian representative, טִפְסָר, is compared with a "swarm of locusts," and appears elsewhere only in Jer 51:27, where it apparently denotes an official in the context of military action against Babylon.[106] Most likely a loan word, the sense of טִפְסָר appears to be close to "scribe," apparently referring to an individual who can appear in military, economic, or other contexts in which written records of one sort or another are required.[107] Akkadian analogues for both words appear (*manzazu*, *ṭupšarru*) in Neo-Assyrian sources, with both terms overlapping "astrologers, augurs, magicians" if *ṭupšarru* occurs with an appropriate modifier.[108]

101. Avraham Faust, "The Interests of the Assyrian Empire in the West: Olive Oil Production as a Test-Case," *JESHO* 54 (2011): 62–86.

102. Moshe Elat, "Phoenician Overland Trade within the Mesopotamian Empires," in *Ah, Assyria! Studies in Assyrian History and Ancient Near Eastern Historiography Presented to Hayim Tadmor*, ed. M. Cogan and I. Eph'al, ScrHier 33 (Jerusalem: Magnes, 1991), 22–23; Saggs, *The Might That Was Assyria*, 177–79.

103. The data is presented in detail by Moshe Elat, "The Economic Relations of the Neo-Assyrian Empire with Egypt," *JAOS* 98 (1978): 20–34.

104. Elat, "Phoenician Overland Trade," 27, 28.

105. *HALOT*, 601.

106. Gerald L. Keown, Pamela J. Scalise, and Thomas G. Smothers, *Jeremiah 26–52*, WBC 27 (Dallas: Word, 1995), 351, translate טִפְסָר, as "recruiter (scribe)." Allen, *Jeremiah*, 524, translates it as "strategist," with a nod to the Akkadian loanword.

107. *HALOT*, 379.

108. Kevin J. Cathcart, "Nahum," *ABD* 4:998, following Simo Parpola, *Letters from Assyrian Scholars to the Kings Esarhaddon and Assurbanipal*, AOAT 5 (Neukirchen-Vluyn: Neukirchener Verlag, 1970–1971), 1:2. In the case of *ṭupšarru*,

Apart from a general association of divination and the royal court with Assyrian diplomacy and thus with decisions related to economic affairs, these divinatory connotations do not suit the Nahum context well, nor is *ṭupšarru* modified in any way, so we should see these individuals in a more general association with the royal court, albeit as distinct from the "merchants" mentioned in 3:16.[109]

Unlike the previous section, no explicit reference is made to Assyria's defeat and destruction in connection with the disappearance of the empire's economic and royal personnel.[110] Their complete disappearance suits Nahum's purposes perfectly, however. The image emphasizes the transience of this host of ravaging merchants, who will disappear entirely along with the empire they served, and their whereabouts will be unknown (3:17g). This point is emphatically reiterated by the last line of the section: "Where are they?" (3:17h).[111]

5. The Final Dirge for the Assyrian King (3:18–19)

This subunit, a dirge that closes the book, follows three taunts that cast doubt on Assyria's ability to remain indefinitely on the world stage, regardless of its military might, political alliances, battle-readiness, and economic strength. The dirge's semantics do not go beyond those of the taunts, which also announced the empire's downfall, but its focus on the king is paralleled only in 1:14. Like that announcement that YHWH will do away with the Assyrian monarch as despicable (despite his claims to the contrary), this final address to Assyria exposes the ultimate insignificance of the king and echoes the book's repeated condemnations of the empire's treatment of other nations as the ground for its destruction. The end of the Assyrian Empire is presented in terms of its population (3:18) and of the king himself (3:19a–b) and meets with applause on the part of all who hear the news. The empire's fall will come about because of the king's "evil" (רָעָה).

A dirge typically eulogizes the deceased. Since in the book's perspective Assyria is not yet dead (1:12), this dirge is prospective, meaning it anticipates the empire's certain demise.[112] Far from eulogizing Assyria, Nahum spells out the mortal danger that threatens the empire only to announce that all who hear of its inevitable passing will rejoice![113] This dirge is thus bitterly sardonic, since dirges normally lament "the irreplaceability and incomparability of the dead person."[114]

---

it appears in a syntagm that specifies that the *ṭupšarru* reads an omen series; Karen Radner, "The Assyrian King and His Scholars: The Syro-Anatolian and the Egyptian Schools," in *Of God(s), Trees, Kings, and Scholars: Neo-Assyrian and Related Studies in Honour of Simo Parpola*, ed. M. Luukko, S. Svärd, and R. Mattila, StOr 106 (Helsinki: Finnish Exegetical Society, 2009), 222. Parpola, *Letters from Assyrian Scholars*, xiv, defines the *ṭupšarru* as "experts in the art of interpreting celestial, terrestrial and teratological portents, and establishing the calendar and the ominous significance of days and months." However, the term by itself need not have a divinatory connotation; an Assyrian king, probably Esarhaddon, mentions "Egyptian scribes" alongside "veterinarians" in a description of his Egyptian spoils of war; cf. Leichty, *The Royal Inscriptions of Esarhaddon*, 55. Radner, "The Assyrian King," 222–23, notes a reference to a "scribe (*ṭupšarru*) of the tablet house."

109. Cf. Berlejung, "Erinnerungen," 342, who asserts that both offices "had significant roles in the Neo-Assyrian Empire in terms of military efficiency and management" (author's translation).

110. It is difficult to correlate the rising of the sun with danger, whether for locusts or in general.

111. Although emended or moved by *BHS*, the verse's final word is clearly present in L and reflected in many of the versions; cf. Gelston, *The Twelve Minor Prophets*, 91.

112. Some biblical dirges are proleptic, e.g., Ezek 26–28; cf. Goering, "Proleptic Fulfillment," 503.

113. See the comments of Goering, "Proleptic Fulfillment," 492–94, 503; Gale A. Yee, "The Anatomy of Biblical Parody: The Dirge Form in 2 Samuel 1 and Isaiah 14," *CBQ* 50 (1988): 565–86; Hedwig Jahnow, *Das hebräische Leichenlied im Rahmen der Völkerdichtung*, BZAW 36 (Giessen: Töpelmann, 1923).

114. Jahnow, *Das hebräische Leichenlied*, 97–98, with reference to 2 Sam 1:19–27, cited and translated in Goering, "Proleptic Fulfillment," 493.

The dirge has three parts. The first two announce the collapse of the Assyrian state in terms that stress its (now meaningless) relationship to the king (3:18) and his fatal prognosis (3:19a–b). The final section includes a response of widespread joy rather than sorrow at the king's demise, which is proof of YHWH's righteous punishment of him and his empire.

The indentation of 3:18c–e highlights the effect of three successive parallel lines that reinforce 3:18a,[115] and the whole dirge is indented from the mainline as direct discourse. In Nah 3:19d the subordinating conjunction כִּי signals the ground for the action in 3:19c.

This section is explicitly addressed to the king of Assyria (3:18b) as a masculine-singular subject. The directness of the speech is emphasized by the use, in every one of this section's lines (apart from the vocative in 3:18b and the implicit cataphoric reference in 3:19e) of a second-person singular suffix on a noun "belonging to" the king. The king is the target of YHWH's wrath (cf. 1:14) and the representative of the empire, so that when he falls, it falls with him.

The Collapse of the State (3:18)

The collapse of the Assyrian state, implying the king's inability to watch over and protect its citizens, is presented in order of descending rank. First, the king's nobles are so highly placed that Nahum attributes to them a quasi-royal role by referring to them as "shepherds," a term often used by the king of himself to underline his guiding and protective role. This overlap in terms of responsibility (if not in rank as recognized by the royal court) is occasionally attested in Neo-Assyrian history, especially in times of upheaval: Shamshi-ilu, a *tartānu* or commander-in-chief responsible for the northwest regions of the empire during the tumultuous first half of the eighth century, gave himself the title of "ruler of Hatti, Guti, and all Namri"[116] (roughly from the northern Levant to the Zagros Mountains on Assyria's northeastern border) and recorded his military exploits on two enormous stone lions in typical royal style. In Nahum's vision, these normally vigilant governors are said to be "dozing" or "drowsy," which clearly bodes ill for their metaphorical sheep.[117] Much as the empire's "shepherds" are dozing, its "nobles" "sit still" (3:18b).[118] While it is difficult to specify what offices these persons held, their inactivity (due to insouciance?) is clearly inappropriate and leads directly into a picture of the citizens under their care being scattered abroad (cf. 1 Kgs 22:17).[119]

After two lines that describe the failure of Assyria's leaders to exercise proper oversight and care for their people follow two lines that describe the result in terms of the empire's population. Both lines use the image of dispersion: Assyrians are "scattered" over hill and dale (פוש), and given the delinquency or inability of the "shepherds" and "leaders" there is no one who will "gather" them (קבץ; cf. Isa 13:14; literally, Jer 49:5). The verb "scatter" is very rare, and given its sound (*pûš*) is probably meant to recall the "scatterer" of 2:2[1] (a participial form of *pûṣ*).

115. Cf. Fokkelman, *Major Poems of the Hebrew Bible*, vol. 1, 54–55.

116. Wayne Horowitz, *Mesopotamian Cosmic Geography* (Winona Lake, IN: Eisenbrauns, 1998), 82–83.

117. Cf. William C. Williams, "נום," *NIDOTTE* 3:60–61.

118. Gerald H. Wilson, "שכן," *NIDOTTE* 4:109–10, argues that the verb denotes immobility following movement. While LXX has translated this as a verb of sleep, the MT tradition attests no variants; cf. Gelston, *The Twelve Minor Prophets*, 114*. The use of ישן, "sleep," with נום, "slumber, doze," in Ps 121:4; Isa 5:27 weighs in favor of emending the text here, but the parallel use of נום, "slumber, doze," and שכב, "lie down," in Isa 56:10 complicates the question, as does the use of ישב, "sit," for Babylon's exhausted defenders in Jer 51:30 (noted by Spronk, *Nahum*, 142–43). Since the text makes good sense as is, I favor retaining the reading attested in MT.

119. Nahum's assertion here overturns the description of Assyria as watchful and vigilant in Isa 5:27, where the verb נום, "slumber, doze," also appears. A double entendre involving sleep as death (cf. Job 14:12; Pss 22:16; 49:12; 94:17; ישן is in

However, the one responsible for scattering Assyria is not in focus here, and the perspective is limited to the final outcome of the attack on Assyria.

The choice of this image of Assyrians scattered over their land like sheep without a shepherd was likely motivated by the frequency with which Neo-Assyrian kings referred to themselves as the "shepherd" of their land and people, pasturing and protecting the flock and gathering wandering sheep.[120] As such, this verse "inverts a stereotypical image of the prestige used in royal self-glorification in the ancient Near East and uses it against the Assyrian king and his officers, whose shepherd-function YHWH finally abrogates."[121] Additional irony arises from the fact that Neo-Assyrian treaties sometimes threatened the treaty-breaker with "the dispersion of his people."[122]

The Prognosis: Death of the King (3:19a–b)

The book of Nahum closes with decisive finality by announcing the certain death of the Assyrian king, still addressed with second-person masculine grammar as in 3:18. The book's last lines begin with a double assertion that the Assyrian king, and thus his empire, cannot and will not recover from the judgment that Nahum sees looming over them. First, 3:19a affirms that there is no "healing" or "amelioration" (כֵּהָה) possible for his fracture (שֶׁבֶר), and 3:19b reinforces this by qualifying his "wound" as "severe."[123]

The motif of the mortal wound is well attested in the ancient Near East, particularly in Neo-Assyrian treaties of the seventh and eighth centuries.[124] At roughly the same time that Nahum was composed, Esarhaddon boasted that he inflicted such a wound on the rebellious Egyptian vassal king Taharqa: "By means of arrows, I inflicted him five times with wounds from which there is no recovery."[125] Similarly, Esarhaddon threatened four times those vassals who would break his succession treaty with "an unhealing sore," and in another treaty he repeats that threat against Baal of Tyre.[126] In these treaties, as in Nahum, the attribution of a fatal wound to an enemy is tantamount to announcing his death but preserves the prospective aspect in which the dying enemy has not yet met his fate.

The Reaction: Universal Joy (3:19c–d)

Against the somber background of Assyria's inevitable demise arises a reaction of unmitigated joy! While hardly unexpected, the contrast is as stark as can be imagined. Although Nahum is addressed to

---

parallel with נום in Isa 5:27; Ps 121:4) is possible but unlikely here because there is no explicit violence against these "shepherds," whose literal sleep or inattention allows their "sheep" to stray. Cf. the discussion in Fabry, *Nahum*, 222.

120. So also Berlejung, "Erinnerungen," 343–44, 347. Among numerous references, see Royal Inscriptions of the Neo-Assyrian Period, "Tiglath-pileser III 35, ii 17"; "Sennacherib 001, 93"; Esarhaddon 033, i, 9"; http://oracc.museum.upenn.edu/rinap/pager. Although the motif has a long history in the ancient Near East, Nahum's familiarity with Neo-Assyrian ideology favors seeing a close connection here; cf. Timmer, "Nahum's Representation of and Response to Neo-Assyria," 349–62.

121. Berlejung, "Erinnerungen," 344 (author's translation).

122. Parpola and Watanabe, *Neo-Assyrian Treaties and Loyalty Oaths*, 4 (text 1, 17′).

123. שֶׁבֶר can involve broken bodily limbs (Lev 21:19 and a few other texts) but more often refers to the collapse of structures or a lack of well-being. Healing language is used of שֶׁבֶר or מַכָּה in Isa 30:26; Jer 6:14; 8:11; 10:19; 30:12, 15; Hos 5:13; Mic 1:9. Among these, Isa 30:26; Jer 10:19; 30:12 are particularly close to Nah 3:19.

כֵּהָה occurs only here in Biblical Hebrew. Spronk, *Nahum*, 143, favors retaining the text as transmitted by MT, in part because of the alliteration (with כ) it shares with other lexemes in the verse. Some suggest reading גֵּהָה, but this too is a *hapax legomenon* (Prov 17:22). *Niphal* חלה is parallel to "incurable pain" (with אָנוּשׁ) in Isa 17:11 and Jer 30:12; it is mourned for and apparently without healing in Jer 14:17, 19.

124. Johnston, "Nahum's Rhetorical Allusions to Neo-Assyrian Treaty Curses," 429; Russell Mack, *Neo-Assyrian Prophecy and the Hebrew Bible: Nahum, Habakkuk, and Zephaniah*, PHSC 14 (Piscataway, NJ: Gorgias, 2011), 216.

125. Leichty, *The Royal Inscriptions of Esarhaddon*, 185 (I owe this reference to Berlejung, "Erinnerungen," 344).

126. "The Vassal Treaties of Esarhaddon," trans. Erica Reiner (*ANET*, 538–39); "Treaty of Esarhaddon with Baal of Tyre," trans. Erica Reiner (*ANET*, 534).

Judeans, the end of Assyria will be witnessed by many other states (cf. 3:7), and all who hear of it will clap their hands in jubilation (cf. Pss 47:2[1]; 98:8; Isa 55:12 uses מחא instead of תקע).[127] As was the case with the audience in 3:7a, the placement of "all those who see/hear" of the fall of Assyria before the verb (thus before its fall) emphasizes the communicative nature of YHWH's work of judgment—the audience's reaction is subsequent to the event in time, but preeminent in terms of focus. The reason is indicated by the כִּי that subordinates this clause to those preceding it and is expressed in the language of moral evaluation—Assyria's "evil" (רָעָה) has "passed over" (cf. the ironic reuse of this verb in connection with flood language in 1:8) everyone in its orbit "ceaselessly" (תָּמִיד; cf. the use of the verb עבר with the same sense in 2:1[1:15], where this outcome is anticipated).

The only other use of רָעָה, "evil" in Nahum appears in 1:11, where it describes the "wicked" opposition of the empire's plots to YHWH and his claims.[128] Those who first heard or read Nahum's message would have known (probably by direct experience) the concrete expression of Assyria's power and voracious appetite for conquest and would have qualified it as evil themselves. The use of the same term in Nah 1:11 reminds the reader, however, that what is "evil" on the horizontal level in terms of how one person or group treats another is, above all, "evil" with respect to YHWH, in whose world such acts are committed and to whom all are accountable (cf. 1:2–8). This dirge closes the book of Nahum by confirming in concrete, historical language that YHWH will not leave unpunished those responsible for evil and that his victory over evil is good for those whom it delivers.

Canonical and Theological Significance

YHWH's Glory and Justice (3:1–7)

Although Assyria's destruction is "good news" (in a nonsalvific way) to the entire ancient Near East, the book of Nahum as a whole presents it especially as the demonstration of YHWH's justice in the undoing of an impressive charlatan that had usurped YHWH's role and authority. This passage focuses on Assyria's usurpation of power over life and death in its violence and its forcing human beings to serve a master that laid claim to rights and honors that belong only to YHWH. As the gracious, good Creator, YHWH by definition cannot exploit his creatures (cf. 1:7). His destruction of Assyria demonstrates his compassion for the many nations who were its victims and reasserts the inviolability of his unique glory.

The book of Revelation clearly develops this line of thought in connection with Rome, especially in Rev 17:1–19:10. John presents the empire of his day as "a seductive whore and a scheming witch" in order to help his readers "perceive something of Rome's true character—her moral corruption behind the enticing propagandist

127. Cf. Nili Fox, "Clapping Hands as a Gesture of Anguish and Anger in Mesopotamia and in Israel," *JANES* 23 (1995): 49–60, esp. 54. Idioms that use ספק, "slap, clap," שׂפק, "slap, clap," or *hiphil* נכה, "hit, strike" (Job 27:23; Lam 2:15; Ezek 6:11; 21:14, 17) express other sentiments.

128. There may be an ironic use of the homophonic root רעה, "shepherd," in 3:18.

illusions of Rome which they constantly encountered in their cities."[129] This self-aggrandizement, concretely expressed in the imperial cult, involved the same idolatry we have seen in Nahum's depiction of Neo-Assyria, and John's use of the sobriquet "Babylon" at various points in his book hints that he sees essential continuity between all power structures (political or not) that elevate themselves to the level of deity (Rev 16:19; 17:5; 18:2, 10, 21).[130] This has reference especially to their authority and thirst for glory, which stand in opposition to God's throne and worship (e.g., Rev 4, and note that the destruction of Rome/Babylon leads to worship of God, Rev 19:4).[131] God's just destruction of "Babylon" similarly liberates or vindicates (in a general sense) not only his people but "all who have been slain on earth" (Rev 18:24), leading to worship (Rev 19:1–6).

The simultaneously Christocentric and Trinitarian worship that Revelation presents draws most frequently on God's designation of Jesus Christ as the one through whom he will judge the world (Rev 22:12) and as the way to be delivered from his wrath (22:14; for the two together, note especially 1:5–7 and the lion/lamb pair in Rev 4–5). The final judgment unites the two emphases of Nahum's opening vision, in which God alone is judge and deliverer, and it arrives at that final point after pausing to witness the humiliation and destruction of all power that sets itself up in defiance of God's exclusive claims. Believers who read Nahum are encouraged to deconstruct the (often veiled) claims that any and all things outside God make on their heart, mind, and body and to serve the one true God at all costs, knowing that the names of those who serve God alone are written in the Lamb's book of life (Rev 12:11; cf. 18:4; 19:5).[132]

YHWH's Irresistible Judgment (3:8–11)

The point of this taunt is to establish that despite all its power and defenses, Nineveh will fall under YHWH's judgment just as Thebes fell to Assyria. In Nahum, the validity of the taunt is guaranteed first of all by YHWH's perfect justice, from which there is no escape (1:3b, 6, 8). Before the final conflagration, however, YHWH brings about his judgment only in partial, incomplete ways. Thus the destruction of Assyria on the historical scene stops short of the eschatological judgment sketched in 1:2–8. While other passages in Nahum stress the reasons for Assyria's punishment, here the emphasis falls on its certainty, despite factors that might suggest otherwise.

This message appears in various forms in both Testaments and is foundational to believers' hope, confidence, and peace. From the very beginning God promised to

129. Richard Bauckham, *The Theology of the Book of Revelation*, NTT (Cambridge: Cambridge University Press, 1993), 18.

130. Cf. Ibid., 102; Gregory K. Beale, *The Book of Revelation: A Commentary on the Greek Text*, NIGTC (Grand Rapids: Eerdmans, 1999), 843.

131. Bauckham, *The Theology of the Book of Revelation*, 39, rightly traces God's conflict with Rome in Revelation back to the vision of the heavenly throne in Rev 4.

132. Beale, *The Book of Revelation*, 174, summarizes the book's message in light of Rev 22:9 as "the sovereignty of God

ensure the victory of his people over their opponents (Gen 3:15), and Israel's history (despite its consistently limited military might) bears eloquent witness to YHWH's saving power as he delivers them from Egypt, from Aram/Syria during Elijah's ministry (e.g., 1 Kgs 20), from Assyria during the reign of Hezekiah (2 Kgs 18–19), and from Babylon in order to secure his people's return from exile (Ezra 1:1–4).

Moving into the NT, Nahum's strong emphasis on the religious nature of Assyria's opposition to YHWH and his people helps explain the Gospels' emphasis on the spiritual nature of the kingdom that Christ brings (Matt 12:28; John 18:36). The book of Revelation stands out as an extended analysis of the ways that supernatural opposition to God and his people makes use of political and military power and institutions, bringing Nahum's analysis of Assyria to its fullest expression. In the context of the whole Bible, Nahum's message that the Assyrian oppressor, thus far unstoppable, will all the same be unable to escape YHWH's judgment encourages the reader to maintain faith in God's justice (especially when under persecution, Rev 6:9–11), to remain patient and faithful while the empire is at full strength (Rev 12:17), and to observe soberly the fulfillment of the threatened punishment in due time (Rev 11:15–19, etc.).

Deconstructing Human Self-Confidence (3:12–15c)

This taunt focuses on military might as the ground of Assyria's confidence that no enemy can defeat it. In the book of Nahum, this confidence is not simply a military calculation but the assertion that Assyria is beyond the reach of YHWH himself, despite his being the sole creator and sole guarantor of universal justice. The taunt puts Assyria in its place, debunking its arrogant claims to be master of its own destiny by asserting that it is far less powerful than it thought itself to be. Then as now, human power, whether wielded individually, collectively, or by an elite, is used wrongly unless it is consecrated to the service of YHWH and his glory.[133] Much like Nahum's message recognizes the interrelation of spiritual and earthly powers and the often surprising fragility of the powerful, the gospel highlights the power of God in the apparent weakness of those who serve him faithfully. This paradox is clearest in our Lord's example (Acts 8:32–35; 2 Cor 13:4), but biblical writers repeatedly apply it to the Christian life (2 Cor 11:29–30; 12:9) and ministry (1 Cor 2:3–5). As Western culture is on the verge of completing the long process of shuffling off the Judeo-Christian veneer it has carried for centuries, this truth is both a caution and an encouragement. On the one hand it warns against seeking to advance one's (Christian?) cause in one's own power, and on the other encourages the church to

and Christ in redeeming and judging brings them glory, which is intended to motivate saints to worship God and reflect his glorious attributes through obedience to his word."

133. See J. Gordon McConville, *God and Earthly Power: An Old Testament Political Theology*, LHBOTS 454 (London: T &T Clark, 2006), 12–29.

continue in the faithful exercise of its mission in dependence upon its king, whose power is unlimited and who makes his strength perfect in our weakness.

Although Assyria is beyond repentance in Nahum, one can never be certain that an individual or group is beyond repentance. Outside the context of the unique case of Assyria in the seventh century BCE, this taunt is like other biblical arguments meant to deprive those not yet reconciled to God of their reasons for remaining in that situation. Like Jesus's statement to some of the Pharisees that "if you were blind, you would have no guilt; but now that you say, 'We see,' your guilt remains" (John 9:41 ESV), and Paul's exploration of innate human sinfulness in Rom 1–3, Nahum's dismissal of human pretensions to be beyond the reach of divine justice challenges his audience to reevaluate the foundations of their beliefs in light of God's character and actions. The larger context of this taunt affirms that YHWH is indeed a shelter to those who see their need of one, and in the context of Nah 1:2–8, the fall of Assyria is a faint shadow of the judgment that looms over all who are unreconciled to God (John 3:18).

The gospel unflinchingly presents Jesus Christ as the only refuge from the wrath of God against sin, and Nahum reminds us that as only the sick need a physician, only those whose self-confidence in ultimate matters has been shaken will turn to Christ and find deliverance from sin's guilt and power. Each of us has to do with a God who transcends all human categories and standards. One may be powerful, intelligent, and immune to critique or attack on the human level, but human ability or accomplishment is of no account in the eyes of the God to whom each of us must give account. Far more so than in Nahum's taunt, the realities of the gospel invert the world as we naturally see it, and our well-being in every sense depends on seeing ourselves in relation to God on Scripture's terms rather than self-confidently persisting in our autonomy and independence. Those who jettison trust in themselves find genuine security in God and need not pursue cheap and ultimately ineffective imitations.

Human Transience (3:15d–17)

This taunt eschews the usual presentation of Assyria as a military state in favor of its economic facet. Despite the empire's well developed, effective, and widespread economic apparatus, Nahum announces that it will disappear almost overnight. As before, the certainty of this unexpected event depends on YHWH's truthfulness in promising to rid the world of evil and specifically to free Judah and similar states from the clutches of the Neo-Assyrian Empire.

Nahum's claims would have appeared incredible to many, including many in Judah, since Assyria was the largest and most developed empire the world had seen. Yet Assyria, like empires before and after it, disappeared from the scene regardless of its very focused efforts to remain in power. While the twenty-first century still witnesses the existence of substantial world powers, we cannot understand Nahum's message in simple geopolitical terms. This is not only because the distinction between Israel and the "nations" is undone in the NT, with membership in the people of God being presented in terms of one's faith in Christ and repentance from sin, but also because Nahum does not critique Assyria as nothing more than a political power. Rather, he focuses on its propagandistic metanarrative, which was designed to persuade lesser powers to come under its aegis and to convince those already under its control that it would meet all their needs and was worthy of their unreserved commitment and complete trust.

Today, such metanarratives are often transmitted more clearly at the level of culture than at the level of nation-states.[134] Cultures based on a secular metanarrative give those who espouse them significance, identify and grant access to fulfillment and standing, and exercise a formative influence on many areas of their lives, especially their moral values and beliefs.[135] It is essential that those who preach the gospel explore the various worldviews that their hearers hold or by which, at least, they are invariably influenced in their cultural setting. Like the Enlightenment worldview's fall from supremacy, the worldviews that have arisen in its place are similarly ephemeral, appearing for a brief time before giving way to the next best thing. The critical feature of their passing is of course their epistemological insufficiency, which leaves those who embrace them adrift until the next thing.

Whether tied to a nation-state or some nonpolitical source, metanarratives at odds with the biblical worldview inevitably offer permanence where none is to be found. The gospel, by contrast, offers the deepest possible sense of belonging, permanence, and significance on the basis of a restored relationship with one's creator and judge through repentance and trust in him as one's redeemer (e.g., 1 Pet 2:4–10). The hope the gospel offers (1 Pet 1:3–9) outweighs whatever price believers pay here and now as they follow and bear witness in word and deed to the Son of God who died for them (1 Pet 1:18–21) and will judge the living and the dead (1 Pet 4:5).

Materialism (3:15d–17)

While power, pleasure, and other things are frequently used as analgesics against the throbbing awareness of human transience and accountability to God, the economic focus of this taunt highlights the relevance of Scripture's teaching on

134. Helpful discussions of these issues appear in D. A. Carson, *The Gagging of God: Christianity Confronts Pluralism* (Grand Rapids: Zondervan, 1996), and David F. Wells, *Above All Earthly Pow'rs: Christ in a Postmodern World* (Grand Rapids: Eerdmans, 2005).

135. Greg Forster "To Love the World: The Irony, Tragedy, and Possibility of *To Change the World*," in *Revisiting 'Faithful Presence'*: To Change the World *Five Years Later*, ed. C. Hansen (Deerfield: The Gospel Coalition, 2015), 17–18, argues that "the concept of culture emerged to fill the gap between religion and social order in the modern world," and that "when it is detached from revealed religion that transcends culture, the ideal of culture leads first to racism and nationalism, then to relativism and nihilistic despair."

wealth and material possessions.[136] Despite the fact that the OT connects material well-being and covenant fidelity in various contexts (e.g., Deut 28:1–14), it also frequently cautions against the abuse of one's wealth (Amos 4:1). Indeed, it is hard to imagine a more convincing argument against the absolute good of wealth and material possessions than the admission in Ecclesiastes that when these are pursued "under the sun" rather than in the fear of YHWH, they are meaningless (Eccl 2:1–11). Although the NT nowhere connects material wealth and a healthy relationship with God, it still affirms that earthly goods have their place when properly used, and a number of wealthy individuals played important roles as supporters of Jesus and the apostles (Luke 8:1–3; Acts 16:14–15).[137] In contrast, not only were Assyria's riches often obtained through violent conquest, but its self-centered imperialism involved the accumulation of wealth in the hands of the elite, where it fostered pride and autonomy. Despite the massive amount of wealth it accumulated, the Assyrian Empire disappeared from the world scene nearly overnight (cf. Jas 1:9–11). Material wealth is indeed "a particularly telling area for determining one's religious commitment," and Nahum's condemnation of Assyria's ill-gotten and misused wealth is complemented by Jesus's admonition to "seek first the kingdom of God and his righteousness."[138] In so doing our use of material means will be pleasing to God, who will bless them for his glory (Matt 6:19–21).

Divine Justice and Mercy (3:18–19)

Taken together, the books of Jonah and Nahum help the reader see that YHWH's punishment of Nineveh is not premature, nor is YHWH without mercy (cf. also 1:7). The biblical presentation attributes repentance to Nineveh in the eighth-century setting of Jonah, although there is no mention of Nineveh putting aside its gods as converts to faith in YHWH do.[139] It would appear that after this temporary change of heart, Nineveh fell back into its habitual violent behavior (Jonah 3:8), so that by the time of Nahum some one-hundred years later, the time for Assyria's genuine repentance had come and gone.

While Nahum by itself is a clear testament to YHWH's just wrath as the expression of his vengeance against sinners (cf. 1:2), divine mercy is hardly absent from the book (1:3a, 7). Further, comparison of its message with that of Jonah makes

136. Note, however, Carl Trueman's incisive analysis of the centrality of entertainment in contemporary American culture in "Lost in Xanadu: Life in the Pleasure-Dome Makes the Church's Task Incalculably Difficult," http://www.firstthings.com/blogs/firstthoughts/2016/08/lost-in-xanadu.

137. Throughout this paragraph I draw on some points made by Craig L. Blomberg, *Neither Poverty nor Riches: A Biblical Theology of Material Possessions*, NSBT 7 (Grand Rapids: Eerdmans, 1999).

138. Ibid., 244.

139. Ludwig Schmidt, *'De Deo': Studien zur Literarkritik und Theologie des Buches Jona, des Gespräches zwischen Abraham und Jahwe in Genesis 18:22f. und von Hi 1*, BZAW 143 (Berlin: de Gruyter, 1976), 84–86, and Hartmut Gese, "Jona ben Amittai und das Jonabuch," *TBei* 16 (1985): 256–72, also note that Nineveh does not abandon her gods. The examples of Ruth and Naaman present a more comprehensive conversion to YHWH; cf. Walton, "The Object Lesson of Jonah 4:5–7," 47–57.

clear that neither attribute can be separated from the other (cf. esp. Nah 1:3a–b with Jonah 3:10–4:2). This same reality appears in Nahum's use of the root שמע in 3:19, used with reference to news regarding Assyria only one other time, in 2:1[1:15]. The announcement there to Judah that Assyria will no longer oppress them and the affirmation here that it will be done away with remind the reader that YHWH's just intervention involves not only punishment of the guilty but deliverance of those who trust in him.

The ultimate fulfillment of the judgment announced in 1:2–8 and partially fulfilled in Assyria's fall will be realized in the full and final salvation of those who have put their trust in Christ, who died for their sins and rose again for their justification (Rom 4:25). He will deliver them from all oppression (Rev 7:9–17), while those who persist in rebellion against him will be eternally condemned (Rev 9:20–21; 16:9, 11, 21; 19:19; 20:15). Those who read Nahum well cannot but take these realities to heart and so renew their commitment to spreading by word and deed the gospel to which Nahum bears witness. They can do so confident in the power and grace of the Lord Jesus Christ as more than sufficient to overcome all obstacles, even those that set themselves directly against the progress of the gospel. In sharp contrast to every human kingdom, his dominion is "an everlasting dominion" (Dan 7:14), and the rapid growth of the early church in the face of significant opposition bears eloquent witness to the power of its ascended king as he reigns through the Holy Spirit (Acts 1:6–8; 2:32–33; 1 Cor 15:25).

Scripture Index

Genesis

2:16; 12:20 108
3:15 176
4:7 159
10:32 159
11:3 167
13:2 .... 135, 136
15 105
15:7 72
16:4, 5 113
17 105
18:19 88
28:6 108
28:12 132
28:20–22 115
29:19 159
31:1 136
32 124
32:27–28 43
34:2 155
42:10 159
42:11 74
42:13 159
44:8 135
49:23 78

Exodus

1:11–12 106
1:14 167
4:14 79
6:2 72
6:2–8 72
6:27 74
7:5, 17 72
14–15 47
14:4 72
14:6 142
14:12 159
14:17 47
14:18 72
15 47
15:6 80
15:7 103
19:5–8 105
20 .... 74, 75, 76, 79
20:5 .... 74, 75
20:5–6 47
20:5–7 .... 43, 77
20:6 47
20:23 135
22:22–24 79
23:14–17 114
23:33 105
28:10 110
29:46 72
32 79
32–34 .... 79, 94
32:11 .... 48, 79
32:12 86
32:25–28 79
32:33 88
32:33–35 79
32:35 88
33:12 88
33:19 88
34 .... 76, 80, 88, 93
34:6 79
34:6–7 .... 47, 48, 61, 76, 77, 79
34:7 .... 80, 106
34:7b 76
34:14 .... 74, 75
34:18, 22 114

Leviticus

8:18 156
16:12 87
18:8 156
20:3 109
20:18 132
21:19 173
26 106
26:14–39 106
26:40–45 106
27:2–8 115
27:9–13 115

Numbers

6:26 114
8:22 108
10:35–35 47
14:17–18 76
22:18 135
23:9 87
24:13 135
25:4–5 86
25:11 74
32:36 124

Deuteronomy

1:28 137
4:24 .... 74, 75
4:37 .... 48, 79
5:9 .... 74, 75

6:15 . . . 74, 75
7:24 . . . 109
8:2–3, 16 . . . 106
9:29 . . . 48, 80
13:14 . . . 104
16:1–17 . . . 114
17:18 . . . 67
20:8 . . . 137
22:28 . . . 155
28 . . . 106
28:1–14 . . . 179
28:15–68 . . . 106
28:16, 22 . . . 84
30 . . . 106, 107
30:6 . . . 106
32:8 . . . 132
32:15 . . . 157
32:16, 21 . . . 74
32:22 . . . 87
32:41, 43 . . . 78
33:15 . . . 85
34:10 . . . 88

Joshua

2:10 . . . 82
2:11 . . . 137
4:23 . . . 82
5:1 . . . 82, 137
6:24 . . . 135
7 . . . 47
7:5 . . . 137
7:26 . . . 86
11:6 . . . 47, 143
17 . . . 124
22:12 . . . 122
22:33 . . . 122
24 . . . 74
24:19 . . . 74

Judges

4:17 . . . 114
5:28 . . . 142
6:3 . . . 122
6:28 . . . 132
9:6 . . . 132
9:15 . . . 84
15:10 . . . 122
17:13 . . . 159

Ruth

1:16 . . . 57
3:10 . . . 159

1 Samuel

2:8 . . . 85
2:30 . . . 113
2:32 . . . 159
3:1 . . . 68
8:12 . . . 142
11:11 . . . 166
15:2–3 . . . 44
24:3 . . . 87
24:13 . . . 75
24:21 . . . 109
28:18 . . . 86

2 Samuel

1:19–27 . . . 171
5:20 . . . 49
7 . . . 105
7:20 . . . 88
8:11 . . . 135
10:3 . . . 158
13:12 . . . 155
13:14 . . . 156
14:8 . . . 108
17:10 . . . 137
20:15 . . . 161
23:19 . . . 103

1 Kings

1:47 . . . 110, 159
2:43 . . . 108
4:33 . . . 84
5:6 . . . 84
11:5 . . . 156
11:10, 11 . . . 108
11:39 . . . 106
12:26–33 . . . 42
14:22 . . . 74
14:25–28 . . . 162
20 . . . 176
20:10 . . . 166
20:13 . . . 72
20:26–30 . . . 44
21:8–10 . . . 67
21:10, 13 . . . 104
21:23 . . . 161
22:3 . . . 42
22:17 . . . 172

2 Kings

5:17 . . . 57
8:7–15 . . . 44
8:12 . . . 163
8:28 . . . 42
9:25 . . . 68
10:32–33 . . . 42
13:14–19 . . . 44
14:9 . . . 84
14:25 . . . 42
16 . . . 152
16:5–10 . . . 101
16:7–10 . . . 39
17 . . . 80
17:11, 17–18 . . . 81
17:24, 30–31 . . . 39
17:36 . . . 48, 80
18 . . . 152
18–19 . . . 176
18:13–19 . . . 45
18:22 . . . 100
18:29–35 . . . 39
18:33, 35 . . . 101
19 . . . 83
19:17 . . . 82
19:19 . . . 101
19:21–28 . . . 45
19:23 . . . 84
19:24 . . . 82, 83
19:25 . . . 83

19:32 . . . 105
19:35–36 . . . 105
21:1–18 . . . 40
21:9 . . . 40
21:13 . . . 40
22:14–20 . . . 40
23:21–25 . . . 114
23:25 . . . 40
37 . . . 45

1 Chronicles

14:11 . . . 49
16:40 . . . 108
18:3 . . . 132
19:3 . . . 158

2 Chronicles

4:27 . . . 103
12:7 . . . 87
16:8 . . . 162
20:34 . . . 132
24:27 . . . 68
33:1–17 . . . 40
34:21, 25 . . . 87

Ezra

1:1–4 . . . 176
3:7 . . . 84
7:15 . . . 135

Nehemiah

1:10 . . . 48, 80

Esther

2:10, 20 . . . 108
4:5, 8, 17 . . . 108

Job

2:3 . . . 134
2:11 . . . 158
3:24 . . . 87
9:17 . . . 81
10:10 . . . 87
13:25 . . . 104
14:12 . . . 172
15:33 . . . 155
21:18 . . . 104
21:19–20 . . . 163
24:21 . . . 159
26:12 . . . 79
27:20 . . . 81
27:23 . . . 174
28:10 . . . 87
34:13 . . . 85
36:32 . . . 108
38:11 . . . 135
39:5 . . . 107
40:4 . . . 113
42:11 . . . 158

Psalms

1:4 . . . 104
2 . . . 47
2:3 . . . 107
2:12 . . . 42, 89
5:12 . . . 42
7:11 . . . 86
9 . . . 95
9–10 . . . 95
9:14–15, 20–21 . . . 95
10:1, 12–15 . . . 95
18:4 . . . 83
18:8–16 . . . 72
18:15–19 . . . 83
18:48 . . . 75
22:14 . . . 137
22:16 . . . 172
24:1 . . . 85
24:2 . . . 83
25 . . . 95
29:5 . . . 84
29:10 . . . 83
31:2 . . . 88
31:20 . . . 42
34:8 . . . 88
35:5 . . . 104
37:28 . . . 109
37:40 . . . 42
38:3 . . . 86
41:5 . . . 109
47 . . . 62
47:2 . . . 174
47:5 . . . 124
48:14 . . . 161
49:12 . . . 172
49:19 . . . 159
60:5 . . . 163
64:11 . . . 42
65:7 . . . 79
66:6 . . . 83
69:21 . . . 158
69:24 . . . 86
69:32 . . . 159
74:17 . . . 132
75:9 . . . 163
77:16–19 . . . 83
78:49 . . . 86
78:58 . . . 74
83:13 . . . 104
83:16 . . . 81
85:5 . . . 124
85:10 . . . 91
88:7 . . . 106
89:9 . . . 83
90:2 . . . 85
90:15 . . . 106
93 . . . 62
94:17 . . . 172
96–99 . . . 62
98:8 . . . 174
102:10 . . . 86
102:11 . . . 86
103:9 . . . 78
104:7 . . . 135
106 . . . 82
106:2 . . . 72
106:9 . . . 82, 83
107:14 . . . 107
107:17 . . . 106
110 . . . 47
114:3, 5 . . . 135

114:4, 6 ... 72, 85
119 ... 95
119:67, 71 ... 106
121:4 ... 172, 173
122:7 ... 161
135:3 ... 88
137:9 ... 163
146 ... 62
147:5 ... 79

Proverbs

1:11, 16, 18 ... 78
1:27 ... 81
8:25 ... 85
10:25 ... 81
15:2, 13 ... 159
17:22 ... 159, 173
22:24 ... 77
27:5 ... 132
29:22 ... 78
30:1 ... 68
31:1 ... 68

Ecclesiastes

2:1–11 ... 179
11:9 ... 159

Song of Solomon

2:8 ... 114
4:10 ... 159

Isaiah

1 ... 40
1–3, 5 ... 60
1:1 ... 68
2 ... 85
2:7 ... 136
2:13 ... 84
2:19, 21 ... 87
5:24 ... 103–4
5:27 ... 172, 173
5:29 ... 142
7–8 ... 39, 101
8:7 ... 122
8:7–8 ... 130
10:5 ... 86
10:5–19 ... 147
10:13 ... 147
10:16 ... 136, 147
10:17 ... 103
10:25 ... 86
10:27 ... 107
11:6 ... 143
11:15 ... 83
13:1 ... 68
13:5 ... 86
13:7 ... 137
13:7–8 ... 137
13:9 ... 86
13:9–13 ... 86
13:13 ... 86
13:14 ... 172
13:16 ... 163
14:25 ... 107
14:32 ... 44
17:11 ... 173
17:13 ... 81, 104
18:2 ... 44
19:1 ... 137
19:4 ... 68
19:5 ... 83
19:5–7 ... 82
19:5–8 ... 161
19:14 ... 103
19:16 ... 166
21:3 ... 137
22:24 ... 136
24:4 ... 85
26:1 ... 161
26:21 ... 86
28:4 ... 166
28:7 ... 137
29:5 ... 104
29:6 ... 81
30:20 ... 134
30:26 ... 173
30:27 ... 86
32:15–17 ... 114
33:11 ... 104
36 ... 152
36:10 ... 122
36:18 ... 101
36:18–20 ... 101
36:20 ... 101
37 ... 83
37:4 ... 101
37:6 ... 101
37:11–13 ... 101
37:17 ... 101
37:18 ... 82
37:20 ... 101
37:25 ... 82, 83
38:14 ... 134
40:24 ... 81, 104
41:2 ... 104
41:16 ... 81
41:23 ... 159
42:13 ... 74
42:15 ... 72, 82, 83, 85
44:27 ... 82
47:14 ... 104
48:19 ... 109
49:26 ... 163
50:2 ... 80, 82
51:10 ... 82, 83
51:17–23 ... 103, 163
51:19 ... 158
52:1, 7 ... 45
52:7 ... 114
52:8 ... 124
55:12 ... 174
56:10 ... 172
57:13 ... 89
59:11 ... 134
59:17 ... 74
59:18 ... 86
60:13 ... 84, 136
63:6 ... 163
64:11 ... 106
64:12 ... 106

65:25 143
66:12 136
66:14 86
66:15 81
66:22 109
66:24 92

Jeremiah

1:5 88
2:20 107
2:23 159
3:5, 12 78
4:13 81
4:23–26 72
4:24 85
5:5 107
5:14 143
6:14 173
6:29 87
7:5 159
7:20 87
8:11 173
10:4 137
10:10 86
10:12 85
10:19 173
11:20 75
13:22 155, 156
13:24 105
13:26 155, 156
14:1–7 84
14:13 114
14:17, 19 173
14:21 157
15:7 167
18:5–10 92
18:7–8 44
18:18 100
21:3–7 47
23:16 68
23:19 81
23:33, 34, 36, 38 68
25:15–19 103
25:15–29 163
27:1–11 44
27:2 107
27:5 79
30:6 137
30:8 107
30:12, 15 173
30:23 81
31:33 105
32:17 79
33:11 88
39–40 44
42:18 87
44:6 86, 87
46:7–8 49
46:9 162
47:2 49
49:5 172
49:7–12 103
49:12 163
49:20 100
49:37 86
50:25 86
50:31 142
50:37 166
50:45 100
51:7–8 163
51:15 85
51:25 142
51:27 170
51:30 166, 172
51:36 82
51:39 163
51:45 86
51:57 163

Lamentations

2:5 47
2:6 86, 155
2:8 161
2:14 68
2:15 174
4:21 103, 163

Ezekiel

5:13 86
6:11 174
7:17 137
12:10 68
16:36 156
16:37–39 155
21:12 137
21:14, 17 174
22:20 87
22:22 87
23:31–34 103, 163
24:8 75
24:12 87
26–28 171
26:3 142
28:2 134
28:22 142
29:3–5 161
29:21 72
30:5 162
30:12 161
32:5 114
36:5–6 74
38:19 74
39:25 74

Daniel

2:35 104
7:14 180
9:11 87
9:27 87
11:7 161
11:10, 40 49

Hosea

2:5 156
4:15 81
5:5 124
5:10–15 81
5:13 173
7:10 124
7:15 104, 134

10:14 . . . 163
12:2 . . . 81
13:3 . . . 104
14:1 . . . 163

Joel

1:6 . . . 122, 142
2 . . . 76
2:5 . . . 104
2:13 . . . 76
2:18 . . . 74
2:27 . . . 72
3:12 . . . 12
3:17 . . . 72
4:12 . . . 12
4:17 . . . 115

Amos

1:14 . . . 81
2:4–6 . . . 60
3:2 . . . 88
4:1 . . . 179
4:7–8 . . . 84
6:1–3 . . . 147
6:2 . . . 159
6:4–7 . . . 147
6:7 . . . 147
6:8 . . . 124
8:7 . . . 124
9:9–10 . . . 125
9:11–15 . . . 124

Obadiah

16 . . . 103, 163

Jonah

1:2 . . . 67
3:3 . . . 67
3:8 . . . 179
3:9 . . . 86
3:10–4:2 . . . 180
4 . . . 76
4:1–2 . . . 92
4:2 . . . 76, 77
4:11 . . . 67

Micah

1:9 . . . 173
2:1–5 . . . 147
2:3, 5 . . . 147
2:7 . . . 159
3 . . . 40
5:14 . . . 86
7 . . . 76
7:14 . . . 84
7:18–20 . . . 77

Nahum

1 . . . 82, 83, 95
1:1 . . . 53, 65, 66, 69, 72, 89, 97, 100, 128
1:1–2 . . . 73
1:1–10 . . . 65
1:1–11 . . . 65
1:1a . . . 66
1:1b . . . 66, 73
1:1b–3b . . . 72, 74
1:2 . . . 47, 59, 70, 72, 73, 75, 80, 179
1:2–3 . . . 43, 61, 77
1:2–3b . . . 70, 71, 74, 81, 85, 86, 87, 90
1:2–5 . . . 42, 70, 72
1:2–6 . . . 88
1:2–8 . . . 33, 41, 43, 44, 46, 49, 52, 54, 58, 59, 61, 65, 66, 69, 70, 71, 72, 73, 79, 88, 89, 90, 91, 92, 93, 95, 96, 97, 100, 115, 116, 117, 118, 122, 125, 142, 155, 163, 174, 175, 177, 180
1:2a . . . 73, 74, 75, 80
1:2a–d . . . 71, 79
1:2a–3a . . . 70, 72
1:2a–3b . . . 65, 69, 70, 88
1:2b . . . 73, 76, 79, 80
1:2c . . . 73, 76, 77, 78, 80, 100
1:2c–d . . . 79
1:2d . . . 73, 76, 77, 78, 80, 100
1:3 . . . 47, 73, 79
1:3–5 . . . 94
1:3a . . . 71, 73, 76, 79, 80, 81, 85, 86, 89, 90, 179
1:3a–b . . . 180
1:3b . . . 70, 71, 73, 76, 80, 81, 93, 175
1:3b–5 . . . 87
1:3b–6 . . . 86, 89
1:3c . . . 72
1:3c–d . . . 71
1:3c–5 . . . 46, 65, 69, 70, 81, 86, 87, 90
1:3c–5d . . . 90
1:3c–5e . . . 71, 86
1:4 . . . 73, 82, 83, 135
1:4a . . . 46, 70, 82, 83
1:4a–b . . . 70
1:4a–c . . . 71, 83, 84
1:4b . . . 46, 70, 82
1:4c . . . 72, 82
1:4c, d . . . 46
1:4c–5b . . . 70
1:4d . . . 83, 84
1:4d–e . . . 71, 84
1:5 . . . 73, 81, 84
1:5a . . . 87
1:5a–c . . . 84
1:5a–e . . . 71
1:5b . . . 87
1:5c . . . 46, 70, 81, 85
1:5d . . . 46, 81, 85
1:5d–e . . . 70, 85
1:5e . . . 85
1:6 . . . 73, 85, 87, 88, 90, 93, 94, 95, 175
1:6–8 . . . 65, 69, 70, 71, 85, 87
1:6a . . . 72
1:6a–b . . . 70, 71, 86, 87
1:6b . . . 72, 87
1:6c . . . 70, 87
1:6c–d . . . 71, 72
1:6d . . . 85, 87
1:7 . . . 14, 42, 61, 62, 73, 81, 85, 86, 88, 90, 94, 103, 163, 174, 179
1:7–8 . . . 88, 90, 95
1:7a . . . 72, 88
1:7a–c . . . 71
1:7b . . . 88, 89
1:7b–c . . . 72

1:8......45, 47, 49, 61, 70, 73, 75, 89, 90, 93, 94, 105, 175
1:8a........................89, 100
1:8a–b..........................71
1:8a–c..........................72
1:8b.........................89, 93
1:9..........47, 69, 75, 96, 100, 102, 103, 104, 142, 152
1:9–10.........97, 99, 100, 103, 104, 109, 114, 152
1:9–11............. 41, 48, 142, 163
1:9–14..........................67
1:9–2:1 ....54, 65, 68, 96, 97, 98, 99, 116, 118, 119
1:9–3:19.......... 53, 58, 59, 60, 61
1:9a...................99, 100, 104
1:9a–c..........................98
1:9a–10c........................98
1:9b...........................100
1:10................. 103, 167, 168
1:10a..........................103
1:10a–c.........................98
1:10b..........................103
1:10c..........................103
1:11...75, 98, 100, 104, 105, 115, 174
1:11–12........................114
1:11–13.....................97, 99
1:11–13b 98
1:11a, b.......................105
1:12....34, 48, 58, 60, 68, 75, 93, 105, 106, 109, 115, 117, 124, 138, 141, 152, 171
1:12–13............. 41, 42, 68, 104
1:12–14.........................68
1:12a–c.........................98
1:12b.............. 33, 99, 105, 165
1:12c..................99, 105, 163
1:12d.....................106, 115
1:12d–e........... 98, 105, 107, 124
1:12d–13 105
1:12d–2:1.......................99
1:12e..........................115
1:13...................45, 62, 107
1:13a–b.........................98
1:14....41, 48, 59, 67, 75, 97, 99, 102, 104, 108, 109, 110, 111, 112, 114, 115, 122, 132, 133, 142, 152, 156, 157, 163, 171, 172
1:14a–b.........................98
1:14a–e.........................98
1:14b................ 111, 113, 115
1:14b–d 99, 113
1:14b–e........................109
1:14c..................98, 111, 112
1:14d......................98, 113
1:14e..................98, 99, 113
2 142
2:1......43, 45, 62, 67, 68, 70, 89, 97, 99, 100, 105, 109, 114, 115, 116, 124, 146, 166, 174, 180
2:1–3:19 41
2:1a...........................114
2:1a–b..........................98
2:1a–f..........................98
2:1b...........................114
2:1c...........................114
2:1c–d..........................99
2:1c–f..........................98
2:1d...........................114
2:1e...........................115
2:1e–f..........................99
2:1f...........................115
2:2.......54, 118, 119, 122, 123, 126, 127, 128, 129, 130, 132, 134, 135, 136, 137, 138, 172
2:2–11.........41, 51, 53, 54, 97, 99, 118, 119, 122, 133, 135, 137, 138, 139, 141, 146
2:2–14...65, 69, 97, 118–45, 120, 138
2:2a–e.........................120
2:2c...........................124
2:3.........33, 43, 62, 107, 116, 117, 118, 119, 124
2:3–4..........................125
2:3–11.........................135
2:3a...........................119
2:3a–c.........................120
2:3b–c....................119, 124
2:4.......54, 123, 125, 126, 127, 128, 129, 130, 134, 135, 136, 137
2:4–5.....................138, 152
2:4–6..........................123
2:4–11........67, 119, 122, 123, 125, 152, 157
2:4–14.........................118
2:4a–e.........................120
2:4a–11e.......................120
2:4c...........................126
2:4d...........................126
2:5.......54, 123, 126, 127, 129, 130, 133, 134, 135, 136, 137
2:5a...........................128
2:5a–d....................120, 122
2:5d...........................128
2:6... 54, 60, 123, 126, 127, 128, 129, 130, 133, 134, 135, 136, 137
2:6–9..........................138
2:6a–d.........................120
2:7...........49, 123, 126, 127, 128, 129, 130, 131, 132, 134, 135, 136, 137
2:7–8.....................123, 133
2:7–9...........................54
2:7a...........................131
2:7a–b.........................120
2:7b...........................131
2:8...........60, 122, 123, 126, 127, 129, 130, 132, 133, 134, 135, 136, 137
2:8a–e.........................120
2:9..........123, 126, 127, 129, 130, 133, 134, 135, 136, 137
2:9–11....................123, 162
2:9a...........................134
2:9a–e.........................121
2:9b...........................134
2:9b–c.........................133
2:9b–e.........................134
2:9c–d.........................122
2:10.......54, 67, 122, 123, 126, 127, 129, 130, 133, 134, 135, 136, 137, 138, 152, 162
2:10a–b............. 122, 135, 158
2:10a–d 121
2:10d..........................136

2:11 . . . 60, 122, 123, 126, 127, 129, 130, 133, 134, 135, 136, 137, 138, 163, 164
2:11a–e . . . 121
2:11b . . . 164
2:11b–e . . . 122
2:11b, d . . . 137
2:11c, e . . . 137
2:12 . . . 139, 141, 143
2:12–13 . . . 139, 144, 152
2:12–14 . . . 45, 48, 49, 51, 55, 67, 119, 122, 138, 146, 152, 153
2:12a . . . 141
2:12a–e . . . 121
2:12a–14f . . . 121
2:12b . . . 141
2:12b–e . . . 122
2:12c–e . . . 122
2:12e . . . 141
2:13 . . . 41, 59, 75, 122, 141, 142, 143
2:13a–d . . . 121
2:14 . . . 45, 51, 60, 68, 75, 102, 108, 115, 116, 122, 139, 141, 142, 143, 153, 155, 163, 166, 167, 168
2:14a–f . . . 121
2:14b . . . 122
2:14c . . . 142
2:14d . . . 142, 144
2:14e . . . 142, 144, 152
2:14f . . . 142
3 . . . 113
3:1 . . . 67, 147, 152, 153, 154, 155, 156
3:1–3 . . . 153
3:1–4 . . . 41, 59, 60, 153, 158, 164, 168
3:1–7 . . . 55, 67, 147, 174
3:1–19 . . . 65, 69, 97, 138, 148
3:1a . . . 152, 153, 154
3:1a–d . . . 148, 153
3:1a–4 . . . 153
3:1a–7e . . . 148
3:1b . . . 152, 153
3:1b–d . . . 147, 152
3:1d . . . 152
3:2 . . . 153
3:2–3 . . . 152, 153, 155
3:2–4 . . . 153
3:2a–b . . . 153
3:2a–3g . . . 148
3:2c–d . . . 153
3:3 . . . 162
3:3a–g . . . 147
3:3d–e . . . 153
3:3f . . . 153
3:3g . . . 153
3:4 . . . 67, 152, 153, 154, 155, 156
3:4–6 . . . 133
3:4–7 . . . 51, 156
3:4a . . . 147, 153
3:4a–d . . . 148
3:4b–d . . . 147
3:5 . . . 45, 51, 102, 142, 155, 163, 166
3:5–6 . . . 142, 155, 158
3:5–7 . . . 33, 41, 68, 75, 147, 153
3:5a . . . 156
3:5a–6c . . . 148
3:5c–e . . . 156
3:5c–6c . . . 155
3:5d . . . 155
3:5e . . . 155
3:6 . . . 158
3:6a–c . . . 156
3:7 . . . 68, 158, 174
3:7a . . . 158, 174
3:7a–e . . . 149
3:7c . . . 158
3:7c–e . . . 155
3:7d . . . 158
3:8 . . . 33, 163
3:8–9 . . . 158, 160
3:8–11 . . . 51, 52, 55, 158, 164, 175
3:8–19 . . . 41
3:8a . . . 159, 163
33:8a–9c . . . 149
3:8a–11c . . . 149
3:8b . . . 161
3:8b–e . . . 159
3:8c . . . 161
3:8d . . . 161
3:8d–e . . . 161, 162
3:8e . . . 161
3:9 . . . 162
3:9a–c . . . 159
3:9b–c . . . 159
3:10 . . . 159, 162, 163
3:10a–b . . . 162
3:10a–e . . . 149, 159
3:10b–e . . . 159
3:10c . . . 163
3:10d–e . . . 163
3:11 . . . 88, 103, 159, 163
3:11a . . . 163
3:11a–c . . . 149
3:11b–c . . . 159
3:11c . . . 159, 163, 164
3:12 . . . 164, 167
3:12–13 . . . 165
3:12–15c . . . 55, 158, 164, 176
3:12a . . . 164, 167
3:12a–13d . . . 150
3:12a–15c . . . 150
3:13 . . . 167
3:13a . . . 166
3:13a–b . . . 164
3:13b . . . 166
3:13d . . . 167, 168
3:14 . . . 165, 167
3:14–15c . . . 167
3:14a–15c . . . 150
3:14b . . . 167
3:14b–e . . . 164
3:14c . . . 167
3:14d . . . 167
3:14e . . . 167, 168
3:15 . . . 115, 167, 168
3:15a . . . 168
3:15b–c . . . 164
3:15c . . . 168, 169
3:15d . . . 169
3:15d–e . . . 150, 169
3:15d–17 . . . 56, 164, 168, 177, 178
3:15d–17h . . . 150

3:15e . . . 169
3:16 . . . 169, 170, 171
3:16–17 . . . 60
3:16a . . . 169, 170
3:16a–b . . . 150
3:17 . . . 169, 170
3:17a–b . . . 169
3:17a–h . . . 150
3:17c–e . . . 169
3:17e . . . 169
3:17g . . . 171
3:17h . . . 171
3:18 . . . 56, 114, 126, 171, 172, 173, 174
3:18–19 . . . 56, 171, 179
3:18a . . . 172
3:18a–e . . . 151
3:18a–19d . . . 151
3:18b . . . 56, 172
3:18c–e . . . 172
3:18e . . . 56
3:19 . . . 33, 75, 89, 105, 116, 158, 173, 180
3:19a . . . 56. 173
3:19a–b . . . 56, 151, 171, 172, 173
3:19b . . . 173
3:19b, c . . . 56
3:19c . . . 172
3:19c–d . . . 151, 173
3:19d . . . 172
3:19e . . . 172

Habakkuk

1:1 . . . 68
1:2–4 . . . 40
2:16 . . . 163
3:3–11 . . . 72
3:6 . . . 85

Zephaniah

1 . . . 43
1:4–5 . . . 40
1:12 . . . 159
1:14–15 . . . 88
1:18 . . . 74
2:2 . . . 104
3:1–4 . . . 40
3:1–8 . . . 147
3:8 . . . 74, 86, 147

Haggai

2:8 . . . 135

Zechariah

1:14 . . . 74
8:1 . . . 74
9:1 . . . 68
9:4 . . . 161
9:7 . . . 156
10:11 . . . 82
12:1 . . . 68
12:2 . . . 163
13:9 . . . 87

Malachi

1:1 . . . 68
3:2 . . . 87
4:1 . . . 104

Matthew

6:19–21 . . . 179
8:11 . . . 145
10:32–33 . . . 145
12:28 . . . 176
24:13 . . . 145
25:34–40 . . . 145

Luke

8:1–3 . . . 179
13:34 . . . 89
18:13 . . . 134

John

3:18 . . . 177
9:41 . . . 177
14:1–3 . . . 145
17:24 . . . 145
18:36 . . . 117, 176

Acts

1:6–8 . . . 180
2:32–33 . . . 180
8:32–35 . . . 176
16:14–15 . . . 179

Romans

1–3 . . . 177
1:18 . . . 102
3 . . . 93
4:25 . . . 144, 180
5:1 . . . 144
5:8–11 . . . 117
8:17 . . . 145
8:18–25 . . . 145
8:22 . . . 143
11:22 . . . 91

1 Corinthians

2:3–5 . . . 176
15:25 . . . 180
15:26 . . . 145
15:49 . . . 145

2 Corinthians

5:18–21 . . . 117
11:29–30 . . . 176
12:9 . . . 176
13:4 . . . 176

Ephesians

1:19–23 . . . 117
2:14–17 . . . 117
3:21 . . . 62
4:8–10 . . . 117
6:10–20 . . . 117

Colossians

1:20–22 . . . 117
2:15 . . . 117
2:16–23 . . . 117
3 . . . 117

2 Timothy

1:12 . . . 117
2:12 . . . 145

3:12 . . . 145
3:16–17 . . . 9

Hebrews

12:27 . . . 117

James

1:2–4 . . . 145
1:9–11 . . . 179

1 Peter

1:3–9 . . . 178
1:18–21 . . . 178
2:4–10 . . . 178
2:24 . . . 92
3:18 . . . 92
3:14–16 . . . 117
4:5 . . . 178
5:10–11 . . . 62

2 Peter

3:10–12 . . . 92

Revelation

1:5 . . . 145
1:5–7 . . . 175
4 . . . 175
4–5 . . . 62, 145, 175
5:5 . . . 145
5:5–6 . . . 145
6 . . . 145
6:9–11 . . . 176
7:9–17 . . . 180
9:20–21 . . . 180
11:15–19 . . . 176
12–13 . . . 117
12:11 . . . 175
12:17 . . . 176
14:3 . . . 62
15:3–4 . . . 62
16:5–7 . . . 62
16:9, 11 . . . 180
16:19 . . . 175
16:21 . . . 180
17:1–19:10 . . . 174
17:5 . . . 175
18:2, 10, 21 . . . 175
18:4 . . . 175
18:24 . . . 175
19:1–6 . . . 175
19:4 . . . 175
19:5 . . . 175
19:19 . . . 180
20:11 . . . 92
20:15 . . . 180
21:1 . . . 92
22:9 . . . 175
22:12 . . . 175
22:14 . . . 175

Subject Index

Abdi-Milkuti, 37, 102
abuse of power, 33
acrostic, 72, 73, 74, 79n. 42, 88, 95
Adad-nirari II, 110, 141
Anshar-Assur, 38
Assur, 111, 111n. 63
Assur-etillu-ili, 114
Assur-uballit, 114
Assurbanipal
    and Babylon rebellion, 40
    and conquest of Thebes, 37, 135–36, 160, 163
    death of, 114
    and extent of Assyrian empire, 39, 40
    and flood imagery, 49n. 63
    lion hunts of, 50, 140, 144
    name-centered self-glorification of, 110–11
    palace of, 139n. 91, 139n. 93, 140
    plunder from Judah of, 108
    reign of, 39
    religious ideology of, 37, 37n. 22, 38
    and royal burial, 113
    and temple of Ishtar, 133
    violence of, 36, 37n. 22
Assurnasirpal II, 35, 38, 49
Assyria. *See also* Nineveh
    abuse of power of, 33, 60
    anticipation of fall of, 54–55, 99, 118–45
    arrogance of. *See* pride of
    autonomy of, 33, 59, 60, 92, 97, 142, 147, 155, 179
    and Babylonian rebellion, 40
    burning of chariots of, 142–43n. 113, 143
    call to expand its personnel, 150, 169–70
    call to prepare for attack against, 122–23, 138, 150, 164, 165, 167–68
    celebration at collapse of, 62, 99, 114–15, 116, 158, 171, 173–74
    certainty of punishment of, 175–76
    collapse of state of, 151, 172–73
    conquest of Thebes, 33, 37, 51, 55, 149, 158, 159, 160, 162–63
    death of kings of, 99, 112–14, 116, 118, 151, 171
    deconstruction of pride of, 146–80
    dirge for king of, 151, 171–74
    divine mocking of, 45, 50, 97, 122, 123, 124, 138, 147, 158, 164
    economic personnel of, 150, 170
    and Egypt, 37, 159–60, 162
    elimination of legacy of, 109–11
    exposure and shame of, 155–57, 158
    extent of empire of, 39–40, 122, 159–60
    fall of as partial fulfillment of God's commitment to destroy those who oppose Him, 33, 40, 59–60, 61, 62, 69, 91, 116, 118, 142
    first address to, 98, 99, 100–103
    and flood imagery, 45n. 54, 49, 49n. 63, 89–90
    fortresses of, 165
    four announcements of destruction of, 96–117
    general population, innocence of, 60
    God's commitment to destroying, 121, 122, 142–44, 152, 155, 163, 165
    ideology of kingship of, 37–39, 101–2, 109–12, 111n. 57, 113, 118, 142n. 109, 154, 157
    idolatry of, 96, 102, 112, 142, 146, 175
    imperialism of, 33, 37–39, 144, 154, 154n. 18
    important gods to, 111–12
    and Jonah, 57
    and Judah, 35–36, 38–39, 42–43, 45n. 52, 54, 75, 100–101, 102, 107–8
    and lion imagery, 45n. 54, 49–50, 51, 119, 122, 139–44, 139n. 91
    as militarily established empire 34–35, 37–39, 51, 138
    opposition to God of, 48, 54, 59, 96, 100–102, 118, 154, 155, 174
    palace personnel of, 150, 169, 170–71
    propaganda of. *See* propaganda, Assyrian
    punishment of, 147, 148, 155–57, 158
    reasons for destruction of, 59, 92, 96, 142, 147, 152–54, 157, 171
    removal and destruction of religious images in, 111–12, 116, 118, 120, 132–34, 138
    scattering of people of, 171, 172–73
    second address to, 98, 99, 108–14
    significance of fall of for Judah, 59, 81, 99, 107–8, 114–16, 118, 119, 124–25, 124n. 13, 138
    and siege of Jerusalem, 39, 101, 104–5
    violence of. *See* violence, Assyrian
    vulnerability of, 150, 159, 160, 164, 165–67
    wealth of, 55, 143, 152, 153, 160, 170, 179
autonomy
    Assyrian, 33, 59, 60, 92, 97, 142, 147, 155, 179
    human, 33, 75

Babylon
    army of, 126, 126n. 26
    destruction of, 131, 131n. 45
    divine wrath against, 86n. 70, 86n. 71
    and fall of Nineveh, 54, 60, 125, 126, 126n. 29, 130, 131, 136, 138
    rebellion of, 37n. 22, 40
    shields of, 125, 125n. 19

Bashan, 42, 42n. 42, 46, 71, 83–84, 84n. 59
Black Obelisk of Shalmaneser III, 34, 34n. 4
Book of the Twelve, the, Nahum in, 56–58

Carmel, 42, 46, 71, 84
catchwords, 53, 164, 168
challenge formula, 142, 155
Chaoskampf motif, 83
Christ. *See* Jesus Christ
clauses, in Nahum
- coordination of, 53, 70, 122, 159, 169
- head, 53
- independent, 76
- nominal. *See* nonverbal
- nonverbal, 52, 70, 74, 49n. 36, 128, 153, 164
- primary, 53
- subordination of, 53, 53n. 70, 70, 72, 99, 119, 147, 159, 164, 169, 174
- verbal, 53, 70, 72, 74, 153, 164

commentary format, 10–12
condemnation of Nineveh
- first, 147, 148, 152
- second, 148, 152–53
- third, 148, 153–54

Dadusha, 109
deliverance
- of Israel, 72, 80, 104, 176
- of Judah, 33, 43, 46, 54, 62, 69, 81, 90–91, 96, 107, 114–16, 146
- limited, 59, 60, 61, 81, 116
- of Nineveh, 92
- as not to be presumed, 85, 86
- of those who trust in God, 33, 42, 59, 62, 63, 69, 71, 88–89, 91, 96, 180

Dor, 42

Edom, 44, 164, 165
Egypt, 37, 86n. 70, 159–60, 162, 170
Ekron, 36, 170
Eltekeh, battle at, 159, 162
Esarhaddon
- armory of, 108
- comparison of foes to women, 166
- conflicts of with Egypt, 39, 160, 163n. 62
- divination and astrology at court of, 154
- and lion imagery, 50, 141
- military campaigns of, 37, 39, 160
- and mortal wound motif, 173
- name-centered self-glorification of, 101, 110
- religious ideology of, 101, 102
- violence of, 35

figs, imagery of, 164, 164–65n. 69, 165–66
flood, imagery of, 45n. 54, 49, 49n. 63, 89–90, 132, 141, 174

genre 72, 73, 99, 159, 164n. 69
Gilead, 42
God
- anger of. *See* wrath, divine
- character of, 46–47, 48, 58, 61, 70, 71, 73, 74–81, 86, 92–93
- commitment of to destroying Assyria, 54, 121, 122, 142–44, 152, 155, 163, 165
- covenant with Israel of, 74, 79, 105–6
- definitive judgment of, 78, 89, 90, 91, 93, 96, 102–3, 175–76
- as deliverer, 33, 59, 61, 62, 70, 175, 176
- and deliverance of Israel, 72, 80, 104, 176
- and deliverance of those who trust in Him, 33, 42, 54. 59–63, 69, 71, 88–89, 91, 96, 118, 180
- destruction (punishment) of enemies of, 54, 70, 71, 72, 80, 83, 89, 90, 91, 118, 122, 142, 155
- as Divine Warrior, 33, 47, 59, 84n. 64, 93
- effect of intervention of on humans, 70, 71, 80, 81, 85–90
- effect of intervention of on natural world, 70, 71, 72, 81–85
- and eradication of name of Assyrian king, 110
- and fall of Nineveh, 55, 142, 147, 148, 155–57, 158
- global scale of wrath of, 58, 69, 75, 86, 87, 89, 90, 93, 96
- glory of, 69, 74, 75, 78, 174–75
- goodness of, 47–48, 88
- graciousness of, 76, 88, 107
- jealousy of, 47, 75n. 19
- justice of. *See* justice, divine
- judgment of, 81, 175
- mercy of, 80, 91, 92, 179–80
- name of, 12
- patience of, 61, 71, 76, 79, 80–81, 85, 116
- personal knowledge of those He delivers, 54, 88
- power of, 46, 79, 80, 81, 88, 102
- as refuge, 47, 48, 63, 88, 89, 115, 163, 177
- retribution of. *See* vengeance, divine
- self-identification of, 72, 74
- unchanging character of, 93
- vengeance of. *See* vengeance, divine
- willingness of to forgive, 76, 79, 88
- wrath of. *See* wrath, divine
- zeal of, 70, 74, 75, 79, 80, 89, 91, 94

happiness, pursuit of, 33
Hezekiah, 39, 42, 45, 101, 104, 176
hypotaxis, 52n. 77

idolatry, 40, 74, 79, 96, 112, 142, 146, 175
imagery
- burning chariots, 142–43n. 113, 143, 168
- chaff consumed by fire, 103
- figs, 164, 164–65n. 169, 165–66
- flood, 45n. 54, 49, 49n. 63, 89–90, 132, 174
- gate-bars, 166
- intoxication, 163–64
- lion, 45n. 54, 49–50, 51, 119, 122, 139–43, 144, 168
- locusts, 164, 168–69, 169n. 98
- prostitute, 51, 147, 154, 155, 156n. 27, 157
- shepherd, 50, 101, 139, 140, 144, 172–73
- storm, 81
- terminal, 89
- thorns, 103
- water, 82–83, 134
- whirlwind, 81
- withering, 83–84
- yoke and cords, 107–8

intervention, divine
- and drying up of waters, 71, 81, 82–83

global focus of, 69, 75, 78, 82, 84, 85, 96
and humanity, 70, 81, 84, 85–90
and the natural order, 70, 72, 81–85, 94
and removal of fertility, 71, 83–84, 94
and seismic upheaval, 71, 84–85, 94
intoxication, imagery of, 163–64
Isaiah, 44, 45, 101
Ishtar, 37, 51, 89n. 83, 111, 111n. 60, 132–34, 133n. 58, 133n. 67, 138
Israel. *See* Judah

Jacob, 43
Jeremiah, 44
Jerusalem, Assyrian siege of, 39, 101, 104–5
Jesus Christ, as center of salvation history, 33, 93, 144–45, 175, 177, 180
Jonah, 44, 57, 57n. 86, 58, 58n. 89, 76, 179
Josiah, 40, 42
Judah
in the Assyrian Empire, 35–36, 38–39, 42–43, 45n. 52, 54, 75, 100–101, 102, 107–8
Assyrian rule of as God's punishment, 105, 106–8
celebration of, 62, 114–15, 116, 118, 173–74
covenant of with God, 74, 79, 105–6
decline of, 39–40
deliverance of, 33, 43, 46, 54, 62, 69, 81, 90–91, 96, 107, 114–16, 146
first address to, 98, 99, 104–8
four announcements of deliverance of, 96–117
idolatry of, 40, 74, 79
limited deliverance of, 59, 60, 61, 81, 116
punishment of by God, 78, 79, 105–7, 115, 124
religious condition of, 40, 41–42, 43, 48, 60, 106, 124
restoration of, 58, 62, 118, 119, 124–25, 124n. 13, 138
second address to, 98, 99, 114–16
significance of fall of Assyria to, 59, 81, 99, 107–8, 114–16, 118, 119, 124–25, 138, 146
violence in, 40

justice, divine
as common to both deliverance and punishment, 91, 93
emphasis on in Nahum, 61
finality of, 80
global, 59, 69
and mercy, 91, 179
as vengeance against those who oppose God's will, 70, 75, 81, 88, 174

Karnaim, 42
Kush, 162

Lebanon, 46, 71, 84, 84n. 60, 94
Libya, 162
lion imagery, 45n. 54, 49–50, 51, 119, 122, 139–43, 144, 168
locusts, imagery of, 164, 168–69, 169n. 98

Manasseh, 39, 40, 45n. 52, 108
Marduk, 38
materialism, 33, 178–79
Medina-Habou, 162
Megiddo, 42
Memphis, conquest of, 160
Micah, 76

Naaman, 57, 57n. 88
Nabu, 112, 133
Nabu-zer-kitti-lisir, 102
Nahum
addressees in, 99, 100, 104, 108–11, 114, 123, 128, 132, 159, 165, 169, 172, 173–74
acrostic in, 72, 73, 74, 79n. 42. 88, 95
and Assyrian propaganda, ironic reuse of, 45, 49–51, 83n. 55, 89–90, 110–11, 132, 138, 166, 169–70, 173
and Assyrian vulnerability, 165–67
audience of, 41–45, 67–68
author of, 41, 53, 65, 66, 67, 68n. 12, 100, 104, 105, 114, 122, 155, 156
binary approach of, 48–49, 61, 75, 87, 90, 95
in the Book of the Twelve Minor Prophets, 56–58
call to prepare for God's attack on Assyria, 122–23
canonical significance of message of, 91–95, 116–17, 144–45, 174–80
catchwords in, 53, 164, 168
Chaoskampf motif in, 83
clauses in. *See* clauses, in Nahum
as comfort and encouragement 41, 45, 68, 97
as compared to Jonah, 57, 92
and deconstruction of Assyria's pride, 146–80
as dirge for Assyrian king, 171–74
divine origin of, 68
fall of Assyria anticipated, 54–55, 138–44
fall of Nineveh anticipated, 125–38
finality of, 69, 173
first address to Assyria, 98, 99, 100–103
first address to Judah, 98, 99, 104–8
first person speech in, 104, 108, 156
genre of, 72, 73, 99, 159, 164n. 69
global context of, 46, 54, 58, 59, 65, 67, 69, 78, 82, 84, 91, 96
historical background to, 33–40
and hope in God, 117, 144–45
as hymn, 72, 73
imagery in. *See* imagery
introduction to, 33–64
irony in, 49, 51, 119, 123, 128, 173
literary context of, 65, 69, 96–97, 118–19, 146
literary form of, 70, 72–73, 97, 99, 119, 122, 148
message of, 33
as oracle against a foreign nation, 44–45, 53, 65, 66, 69
outline of, 63–64, 66, 71, 98, 120–21, 148–51
practical significance of message of, 91–95, 116–17, 144–45, 174–80
prolepsis in, 51–53, 119, 122, 123, 136, 138, 144
purpose of, 62
relation to other Old Testament texts, 75–76, 77, 78, 79, 80, 81, 82, 93, 114
rhetorical aims and strategies of, 41–53
sarcasm in, 55, 138, 150, 164, 165, 167–68, 169
second address to Assyria, 98, 99, 108–14

second address to Judah, 98, 99, 114–16
second person speech in, 41, 56, 70, 96, 97, 105, 108, 169, 172
speaker of. *See* author of
structure and message of, 53–56
synecdoche in, 67
taunts in, 50, 53, 55, 56, 146, 147, 149, 158–71
theological message of, 33, 58–62
third person speech in, 41, 70, 97, 100
translation of, 29–31, 66, 71, 98, 120–21, 148–51
as vision, 68, 68n. 12, 69
as woe oracle, 55, 147, 148, 152–58

Nebuchadnezzar, 44
Nebuzaradan, 44
Nineveh. *See also* Assyria
anticipation of fall of, 120–21, 125–38
army that threatens, 125–26
canals and moats of, 129, 130, 130n. 39, 131
city wall and gates of, 127–28, 127n. 26
condemnation of, 147, 148, 152–54
deceit of, 152, 153, 154, 154n. 18, 156, 157
divine wrath at, 86n. 71
exposing and shaming of, 155–57, 158
fall of city of, 33, 49, 51, 54, 55, 67, 69, 111, 113, 116, 122, 125, 146, 152
fall of palace of, 122, 129–32
fleeing of defenders of, 134–35, 138
as focus of introduction to Nahum, 65, 66, 67
geographical perspective with respect to, 123, 126, 127, 129, 130, 134, 135, 136, 137
God's punishment of, 55, 142, 147, 148, 155–57, 158
God's sparing of, 76
ineffectiveness of defenders of, 128-29, 138
initial assault on, 122, 125, 126–28, 138
likeness to Thebes, 51, 55, 149, 158, 159, 160, 161, 163–64
plundering of wealth of, 122, 125, 135–36, 138
as prostitute, 51, 147, 154, 155, 156n. 27, 157
realization of defeat of, 122, 125, 134, 136–37, 138
relocation of citizens of, 60, 122, 162, 164
repentance of, 57–58, 179
role of water in fall of, 130–32
as royal residence, 111
temple of Ishtar in, 133

Ninurta, 111, 111n. 63

oracle. *See also* prophecies
against foreign nations, 44, 45
as genre, 66–67, 66n. 4
Nahum as, 53, 65, 66
woe, 55, 147, 148, 152–58

Pax Assyriaca, 39
Phoenicia, 160
poetics, 52
propaganda, Assyrian
Assyrian, 35–36, 45, 45n. 54, 49
God in, 100, 101
imagery in, 45n. 54, 83n. 55, 169, 173
ironic reuse of, 45, 49–51, 83n. 55, 89–90, 110–11, 132, 138, 166, 169–70, 173
promoting deceit and exploitation, 154, 178
self-idolizing, 101, 118, 138
of violence of, 35–36
prophecies, 44–45, 67, 99. *See also* oracle: against foreign nations
prostitute, imagery of, 51, 147, 154, 155, 156n. 27, 157
Put, 162

Ramses III, 162
Ruth, 57, 57n. 88

Samerina, 39
Sanda-uarri, 37, 102
Sargon II, 35, 39, 111, 141, 169
Sennacherib, 36, 37, 39, 43, 45, 101, 103, 110, 111, 126, 127, 129, 131–32, 141, 157n. 33
arrogance of, 157n. 33, 169
destruction of Babylon, 131
Egyptian resistance to, 159–60, 162
and Judah, 43, 45, 101, 104
and lion imagery, 141
and locust imagery, 169
military campaigns of, 36, 39
and palace of Nineveh, 110, 111, 131–32
and planting of fig trees, 166
reign of, 39
religious ideology of, 37–38
and river wall in Nineveh, 127
violence of, 36
waterworks projects of, 129, 131n. 45
widening of streets of Nineveh, 126–27
Shalmaneser I, 111
Shalmaneser III, 34, 49, 50
Shalmaneser V, 39
Shamash-shum-ukin, 37
shepherd, imagery of, 50, 101, 139, 140, 144, 172–73
Sidon, 37, 160
Significance
canonical, of message of Nahum, 91–95, 116–17, 144–45, 174–80
of fall of Assyria to Judah, 107–8, 114–16, 118, 124–25
practical, of message of Nahum, 91–95, 116–17, 144–45, 174–80
pursuit of, 33
Sin-shar-ishkun, 114
storm, imagery of, 81
synecdoche, 67

Taharqa, 37, 160, 162, 173
Tanwetaman, 160
taunts
economic, 56, 150, 168–71
historical, 55, 149, 158–64
military, 55, 150, 164–68
Thebes
apparent strength of, 149, 158, 160–62
Assyrian conquest of, 33, 37, 51, 55, 149, 158, 159, 160, 162–63
defenses of, 162
Nineveh likeness to, 51, 55, 149, 158, 159, 160, 161, 163–64
water in, 161
theodicy, 56
Tiglath-pileser I, 49–50, 156
Tiglath-pileser III, 35, 39, 49, 49n. 63, 101, 157n. 33, 159
Tyre, 160

vengeance, divine
- against human opposition to God's will, 70, 73, 74, 75, 78, 79, 91, 94, 102
- finality of, 78
- and God's character, 71, 73, 76, 77, 78
- for God's glory, 102
- destructive nature of, 54
- emphasis on in Nahum, 61
- global, 54, 59, 91

violence, Assyrian
- as empire-building strategy, 35–36, 112
- human toll of, 152–53
- and ideology of other as less than human, 36–37n. 16, 157
- and lion imagery, 141, 142, 143
- as reason for God's punishment, 55, 59, 92, 97, 122, 142, 143, 152, 174

whirlwind, imagery of, 81

wrath, divine
- against enemies, 43, 47, 76, 78, 79, 86, 89, 179
- compared to breaking up cliffs, 87, 87n. 73
- compared to fire, 87, 87n. 72
- destructive, 71, 87–88
- dreadful, 71, 77–78
- emphasis on in Nahum, 61
- escape from, 81, 88, 89, 91, 96
- finality of, 78, 89, 90, 91, 93, 96
- global focus of, 58, 69, 75, 86, 87, 89, 90, 93, 96
- leading to vengeance, 48
- and the natural order, 86, 87
- rhetoric of to promote faith response, 60, 61, 62, 88, 90, 95, 117, 176
- significance of for humanity, 70, 72, 85, 86
- varying severity of, 86–87

Yahdun-Lim, 109

YHWH. *See* God

yoke and cords, metaphor of, 107–8

Author Index

Abusch, Tzvi, 51
Allegro, John M., 141–42
Allen, Leslie C., 107, 155, 170
Andersen, Francis I., 44, 66, 74, 76, 124
Anderson, Arnold A., 142
Armerding, Carl E., 75, 81, 114
Arnold, Bill T., 78
Ataç, Mehmet-Ali, 136, 142, 143
Aufrère, Sydney H., 162
Averbeck, Richard E., 83

Baker, David W., 106
Baloian, Bruce, 79
Barnett, Richard D., 140
Barr, James, 89
Bauckham, Richard, 175
Baumann, Gerlinde, 70, 82, 86, 87
Beale, Gregory K., 175
Beaulieu, Paul-Alain, 111, 154
Becking, Bob, 75, 112
Ben Zvi, Ehud, 56
Benun, Ronald, 95
Berlejung, Angelika, 50, 51, 128, 144, 165, 167, 171, 173
Berlin, Adele, 52
Beyer, Brian E., 78
Block, Daniel I., 122
Blomberg, Craig L., 179
Bosman, Hendrik L., 114
Brooke, George J., 57
Brown, William, 73
Bussmann, Hadumod, 67
Buth, Randall, 70, 74, 76, 79, 80
Butler, Judith, 139
Byargeon, Rick W., 84

Carson, D. A., 178
Cassin, Elena, 139, 141
Cathcart, Kevin J., 103, 170
Charles, J. Daryl, 135
Christensen, Duane L., 65, 124, 126, 128, 131, 132, 137, 138, 142, 159, 164, 166
Cifarelli, Megan
Codella, Kim, 111
Cogan, Mordechai, 83, 101, 112, 114, 163
Cole, Steven W., 166
Cook, Greg, 76
Cook, Gregory D., 95, 156
Cook, John A., 104, 122
Cook, Paul M., 44
Cooley, Jeff, 110
Craigie, Peter C., 155, 167
Crouch, Carly, 38, 83
Curtis, John, 139

Davies, Philip R., 154
Day, John, 83
Dearman, J. Andrew, 124
De Backer, Fabrice, 125, 126
Dehenin, Evelyne, 125
Delcor, Mathias, 134
de Moor, Johannes C., 78
Desjarlais, Robert R., 159, 165
Dick, Michael B., 139, 140
Dietrich, Manfried, 153
Dozeman, Thomas, 76
Dreytza, Manfred, 81
Drinkard, Joel F., 155, 167
Driver, G. R., 89
Duff, R. Antony, 157
Durand, Jean-Marie, 67

Elat, Moshe, 170
Emerton, J. A., 155
Eph'al, Israel, 34
Estelle, Bryan D., 44

Fabry, Heinz-Josef, 50, 58, 70, 75, 83, 84, 88, 99, 103, 104, 105, 109, 126, 128, 129, 131, 132, 136, 138, 152, 167
Fales, Frederick M., 34, 35, 36, 38, 39, 111, 125, 126, 127, 167
Fantuzzo, C. J., 95
Faust, Avraham, 170
Fischer, Georg, 155
Floyd, Michael H., 41, 43, 45, 51, 66, 72, 81, 104, 109, 138, 147, 153, 159, 164
Fohrer, Georg, 41
Fokkelman, Jan P., 159, 164, 172
Follingstad, Carl M., 103
Forster, Greg, 178
Frame, Grant, 40
Freedman, David N., 44, 66, 124
Fuchs, Andreas, 34, 35, 131, 142, 143, 165
Futato, Mark, 82

Gamberoni, Johann, 89
Gansell, Amy R., 133
Garcia-Martintez, Florentino, 141
Garelli, Paul, 38
Gelston, Anthony, 89, 103, 124, 141, 143, 171, 172
Gerstenberger, Erhard S., 106
Gese, Hartmut, 179
Gitin, Seymour, 165
Goering, Greg S., 52, 171
Goldsworthy, Graeme, 58, 117
Golvin, Jean-Claude, 162

Gordon, Robert P., 67, 88
Goyon, Jean-Claude, 162
Grayson, A. Kirk, 33, 34, 38, 50, 111, 112, 133, 135
Grisanti, Michael A., 156
Guillaume, Philippe, 57
Guthrie, Donald, 79

Hall, Gary H., 154
Hallo, William W., 110
Hamilton, R. W., 133
Hamilton, Victor P., 43, 124, 137
Harré, R., 60
Harris, Rivkah, 133
Hartley, J., 100
Hartog, Pieter B., 143
Harvey, John E., 107
Heard, Warren J., Jr., 162
Hess, Richard, 43
Hill, Andrew E., 89
Hillers, Delbert R., 152
Holloway, Steven W., 109, 112
Holmstedt, Robert D., 52, 53, 130
Horowitz, Wayne, 172
Huddleston, John R., 161

Isaksson, Bo, 53, 70

Jacobsen, Thorkild, 129
Jahnow, Hedwig, 171
Jakob, Stefan, 104
Jeremias, Jorg, 72
Johnson, Elsie, 79
Johnson, Eric L., 92
Johnston, Gordon H., 50, 89, 109, 110, 123, 131, 137, 143, 169, 173

Kalami, Isaac, 101
Kelley, Page H., 155, 167
Kennedy, James M., 82
Keown, Gerald L., 170
Kessler, Karlheinz, 165
Knowles, Murray, 154
Koopmans, William T., 78
Kraus, Hans-Joachim, 124
Kroeze, Jan H., 70, 77, 80, 88, 100, 103, 107, 110, 147, 153
Kuhrt, Amélie, 126, 159
Kutsch, Ernst, 112

Lane, Daniel C., 106
Langenhove, L. V., 60
Leichty, Erle, 35, 37, 50, 84, 101, 102, 107, 108, 135, 136, 141, 166, 171, 173
Lerner, Gerda, 156
Levy, Elisabeth, 136
Lewis, C. S., 116
Lewis, Theodore J., 104
Lipiński, Édouard, 75, 166
Liverani, Mario, 38, 102, 113
Livingstone, Alasdair, 38, 111
Lloyd, Seton, 129
Locher, Clemens, 164
Loewenstamm, Samuel E., 103
Longman III, Tremper, 47, 52, 68, 82, 84, 86, 103, 104, 107, 124, 134, 136, 147, 152
Luc, Alex, 81
Luckenbill, Daniel D., 50, 127, 131, 133, 157, 166, 169
Lumsden, Stephen, 36

Machinist, Peter, 45, 49, 130, 131
Mack, Russel, 173
Mann, Thomas W., 83
Marrow, William, 144
Mateo, José, 164
May, Natalie N., 139, 143
McConville, J. Gordon, 176
McKane, William, 155, 157
McNutt, Paula, 42
Meier, Samuel A., 108
Melchert, H. C., 67
Melville, Sarah C., 36, 37, 38, 49, 107, 110, 141
Merwe, Christo H. J. van der, 70, 77, 80, 88, 100, 103, 107, 110, 147, 153
Millard, Alan, 88, 112
Miller, Patrick D., 106
Moo, Douglas, 92
Moon, Rosamund, 154
Morgan, Christopher, 110
Morgan, Maurya P., 143
Mori, Lucia, 166

Naudé, Jackie A., 70, 77, 80, 88, 100, 103, 107, 110, 147, 153
Niehaus, Jeffrey J., 50
Nissinen, Martti, 38, 67, 111
Nogalski, James D., 56

Oates, Joan, 40, 114
O'Brien, Julia M., 156
O'Connor, Michael, 74
Oded, Bustenay, 37
Olivier, J. P. J., 80
Oppenheim, A. Leo, 33, 108
Oswalt, John, 92, 137

Pajunen, Mike, 57
Park, Grace J., 103
Parker, Bradley J., 102, 165
Parker, Simon B., 84
Parpola, Simo, 43, 67, 108, 110, 170, 171, 173
Patterson, Richard D., 52
Peels, H. G. L., 47, 74, 75, 78
Perlitt, Lothar, 66, 72, 83, 86, 100, 104, 107, 109, 124, 128, 153, 157, 159
Piepkorn, Arthur Carl, 111, 136, 143, 163
Pinker, Aron, 125, 126, 130, 133
Polak, Frank, 105
Polz, Daniel C., 161
Porter, Barbara N., 111, 133
Porter, Stanley, 117
Propp, William H. C., 47
Purcell, William L., 94

Raabe, Paul, 44, 163
Radner, Karen, 144, 171
Ramsey, Thor, 89
Reade, Julian, 36, 127, 129, 131, 133
Redford, Donald B., 159, 162
Reid, Daniel G., 47
Renaud, Bernard, 68, 126, 128, 138, 158

Renz, Thomas, 72, 93, 95, 154
Reuter, E., 75
Reynolds, Frances, 166
Richardson, Seth, 101
Ringgren, Helmer, 80
Ritner, Robert K., 38, 67
Rivaroli, Marta, 131, 132
Roberts, J. J. M., 68, 73, 83, 84, 87, 93, 96, 103, 104, 113, 114, 116, 125, 128, 134, 138
Robinson, David, 136
Rogerson, John W., 154
Rooker, Mark F., 84
Roth, Martha T., 156
Russell, John M., 35, 67

Saggs, H. W. F., 40, 107, 112, 113, 114, 130, 170
Sanders, Seth L., 67
Scalise, Pamela J., 170
Scharbert, Josef, 113
Schart, Aaron, 56, 76
Schmidt, Ludwig, 179
Schoville, Keith N., 78
Scoralick, Ruth, 74, 78, 80
Scurlock, Joann, 130
Seow, C. L., 38, 67
Sherwin, Simon, 142
Simkins, Ronald A., 41
Smith, Robert H., 84
Smothers, Thomas G., 170
Snowball, David, 94
Spalinger, Anthony J., 162
Spieckermann, Hermann, 76
Spronk, Klaas, 34, 65, 68, 72, 74, 79, 84, 88, 89, 103, 104, 105, 107, 108, 109, 111, 128, 132. 137, 139, 142, 143, 144, 152, 159, 161, 168, 172, 173
Strawn, Brent A., 49, 50
Stronach, David, 111, 127, 168
Struthers, Gale B., 79
Stuart, Dougals, 115
Sweeney, Marvin A., 56, 83

Tadmor, Hayim, 49, 83, 84, 101, 157
Talmon, Shemaryahu, 110
Tengberg, Margareta, 165
Thompson, R. Campbell, 133
Tidiman, Brian, 66, 124, 126, 131, 137, 139, 153, 154, 168
Tigchelaar, Eibert J. C., 141
Timmer, Daniel C., 37, 43, 44, 45, 48, 57, 60, 79, 92, 99, 101, 173
Travers, Michael E., 52
Trueman, Carl, 179
Tucker, Gene M., 76

Van De Mieroop, Marc, 131
Vanderhooft, David S., 134
VanGemeren, Willem, 86, 147
Vanhoozer, Kevin J., 46, 57
van Koppen, Frans, 109
van Leeuwen, Cornelis, 80
Van Til, Cornelius, 78
Verderame, Lorenzo, 154
von Weissenberg, Hanne M., 57

Wakely, Robin, 80, 115
Waltke, Bruce K., 74, 78, 105
Walton, John H., 57, 179
Warmuth, Georg, 80
Watanabe, Kazuko, 110, 173
Watts, J. D. W., 83, 89
Weissert, Elnathan, 38, 139, 140, 143
Wells, David F., 178
Wendland, Ernst, 62, 104, 116
Wenham, G. J., 124
Widmer, Michael, 76, 79
Wiggermann, F. A. M., 112
Wiklander, Bertil, 86
Wildberger, Hans, 137
Williams, Michael J., 90
Williams, William C., 172
Wilson, Gerald H., 172
Winter, Irene J., 36, 142
Wiseman, Donald J., 130
Wöhrle, Jakob, 76
Wolf, Herbert M., 130
Wolters, Al, 89, 92
Wright, C. J. H., 85

Yadin, Yigael, 128
Yamada, Shigeo, 49, 84, 101
Yee, Gale A., 171
Youngblood, Kevin J., 57, 76
Younger, K. Lawson Jr., 38, 102
Younker, Randall W., 84
Yus, Francisco, 164

Zehnder, Markus, 37, 102, 157, 166
Zewi, Tamar, 52, 53, 74

Zondervan Exegetical Commentary on the Old Testament

Ruth

A Discourse Analysis
of the Hebrew Bible

Daniel I. Block

With careful discourse analysis and interpretation of the Hebrew text, the authors of the Zondervan Exegetical Commentary on the Old Testament series trace the flow of argument in each Old Testament book, showing that *how* a biblical author says something is just as important as *what* they say.

Ruth is widely recognized as a superlative literary achievement of ancient Israel. With its sensitive portrayal of women in crisis, its admiration for a righteous man, and its profound theology of providence it offers hearers in every age a window into life in the ancient Near East, inspiration for good and godly living, and reason to wonder at the common roots of Israel's royal and messianic hope. Bridging the historical and theological gap between Judges and Samuel, the book of Ruth explains specifically first how David, the most important character in the Hebrew Bible, could emerge from the spiritual and ethical morass of the premonarchic period, and second to account for the Moabite blood in this king's veins.

Available in stores and online!

ZONDERVAN
ACADEMIC